THE
FRENCH
REVOLUTION

*A Document
Collection*

THE
FRENCH
REVOLUTION

A Document Collection

Laura Mason
University of Georgia

Tracey Rizzo
University of North Carolina
at Asheville

Houghton Mifflin Company   Boston New York

Editor in Chief: Jean L. Woy
Assistant Editor: Leah Strauss
Senior Project Editor: Christina M. Horn
Associate Production/Design Coordinator: Jodi O'Rourke
Manufacturing Coordinator: Andrea Wagner
Senior Marketing Manager: Sandra McGuire

Cover Image: Lesur (Les Frères), *Le cri français.* Art Resource, NY.

Cover Design: Minko T. Dimov, MinkoImages.

ABOUT THE AUTHORS

LAURA MASON

Associate professor of history at the University of Georgia, Laura Mason holds a Ph.D. from Princeton University. A specialist in the French Revolution and cultural history, she is the author of *Singing the French Revolution: Popular Culture and Politics, 1787–1799,* as well as articles in French cultural history and in history and film.

TRACEY RIZZO

Tracey Rizzo is assistant professor of history and interim director of women's studies at the University of North Carolina at Asheville. She earned her Ph.D. from the University of Oregon, where she specialized in eighteenth-century France and European women's history. She has written and spoken widely on women in the French Revolution and Old Regime France and Haiti and is currently revising her manuscript on pre-Revolutionary court cases for publication.

CONTENTS

PART TWO

From Liberal to Republican Revolution (1789–1792)

89

PART THREE

The Republican Crisis (1793–1795)

189

CHAPTER 8: POPULAR MOVEMENTS BEYOND
             THE CONVENTION   197

PREFACE

Scholarship on the French Revolution has experienced a dramatic transformation since the late 1970s. Historians have extended scholarship beyond traditional social interpretations and political narratives, to incorporate popular culture, women's activism, changing sexual ideologies, and the activities of religious, social, and racial minorities into new syntheses that underscore the extraordinary richness of the French Revolution as a founding moment in Western history. Just as the thematic content of the Revolution has been broadened, so have its chronological and geographic boundaries been expanded. Scholars are increasingly lengthening their view beyond the fall of Robespierre to investigate the legacies of the Thermidoran Reaction and Directory, and they are reorienting traditionally Eurocentric perspectives by examining the dynamic of the Revolution in the Caribbean. In spite of this outpouring of innovative scholarship, there has not been a documentary collection in English to complement such work until now.

Our purpose is not simply to substitute new interpretations of the Revolution for old but to make available a more comprehensive picture. This collection integrates documents that reflect new trends in Revolutionary scholarship with documents that illustrate the insights and arguments of more traditional histories. We have included the voices of philosophes and legislators alongside those of sans-culottes, women, peasants, and the free blacks and slaves of Saint Domingue; we include, as well, the testimony of revolutionaries and counter-revolutionaries alike. Reflecting this mixture of old and new, the collection combines documents that are currently available with those that, until now, have been allowed to fall out of print, have remained untranslated, or have never been published.

To facilitate introductory teaching on the French Revolution, we have organized selections chronologically, in chapters that stretch from the Old Regime to the empire of Napoleon Bonaparte. Each document is preceded by an introduction that offers immediate context, and the collection's four parts begin with short narrative histories of the Revolution that provide students with the broader setting. Students and instructors may use this book either by following the traditional chronology that the chapters trace or by grouping documents thematically. We have facilitated both approaches by including a chronology of the major developments of the Revolution at the beginning of the book. Further, we hope to encourage independent undergraduate research on the collection's principal themes by including a bibliography of important secondary sources at the end of the book. In general, our belief that students should work with historians' tools, interpreting primary sources of all types, visual as well as written, has shaped what materials we make available here.

This has been a collaborative project and such work, almost inevitably, allows each partner to bring unique skills and vision to the project. While Laura Mason contributed experience and leadership commensurate with her training and orientation as a specialist of the French Revolution and of popular culture, Tracey Rizzo, a generalist devoted to undergraduate teaching, brought insights based on her intensive work in the classroom and her expertise in women's studies, Caribbean history, and eighteenth-century France. Each has signed the individual translations for which she is responsible. Laura Mason wrote the general introduction and the section introductions; she also conducted the research necessary to gather the documents included here from the National Archives in France. Tracey Rizzo conducted research at the New York Public Library, the Newberry Library, Queens University Library, and Emory University Special Collections.

We have accrued many debts in completing this collection. We are grateful to Keith Mahoney, Leah Strauss, and Christina Horn of Houghton Mifflin for their patience, encouragement, and excellent editorial advice, and to James Miller for project organization and development. At several stages during the project, reviewers provided valuable and perceptive advice on selections, organization, and chronological introductions. We would like to thank the following individuals: Gail Bossenga, University of Kansas; Jack Censer, George Mason University; Suzanne Desan, University of Wisconsin; Michael Fitzsimmons, Auburn University; Gary Kates, Trinity University; Paul Spagnoli, Boston College; and Donald Sutherland, University of Maryland.

In addition, Tracey Rizzo wishes to thank Douglas Palmer and Raymond Birn of the University of Oregon for excellent suggestions for documents. For invaluable strategic advice when she needed it most, she thanks Barbara Corrodo Pope and Judith Zinsser. For secretarial help she thanks Vivian Coman, Brenda Abell, and Susan Pendakur. For release time from her normal teaching load, she thanks the University of North Carolina at Asheville, and for consumer-testing these documents she thanks her challenging students in History 362. For help with selections, translations, eleventh-hour editorial decisions, and integrating love for French history into daily life, she expresses deeply felt gratitude to Kenneth Banks, her husband and collaborator in all things. She would also like to thank the National Endowment for the Humanities for enabling travel to the New York Public Library and the Newberry Library.

Laura Mason thanks Jack Censer, Suzanne Desan, Peter Jones, Michael Kwass, and Bryant Ragan, Jr., for offering enormously helpful suggestions on documents and the overall conception of the collection. Peter Hoffer provided much-appreciated assistance in helping to get this project off the ground. Bonnie Cary lent prompt and essential secretarial support. Thanks, as well, to the Humanities Center of the University of Georgia, which provided release time to develop the project. A University of Georgia Junior Faculty Research Grant enabled her to travel to the National Archives in Paris to collect documents.

L. M.
T. R.

CHRONOLOGY

1787

February 22–May 25	Assembly of Notables
November 19	Royal Session of the Parlement of Paris; Edict of Toleration granted to Protestants

1788

August 8	Louis XVI convokes the Estates General
August 25	Necker appointed finance minister
December 27	Doubling of the number of representatives for the Third Estate is approved

1789

February–June	Elections to Estates General; drafting of *cahiers*
May 5	Opening session of the Estates General
June 17	Deputies of the Third Estate declare themselves the National Assembly
June 20	Tennis Court Oath
June 23	Royal Session of the Three Estates
June 27	Louis XVI orders clergy and nobility to join the Assembly
July 11	Dismissal of Necker
July 13	Parisian electors form a standing committee and a citizens' militia
July 14	Fall of the Bastille
July 16	Necker recalled
Late July–early August	Great Fear
August 4	Assembly abolishes feudal dues, other privileges
August 26	Assembly adopts "Declaration of the Rights of Man and Citizen"
September 11	Assembly grants king suspensive veto
October 5–6	Parisian women lead a march to Versailles, escort royal family to Paris after massacring palace guards
October 29	Assembly votes distinction between "active" and "passive" citizens

December 19	Creation of assignats
December 22	France divided into departments

1790

February 13	Assembly suppresses religious orders
May 21	Assembly divides Paris into forty-eight sections
June 19	Assembly abolishes hereditary titles
July 12	Assembly approves Civil Constitution of the Clergy
July 14	First Festival of Federation at Champ de Mars
October 23	The king approaches foreign powers to discuss possible intervention
Late October	Revolt of mulattoes led by Vincent Ogé in Saint Domingue
November 27	Clergy required to swear civic oath

1791

January 3	Nonjuring priests barred from public exercise of duties
February 25	Execution in Saint Domingue of Vincent Ogé
March 2	Allard Law suppresses guilds
March 10	Pope Pius VI condemns Civil Constitution of the Clergy and revolutionary principles
May 15	Assembly grants rights to free blacks born of free parents
June 11	Voltaire's ashes transferred to Pantheon
June 14	Le Chapelier Law prohibits workers' organizations
June 20–21	Royal family attempts to flee the country; arrested at Varennes
July 17	Champ de Mars massacre by the National Guard under Lafayette's command
August 5	French nation promises not to engage in wars of conquest
August 22	Slave rebellion erupts in Saint Domingue
August 27	Declaration of Pillnitz issued by Austria and Prussia, threatening action against the Revolution
September 14	Louis XVI accepts the new constitution
September 24	Rights of free blacks rescinded
September 27	Rights granted to all Jews in France
September 30	National Assembly renamed Legislative Assembly

1792

March 24	Rights of free blacks reinstated
April 20	France declares war on Austria
April 24	Rouget de l'Isle composes the "Marseillaise"
April 25	First use of the guillotine
June 13	Prussia declares war
June 20	Crowds invade Tuileries Palace
July 25	Brunswick Manifesto threatens invasion of Paris if rebels do not submit to the king
July 27	"Émigré" properties confiscated
August 10	Insurrection in Paris; creation of the revolutionary Commune of Paris
September 2	Fall of Verdun
September 2–6	Prison massacres in Paris
September 20	French victory at Valmy; decree enabling divorce; secularization of baptism, marriage, and death rites; civil rights for actors, "illegitimate" children; Legislative Assembly dissolves itself
September 21	First session of National Convention abolishes monarchy
September 22	National Convention proclaims a republic
November 19	Decree promising aid to all peoples "seeking to recover their liberty"
December 11	Trial of Louis XVI opens

1793

January 21	Louis XVI guillotined
February 1	France declares war on Britain and Holland
February 24	Convention decrees mass conscription of three hundred thousand men
March 7	France declares war on Spain
March 10	Revolutionary Tribunal created
March 11	Civil war breaks out in the Vendée
April 5	Treason of General Dumouriez, who goes over to the Austrians
April 6	Committee of Public Safety created
May 31	Insurrection of Paris sections against Girondins
Early June	Federalist revolts begin in western France

June 2	Girondins purged from the National Convention
June 3	Sale of confiscated émigré properties
June 24	Constitution of Year I adopted
July 13	Marat assassinated by Charlotte Corday
July 26	Death penalty for grain hoarders decreed
July 27	Robespierre elected to Committee of Public Safety
August 1	Adoption of metric system
August 10	Louvre opened to the public as a museum
August 23	"Levy in mass" decreed
August 29	Toulon occupied by English
September 5	Convention adopts "Terror as the order of the day" in response to popular insurrection in Paris
September 9	Creation of revolutionary army
September 17	Law of Suspects passed
September 23	Port-au-Prince renamed Port Républicain
September 29	General "maximum" on wages and prices decreed
October 5	Revolutionary calendar introduced
October 9	Lyons falls to republican forces
October 10	Government is voted "revolutionary until peace"
October 16	Execution of Marie Antoinette
October 30	Women's clubs outlawed
October 31	Execution of Girondins
November–December	De-Christianization: churches in and around Paris closed
December 19	Recapture of Toulon from English; principle of free primary education adopted
December 23	End of war in the Vendée; government victorious

1794

February 4	Abolition of slavery
March 3	Ventôse decrees passed to aid "needy" patriots
March 24	Execution of militant sans-culottes, including Hébert
April 5	Execution of Danton and his supporters
April 14	Rousseau's ashes transferred to Pantheon
May 6	Toussaint L'Ouverture takes command of slave insurrection in Saint Domingue
May 7	Decree recognizing the existence of a Supreme Being
June 8	Festival of the Supreme Being

June 10	Law of 22 Prairial eliminates due process
June 26	Victory at Fleurus
July 27	Defeat of Robespierre on the floor of the Convention
July 28	Execution of Robespierre, Saint-Just, and twenty other Robespierrists
August 1	Law of 22 Prairial rescinded; prisoners released
November 12	Jacobin Club closed
December 24	Abolition of the maximum

1795

January 19	First performance of "The People's Awakening"
February 21	Freedom of worship and separation of church and state decreed
April 1	Military suppression of sans-culotte insurrection in Paris
April 5	Peace of Basel with Prussia
May 4	Prison massacre in Lyons
May 16	Hague peace treaty; France recognizes Batavia as a "sister republic"
May 20–23	Prairial insurrection and defeat of sans-culottes in Paris
May 24	Prohibition against women participating in political assemblies or gathering in groups of more than five persons
May 31	Revolutionary Tribunal abolished
June 8	Death of Louis XVII in prison
July 24	Louis XVIII publishes Declaration of Verona in France and England
July 21	Defeat of émigré army at Quiberon
July 22	Peace of Basel with Spain
August 22	Constitution of Year III adopted
October 1	Annexation of Belgium
October 5	Vendémiaire uprising in Paris
October 26	National Convention dissolved
October 31	Election of the Directory

1796

| March 2 | Napoleon named commander in chief of the army in Italy |

April 15	Decree calling for death penalty against those who promote royalism or the restoration of the constitution of 1793
May 10	Arrest of Babeuf and "Conspirators of Equality"

1797

February 2	Surrender of Mantua
February 4	Return to metallic-based currency
July 25	Government bans political clubs
May 27	Execution of Babeuf and co-conspirators
July 9	Cisalpine Republic established
September 4	Fructidor coup against Councils; elections annulled in many departments
September 8	Press freedom restricted
October 18	Treaty of Campo Formio with Austria

1798

March 22	Helvetic Republic proclaimed
April–December	Second Coalition formed against France
May 11	Floréal coup by Directory against the left
May 19	Napoleon leaves for Egypt

1799

May 16	Sieyès is elected to the Directory
June 18	Prairial coup by the Directors
October 16	Napoleon returns to Paris
October 23	Lucien Bonaparte elected president of the Council of Five Hundred
November 9–10	Brumaire coup of Napoleon, Sieyès, and Roger Ducos
December 25	Constitution of Year V enacted

1800

January 13	Bank of France established
February 17	Prefectures organized
May 15–23	Napoleon crosses the Alps
December 24	Attempted assassination of Napoleon

1801

January 5	Jacobins proscribed
February 8	Peace of Lunéville with Austria
July 16	Concordat with papacy concluded

1802

February 5	Expedition to Saint Domingue
March 27	Treaty of Amiens
April 1	Germinal Purges
April 8	Organic Articles promulgated
May 19	Legion of Honor created by Napoleon
May 20	Slavery reestablished
August 2	Napoleon proclaimed consul for life

1803

April 7	Death of Toussaint L'Ouverture in France after eight months in prison
April 12	Workers required to carry "livret" by decree
May 2	Diplomatic relations with Britain broken
May 3	Louisiana ceded to United States for 80 million francs

1804

January 1	Saint Domingue declares independence from France; renamed Haiti
March 20	Duc d'Enghien executed
March 21	Civil Code promulgated
December 2	Napoleon proclaimed emperor

INTRODUCTION

n 1789 the glassmaker Jacques-Louis Ménétra was fifty-one years old. A workingman whose most unusual quality was his desire to record the events of his life, Ménétra was on the threshold of old age.

> I was enjoying myself and watching my days go by when the French Revolution came suddenly and revived all our spirits. And the word liberty . . . invigorated us all. People rushed to arms and supported those who called themselves the fathers of the people. This revolution was supposed to secure the happiness of the French people by confining the king to his throne and returning to all the rights that the parlements, the priesthood, the nobility had usurped under the leadership of ministers [who were] inept [and . . .] who thought only of their pleasures and their ambition, trampling the constitution of the state underfoot.*

As a Parisian, and one who was well integrated into the life of his neighborhood and his city, Ménétra was quickly swept into the revolutionary maelstrom: he was elected lieutenant of the local guard unit and later served as a minor bureaucrat; his daughter benefited from the Legislative Assembly's legalization of divorce, and his son served in the revolutionary armies; he saw friends executed during the Terror and others die fighting the royalist insurrection of 13 Vendémiaire. And when it was over, he could only say: "When I am with old friends I think about all that has happened. We recount what we have seen, what we have felt, the good and the evil that the Revolution has done. . . . We are beginning to see the twilight of the times in which our fathers were happy."

Ménétra's experiences of hope and disappointment, chaos, confusion, and improvisation were shared by the men and women throughout France and Europe who lived through the decade of the French Revolution. And like Ménétra, many of them recognized that the world they had known as children was being swept away forever, for the French Revolution changed Europe as profoundly as it touched Ménétra's own life. It gave birth to new government institutions, social

---

*Quotes from Jacques-Louis Ménétra, *Journal of My Life*, trans. Arthur Goldhammer (New York: Columbia University Press, 1986), pp. 217, 237.

structures, and political practices; it reshaped culture across the continent, making its way into painting, literature, and music; it even reached into families, to change relations between husbands and wives, brothers and sisters, fathers and sons. In short, the French Revolution helped to sweep away a society that had developed steadily over several hundred years, to initiate the arduous process of creating the world we live in now, the period that we know as modern.

Prerevolutionary Europe had by no means been static, but it was visibly linked to the medieval and Renaissance worlds from which it had emerged. The populations of most countries were organized into estates, a rigid system of social hierarchy which fixed an individual's status at birth and determined his or her rights and duties. Perched above these societies of orders were sovereigns who claimed to rule by God's authority, and who shared power with tiny and privileged minorities of the population. Rights and duties were local, not universal, and the extent to which individuals enjoyed freedom of speech, press, or conscience was dependent on the sovereign's good will or the subjects' own craftiness. At the base of these societies was a populous peasantry who produced the agricultural wealth of sovereign states while themselves living under fiercely difficult conditions. Burdened by the plethora of dues, fees, and taxes that they owed to landlord, church, and king, most peasants sustained themselves and their children without the least modicum of security. Famine and epidemics swept the countryside even in the eighteenth century, and only a very few years of shortage were enough to drive whole families into destitution.

Revolutionaries in France attacked every dimension of this world, which they quickly came to define as the Old Regime. They created a legislature that drew its authority from the sovereign power of the people. They institutionalized the principle of equality before the law by establishing uniform taxes and legal codes, and by abolishing restrictions on the exercise of professions. They eliminated the feudal dues that had burdened and humiliated the peasantry. They upheld free press, free speech, and freedom of conscience not as the benevolent gifts of the head of state but as the fundamental rights of free citizens. And then they went further still, abolishing the monarchy and, for the first time in European history, declaring universal male suffrage.

Had the French kept these innovations firmly within their borders, we would nonetheless find their achievements worthy of note. But the Revolution resonated across Europe and eventually throughout the world. "Patriots" elsewhere had challenged their governments even before 1789, demanding greater rights and broader representation. After 1789 many drew new strength from the example of the French: writers praised the Revolution in poems and prose, political treatises and newspaper articles; reform movements emerged as far away as Poland to the east and the Caribbean and Latin America to the west. French revolutionary armies also played a part in disseminating revolutionary practices and ideology. Declared liberators by the republican government in 1792, they attempted to dismantle feudalism and disseminate republican principles in the regions they conquered. By the end of the century, France could lay claim to five "sister republics," which included parts of the Netherlands in the north and more than two thirds of the Italian peninsula in the south.

Efforts to reform and revolutionize also excited reaction. For the first time in European history, it became necessary to defend the very existence of monarchy and social hierarchy, and the Revolution's opponents did so with sword and pen alike. Scarcely a year after the taking of the Bastille, Edmund Burke published *Reflections on the Revolution in France*, which laid the foundation for two centuries of conservative thought by condemning revolutionaries for shattering an organic political order and innovating on the basis of unproven theories. By the time of the revolution of August 1792, France would face the armies of Austria, Prussia, Spain, and England, raised by the crowned heads of those countries against their unruly neighbor. Republican armies that claimed to liberate would meet opposition from the peasants, upon whom they imposed new taxes and new laws, and in whom they revived traditional loyalties and provoked new senses of regional identity. Ironically, the revolutionary movement that celebrated the universal appeal of its most fundamental principles would also plant the seeds of later nationalist movements.

Many who, like Ménétra, lived through the revolutionary decade would try with varying degrees of success to make sense of their experience, while their successors in the nineteenth and twentieth centuries would define political ideologies—liberalism, socialism, conservatism—by founding them on opinions about the Revolution. Alongside such ordinary men and women, there emerged as well generations of historians who have debated the causes and significance of the French Revolution in light of their own political and social concerns. During the nineteenth century, many scholars wrote what were primarily political histories of the Revolution, which echoed ongoing struggles in France between monarchism and republicanism, secularism and clericalism. The most important such history was that of Alexis de Tocqueville, who, instead of examining the events of the Revolution itself, focused on its long-term origins and outcomes. Trying to make sense of modern political practices and the decline of the aristocratic heritage that had dominated early modern Europe, Tocqueville tried to look beyond what revolutionaries themselves said about their actions. Thus, he argued that the Revolution did not mark a radical break with the past in French history. Rather, it completed a centuries-long process of political centralization that had been initiated by the kings of France. For Tocqueville, then, the Revolution's most significant achievement was not to have brought a new world into being, but to have completed a much older project of draining power away from the nobility to create a political system in which all citizens were equally subject to the centralized state.

By the early twentieth century, a secular and democratic Republic had been firmly established in France, but new events, in particular the Bolshevik Revolution in Russia, helped to provoke new questions. The pioneering studies of the first half of the twentieth century emphasized social and economic rather than political issues; they may almost uniformly be characterized as histories "from below," which examined the aspirations and activities of peasants and urban workers. By intellectual affiliation and political inclination many of these histories were also informed by Marxism. Although they emphasized social class and asserted that the Revolution had indeed marked an important break between the premodern and modern worlds, historians such as Albert Mathiez, Georges Lefebvre, and Albert Soboul shared Tocqueville's concern with long-term causes and consequences. They argued that the French Revolution was produced by an economically powerful bourgeoisie struggling to throw off the legal and political constraints of the feudal world. In the long run, they claimed, the French Revolution helped to facilitate the emergence and development of capitalism.

The Marxist interpretation of the Revolution was dismantled by Anglo-American historians writing in the 1950s, '60s, and early '70s, during the Cold War. "Revisionism" was initiated by the English historian Alfred Cobban, who argued that the Revolution was not begun by a rising bourgeoisie; rather, it was the work of men who were well integrated in the Old Regime economy and who resisted the changes being wrought by capitalism. Cobban's broadside and largely theoretical attack was sustained in subsequent years by the monographs of historians who demonstrated the extent to which the Old Regime bourgeoisie and nobility shared similar economic interests and aspirations. In 1967, George V. Taylor took revisionism to its furthest logical point by declaring that the French Revolution "was essentially a political revolution with social consequences and not a social revolution with political consequences."*

By the 1970s historians could say that the Marxist interpretation of the Revolution had suffered serious structural damage, and they began to ask what new structure they might build in its place. They knew what the Revolution was not, but what was it? One particularly promising avenue of research was suggested by the French historian François Furet and the American historian Lynn Hunt, who asserted that the Revolution was significant as a pivotal moment in the constitution of modern political culture. Although Furet and Hunt disagreed about the merits of the revolutionary moment, they shared the desire to shift attention away from Marxist and revisionist emphases on the Revolution's origins in order to focus on the event itself, and both argued that the Revolution produced fundamentally new kinds of political behavior. Furet and Hunt encouraged other historians to examine the relationships among language, cultural practices, and politics during the French Revolution.

Although Furet and Hunt suggested a new methodology for studying the Revolution, they did not impose a single, defining paradigm. In the absence of any particular orthodoxy, a broad range of approaches has flourished in the past fifteen years, allowing historians to bring new insights to this multifaceted event. Some scholars have labored to reconcile the social interests of the Marxists with the cultural and political interests of the postrevisionists; others have integrated the experiences of neglected groups—women, slaves, Jews—into our broader picture of the course and consequences of the Revolution; still others have used new methods to reinterpret old subjects—the question of origins, the experience of the peasantry, the conduct of legislative politics, the role of religion—about which we once thought debate concluded. This is not to say that today's histori-

---

*Quoted in William Doyle, *Origins of the French Revolution*. 2d ed. (Oxford: Oxford University Press, 1988), p. 20.

ans have somehow miraculously freed themselves from the period in which they live. Rather, historians writing at the end of the twentieth century are as enmeshed in their own history as were our forebears. Contemporary work reflects the emergence of new political practices and objectives at the end of the Cold War, the more explicit integration of women and minorities into education and public affairs, the growing self-consciousness of postcolonial peoples, and, of course, reactions against all of these movements.

This collection is designed to integrate documents that reflect contemporary historiographic concerns with those that treat more classical objects of study. In other words, it is our hope that students may use this collection to examine political, social, and cultural dimensions of the Revolution; to consider the experiences of women and slaves, as well as those of peasants and artisans, and the leaders of revolutionary and counter-revolutionary movements. Students of the French Revolution stand to learn a great deal from the enormously rich and important secondary literature on the subject, but it is equally important to have access to the words of the actors themselves. Primary sources allow readers to consider the possibilities and constraints that revolutionaries confronted, to examine the choices that they made and the sense they conferred on their experience. And they provide us with the opportunity to address the difficult issue that has plagued commentators for more than two centuries, that of distinguishing between judging the Revolution as a political event and understanding it historically. For however much contemporary concerns may shape the questions asked about the Revolution, and however much we may agree or disagree with particular revolutionary achievements, we must strive to understand what the actors themselves thought they were doing and why they made the particular choices that they did. Without historical understanding, judgment becomes nothing more than prejudice and contemporary concerns mere anachronism.

ONE

From Old Regime to Revolution ## 1610–1789

*H*istorians have retrospectively offered very plausible explanations of the causes of the French Revolution, but it was, at the time, an event that took witnesses and participants alike by surprise. France was the most powerful and most densely populated state in eighteenth-century Europe, ruled not by a despot but by a reforming monarchy. By the late 1780s, however, the weight of growing debt made clear that the king could neither continue to borrow nor accomplish reform without negotiating new fiscal arrangements with his subjects. And so Louis XVI agreed to convoke the Estates General, a representative institution that had last met in 1614. In agreeing to convoke the Estates General, the king set in motion a remarkable process of politicization that rapidly outpaced his intentions. Political discussion would give way to political action, moving the new nation from reform to revolution. Within a year, Louis XVI would find that he had lost his status as the sole and divinely ordained ruler of France to become the head of a constitutional government.

Prerevolutionary France

We would have only a very incomplete sense of what the Revolution achieved if we knew nothing of what it swept away. Therefore, it is worth pausing for a

---

The Tennis Court Oath The deputies of the new National Assembly swear not to separate until they have given France a constitution. *(Corbis-Bettman)*

moment to consider the society, politics, and culture of prerevolutionary France, a world that the revolutionaries would quickly come to characterize as the Old Regime.

Since about the eleventh century, French society had been divided into three legal categories, or estates, which determined its members' rights and duties and which supposedly expressed their principal contributions to the realm. The First Estate encompassed those who prayed (the clergy); the Second Estate, those who fought (nobles); and the Third Estate, those who worked (everyone else). After centuries of economic and political change, however, none of these groups were homogeneous entities. The members of the First Estate, for example, included wealthy, powerful, and cultivated archbishops as well as parish priests whose incomes and education scarcely distinguished them from poor parishioners. Members of the Second Estate monopolized the most important positions in royal administration, the army, church, and magistracy but here too there was great diversity; in addition to differences in wealth, there were differences in function, for the Second Estate grouped sword nobles, ancient military families whose wealth was based on land, with robe nobles, whose prestige was based on the possession of offices in the king's law courts, such as the parlements.

It was the Third Estate, however, that included the greatest variety of fortunes, occupations, and circumstances, and the largest number of people (97 percent of the population, or about 26 or 27 million people in 1789). In the overwhelmingly agricultural economy of the Old Regime, most members of the Third Estate were peasants: men and women who worked the land and whose conditions ranged from landless laborers teetering on the brink of homelessness and destitution to affluent landholders whose holdings and income rivaled those of lesser nobles. The vast majority of city dwellers were also members of the Third Estate: laborers, artisans, traders, and shopkeepers who fueled France's commercial and manufacturing economies. Finally, perched at the pinnacle of the Third Estate were administrators and lawyers, merchants and bankers. These men and their families—often called the bourgeoisie—were sometimes wealthier and often better-educated than the nobles who could claim to be their political and social superiors.

Ruling over this shifting and multifaceted society was a monarchy that had enjoyed almost a millennium of rule. The kings of France had struggled steadily since the thirteenth century to extend their rule, and by the eighteenth century the crown could claim sovereignty over a geographic area slightly smaller than the state of Texas, and it declared itself absolute, the source of all law. There was some basis to the claim of absolute power, for the king of France appointed his own ministers and benefited from a growing bureaucracy that extended his reach well beyond the royal palace at Versailles. However, he was also limited by tradition and by regional and corporate privileges. Equally important, he faced opposition from the royal law courts—the thirteen parlements of France. Although French magistrates served in royal law courts, they were not appointed by the king; rather, they owned and bequeathed their offices and so possessed a powerful sense of professional security and corporate unity. Having been tightly reined in by Louis XIV, the parlements enjoyed a resurgence of power after his death at

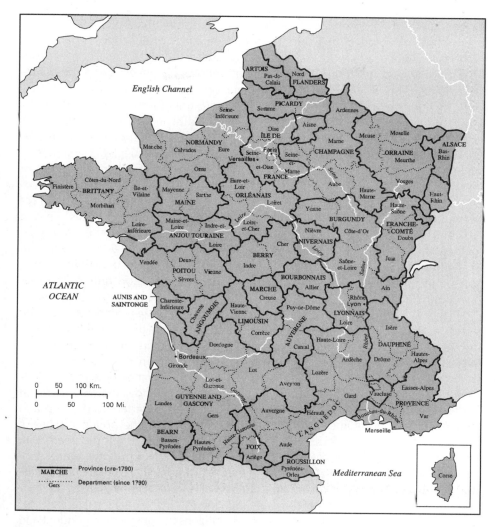

France's Provinces and Departments
The administrative departments of France, created by the National Assembly in 1791, are superimposed over traditional provincial divisions.

the beginning of the eighteenth century. Claiming to act as bulwarks against despotism, parlementary magistrates debated religious policy with the king and opposed his efforts to impose new taxes upon traditionally privileged groups. Parlementary opposition would prove instrumental in producing the deadlock that would lead to the calling of the Estates General in 1789.

While the king had to negotiate the limits imposed by tradition, privilege, and the parlements, he also had to contend with new intellectual forces that were emerging during the eighteenth century. Certainly the most powerful philosophical movement was that of the Enlightenment. Enlightenment thinkers adopted methods of observation and inductive reasoning that others had applied to the physical world during the Scientific Revolution; now they turned those methods on the social world. Arguing that no subject ought to be sheltered from the searching light of reason, Enlightenment philosophes investigated the nature and origins of good government, the foundation and structure of different societies, the purpose of law, and the value of religious toleration. The baron de Montesquieu, for example, urged readers to think critically about French government by comparing it to governments elsewhere in the world. Voltaire, a prolific essayist and historian, popularized Newtonian science and struggled passionately against religious prejudice. Certainly, the most important intellectual project of the century was the *Encyclopedia*, which gathered essays by European philosophers that summarized useful knowledge while developing subtle critiques of religious intolerance and prohibitions against the free circulation of ideas. Among the contributors to the *Encyclopedia* was Jean-Jacques Rousseau. Although Rousseau was far more critical of the social value of knowledge than were the other philosophes, he too defended the individual's right to question existing mores and institutions, basing that right on private conviction rather than reasoned knowledge.

The new intellectual forces of the eighteenth century were not based on the content of ideas alone; they were also based on new forms of sociability and new ways of understanding intellectual exchange. Educated men and women did not learn about the Enlightenment simply by reading books in the privacy of their homes; rather, they had access to a network of institutions that made different kinds of information available and that provided arenas for critical discussion. Provincial academies organized essay competitions that encouraged writers to develop and publicize reasoned arguments about the economic, social, and political issues of the day; local reading societies charged small fees to provide their members with subscriptions to a wide range of political and cultural journals; masonic lodges promoted democratic practices and a sense of fraternity among their members. Increasingly, philosophers and politicians alike referred to "public opinion," by which they meant not the unstable beliefs of disparate individuals but the universal and rational judgments of men who met together as private citizens to consider the conduct and outcome of public affairs. Although public opinion was explicitly regarded as the political judgments of an educated minority, peasants and poor city dwellers also expressed their opinions, albeit in more traditional ways: the king and his officials attended closely to applause on parade routes, songs and gossip, and local riots, hoping to measure the popular mood in this way and keep the peace of the realm.

From Reform to Revolution

By the late 1780s it had become apparent that the government was going bankrupt. The crown's financial difficulties dated to French participation and losses in the costly Seven Years' War (1756–1763), and they worsened during the intervening period thanks to debt service and further borrowing to help finance the American War of Independence. Having made minor economies, the greatest difficulty the crown faced was its inability to increase revenue because of France's archaic tax system. For among the most significant privileges that the king's subjects possessed were their exemptions from particular kinds of taxes. In particular, clergy and nobles—holders of much of the kingdom's land—were largely exempt from the principal land tax, the *taille*.

By 1786 the king could point to a long and worthy line of finance ministers who had tried to alleviate the monarchy's fiscal troubles. Some had instituted new and supposedly temporary taxes, others had tried to free trade to improve the economy, still others had taken further loans in an effort to improve public confidence. In many cases, however, ministerial innovation provoked opposition from the populace at large and from the parlements in particular, who believed that the crown's attempts to impose reforms from above threatened to become despotic. Having failed to find a lasting solution, the king convened a special Assembly of Notables in 1787, which he hoped would accept and help to popularize his current minister's reforms. But the notables proved as suspicious of royal motives as had been the public and the parlements. After months of fruitless negotiations, they concluded that only the Estates General—a representative body elected by the king's subjects—had the authority to agree to the proposed reforms and, above all, to the restructuring of taxes. The parlements concurred. In 1788 the king acquiesced and agreed to convoke the Estates General.

The Estates General had last met in 1614 and French society had undergone enormous change since then. In 1614 the dominance of the first two estates was reflected in the fact that, although they collectively constituted less than 4 percent of the population, each had the same number of representatives as the Third Estate. Furthermore, the Estates General traditionally voted by order, and the first two estates regularly outvoted the Third. By the end of the eighteenth century, however, the Third Estate had gained a great deal of economic and political vitality, and its members wanted representation in the Estates General to reflect that. Leaders of the Third Estate and their allies among the clergy and nobility demanded that the Third Estate be allotted twice the number of delegates as either of the other estates and that votes be counted by head, not by order. Early in 1789 a liberal cleric, the abbé Sieyès, weighed in with *What Is the Third Estate?*, asserting that because the Third Estate encompassed the truly productive members of French society, it constituted the nation. Bowing to popular pressure, Louis agreed to double the number of delegates of the Third Estate, but he remained silent on the question of vote by order or by head, so laying the groundwork for the eventual paralysis of the Estates General.

Once the number of delegates to be elected had been determined, the king's subjects could proceed to electoral assemblies, at which they were also expected to draw up *cahiers de doléances* (lists of grievances) to instruct the king and their delegates. These *cahiers*—composed by peasants and city dwellers, nobles and clergy, by a few women as well as by men—provided an extraordinary glimpse into the political concerns of France on the eve of Revolution as they detailed demands for legal and fiscal reform while expressing reverence for the king and respect for the existing social hierarchy.

The 1,200 deputies to the Estates General assembled at Versailles on May 3, 1789, and almost immediately encountered obstacles. At the opening session, the minister of finance, Jacques Necker, spent three hours delivering a rambling speech on the crown's financial difficulties; then he and the king withdrew without having offered proposals for debate or a solution to the question of whether delegates should vote by order or by head. Left to themselves, the delegates of the Third Estate continued to demand voting by head while the other two orders clung to the vestiges of tradition; thus, rather than attending to France's financial woes, the Estates General drifted in a state of stalemate for weeks. Finally tiring of the enforced calm, the Third Estate seized the initiative in early June by issuing a final invitation to the other estates to join them. When a number of clergy did so, the deputies gathered and declared themselves a National Assembly on June 17. A few days later, they adopted the Tennis Court Oath, vowing not to separate until they had produced a new constitution.

Moved by the initiative of the Third Estate, Louis XVI met with the assembled delegates and promised new reforms. Had the king made such proposals even a few weeks earlier, he would have been hailed as benevolent and far-sighted. But by late June he seemed only to be catching up with a reforming spirit that continued to elude him; then he made matters worse by insisting that the orders meet and vote separately. The new National Assembly stood its ground. In the face of their intransigence, Louis backed down and instructed the nobles and remaining clergy to join the new legislative body to deliberate in common and vote by head. Once again he had made concessions too late and once again lost the opportunity to lead the way.

The Assembly set to work, but not without a certain fearfulness, for on the advice of a conservative faction at court, Louis had begun to mass troops nearby. Rumors circulated that the king hoped to suppress the Assembly by armed force; his dismissal of the popular reform minister, Necker, on July 11 only seemed to confirm those fears. As the threat of violence lingered before them, initiative passed from the deputies in Versailles to the citizens of the capital. By mid-June, Paris was already in a state of turmoil because of ongoing economic difficulties and the ready circulation of political rumors. When news of Necker's fall from power reached them, Parisians began to fear that royal troops would be sent to the capital as well as to Versailles. Tensions ran high on July 12 and 13 as orators spoke energetically of the impending crisis and Parisians organized themselves into militia. On the afternoon of July 14 a crowd composed largely of skilled workers surrounded the medieval fortress and prison of the Bastille to demand arms with which to defend themselves. The crowd sent delegates to negotiate with the commander of the fortress, and when the delegates were too long in returning, the artisans stormed the fortress. They defeated the king's troops in a victory that was stunning for its unexpectedness; simple working people had overcome one of the greatest symbols of monarchic power. Frightened, Louis backed down: he recalled the troops stationed near the capital, reappointed Necker, and left the National Assembly to go on with its work.

The Beginning of Popular Revolution

At a point of deadlock, Parisians intervened to protect the new National Assembly from the threat of dispersion; popular and elite political interests coincided, and it is perhaps this coincidence that helps to explain why the taking of the Bastille on July 14, 1789—not the calling of the Estates General or the declaration of the National Assembly—should mark the beginning of the French Revolution. But the taking of the Bastille was a problematic victory, for the men of the National Assembly also knew that when the commander of the fortress surrendered to the crowd, the crowd lynched him and paraded his severed head through the streets. These were the legislators' allies and the tensions inherent in this event would trouble revolutionary governments until 1795, as they found themselves dependent on popular strength that they were not always certain of containing.

The next important act of 1789 was also tied to popular violence, but this time it was associated with rural activism. The peasantry constituted about 80 percent of the population in eighteenth-century France; although there were great extremes of wealth and poverty among peasants, most lived with the knowledge that their labors and careful economies only sufficed for the moment and were unlikely to carry them through hard times. The land was productive—and large-scale landholders did quite well over the course of the eighteenth century—but the average family was burdened by rising rents and a dizzying array of taxes that drained away profit. Equally critical were the archaic and humiliating feudal dues and privileges owed to local seigneurs, which, for example, required peasants to provide free labor to landlords and prohibited them from fishing or hunting in nearby waterways and forests. And, thanks to inflation and the crown's financial difficulties, the amount and number of taxes had risen steadily throughout the century while wages (and most peasants did some wage labor) lagged behind.

The drafting of *cahiers* in early 1789 raised peasants' hopes for the improvement of their condition at the same time that flour shortages and high bread prices provoked uneasiness. So even before the Estates General came to sit, rural unrest shook different provinces as peasants rioted for cheaper bread or refused to pay feudal dues, convinced that the deputies in Versailles would cancel them shortly. Conditions only worsened as summer approached: rumors of trouble in Versailles compounded the anxiety produced by waiting for crops to ripen after a year of shortages. The news of the July insurrections in Paris acted as a spark that touched off the smoldering unrest. Rumors and rioting swept the countryside in an episode of violence that has come to be known as the Great Fear. In many areas, crowds of peasants demanded the records of feudal dues from local seigneurs in order to destroy them; in a few cases, they vandalized and even destroyed local châteaux. Meanwhile, rumors swept the countryside that towns and villages were being overrun by nameless bandits, rumored to be in the pay of aristocrats enraged by reform. Thus, rioting was intensified by bands of peasants, armed for defense, who turned on local elites when the rumored bandits failed to materialize, destroying records of feudal dues and demanding oaths of loyalty to the new order.

News of these events trickled into the National Assembly, exciting the deputies' worst fears that popular violence would rage out of control, sweeping away not only all feudal dues but all property. A small group of deputies undertook to propose the abolition of feudal dues to the Assembly, but what was initiated as a matter of debate swung wildly out of control. On the night of August 4, deputies to the National Assembly engaged in a delirium of renunciation as, in a session that stretched into the small hours of the morning, they gave away their own privileges and those of their peers. Although they would later qualify many of these renunciations, requiring compensation for some of the dues they abolished, they had unequivocally swept away the system of privilege that had defined the rights and duties of the king's subjects for centuries. Henceforth, France could claim to be a nation founded on the principle of equality before the law.

Having taken down the old order, the deputies turned their attention once more to creating the new. In late August they endorsed the "Declaration of the Rights of Man," which swept away many of the inequities of the Old Regime and declared principal rights of the new citizenry. Almost immediately, however, the deputies determined that the Declaration would require some form of assent from the king himself. But how to request royal assent without first determining the limits of the king's power? And so the Assembly found itself confronting the limits of legislative and executive power in the form of a debate over the king's veto. The Monarchiens, admirers of the English system, favored the creation of an upper house similar to the House of Lords and an absolute veto for the king. The Patriots did not want to divide an Assembly so recently united, and they favored a suspensive (temporary) veto. Once the liberal minister, Necker, had circulated the rumor that this was also the king's preference, the Patriots won the day; the suspensive veto was adopted in mid-September, by a vote that fell just short of a two thirds majority.

To modern eyes, the suspensive veto might appear an acceptable compromise, but it was not well received in Paris, where many radicals feared giving any significant power to the king. Thus, anti-veto pamphlets began to circulate in a city that was again experiencing flour shortages and high bread prices. Matters deteriorated still further as news circulated that Louis was dragging his feet on ratification of the decree abolishing feudalism. And then a new regiment arrived in Versailles. Fearing for his safety, the king had summoned the well-disciplined Flanders Regiment to the palace. Upon arrival, they were welcomed by the standing regiment with a banquet at which the soldiers' behavior quickly spiraled out of control; they were reputed to have sung songs insulting the Revolution and to have torn off their revolutionary cockades.

Once again, news from Versailles ignited popular anxieties. On the morning of October 5, several thousand women from throughout Paris gathered and marched off to see the king. Recognized as providers of food for their families, women had traditionally been the principal activists in bread riots, and the October march was provoked, in part, by their desire to win better and cheaper provisioning. But like the insurgents against the Bastille, these women were reaching beyond the objectives of traditional insurrections to involve themselves in revolutionary politics, for they were equally concerned that the king might fall into the hands of counter-revolutionaries. When they reached Versailles, the women sent a deputation to meet the king and then, having won promises of better supplies and lower prices, they settled down to spend the night on the palace grounds alongside troops of national guard that had followed them from Paris. Violence broke out early the following morning when a crowd invaded the palace and killed two guards. Counseled that the best means to calm the crowd was to agree to return to Paris with them, the king gathered the royal family and set off with the women. And so it was that, on October 6, 1789, the market women of Paris returned to the capital with the king, the queen, and the heir to the throne or, as they put it, "the baker, the baker's wife, and the baker's son." Now, they and many others believed, Parisians could protect their beloved king from the influence and possible violence of counter-revolutionaries. Louis XVI never returned to Versailles, and to facilitate its work, the National Assembly moved to the capital a few days later.

While many Parisians celebrated the king's arrival in the capital, other witnesses were deeply troubled by the events of the October days. Henceforth, many would consider the king to be a prisoner of his people. More important, this incursion of the populace into the political process set an important precedent. The taking of the Bastille had been a defensive measure, but the October days were offensive: the crowd had intervened to break a deadlock between king and Assembly and to win legislative action. Then market women and national guard had taken the government to Paris, to the most radical political arena in France. Henceforth, king and Assembly would be subject to pressure from the Paris crowd. And the Paris crowd would, again and again, show itself willing to use force to extract radical measures; it would also pressure the legislature to privilege Parisian interests over those of the countryside, thus eventually helping to divide France. But, for the moment, many believed that the Revolution had been completed and that the only task they now faced was one of creating the new France.

THE PRE-REVOLUTION

1. Charles Loyseau, *A Treatise on Orders* (1610)

·Charles Loyseau (1564–1627) was a jurist and a legal scholar. Writing at a moment of great social change, in particular one during which robe nobles were gaining political power and social esteem, Loyseau produced three legal treatises that have been characterized as describing the "social anatomy of France."* Although Loyseau's explicit goal was to describe the juridical basis of each order, he was also interested in their moral foundations and social functions. His treatise, which, it must be remembered, describes an idealized vision of French society, remained authoritative until the Revolution.

Foreword

It is necessary that there be order in all things, for their well being and for their direction. . . . Inanimate creatures are all placed according to their high or low degree of perfection: their times and seasons are certain, their properties regulated, their effects assured. As for animate creatures, the celestial

---

*J.M.H. Salmon, *Society in Crisis: France in the Sixteenth Century* (London: Methuen, 1979), p. 323.

Source: Keith Michael Baker, ed., *The Old Regime and the French Revolution* (Chicago & London: University of Chicago Press, 1987), pp. 13–31. Translated by Sheldon Mossberg and William H. Sewell, Jr. © 1987 by The University of Chicago. All rights reserved.

intelligences have their hierarchical orders, which are immutable. And in regard to men, who are ordered by God so that they may command the other animate creatures of this world here below, although their order is changeable and subject to vicissitude, on account of the particular liberty that God has given them for good and for evil, they nevertheless cannot exist without order. ...

. . . Since the people is a body with several heads, it is divided by orders, Estates, or particular occupations. Some are dedicated particularly to the service of God, others to protecting the state by their arms, others to nourishing and maintaining it through peaceful occupations. These are our three orders or Estates General of France: the clergy, the nobility, and the Third Estate. But each one of these three orders is again subdivided into subordinate degrees, or subalternate orders, following the example of the celestial hierarchy. . . .

Chapter I. Of Order in General

. . . In France, the three Estates have their order and rank one after the other, the ecclesiastical order being first, followed by the nobility and the Third Estate last. This is true even though there are no statutes to this effect, because laws are scarcely made in matters simply of honor. But the ranks are willingly observed through honor, and certainly they are more honorable when they come from a voluntary respect. . . . For honor and love are two things so sublime and exalted that they cannot be commanded; nor can they be obtained with good grace by force; nor can any action assure them. If one thinks one possesses them by force, this is not love but fear and subjection, not honor but tyranny and oppression. . . . As love is necessary to the world, so are honor and rank; otherwise there would only be confusion among us. But it is necessary to earn both by merit, and maintain them by gentleness.

Thus since the ecclesiastical order is the first among us, it appears that even the least priest, even the lowest tonsured cleric, should take precedence over the greatest gentleman of the court (I refer here to private persons; those whose office gives them a particular rank are another matter) not because of his individual merit, but for the sake of his order and for that of God whose minister he is. . . . But because the ecclesiastical order is considered an exceptional and extraordinary order in the secular domain, our Redeemer having said that his realm is not of this world . . . it is commonly observed at present that those who enjoy some secular dignity do not wish to give place to priests unless they have an ecclesiastical dignity.

Similarly, I say that the least gentleman must take precedence over the richest and most honorable member of the Third Estate, speaking of course of private persons and when it is only a matter of rank among orders; but since the dignity of office is greater, and even enhances that of order inasmuch as order is ordinarily required to hold office, it becomes a difficult issue when a commoner who holds office disputes precedence with a gentleman who does not. . . .

Chapter III. Of the Order of the Clergy

... In this Christian kingdom, we have bestowed on God's ministers the first rank of honor, rightly making the clergy (that is to say, the ecclesiastical order) the first of our three Estates of France. ... In nearly all the states of Christendom the clergy are similarly constituted as a distinct order, as in France, which has always been more Christian and has honored the Church more than any other nation on earth. ...

As in the case of each of the three orders or general Estates of France, there are among the clergy several degrees, or subalternate and partial orders subordinated one to another. ...

Chapter IV. Of the Order of the Nobility in General

... [In France] we have ... that nobility which derives from ancient blood, and that which derives from dignities. The first has no beginning, the second has a beginning; the first is original, the second acquired. We tend to call the latter nobility and the former generosity or gentility, just as we commonly distinguish between noblemen and gentlemen.

To discover the origin of this gentility, or ancient and immemorial nobility, it is necessary to consider that as the Athenians and the Romans first divided their people into patricians and plebeians, so from the first establishment of this monarchy, its people were divided into gentlemen and commoners, the one group destined to defend and maintain the state, either by counsel or force of arms, the other to nourish it by working the soil, engaging in commerce, or practicing the crafts. This division has continued up to the present time. ...

Alternatively, the nobility of France had its origin in the ancient mixture of the two peoples who came together in this kingdom, that is to say, the Gauls and the Franks who conquered and subdued them without attempting to exterminate or drive them away. But the Franks retained this prerogative over the Gauls, that they alone would hold public office, bear arms, and possess fiefs without having to contribute anything either to the lords of particular localities or to the sovereign for necessities of state. Instead, they were obliged only to fight in wars.

As for the conquered people, they were reduced to a condition of partial servitude. ... In addition to being in this condition of partial servitude and being incapable of holding offices, bearing arms, or possessing fiefs, the people were also required to pay the seigneur a tribute or land tax, and occasionally to provide taxes for the unusual needs of the state. ...

Now as the two races mixed and adapted to one another, this initially rigorous exclusion of commoners from holding offices, bearing arms, and possessing fiefs did not continue so strictly. But some vestiges of it still remain. In the case of offices, the principal ones, such as the crown, those in the king's household, and provincial governorships, may only be held by gentlemen. In the case of arms, commoners are not admitted into heavy cavalry regiments, and were not in earlier times allowed to hold important commissions in the infantry. In the case of fiefs, they are still ineligible to hold the principal fiefs and seigneuries, and as for simple fiefs, they must still pay the tax of *franc fief* for the right to hold them. But gentlemen have carefully guarded the liberty of exemption from any subsidies or obligations other than joining the king in war. . . .

Nevertheless . . . our ancient and immemorial nobility, whose beginnings are unknown, does not derive from right of nature, as does liberty, but rather from the ancient law and arrangement of the state. Nobility is not simply a particular privilege, contrary to the common law, but has its origin in a public and general law and proceeds from means established to this effect long ago in each country. Accordingly, it is of much longer duration and is more firmly held than are simple privileges. This is a fundamental point, the basis for deciding an infinite number of questions that arise in this matter.

All this is true of that nobility ("gentility") which exceeds the memory of man. As for the nobility whose origins may be determined, in France it comes from ennoblement by the prince, who is ordained by God to distribute the substantial honors of this world. . . . The prince may ennoble in two ways: by means of a letter written expressly to this end, or by grant and investiture of offices and seigneuries that carry nobility with them, and in which the nobility that derives from dignity properly consists.

This ennoblement purges the blood and the posterity of the ennobled of all stain of commonness, raising him to the same quality and dignity as if his race had always been noble. . . . Nevertheless, because . . . this abolition of servitude or commonness is only an effacing of a mark that remains, it seems more of a fiction than a truth, since the prince cannot reduce being to nonbeing. . . .

Accordingly, in the common opinion, those ennobled either by royal letter or by the dignity of office are less esteemed than nobles by blood, although in fact they enjoy all the same privileges. . . . That is why in France we are so interested in hiding the origins of our nobility, so that we may reduce this type of nobility to that of the immemorial sort. . . .

We have three degrees of nobility in France: simple nobles, whom we call gentlemen and esquires; high nobles, whom we designate as seigneurs and knights; and those of the highest degree, whom we name princes. Each of these three degrees of nobility has its own effects. For simple nobility affects the blood and passes on to posterity in such a way that the older it is the more honorable it becomes. High nobility does not descend to posterity, at least in the same degree, but rather it is personal, being conferred upon the person for his particular merit, such as knighthood (which is a perfect order that perishes with the person), or by reason of his office or seigneurie (and in the latter case, it perpetually follows the office or seigneurie). Finally, princehood can come only from blood, but resides there in a manner opposite to that of simple nobility; for it is of a higher rank according to its recentness and its nearness to its source.

Chapter V. Of Simple Gentlemen

. . . The true rights of the nobility are as follows. First, as to power, it has been said in the first chapter that orders have no particular power, as offices have, but that they only produce an aptitude for offices, benefices, and seigneuries. This is confirmed above all in the order of the nobility. . . .

. . . As for the honor pertaining to nobility, since it is the true effect of orders to produce honorable rank, as their name denotes, it is altogether reasonable that the nobility, which risks its life for the defense of the state, be honored by the people as its protector. Consequently, it is an established right among us that members of the order of the nobility outrank and take precedence over members of the Third Estate. . . .

As for other marks of honor, nobles have the right to call themselves Esquire and to bear coats of arms, even if they are men of the city and of the long robe, ennobled only by their offices. Moreover, all nobles (except those of the long robe) have the right to carry a sword as the ornament and sign of nobility, and in France they are even entitled to wear it in the king's own chambers. . . .

It is a matter of debate whether commoners are formally obliged to salute nobles, as the latter believe, even though the contrary is true. For . . . the salute is a recognition and obligation of subjection, which is formally owed only by subjects to those who command them, either by right of possession (as their seigneurs) or by the exercise of public function (as their magistrates). As a matter of honor and propriety, a salute is given to members of the high nobility, namely great lords and holders of high office, and all those entitled to call themselves knight; and from this same sense of propriety, we salute senior members of our families. But the most well-bred and cultivated among us salute all honorable persons, just as they salute family members of equal rank, and friends, as a matter of simple civility and courtliness. But these latter actions belong to the domain of manners, not law.

As for profits and pecuniary emoluments, it has been said above that there are none that pertain purely to orders as such. But the privileges of the nobility are yet very great. They include exemption from the *taille* and all other personal taxes levied for purposes of war. It is certainly a very reasonable privilege that those who contribute their lives for the defense of the state be exempt from contributing their goods. For the same reason, gentlemen are exempt from lodging soldiers in their homes. Gentlemen also have the privilege of hunting game in authorized places, seasons, and manners, a privilege which is justly denied to the common people for fear that it would lead them to abandon their ordinary employment to the public detriment. The hunt has also for good reason been limited to the nobility, so that nobles can maintain in peacetime an exercise resembling war. . . .

It is another privilege of gentlemen that when they commit a crime, they are not punished as rigorously as the common people. . . . This is true in terms of severity of judgments and the nature of punishments (there are some punishments to which gentlemen are never condemned, such as hanging and flogging; on the contrary, common people are never decapitated . . .). It is also true that nobles receive grace and forgiveness from the prince more readily than do commoners. . . .

But there are two exceptions to this rule. The first consists in the fact that crimes repugnant to nobility, such as treason, larceny, perjury, or double-dealing are aggravated and made more serious by the dignity of the person committing them. . . . The second consists in the fact that corporal punishments inflicted on gentlemen are milder, but pecuniary punishments must be harsher. . . .

Activities leading to the forfeiture of nobility are those of the pleading attorney, clerk of the court, notary, sergeant, clerk, merchant, and artisan of all trades except glass-making. . . . What is at issue here is the fact that these activities are performed for profit. For rightly speaking, it is sordid profit that derogates from nobility, whose proper characteristic is living off rents or at least not selling its labor. On the other hand, the employments of judges, advocates, doctors, and professors of the liberal arts do not derogate from nobility, even when nobles live by means of these professions, because this kind of profit (which proceeds from the work of the mind not the hands) is honorary rather than mercenary.

Tilling the fields does not derogate from nobility, not because of its utility (as is commonly thought) but because nothing a gentleman does for himself, and without taking money from another, implies derogation. . . .

Chapter VIII. Of the Orders of the Third Estate

Inasmuch as order is a species of dignity, the Third Estate of France is not properly an order. For since it comprises all the rest of the people apart from the clergy and the nobility, this would imply that all the people of France without exception were in dignity. But inasmuch as order signifies a condition or occupation, or a distinct kind of person, the Third Estate is one of the three orders or general Estates of France. In ancient Gaul, it was not taken into account or held in any respect or regard, as Caesar says in Book VI of *De Bello Gallico*. And following Caesar, M. Pasquier appropriately remarks in his *Livre des Recherches* that during the first two dynasties of our kings there was no mention of the Third Estate, nor were the simple people called to the general assemblies held to reform the state: assemblies then called parlements, which we now call Estates General. These assemblies comprised only the prelates and the barons, that is to say the principal persons of the clergy and of the laity. . . . Pasquier adds that in the third dynasty our kings had adopted the custom of asking the common people for aid or subsidies for the necessities of war. In order to secure the people's consent (without which, at that time, no levy of funds could be raised) the kings henceforth summoned it to these assemblies which, for this reason, were called Estates General. This is why the common people is called the Third Estate . . . because it was added to the two others, which had been established a long time before. And this Third Estate of France enjoys much greater power and authority in our time than it did formerly, because nearly all of the officeholders of justice and finance belong to it, the nobility having scorned letters and embraced idleness. . . .

The term "Third Estate" is more comprehensive than that of "bourgeois," which comprises only the inhabitants of the towns, that in old French (and still today in German) are called bourgs. . . . Furthermore, the term "bourgeois" does not properly comprise all the inhabitants of the towns. For nobles, even if they make their home in the towns, do not qualify as bourgeois because the nobility is an order completely separate from the Third Estate, to which the bourgeoisie belongs. . . . Moreover, base persons among the common people have no right to call themselves bourgeois, since they have no share in the honors of the city nor any voice in the assemblies, in which rights bourgeoisie consists. . . .

What is more, properly speaking, bourgeois are not found in all towns but only in privileged towns, those which have the right to corporate and communal forms of government. For to be a citizen or bourgeois . . . is to participate in the rights and privileges of a city; so that if the city has no communal government and corporate existence, neither officeholders nor privileges, it can have no bourgeois. . . .

In France, as in ancient Rome, there are several orders or degrees of the Third Estate . . . men of letters, financiers, those serving the courts, merchants, husbandmen, ministers of justice, and laborers. It is necessary to speak of each separately.

For the honor which is due to knowledge, I have put men of letters in the first rank. . . . Our men of letters are divided into four principal faculties, or branches of knowledge: theology, jurisprudence (under which are included civil and canon law), medicine, and the arts, which comprise grammar, rhetoric, and philosophy. . . .

In my opinion, financiers must rank after men of letters. . . . By financiers, I mean all those who undertake the handling of finances (that is to say, the king's monies) whether they hold offices or not. For we are speaking here of orders, or rather of mere occupations, which are compatible with offices. It is true that in earlier times the tasks of finance were not offices, but simple commissions. . . . The majority of these were conferred by the people when it granted a levy to the king and named particular persons to allocate the levy equally. . . . But since venality of offices has become customary, even the most minor financial operation has been made into an office. And because these offices ordinarily carry little honor or power, their remuneration is generally very high; added to which it is expected that, as those who pick peas keep a few in their hands, so those who handle finances keep their share—which they rarely forget to do. . . .

Next come practitioners or men of affairs . . . all those who, apart from judges and advocates, gain their living by the business and legal transactions of others. They are of two kinds: those of the long robe, namely clerks of the court, notaries, and attorneys . . . ; and those of the short robe, namely sergeants, trumpeters, appraisers, vendors, and others like them. . . .

After the principal practitioners . . . come the merchants, as much for the utility, indeed the public necessity, of commerce . . . as for their usual opulence, which brings them credit and respect. In addition to the latter, their ability to employ artisans and laborers brings them much power in the towns. Thus merchants are the last group among the people to receive honorable titles, to be called "honorable men" or "honest persons" and "bourgeois of the town." Titles such as these are attributed neither to husbandmen, nor to sergeants, nor to artisans, and still less to laborers, all of whom are reputed to be vile persons, as will shortly be explained.

Husbandmen must, in my opinion, follow merchants and precede practitioners of the short robe . . . since in France rural life is the ordinary occupation of the nobility, while commerce brings derogation of nobility. It is true that by husbandmen I mean those ordinarily engaged in tilling for others as tenants, an exercise which is as strictly forbidden to the nobility as is commerce. But be that as it may, there is no life more innocent, no gain more in accord with nature than that of tilling the soil, which philosophers have preferred to all other vocations. In France, however, administrative policy has lowered them so much, even oppressed them, by taxes and by the tyranny of the gentlemen, that one is astonished that they can subsist, and that there are enough of them to provide nourishment for us all. Thus one sees that the majority prefer to be valets and carters for others, rather than masters and farmers in their own right.

In any case, today we consider common husbandmen and all other men of the village, whom we call peasants, as vile persons. . . .

The artisans, or tradesmen, are those who exercise the mechanical arts, which are so named to distinguish them from the liberal arts. This is because the mechanical arts were formerly practiced by serfs and slaves, and indeed we commonly call mechanical anything that is vile and abject. Nevertheless, because the mechanical arts demand considerable skill, masterships have been created in them, just as in the liberal arts. . . .

Although artisans are properly mechanics and reputed to be vile persons, there are certain trades in which manufacture and commerce are combined. . . . Inasmuch as they participate in commerce, these trades are honorable, and those who exercise them are not numbered among the vile persons . . . but may be addressed as "honorable men" and "bourgeois" like other merchants. . . .

On the other hand, there are trades which reside more in bodily strength than in the practice of commerce or in mental subtlety, and these are the most vile. . . .

For all the more reason, those engaged neither in manufacture nor commerce, and who gain their living only by the labor of their arms, whom we call *gens de bras*, or mercenaries, such as porters, masons' laborers, carters, and other day laborers, are the most vile of the common people. For there is no worse occupation than having none at all. Still, those who are occupied in gaining their living by the sweat of their brow, according to the command-

ment of God, are far better to be maintained than so many able-bodied beggars, with whom France is filled at present, because of excessive taxes. . . .

2. The Parlement of Paris

The parlements of France, thirteen in number by the eighteenth century, were
formally defined as the king's law courts. In practice, they did far more than simply administer justice: they played an integral part in politics and administration
as well. Traditionally, the king was required to register all new laws and edicts
with the parlements, which in turn had the right to remonstrate, or criticize
those edicts, if they contravened customary law or the fundamental rights of the
king's subjects. If the king refused to accept the parlement's suggestions, the parlement might, in rare cases, refuse to register the edict. In the absence of regular
meetings of the more representative Estates General, the parlement could plausi-
bly claim to represent the popular will, even though its members were not
elected; they held their offices as personal property. The first of the following selections is drawn from a *lit de justice*, a session in which the king imposed his
will on the parlement. Here, the parlement justifies the role that it has historically played in the political life of the realm. The second selection illuminates
the precarious position that parlements often occupied on the cusp of tradition
and progress as they protested reforms proposed by the Physiocratic minister
Turgot.

A. *Lit de Justice* to Register the Edict of November 1770 (DECEMBER 7, 1770)

Sire,

Nothing could be more painful for your parlement and nothing, it may be
said, does your parlement deserve less than to see itself accused, with other
companies of the magistracy, of a crazed and criminal plot to obscure and
weaken the inviolable rights of your sovereign authority.

Source: Jules Flammermont, ed., *Remontrances du Parlement de Paris au XVIII⁰ Siècle* (Paris, 1848),
pp. 158–163, 308–311. Translated by Laura Mason.

Your parlement, Sire, always worked to strengthen and increase this sacred authority, which it regards as the soul of the state and the founding principle of its very existence.

If the pride of the great vassals was forced to humiliate itself before the throne of your ancestors, to renounce independence and recognize in their king a supreme jurisdiction, a public power superior to theirs; if the independence of your crown was sustained against the efforts of the court of Rome when all sovereigns had bowed beneath the yoke of Ultramontane ambition; finally, if the scepter was preserved from male to male, to the eldest of the royal house by the longest and happiest succession that exists in the annals of empires; all these services, certainly the most important ever rendered to royal authority and to the state, are due, as history testifies, to your parlement.

And who else, Sire, other than a body that considers danger meaningless when it must prove its faithfulness to its kings, would dare expose itself fighting for them against that which is most fierce and most dreadful? Independent of the duty that requires it to do so, your parlement's very interests, Sire, would compel it to undertake the defense of your authority. . . .

The preservation of this authority will always seem of such great import to your parlement that it would possibly make the sacrifice of accepting the humiliations to the magistracy gathered in the present edict if that were truly useful to the true interests of your authority and did not risk making the liberty, life, honor, and property rights of your subjects the plaything of unforeseen events, which the monarch would soon regret, but too late.

But what advantages, Sire, could your authority find in renewing efforts which experience has already banished several times and which public opinion denounces unequivocally?

Some projects of this sort, presented to kings only to be rejected by them, were aborted before blossoming; some were publicized without effect, their authors winning only shame and disgrace; some, adopted in an initial movement excited by dark devices in the spirit of the Sovereign, vanished with the grim impressions to which they gave rise. Finally, if there are similar projects whose existence the efforts of the powerful sustained with difficulty, this temporary ordeal only made more clear the need to revoke them and allow affairs to return to their old and natural course.

Thus has authority always seen itself decisively compromised by such risky projects; time itself, which reveals all, was not long, Sire, in revealing to the Sovereign that, in the case of those projects, an affected zeal for authority is nothing but the veil that their authors throw over themselves while their true objective is to employ such dangerous projects to satisfy their personal interests and their vengeance, without considering the ills that necessarily result for the state and for the Monarch. . . .

Sire, far from listening to those who use such language with you, far from risking the fatal test of projects about which your people grumble, which make the great moan, which shock Europe and upon which your enemies perhaps found their hopes, condescend, Sire, in withdrawing your edict, in doing justice to your parlement, in leaving it the free exercise of its functions, the integrity of the authority you confided in it, which is and always will be within your domain, authority that parlement has never used and can never use except to strengthen your own, which is its foundation and fundamental principle; condescend to carry out a test that is less lengthy, less painful, less subject to tiring difficulties that are ceaselessly renewed; in short, Sire, a test that will heap glory on your name while insuring your tranquillity; recognize these slanderers of the magistracy as disrupters of the state, as secret enemies of your peacefulness, as ambitious usurpers of your authority; hand them over to the vengeance of the laws; all your subjects will applaud; nations will admire your wisdom; you will soon enjoy a calm that these men will never leave to you because they believe it is in their interest to deprive you of calm for, raised in trouble, trouble alone can sustain and improve their credit. Then you will see your parlement as it is; you will find nothing there, Sire, but respect, submission, love, and fidelity.

[The king persists in his demand that parlement register the edict in question. The president of the parlement responds on the following day.]

Sire,

Your parlement heard with nothing but the keenest and most bitter sadness that the accounts it had the honor to present to you yesterday have been represented to Your Majesty as likely to produce ideas as false as they are injurious to your sacred person.

It was, Sire, possible to represent these acts in such a way only by corrupting the sense of expressions that your parlement had used only to give Your Majesty new assurances of its fidelity, love, and submission, to demonstrate how much the powerful interest of duty, and even the personal interest of each member composing your parlement, obliges him to sustain the sovereign authority of Your Majesty, and to attest that, in a moment of such violent crisis, all the hopes of your people and your parlement rest solely in the personal wisdom of Your Majesty, in his justice and goodness.

Your parlement, Sire, cannot and must not proceed with the registration of an edict whose registration would cover it with shame in the eyes of the people from this moment forward and in the eyes of the Sovereign himself on some day to come;

An edict which so clearly compromises the most precious rights of the subjects of Your Majesty, their property, their liberty, their lives, and their honor;

In short, an edict, Sire, which compromises the dear and sacred interests of Your Majesty by altering the constitution of the Monarchy, destroying solemn and perpetually obeyed forms for the establishment of laws and by forever exposing Your Majesty to all the unforeseen events which the greatest kings are never spared and against which their most certain defense is the zeal, faithfulness, and courage of their courts; this is a truth keenly felt by all of Your Majesty's august predecessors, who sought only to reinforce the courage of their officers of justice, by reassuring them in the most effective way of the preservation of their liberty, their life, their estates, and especially by the king Louis XI, the prince who was most jealous of his power and his authority.

B. Parlementary Remonstrance Against the Edict
Suppressing Guilds and Communities of Arts and Trades
(MARCH 2–4, 1776)

It is time to consider what advantages could be drawn at the present time from the suppression [of the guilds].

This edict can be considered from three points of view alone:

According to the advantages to the administration of suppression;

According to the inconveniences for society of the existence of the guilds;

Or according to their inconveniences for commerce.

As regards advantages, there are none for the administration: the guilds have almost no goods that the treasury can acquire by suppressing them; they have only debts which the justice of Your Majesty would oblige him to satisfy.

Considered from the perspective of the advantages that society draws from them, on the contrary, the guilds offer two that are difficult to deny: easier policing of the capital and greater security within commerce.

The police have only two means available to them: force, which they use only when necessary; the terror impressed by vigilance, whereby the police reign without being felt.

Overwhelmed by the details of a city as great as Paris, the police depend on the intermediary authority of a host of domestic guarantors whose power is more extensive because they exercise immediate surveillance and command by example.

The justification for corporations has been sought in their historical origins, when it ought to have been sought in nature. From the greatest [corps], which are empires, to the least, which are families, men have always united to protect themselves, always commanded or been supervised by parents, responding to general calm with internal calm. It is a chain, all the links of which are joined to the first, the authority of the Throne, which it is dangerous to break.

Above all, there are some classes over which the police must exercise all its vigilance. It supervises the rich from afar; they are interested in good order. But in protecting the poor, it watches their conduct more closely because they only stand to gain from trouble. And what class ought to draw the closest attention of the police other than that class of men who are all the more dangerous because their skills offer them greater means to do harm, and all the more fearsome for having more needs?

It is a vain desire to substitute the ties of a new police for this; it would be necessary to test the effects before pronouncing on its usefulness. But one cannot fruitfully supervise unless one commands. What will become of the authority of masters when their workers, always independent, always free to raise themselves up alongside the masters, can repeatedly escape from their homes? An apprentice, scarcely initiated in the first principles of his art, disdains the advice of his master because he depends on his own activity and talent to work for himself. Who will supervise him in the details of domestic life, who will answer for him to the police?

How frightening does this prospect become, Sire, when applied to those beings born to trouble society, beings among whom passions, less tamed by education, join those activities that one acquires in the midst of the license of cities with the brute energy of nature? What police could be sweeter than that of the guilds? Workers were examined by their masters, masters by the guild officials they had chosen; a correspondence of interests joined all together, harmony reigned within the community. If there is any problem there, it is only the regret that the administration did not make a healthful reform of these establishments which seemed so useful in themselves and so easy to perfect.

But will difficulties cease under the new regime and is it certain that harmony will reign in the proposed neighborhoods as it reigns in the guilds? . . .

Once neighborhoods are formed, what harmony may one expect from a disorganized multitude of interests, which have no affinity other than being gathered together in the same quarter?

How will an agent be chosen? Each wants his equal, no one his superior; if the artisan of the least order and the shopkeeper whose business relations raise him above command at the same time or together, then commerce—which is already too debased—will decline further and further; honest families will distance themselves from a trade that will no longer exist. Moreover, what would be the authority of this agent if he were not the passive executor of the orders of the police (as the edict claims with a clause undreamed of until now)? He will be hated without being feared, he will always act, never foresee and, if he supervises as an immediate subordinate to the magistrate, he may be a tyrant.

When secret movements raise the fear of disorder among the people, will the agent be strong enough to contain the artisans of his district? Will the masters themselves be responsible for workers who have become independent?

Your parlement, Sire, perhaps exaggerates the ills to which this policing would give rise, but what may one not fear when the primary ties that unite all men are dissolved; how will the lieutenant general of police be sufficient for the innumerable disputes that will arise? How will he, already keeping his eyes on the whole of such a large city, pause over the details of such complicated administration? Always obliged to depend on subordinates, who will guarantee that he will never be fooled; and how may direct authority over such a great number of artisans not give rise to individual, petty frauds, to hidden and vexatious maneuvers that will escape the vigilance of the magistrate?

The lieutenant general's power, exercised with absolute orders, his tribunal, which will most often be sovereign, will no longer be arms of the judge of police. The overturning of judicial forms, arbitrariness in decisions, contempt for authority, capriciousness, harshness, oppression, the unexpected abuses of all sorts which the subordinate agents of an independent power allow themselves, are terrible ills for the people. Your love for your subjects, Sire, would not allow them to be exposed to this. . . .

3. Jacques Necker, Preface to the *King's Accounts* (1781)

Because Jacques Necker was a Protestant and a foreigner he was barred from holding the official position of Controller General. Therefore, he was appointed by the king in 1776 with the official title of "assistant to the Controller General"; he was, in effect, the minister of finance. During his tenure, Necker tried to improve the financial condition of the realm by initiating piecemeal administrative reforms and paring away court extravagance. In 1781, in an attempt to initiate public debate about French finances and to strengthen the crown's credit, Necker made the monarchy's revenues and expenses public for the first time. The accounts—the preface to which is included here—demonstrated (erroneously, it would later prove) that there were no deficits in the king's accounts. In spite of this happy conclusion, however, Necker lost his post that same year because of court intrigue. His reforms were repealed.

Sire,

Having devoted all my time and energy to serving Your Majesty since he called me to the post I now hold, it is certainly invaluable for me to offer him a public account of the success of my labors, and the current state of His Majesty's finances.

But, regardless of the value that a faithful servant should place on this rendering of his conduct, I would have renounced this satisfaction, I would have joined this sacrifice to many others had I not believed that the publicizing of such an account and its genuineness could be infinitely useful to the good of Your Majesty's affairs. I wonder if such an institution, become permanent, would not be a source of the greatest benefits. The obligation to reveal all his administration to the light of day will influence the first steps that a minister of finance takes in the career that he must follow. Shadows and obscurity favor negligence; publicity, on the contrary, can only become honor and recompense in proportion to the degree that one understands the importance of his duties and strives to fulfill them. This

Source: Auguste Louis de Stael-Holstein, ed., *Oeuvres complètes de M. Necker*, vol 2 (Paris, 1820). Translated by Laura Mason.

Louis XVI and Benjamin Franklin sign the Treaty of Commerce and Friendship (1778) between France and America. *(Musée de l'Impression sur Étoffes)*

account also puts each member of Your Majesty's counsels in a position to scrutinize and supervise the situation of the finances; important knowledge with which all great deliberations should be associated and to which all should be referred.

At the same time, this hopeful advertisement will increase still more the indifference to those obscure writings with which some try to disturb the peace of the administrator, the authors of which—certain that an elevated soul will not descend into the arena to respond—profit by such silence to upset opinions here and there with lies.

Finally, and this is a point worthy of the most serious consideration, such an institution could have the greatest influence on public confidence.

⌈If one examines the great credit that England enjoys and which is currently its greatest strength in the war, one should not attribute that entirely to the nature of its government, because, regardless of the authority of the monarch of France, since his interests are known always to rest on the foundation of faithfulness and justice, he could easily make all forget that he has the power to dismiss those principles,⌉ it is up to Your Majesty, with his strength of character and virtue, to make this truth felt through experience.⌉

But another cause of the great credit of England is, do not doubt this, the public renown to which the status of its finances is subject. That status is presented to Parliament each year, and printed afterward; and thus all lenders have regular knowledge of the balance being maintained between revenue and expenditure, they are never troubled by suspicions and imaginary fears, the inseparable companions of secrecy.

In France, a great mystery is always made of the status of the finances; or, if they are occasionally discussed, it is in the preambles of edicts and always when we want to borrow; but those words, too often the same to be true, have necessarily lost their authority and experienced men no longer believe them without the guarantee, so to speak, of the moral character of the minister of finance. It is vital to found confidence on a more solid base. I admit that, under certain circumstances, it has been possible to profit from the veil cast over the financial situation to obtain, in the midst of disorder, some mediocre credit that was not warranted; but this momentary advantage, which sustained a misleading illusion and favored the indifference of the administration, was soon followed by unhappy transactions, the memory of which lasts longer and which will take long to correct. It is thus only in the first moments of a great state's inconvenience that the light cast upon the situation of its finances becomes embarrassing; but if this very publicity could have prevented the disorder, what service would it not have done!

The sovereign of a realm like that of France can always, when he wants to do so, maintain the balance between expenditures and ordinary revenue; the diminution of the former, always seconded by the wishes of the public, is in his hands; and when circumstances require, increasing taxes is within his power; but the most dangerous, and the most unjust of resources, is to seek momentary aid with blind confidence and take loans without insuring the interest, or to raise revenues, or to economize.

Such administration, which is seductive because it postpones the moment of difficulty, only increases ills and digs itself deeper into the hole; while another kind of conduct, simpler and more frank, multiplies the means available to the Sovereign and forever protects it from any sort of injustice.

It is thus this broad view of administration on the part of His Majesty which has permitted us to offer a public account of the state of his finances; and I hope that, for the good of the realm and his power, this happy institution will not be temporary! Ah! what is there to fear from such an account if, in order to be the foundation and support of credit, it only does what the simplest rules of morality demand of the Sovereign, which is to say, balance expenditures with revenues, and offer guarantees to lenders whenever the needs of the state have recourse to their confidence!

I will divide the account that His Majesty has permitted me to give him into three parts:

The first will concern the current state of finances, and all transactions related to the royal treasury and public credit.

The second will elaborate on transactions that joined important economies with administrative advantages.

In the third, I will offer an account to His Majesty of general measures whose only end is the greatest happiness of his people, and the prosperity of the state.

This division reminds us, at a single glance, that two great parts of administration are placed in the hands of the minister of finance and, unhappily, the elements of these parts, as well as the knowledge and talent they require, have little in common; nevertheless, if both are not tended equally, ills of all sorts will follow.

A controller general's excellent views on administration would be in vain, he could not long hold his post, and he would undermine his best intentions and talents if, in a ministry as active as his and, above all, in the midst of such difficult circumstances, he did not know how to make timely payments and sustain good credit with resources and wise projects.

If, on the contrary, a minister of finance had mastered this latter science to the highest degree and neglected the other, circumstances would regrettably require leaving an administration in his hands which, as it tends to the present moment, should never sacrifice to it the sources of public prosperity; and which, while applied to finding the resources necessary to the defense of state and the Sovereign's power in the midst of war, should never neglect the happiness of his subjects, for whose maintenance this power is destined.

4. Charles Louis de Secondat Montesquieu, "In What Manner the Laws of Civil Slavery Relate to the Nature of the Climate," *The Spirit of Laws* (1748)

Easily one of the best-known works of the Enlightenment, *The Spirit of Laws* was influential throughout Europe and North America from its date of first publication. Therein, Montesquieu articulates the theory of the separation of powers and distinguishes between types of governments. Preferring monarchy to despotism and democracy to aristocracy, he nevertheless believed that culture and climate determined which sort of government is most suitable to a given people. The same is true of systems of slavery. While he unequivocally condemns slavery as

Source: Charles Louis de Secondat Montesquieu, *The Spirit of Laws*, trans. Thomas Nugent (New York: Colonial Press, 1900), pp. 235–241.

an affront to natural law, he grants that climate and custom may justify its use. His ideas on slavery informed a half century of debate that culminated in the formation of the Friends of the Blacks abolition society in 1788, thus forging a link between the Enlightenment and the early Revolution.

Of Civil Slavery

Slavery, properly so called, is the establishment of a right which gives to one man such a power over another as renders him absolute master of the other's life and fortune. The state of slavery is in its own nature bad. It is useful neither to the master nor to the slave; not to the slave, because he can do nothing through a motive of virtue; nor to the master, because by having an unlimited authority over his slaves he insensibly accustoms himself to the want of all moral virtues, and thence becomes fierce, hasty, severe, choleric, voluptuous, and cruel.

In despotic countries, where there is already a state of political servitude, civil slavery is more tolerable than in other governments. Everyone ought to be satisfied in those countries with necessaries and life. Hence the condition of a slave is hardly more burdensome than that of a subject.

But in a monarchical government, where it is of the utmost importance that human nature should not be debased or dispirited, there ought to be no slavery. In democracies, where there is complete equality, and in aristocracies, where the laws ought to use their utmost endeavors to procure as great an equality as the nature of government will permit, slavery is contrary to the spirit of the constitution: it only contributes to give a power and luxury to the citizens which they ought not to have. . . .

Another Origin of the Right of Slavery

I would as soon say that the right of slavery proceeds from the contempt of one nation for another, founded on difference in customs.

Lopès de Gomara relates "that the Spaniards found near St. Martha several basketfuls of crabs, snails, grasshoppers, and locusts, which proved to be the ordinary provision of the natives. This the conquerors turned to a heavy charge against the conquered." The author owns that this, with their smoking and trimming their beards in a different manner, gave rise to the law by which the Americans became slaves to the Spaniards.

Knowledge humanizes mankind, and reason inclines to mildness; but prejudices eradicate every tender disposition.

Another Origin of the Right of Slavery

I would as soon say that religion gives its professors a right to enslave those who dissent from it, in order to render its propagation more easy.

This was the notion that encouraged the ravagers of America in their iniquity. Under the influence of this idea they founded their right of enslaving so many nations, for these robbers, who would absolutely be both robbers and Christians, were superlatively devout.

Louis XIII was extremely uneasy at a law by which all the Negroes of his colonies were to be made slaves; but it being strongly urged to him as the readiest means for their conversion, he acquiesced without further scruple.

Of the Slavery of the Negroes

Were I to vindicate our right to make slaves of the Negroes, these should be my arguments:

The Europeans, having extirpated the Americans, were obliged to make slaves of the Africans for clearing such vast tracts of land. Sugar would be too dear if the plants which produce it were cultivated by any other than black slaves.

These creatures are all over black, and with such a flat nose they can scarcely be pitied. It is hard to believe that God, who is a wise Being, should place a soul, especially a good soul, in such a black ugly body.

It is so natural to look upon color as the criterion of human nature, that the Asiatics, among whom eunuchs are employed, always deprive the blacks of their resemblance to us by a more opprobrious distinction.

The color of the skin may be determined by that of the hair which, among the Egyptians, the best philosophers in the world, was of such importance that they put to death all red-haired men who fell into their hands.

The Negroes prefer a glass necklace to that gold which polite nations so highly value. Can there be a greater proof of their want of common sense? It is impossible for us to suppose these creatures to be men because, allowing them to be men, a suspicion would follow that we ourselves are not Christians.

Weak minds exaggerate too much the wrong done to the Africans. For were the case as they state it, would the European powers, who make so many needless conventions among themselves, have failed to enter into a general one, on behalf of humanity and compassion?

The True Origin of the Right of Slavery

It is time to inquire into the true origin of the right of slavery. It ought to be founded on the nature of things; let us see if there be any cases where it can be derived thence.

In all despotic governments people make no difficulty in selling themselves; the political slavery in some measure annihilates the civil liberty.

According to Mr. Perry, the Muscovites sell themselves very readily: their reason is evident—their liberty is not worth keeping.

At Achim every one is for selling himself. Some of the chief lords have not less than a thousand slaves, all principal merchants, who have a great number of slaves themselves, and these are also not without their slaves. Their masters are their heirs, and put them into trade. In those states. the freemen being overpowered by the government have no better resource than of making themselves slaves to the tyrants in office.

This is the true and rational origin of that mild law of slavery which obtains in some countries: and mild it ought to be, as founded on the free choice a man makes of a master, for his own benefit; which forms a mutual convention between the two parties.

Another Origin of the Right of Slavery

There is another origin of the right of slavery, and even the most cruel slavery which is to be seen among men.

There are countries where the excess of heat enervates the body, and renders men so slothful and dispirited that nothing but the fear of chastisement can oblige them to perform any laborious duty: slavery is there more reconcilable to reason; and the master being as lazy with respect to his sovereign as his slave is with regard to him, this adds a political to a civil slavery.

Aristotle endeavors to prove that there are natural slaves; but what he says is far from proving it. If there be any such, I believe they are those of whom I have been speaking.

But as all men are born equal, slavery must be accounted unnatural, though in some countries it be founded on natural reason; and a wide difference ought to be made between such countries, and those in which even natural reason rejects it, as in Europe, where it has been so happily abolished.

Plutarch, in the "Life of Numa," says that in Saturn's time there was neither slave nor master. Christianity has restored that age in our climates.

Inutility of Slavery Among Us

Natural slavery, then, is to be limited to some particular parts of the world. In all other countries, even the most servile drudgeries may be performed by freemen.

Experience verifies my assertion. Before Christianity had abolished slavery in Europe, working in the mines was judged too toilsome for any but slaves or malefactors: at present there are men employed in them who are known to live comfortably. The magistrates have, by some small privileges, encouraged this profession: to an increase of labor they have joined an increase of gain; and have gone so far as to make those people better pleased with their condition than with any other which they could have embraced.

No labor is so heavy but it may be brought to a level with the workman's strength, when related by equity, and not by avarice. The violent fatigues which slaves are made to undergo in other parts may be supplied by a skilful use of ingenious machines. The Turkish mines in the Bannat of Temeswaer, though richer than those of Hungary, did not yield so much; because the working of them depended entirely on the strength of their slaves.

I know not whether this article be dictated by my understanding or my heart. Possibly there is not that climate upon earth where the most laborious services might not be performed by freemen. Bad laws having made lazy men, they have been reduced to their slavery because of their laziness.

5. Isabelle de Charrière, *The Nobleman* (1763)

Isabelle de Charrière was born a noblewoman in Switzerland in 1740. She was a talented writer from a young age. Her wit attracted the attentions of Voltaire and the king of Prussia. Representative of the genre of the sentimental tale, which became increasingly popular and feminized in the latter half of the eighteenth century, her widely read writings made her a familiar figure of the Enlightenment. Her first story, *The Nobleman*, published in 1763, is autobiographical, as would be many of her later works. The following excerpt depicts the frustrations endured by the vivacious young protagonist, who is confined by the prejudices and lifestyle of her moribund aristocratic family.

There once stood in one of the French provinces a very ancient castle, inhabited by an ancient scion of a yet more ancient family. Baron d'Aronville—for such was his name—was exceedingly sensible of the value of this ancientry, and in this he was wise, for he owned little else of value. Yet it would have perhaps been better if his castle had been a trifle less ancient, for one of its towers blocked up a portion of the surrounding moat while of the rest you could only perceive a little muddy water, where frogs had taken the place of fish. The Baron's table was frugal, but there hung all around the dining hall the antlers of deer killed by his ancestors. He recalled that on feast days he had the right to shoot and that on fast days he had the right to fish. Thus, contented with the possession of these rights, he was enabled, without any sensation of envy, to permit his pheasants and his carp to be eaten by rich men of ignoble birth. He spent his modest revenues in bringing a lawsuit to prove his right to hang malefactors upon his property. It would never have occurred to him that it would have been possible to put his income to better account or to leave a more valuable heritage to his children than the power of executing jus-

Source: Four Tales, ed. Geoffrey Scott; trans. Sybil Scott (Freeport, N.Y.: Books for Libraries, 1926; reprinted 1970).

tice. His private purse he employed to renew the escutcheons that bordered all his ceilings and to repaint the portraits of his ancestors.

Baroness d'Aronville had been dead for many years and had left him one son, and one daughter, named Julia. The young gentleman might, with good reason, have complained equally of his character and education, but in fact he complained of neither. Content with the name of d'Aronville and the knowledge of his family tree, he dispensed easily with both talent and knowledge. Occasionally he shot, and ate his game in the company of the young woman of the neighboring tavern; he drank heavily and gambled every evening with his lackeys. His person was unpleasing, and keen eyes would have been needed to discern in him those characteristics which, according to some, are the infallible signs of noble birth. Julia, on the contrary, was endowed with beauty, charm, and intelligence. Her father had obliged her to read some treatises on heraldry that had not entertained her, and she herself had read in secret some romances which had entertained her exceedingly. A visit she had paid to a lady of her family in the capital of the province had given her some knowledge of the world; much is not required to render a person genteel who has an observant mind and a generous heart.

A painter, who had been employed to copy her ancestors and their quarterings, had once given her some drawing lessons; she could depict landscapes and embroider flowers. She sewed with skill and sang with taste, and as her person had need of neither art nor magnificence, she was always held to be well dressed. She was vastly vivacious and merry, although tender, and jests on the subject of nobility had been known to escape her, but the respect and friendship she felt for her father had always kept them within bounds. Her father reciprocated her love but he would have preferred her to embroider armorial bearings rather than flowers, and to study the mouse-eaten parchments that enumerated his family titles rather than to read *Télémaque* and *Gil Blas*. It vexed him to observe that modern engravings hung near to the window in her room while the old portraits were banished to a dark recess, and he often scolded her for preferring some pretty and amiable girl from the middle class to a young noblewoman of the neighborhood, who was both plain and sullen. Moreover, he would have liked her to give place only to rank, according to the dates of creation, and Julia never consulted Patents of Nobility, but gave place to age, and would rather have been thought plebeian than proud. From thoughtlessness she might have walked out before a princess, from indifference or civility she might have let everyone precede her.

She did not pretend to excessive cleverness, so that what talents she possessed gave all the more pleasure. She knew very little, but one saw that it was because she had not had the opportunity of learning; her ignorance never bore the appearance of stupidity. Her lively, sweet, and smiling countenance attracted all who beheld it, and her gracious manner completed the prepossession her physiognomy had caused. She had become a great favorite with a Parisian lady whom she had met at her relative's house, and this lady now invited her to stay at her county seat. Julia succeeded in obtaining her father's consent, and after he had counselled her never to forget her rank, he permitted her to depart. Her hostess was very wealthy and had an only son, who was, nevertheless, both amiable and well brought up. He was personable, Julia was pretty; they pleased each other at first sight and did not, at the beginning, think either to show or to conceal their feeling. Soon, however, they let it be understood, and found each other all the more amiable when assured of pleasing. In company, at table, or when walking, Valaincourt would murmur or hint some tender thought to Julia; but as soon as they were alone and they might have spoken freely, he ceased to address her. She was surprised at this and yet satisfied; either she had read or had divined that love is timid when it is ardent and delicate, and although no speech would have pleased her like her lover's, she was equally happy in his silence.

Valaincourt had, however, in addition to the reasons that Julia had surmised, a further reason for silence that she did not know. She had seen that he had fine eyes, fair hair, and beautiful teeth; she had found in him sweetness, intelligence, and generosity, and she had remarked order, decency, and opulence in his home. But she had forgotten to enquire which of his ancestors had been ennobled. Unluckily, it was his father, who, by distinguished services and many virtues, had merited this honor. Wise men might argue that when rank has been acquired in this manner the most recent nobility is the best, that the first noble of his race has the most right to be proud of a title he has won for himself, that its second bearer will be worth more than its twentieth, and that it is to be presumed that Valaincourt more closely resembled his father than Baron d'Aronville resembled his thirtieth ancestor. But wise men are not competent to judge the work of prejudice, and Valaincourt knew of the prejudice and the weight it would have with Julia's father. . . .

6. Jean-Jacques Rousseau, *The Social Contract* (1762)

Although he died more than ten years before the taking of the Bastille, Jean-Jacques Rousseau (1712–1778) would prove to be one of the most influential writers of the Revolution. An early if troublesome associate of the philosophes, Rousseau distanced himself from the mainstream of the Enlightenment in both his works and his lifestyle. He was indeed a man of letters, if not a bona fide resident of the "republic of letters," in terms of the diversity of his accomplishments: musical compositions, a best-selling novel (*La Nouvelle Héloise*), a radical treatise on children's education (*Émile*), and above all his political works, including

Source: Jean-Jacques Rousseau, *The Social Contract and the Discourses* (New York: E.P. Dutton, 1913), pp. 3–4, 10–13, 14–15, 16, in *Western Societies: A Documentary History*, vol. 2, ed. Brian Tierney and Joan Scott (New York: Alfred A. Knopf, 1984), pp. 179–182.

Du Contrat social. His theory of the "general will," articulated in the following selection, was of great importance to revolutionary conceptions of politics.

Subject of the First Book

Man is born free; and everywhere he is in chains. One thinks himself the master of others, and still remains a greater slave than they. How did this change come about? I do not know. What can make it legitimate? That question I think I can answer.

If I took into account only force, and the effects derived from it, I should say: "As long as a people is compelled to obey, and obeys, it does well; as soon as it can shake off the yoke, and shakes it off, it does still better; for, regaining its liberty by the same right as took it away, either it is justified in resuming it, or there was no justification for those who took it away." But the social order is a sacred right which is the basis of all other rights. Nevertheless, this right does not come from nature, and must therefore be founded on conventions. Before coming to that, I have to prove what I have just asserted.

The Social Compact

I suppose men to have reached the point at which the obstacles in the way of their preservation in the state of nature show their power of resistance to be greater than the resources at the disposal of each individual for his maintenance in that state. That primitive condition can then subsist no longer; and the human race would perish unless it changed its manner of existence.

But, as men cannot engender new forces, but only unite and direct existing ones, they have no other means of preserving themselves than the formation, by aggregation, of a sum of forces great enough to overcome the resistance. These they have to bring into play by means of a single motive power, and cause to act in concert.

This sum of forces can arise only where several persons come together: but, as the force and liberty of each man are the chief instruments of his self-preservation, how can he pledge them without harming his own interests, and neglecting the care he owes to himself? This difficulty, in its bearing on my present subject, may be stated in the following terms:

"The problem is to find a form of association which will defend and protect with the whole common force the person and goods of each associate, and in which each, while uniting himself with all, may still obey himself alone, and remain as free as before." This is the fundamental problem of which the social contract provides the solution.

The clauses of this contract are so determined by the nature of the act that the slightest modification would make them vain and ineffective; so that, although they have perhaps never been formally set forth, they are everywhere the same and everywhere tacitly admitted and recognized, until, on the violation of the social compact, each regains his original rights and resumes his natural liberty, while losing the conventional liberty in favor of which he renounced it.

These clauses, properly understood, may be reduced to one—the total alienation of each associate, together with all his rights to the whole community; for, in the first place, as each gives himself absolutely, the conditions are the same for all; and, this being so, no one has any interest in making them burdensome to others.

Moreover, the alienation being without reserve, the union is as perfect as it can be, and no associate has anything more to demand: for, if the individuals retained certain rights, as there would be no common superior to decide between them and the public, each being on one point his own judge, would ask to be so on all; the state of nature would thus continue, and the association would necessarily become inoperative or tyrannical.

Finally, each man, in giving himself to all, gives himself to nobody; and as there is no associate over which he does not acquire the same right as he yields others over himself, he gains an equivalent for everything he loses, and an increase of force for the preservation of what he has.

If then we discard from the social compact what is not of its essence, we shall find that it reduces itself to the following terms:

"Each of us puts his person and all his power in common under the supreme direction of the general will, and, in our corporate capacity, we receive each member as an indivisible part of the whole."

At once, in place of the individual personality of each contracting party, this act of association creates a moral and collective body, composed of as many members as the assembly contains voters, and receiving from this act its unity, its common identity, its life, and its will. This public person, so formed by the union of all other persons, [was] formerly called by its members State when passive, Sovereign when active, and Power when compared with others like itself. Those who are associated in it take collectively the name of people, and severally are called citizens, as sharing in the sovereign power, and subjects, as being under the laws of the State. But these terms are often confused and taken one for another: it is enough to know how to distinguish them when they are being used with precision.

The Sovereign

If the State is a moral person whose life is in the union of its members, and if the most important of its cares is the care for its own preservation, it must have a universal and compelling force, in order to move and dispose each part as may be most advantageous to the whole. As nature gives each man absolute power over all his members, the social compact gives the body politic absolute power over all its members also; and it is this power which, under the direction of the general will, bears, as I have said, the name of Sovereignty.

Again, the Sovereign, being formed wholly of the individuals who compose it, neither has nor can have any interest contrary to theirs; and consequently the sovereign power need give no guarantee to its subjects, because it is impossible for the body to wish to hurt all its members. We shall also see later on that it cannot hurt any in particular. The Sovereign, merely by virtue of what it is, is always what it should be.

This, however, is not the case with the relation of the subjects to the Sovereign, which, despite the common interest, would have no security that they would fulfill their undertakings, unless it found means to assure itself of their fidelity.

In fact, each individual, as a man, may have a particular will contrary or dissimilar to the general will which he has as a citizen. His particular interest may speak to him quite differently from the common interest: his absolute and naturally independent existence may make him look upon what he owes to the common cause as a gratuitous contribution, the loss of which will do less harm to others than the payment of it is burdensome to himself; and, regarding the moral person which constitutes the State as a *persona ficta*, because not a man, he may wish to enjoy the rights of citizenship without being ready to fulfill the duties of a subject. The continuance of such an injustice could not but prove the undoing of the body politic.

In order then that the social compact may not be an empty formula, it tacitly includes the undertaking, which alone can give force to the rest, that whoever refuses to obey the general will shall be compelled to do so by the whole body. This means nothing less than that he will be forced to be free; for this is the condition which, by giving each citizen to his country, secures him against all personal dependence. In this lies the key to the working of the political machine; this alone legitimizes civil undertakings, which, without it, would be absurd, tyrannical, and liable to the most frightful abuses.

The Civil State

. . . Let us draw up the whole account in terms easily commensurable. What man loses by the social contract is his natural liberty and an unlimited right to everything he tries to get and succeeds in getting; what he gains is civil liberty and the proprietorship of all he possesses. If we are to avoid mistake in weighing one against the other, we must clearly distinguish natural liberty, which is bounded only by the strength of the individual, from civil liberty, which is limited by the general will; and possession, which is merely the effect of force or the right of the first occupier, from property, which can be founded only on a positive title.

We might, over and above all this, add, to what man acquires in the civil state, moral liberty, which alone makes him truly master of himself; for the mere impulse of appetite is slavery, while obedience to a law which we prescribe to ourselves is liberty. But I have already said too much on this head, and the philosophical meaning of the word "liberty" does not now concern us.

7. Nicolas Toussaint le Moyne des Essarts, "The Noailles Affair" (1786)

In the 1770s and 1780s accounts of court cases were best sellers. Des Essarts, himself a lawyer, edited and compiled ninety-seven volumes of "causes célèbres." In the following case he features the rhetoric of the aspiring lawyer Barère de Vieuzac (see document 58), who offers a condemnation of aristocratic and paternal privilege in matters of marriage. Des Essarts and Barère alternately narrate the case on behalf of a young woman of the middle class who was seduced and abandoned by a young aristocrat. Here are glimpsed some of the tensions over aristocratic privilege that would explode in a few years.

Miss Noailles was born in Beaucaire on August 4, 1756, the daughter of Sir Claude Noailles, merchant, and Miss Anne Pelissier. She was not of the class of fishermen, but of that of merchants; . . . in a useful class, in an honest station which calls forth abundance and augments national industry. It was in this same city, to Miss Noailles' misfortune, that Chevalier de ———— was born on March 12, 1757. . . .

This family lived with an ease acquired by commerce, and with morals respected by the whole town, until the ill-fated destiny of Miss Noailles called the chevalier to her.

The latter appeared receptive to her charms: she was then eighteen years old, and the chevalier was six months younger. Letters, messengers, and visits were all set in motion. He saw that this young woman was born of an honest family and esteemed in the region; she was linked, by blood, to several important citizens, while he was the youngest [in his family] and legitimate. All these considerations fortified the nascent inclination of Chevalier de ————.

Sir Noailles, a wise father, separated his daughter [from the chevalier], and sent her to Toulouse. After spending a year in that city, she was recalled to

Source: Nicolas Toussaint le Moyne des Essarts, "Affaire de Noailles," in *Les Causes célèbres, curieuses et intéressantes de toutes les cours souveraines du Royaume avec les jugements qui les ont décidées*, case 504 (Paris, 1786), vol. 140, pp. 14–56, 138–144. Translated by Tracey Rizzo.

Beaucaire. But her absence had only augmented the chevalier's passion. Upon her return, he wrote her:

> Miss, allow me this day to offer you my heart, this heart which has searched so for an occasion to tell you that it loves you, that it adores you. Yes, miss, I love you and will love you always. Be persuaded that nothing will be capable of diminishing the love I carry for you. Make me happy forever and give me your heart and your faith.

Letters followed each other rapidly. . . . Miss Noailles did not trust ordinary discourse; she avoided all occasions to see the chevalier; she even made him promise not to appear before her. This resolution aggravated the chevalier. . . .

Years passed; letters remained unanswered. These perpetual difficulties did not cool the chevalier's [ardor]. Ever constant, ever attached to the movements of Miss Noailles, he wanted, moreover, to close the distance that social prejudices put between them. Up to that moment, he had only spoken of his love, but after five years of devotion, he had other views, other means of approaching Miss Noailles. . . . He attacked her heart from all sides; he made much of his constancy; he spoke of his probity, his candor; he signed his letters.

The chevalier, aged 24, was hopelessly in love with her: these vows full of honor and integrity fanned the flames which the virtue of Miss Noailles had seen born with caution. After six years of pursuit and love, [she succumbed and] they flattered themselves that they were born for each other.

However, Miss Noailles always combatted this mutual infatuation; she did not ignore their different ranks. The distance alarmed more than flattered her; yet what confidence did the chevalier ceaselessly inspire! He wrote:

> All men are equal. Nobility should be granted only on the basis of personal merit; wealth comes from chance. One ought to designate as 'noble' the man most worthy of the name. . . . Integrity, humanity, greatness of soul, generosity. These are the charms for me. . . . Yes, miss, I regard you as that which I hold dearest in all the world, as my best friend, indeed as my wife.

Here comes a novel twist. His love became a fury. The respectful and humble lover is no longer an enterprising man. The future husband gave way to the seducer. Fear not, we will retrace only that which the chevalier himself was unafraid to say.

He obtained a house key from a confidante attached to the Noailles family. He then made a duplicate of it; he waited until night came to reveal to all eyes the use he planned to make of it.

In the middle of the night of March 4, 1781, he entered the room of Miss Noailles, who, horrified at this appearance, wanted to repel him. To calm her, the chevalier showed her his father's written consent to their marriage, including a signature and date; he asked her to choose the day.

Miss Noailles could not believe this. Ever in the greatest astonishment, she asked for time to make up her mind. After this interview, the chevalier started to leave her room, engaging her to come hold the light and close the door. Confident, she followed him; once she was at the threshold, the chevalier and unknown accomplices kidnapped her from her father's house, locked her in a carriage, and led her to the Venaissin district. She fainted, and recovered only to find herself deposited at the home of an honest citizen of Montfavet. Thus virtue commands the respect of seducers, even in the bosom of license.

Estranged from her family, torn from its asylum, in the midst of fear, far from the place of her birth, taken without her consent, she employed the only weapons of her sex: tears and prayers. The chevalier consoled her: "I will write and your parents will pardon my mistakes. . . ."

This letter could not dry the tears of the Noailles family. They consulted, they considered bringing criminal charges against the chevalier [. . . but] M. Noailles feared exposing his daughter's future husband to the shame of a trial. It was time for this devotion, so often sworn, to be consecrated by religion. Saturday, September 15, 1781, was the designated day to repair so many errors. They went to hear mass with all the people, and following the custom of the district, they placed themselves at the foot of the altar and took each other in matrimony in the presence of the Supreme Being, and under the eyes of Montfavet's priest and four witnesses. . . .

But now, a new epoch.

The chevalier's eldest brother, the hope of the lineage, descended to the grave. All emotions were turned on the chevalier, the only remaining male in this family. He learned of his brother's death; he hoped this tragedy had softened his uncle's heart [who had opposed his marriage to Catherine] and that misfortune rendered all his family sensitive to the voice of nature. He brought his wife back to Beaucaire. . . .

But the chevalier's imperious uncle was impatient with his nephew's marriage. He could not persuade himself that a commoner had won the chevalier's heart and hand; he wanted to make him reject this union which he believed unequal. . . . [Despite the chevalier's persistent love], his relatives' obsession did not ease for an instant. They repeatedly threatened the chevalier with disinheritance, with naming his sister as heir, unless he renounced his wife. . . .

[They then imprisoned him by *lettre de cachet*.]

All meetings between the two spouses were forbidden. The husband had no other resource than his pen and his heart. . . . Finally, all commerce in letters was interrupted in March 1782. . . . Horrible premonitions accompanied this sad epoch. . . .

[Six months passed.]

Then, the unfortunate wife was confined to her paternal home to perish from sadness and punishment. But [she was] forsaken in the bosom of her family who reproached her, every day, with her dishonor, until she was shocked suddenly by the news that the chevalier had married [someone else] in Marseilles!

The uncle's strategy had been to search for a distant arrangement, which could be hidden from everyone; but the secret was revealed and the Noailles family registered opposition to this marriage on May 23, 1783, in the hands of Marseilles' priests.

The Sirs ———— were set on claiming that there was no marriage [between Catherine and the chevalier] and thus that the son should be declared free. . . .

[A trial ensued.]

Before reporting the court's verdict, we believe that our readers would experience as much pleasure as we have in examining the discourse, as touching as it is energetic, of M. Barère de Vieuzac, addressed on behalf of his client to the chevalier.

"How grand, how respectable is the authority of fathers over their children, above all in matters of marriage; it should however be contained within limits. As holy as it is, this domestic magistracy has limits relative to society's interests . . . fathers cannot serve themselves at all times and on all occasions. . . . We know that nature and law have made as many sovereigns within families as there are fathers; but we want to purify the use of their authority, to mitigate its exercise by the just and ingenious means that our laws have adopted. . . .

"I know, sirs, that the validity of marriages demands the concurrence of religion and civil law, but when nature, religion, and probity have already formed a union, can family interests, the speculations of fortune and vanity, break it? . . .

"With the word 'misalliance' they have hoped to elevate the nobility. Is there among gentlemen, among other citizens, is there one single man who, after having seduced a young woman, after having run off with her, after having made reparations by marriage, can then retract his promises, falsify his words, relegate his victim into the lowest class of citizens? . . .

"A spouse married by the tribunal of honor, engaged before the Supreme Being, should he obey the cupidity of his family or the voice of his conscience? . . .

"The holiness of Christianity has finally banished every difference that fortune puts between men; grace knows no distinctions between people. . . .

"Return then to the spouse whom your heart has chosen, and whom religion has given you; come, she will not reproach you forever for the wrongs she has suffered. Your family has exhausted your devotion; they have seduced you with the lure of fortune, and the hope of a more illustrious marriage, and they have mixed your name up in a shameful trial. She will pardon your mistakes. They have still perhaps invoked the word 'honor' to entice you to repel your wife. Ah, honor! True honor is not always in the glamour of a vain name, nor in brilliant matches; honor is in keeping your promises and respecting your vows.". . .

[The parlement of Toulouse found the chevalier guilty of seduction, but not bigamy, on March 29, 1784. A settlement of 20,000 livres was granted on June 1, significantly less than the 80,000 demanded.]

This verdict, which was loudly applauded, is a monument to the wisdom and enlightenment of the magistrates who delivered it.

8. Louis Sébastien Mercier, *Paris Scenes* (1782–1788)

Louis Sébastien Mercier (1740–1814) was a prolific writer, historian, and dramatist. His most famous work, *Paris Scenes*, is composed of twelve volumes of reflection and commentary on life in the French capital, at once satirical and philosophical. In the following excerpts he weighs the Parisian's volatile character against the strong arm of the state and predicts that the days of violent political turbulence have passed. Employing a popular device, he also compares Parisians with Londoners, assuming the former to be more prone to instability, lacking as they do the "innate political sanity" of the British. During the Revolution, he was a deputy at the Convention who associated with the Girondins and voted against the execution of the king. He was subsequently arrested, but he managed to flee.

Riots

Dangerous rioting has become a moral impossibility in Paris. The eternally watchful police, two regiments of Guards, Swiss and French, in barracks near at hand, the King's bodyguard, the fortresses which ring the capital round, together with countless individuals whose interest links them to Versailles; all these factors make the chance of any serious rising seem altogether remote.

During the past fifty years there have only been two such attempts and both were quelled at once. Paris has had more than a century of peace since the time of the Fronde; what with mounted police and a perpetual garrison in the very heart of the city, sedition finds no rallying point; the length of time this state of things has lasted is perhaps the best guarantee that it will not soon be changed.

There is a law against peasant gatherings, but even supposing the peasantry did assemble, where could they go? And what, no matter how desperate their grievance, could they do? They would have to reckon first with the police, then with regiments, and finally with an army or two.

Source: Helen Simpson, ed. and trans., *The Waiting City: Paris 1782–1788. Being an Abridgement of Louis Sébastien Mercier's "Le Tableau de Paris"* (London: Harrap, 1933), pp. 108–110, 189–190.

If the Parisian, on the other hand—who has his moments of efferves-cence—were to attempt anything of the kind, he would find the door of the huge cage in which he lives promptly shut upon him; no food would be al-lowed to reach him; and an empty belly would soon bring him to his knees.

A handful of watchmen has been known to disperse a group of five or six hundred angry men, and that without difficulty, although the demonstrators at first seemed intractable enough; but a few blows with truncheons and the securing of the ringleaders is, generally speaking, enough to cool them down.

Any attempt at sedition here would be nipped in the bud; Paris need never fear an outbreak such as Lord George Gordon recently led in London, and which took a course unimaginable by Parisians; for it appears that even in disorder the crowds were under some kind of control. For instance, a thing which a Frenchman can hardly credit; the houses of certain unpopular men were fired, but their neighbours not touched; our people in the like circum-stances would show no such restraint.

The Londoner, even up in arms, keeps his head and his temper, and con-centrates his rage upon some definite object; while his inborn political sanity draws a line of conduct beyond which, though provoked, he will not go.

But a Parisian in the same turmoil, and flushed with some early slight successes, would get out of hand at once; it is only the thought of the police and magistrates at his back that keeps him quiet; these curbs removed, there is nothing in our people's own tradition to supply the want; and their vio-lence would be the more cruel, since they lack in themselves all power to control it.

We are not practiced rioters, we Parisians, and possibly for that very rea-son an outbreak (if such a thing were ever to occur) would assume alarming proportions. Still, if it should happen, and were met at the outset with pru-dence and moderation, above all if bloodshed could be avoided, I maintain that the people's ill-humour would evaporate of itself. Certainly this is the course adopted by the magistrates in such troubles as we have had, and their rational firmness prevented the conflagration of discontent from spreading.

This freedom of Londoners, who may in a sense please themselves in mat-ters of revolt, is an ever-present danger to their city; and yet these stone-throw-ers and incendiaries make brave sailors and soldiers; they have not learned to fear. Set over them a strong police force too ready with its weapons, and they will lose their qualities as fighting men; England's loss in energy and courage would outbalance the gain of order. You cannot have a satisfactory population both ways, good fighting men and peaceful citizens; these two spring from dif-ferent stock; and it is the true triumph of government to reconcile them as far as may be; to leave the citizen his freedom against authority. We have not worked out this problem as yet, nor assessed the civic values of pride versus insolence in a people, though we have had examples enough in our own history. Nor have we settled in our minds the difference between disturbance and revolution.

Politically speaking, each generation ought to be allowed its Satur-nalia, there would be no great danger in that. It may be that a few broken windows and constables' heads are necessary for our existence as a fighting race; to say nothing of an occasional rotten apple thrown at the lawyers. But what of certain other intangible, invisible onslaughts? Why leave the schooling of a people's character to an all too zealous, none too tactful, force of police; and how assess the damage, the weakening influence, of such schooling?

Political Character of the Parisian

The citizen of the capital has never given a thought to his political importance. His kings rule as they please, their caprices rouse him only to occasional and puerile outbreaks against their authority; he is neither altogether free, nor wholly a slave. The people make songs on the cannon brought up to quell them; a catchword of the markets puts royalty in its place, they punish the King with their silence, and his reward is in their voices and clapped hands as he passes. Their feeling in this matter is always just; the market is the mint where the King's likeness is struck out for public currency, for good or ill; and the philosopher, taking his time, making his notes, wakes up one day to find that his considered verdict does no more than confirm the swifter judgment of the stalls.

The Parisian's instinct seems to have taught him that the little more liberty he might obtain is not worth fighting for; any such struggle would imply long effort, stern thinking, and these are not in his line. He has a short memory for trouble, chalks up no score of his miseries, and has confidence enough in his own integrity not to dread too absolute a despotism. In the recent rivalry between the laws and the throne he showed fortitude, patience, and great courage; a town besieged could not have borne itself more bravely.

He is a kindly, civil personage enough, and as a rule easily led, but it does not do to mistake his docility for weakness; the Parisian, with a wink, allows himself to be deceived; but I believe that I know him well enough to fear him, if the pressure should ever become too great; the League and the Fronde are sufficient witness to his obstinacy. While his life is bearable it will be borne, he will still set his grievances to music and his tongue, though he holds it in public, will run indoors as before.

Paris lives in darkest ignorance of its place in history; it has forgotten that three centuries back it had an English governor; and that it is less than a hundred years since Marlborough, having broken Villars' line at Bouchain, found the way to the capital open, and Paris dependent upon the hazard of a single battle. As for London, the Parisian knows less of it than he does about Pekin.

chapter 2

FROM ESTATES GENERAL
TO NATIONAL ASSEMBLY

9. Letter from the King for the Convocation of the Estates General at Versailles (JANUARY 24, 1789)

Faced with an ongoing fiscal crisis, Louis XVI convened the Assembly of Notables in 1787 to consult with his ministers about reforming state finances. The assembly included nobles, clerics, and a few important commoners who had been handpicked by the crown. In spite of such careful preparation, however, the notables were not as malleable as the king and his ministers had hoped, and they balked at the most important reform: new taxes. They insisted that only a general assembly representing the entire nation could agree to such measures. When the Paris Parlement refused to ratify a series of short-term fiscal reforms, and political crisis began to spread throughout France in 1788, Louis agreed to convene the Estates General, which had last met in 1614.

Source: Annales du Centre Régional de Documentation Pédagogique de Caen, *Les Cahiers de Doléances de 1789 dans le Calvados.* Nouvelle série #6. Service Éducatif des Archives départementales du Calvados. Translated by Laura Mason.

By the King.

Beloved and loyal supporters, we require the assistance of our faithful subjects to overcome the difficulties in which we find ourselves concerning the current state of our finances, and to establish, as we so wish, a constant and invariable order in all branches of government that concern the happiness of our subjects and the prosperity of the realm. These great motives have induced us to summon the Assembly of the Estates of all Provinces obedient to us, as much to counsel and assist us in all things placed before it, as to inform us of the wishes and grievances of our people; so that, by means of the mutual confidence and reciprocal love between the sovereign and his subjects, an effective remedy may be brought as quickly as possible to the ills of the State, and abuses of all sorts may be averted and corrected by good and solid means which insure public happiness and restore to us in particular the calm and tranquillity of which we have so long been deprived.

For these reasons, we proclaim that it is our will to begin holding the free and general Estates of our Realm on Monday the 27th of next April in our city of Versailles, where we hope and expect to find only the most notable persons of each province, *bailliage*, and *sénéchaussée*. To this end, we command and expressly enjoin you, upon receipt of this letter, to summon and convene in our city of ———— with the shortest possible delay, all those of the three Estates of the *bailliage* (or *sénéchaussée*) of ———— to confer and communicate together reproofs, complaints, and grievances as well as ways, means, and opinions to be conveyed to the general assembly of the aforementioned Estates; and this done, to elect, choose, and appoint ———— and no more from each Order, all persons who, because of the integrity and good spirit that animates them, deserve this great sign of confidence; said convocations and elections will be enacted according to the forms prescribed for the entire Realm, by the Regulations annexed to the present Letter; and the aforementioned delegates will be supplied with instructions and general and sufficient authority to propose, call attention to, advise and consent to all matters concerning the needs of the State, the reform of abuses, the establishment of a permanent and durable order in all parts of the Administration, the general prosperity of our Realm, and the good of each and every one of our subjects; and we assure for our part that the delegates will find all good will and affection to execute and maintain all that shall be agreed between us and the aforementioned Estates, whether regarding taxes to which they shall consent, or the establishment of an unchanging rule in all parts of the Administration and the public order; we promise to ask for and listen favorably to their opinions on all that concerns the good of our people, and to attend to the grievances and proposals that they shall make, in such a manner that our Realm, and especially all of our subjects, feel forever the salutary effects that such a notable Meeting ought to promise.

10. Abbé Sieyès, *What Is the Third Estate?* (JANUARY 1789)

Emmanuel Joseph Sieyès (1748–1836), a priest, wrote this famous tract late in 1788, as France prepared to elect delegates to the Estates General. Once the king had called the meeting, the Paris Parlement determined that the Estates General should be organized according to the "forms of 1614"; in other words, each estate would have an equal number of delegates and they would vote by order. Pointing out that the Third Estate represented the vast majority of the population, many of its members objected strenuously to this limitation of their voice, and demanded that the number of their representatives be doubled and that voting be by head. Sieyès became their spokesperson, and *What Is the Third Estate?* their manifesto.

The plan of this book is fairly simple. We must ask ourselves three questions.

1. What is the Third Estate? Everything.
2. What has it been until now in the political order? Nothing.
3. What does it want to become? Something.

   Who is bold enough to maintain that the Third Estate does not contain within itself everything needful to constitute a complete nation? It is like a strong and robust man with one arm still in chains. If the privileged order were removed, the nation would not be something less but something more. What then is the Third Estate? All; but an "all" that is fettered and oppressed. What would it be without the privileged order? It would be all; but free and flourishing. Nothing will go well without the Third Estate; everything would go considerably better without the two others.

   It is not enough to have shown that the privileged, far from being useful to the nation, can only weaken and injure it; we must prove further that the nobility is not part of our society at all: it may be a burden for the nation, but it cannot be part of it.

   First, it is impossible to find what place to assign to the caste of nobles among all the elements of the nation. I know that there are many people, all too many, who, from infirmity, incapacity, incurable illness, or a collapse of morality, perform no functions at all in society. Exceptions and abuses always exist alongside the rule, and particularly in a large commonwealth. But all will agree that the fewer these abuses, the better organized a state is supposed to be. The most ill-organized state of all would be the one where not just isolated individuals, but a complete class of citizens would glory in inactivity amidst

Source: What Is the Third Estate? trans. M. Blondel (New York: Praeger, 1963), pp. 51–52, 56–57, 65–66, 74–80, 174. Copyright © 1963 by The Pall Mall Press, Ltd.

The taking of the Bastille (July 14, 1789). *(From* Révolutions de Paris, *volume 2. Courtesy Harvard University)*

the general movement and contrive to consume the best part of the product without having in any way helped to produce it. Such a class, surely, is foreign to the nation because of its *idleness*.

The nobility, however, is also a foreigner in our midst because of its *civil and political* prerogatives.

What is a nation? A body of associates living under *common* laws and represented by the same *legislative assembly*, etc. . . .

Some occasionally express surprise at hearing complaints about a threefold "aristocracy composed of the army, the Church, and the law." They insist that this is only a figure of speech; yet the phrase must be understood strictly. If the States-General is the interpreter of the general will, and correspondingly has the right to make laws, it is this capacity, without doubt, that makes it a true aristocracy: whereas the States-General as we know it at present is simply a *clerico-nobili-judicial* assembly.

Add to this appalling truth the fact that, in one way or another, all departments of the executive have also fallen into the hands of the caste that provides the Church, the law, and the army. As a result of the spirit of brotherhood or *comradeship*, nobles always prefer each other to the rest of the nation. The usurpation is total; in every sense of the word, they reign.

If you consult history in order to verify whether the facts agree or disagree with my description, you will discover, as I did, that it is a great mistake to believe that France is a monarchy. With the exception of a few years under

Louis XI and under Richelieu and a few moments under Louis XIV when it was plain despotism, you will believe you are reading a history of a *Palace* aristocracy. It is not the King who reigns; it is the Court. The Court has made and the Court has unmade; the Court has appointed ministers, and the Court has dismissed them; the Court has created posts and the Court has filled them. . . . And what is the Court but the head of this vast aristocracy which overruns every part of France, which seizes on everything through its members, which exercises everywhere every essential function in the whole administration? So that in its complaints the People has grown used to distinguishing between the monarch and those who exercise power. It has always considered the King as so certainly misled and defenseless in the midst of the active and all-powerful Court, that it has never thought of blaming him for all the wrongs done in his name.

Finally, is it not enough simply to open our eyes to what is occurring around us at this very moment? What do we see? The aristocracy on its own, fighting simultaneously against reason, justice, the People, the minister, and the King. The end of this terrible battle is still undecided. Can it still be said that the aristocracy is only a chimera? — composite monster

Let us sum up: to this very day, the Third Estate has never had genuine representatives in the States-General. Thus its political rights are null. . . .

In all countries, the law prescribes certain qualifications without which one can be neither an elector nor eligible for election. For example, the law must decide the age under which one is incompetent to represent one's fellow citizens. Thus, rightly or wrongly, women are everywhere excluded from mandates of this kind. It is unquestionable that tramps and beggars cannot be charged with the political confidence of nations. Would a servant, or any person under the domination of a master, or a non-naturalized foreigner, be permitted to appear among the representatives of the nation? Political liberty, therefore, has its limits, just as civil liberty has. The only question to answer is whether the non-eligibility of members of the privileged orders, which the Third Estate is asking for, is as vital as the other non-eligibilities I have just mentioned. Comparison runs completely in favor of this proposition; for the interests of a beggar or a foreigner might not conflict with the interest of the Third Estate, whereas nobles and clerics are, by their very status, supporters of the privileges which they themselves enjoy. . . .

In accord with these principles, we must not permit men of the Third Estate who are under the exclusive domination of the members of the first two orders to be given the trust of the Commons. It is clear that their dependency makes them untrustworthy; unless they are formally excluded, the lords will not fail to use the influence which they can no longer use for themselves in favor of the men whom they control. Above all, beware, I beg you, of the multifarious agents of feudalism. It is to the odious remnants of this barbaric system that we still owe the division of France, to her misfortune, into three mutually hostile orders. All would be lost if the lackeys of feudalism came to usurp the representation of the common order. . . .

Some people have supposed that they reinforce the difficulties of which we have just disposed by submitting that the Third Estate does not contain enough intelligent or courageous members and so forth competent to represent it, and that it has no option but to call on the leading figures of the aristocracy.... So ridiculous a statement deserves no answer. Look at the available classes in the Third Estate; and like everyone else, I call "available" those classes where some sort of affluence enables men to receive a liberal education, to train their minds, and to take an interest in public affairs. Such classes have no interest other than that of the rest of the People. Judge whether they do not contain enough citizens who are educated, honest, and worthy in all respects to represent the nation properly....

Like civil rights, political rights derive from a person's capacity as a citizen. These legal rights are identical for every person, whether his property happens to be great or small. Any citizen who satisfies all the formal requirements for an elector has the right to be represented, and the extent of his representation cannot be a fraction of the extent of some other citizen's representation. The right to be represented is single and indivisible. All citizens enjoy it equally, just as they are all equally protected by the law which they have helped to make. How can one argue on the one hand that the law is the expression of the general will, i.e., the majority, and on the other that ten individual wills can cancel out a thousand individual wills? Would one not thereby run the risk of permitting a minority to make the law? Which would obviously be contrary to the nature of things....

Justice and reason cannot yield to private convenience. Do not ask what is the appropriate place for a privileged class in the social order. It is like deciding on the appropriate place in the body of a sick man for a malignant tumor that torments him and drains his strength. It must be *neutralized*. The health of the body and the free play of its organs must be restored so as to prevent the formation of one of these malignancies which infect and poison the very essence of life itself.

But the word has gone round: you are not yet fit enough to be healthy! And to this aphorism of aristocratic wisdom, you give credence, like a pack of orientals solacing themselves with fatalism. Sick as you are then, so remain!

11. *Cahiers de Doléances*

In addition to electing deputies to the Estates General, the king's subjects were asked to draw up *cahiers de doléances* (lists of grievances) that might guide the deputies' deliberations. Members of each estate produced *cahiers*, and within

---

Source: Annales du Centre Régional de Documentation Pédagogique de Caen, *Les Cahiers de Doléances de 1789 dans le Calvados.* Nouvelle série #6. Service Éducatif des Archives départementales du Calvados. Translated by Laura Mason.

the Third Estate, they were drawn up by villages, towns, urban guilds, and corporations. Some of the *cahiers* were based on models sent from Paris, and it is quite likely that poorer peasants and villagers felt constrained in expressing their grievances; nonetheless, these lists sketch a remarkable picture of the political and economic concerns of French men (and some women) in 1789. The following *cahiers* are from the province of Brittany.

A. *Cahier* of the Parish of St. Germain d'Airan, Written This First Day of March 1789, According to the King's Wishes

Sire, the inhabitants of this community, assembled by your orders, are so touched by Your Majesty's solicitude for the general good, that all they have in their hearts is the desire to reply with reciprocal love by contributing to the subsidies necessary to sustain the state; in the meantime, the said parishioners have the honor to represent to Your Majesty:

1. That they would desire that in place of regular taxes, a single and unique tax be levied on all property in general, without regard to the status of the property owner. By this means the Prince's income would increase all the more because such taxation would bring about the destruction of *aides*,* salt tax, and *elections*,† useless things that exist only at the expense of the king and his people because of the great costs of tax collection and litigation. *tax farming*

2. That all property be taxed in the parish in which it is situated, again without regard to the status of the property owner, and that the royal coins be paid into the hands of a receiver for each province who will place them in the chest of the royal treasury. By this means, the state will more easily acquit its debts as coins follow the decrees that solicited them. All will take place immediately and without any degree of accountancy. *tax farming inefficient*

3. That His Majesty deign to exact a tribute for each boy subject to the militia lottery, which would spare great expense especially for those who live far from the subdelegation;‡ the poorest and the wealthiest alike will be happy to find that they must pay only three livres annually. Voluntary enlistments, which will multiply steadily under the reign of such a good king, will provide adequate defenders of the French monarchy without expense to the royal treasury.

4. That salt be fixed at a reasonable and equal price throughout the kingdom. By this means, the state will be freed of a heap of clerks who only bankrupt it and commit the most outrageous stupidities. *middle mgm*

---

*Indirect taxes levied on certain consumable goods, such as wine and fish.
†Fiscal districts through which the *taille*, the main direct tax on commoners, was levied.
‡Local administrative unit.

5. That the ecclesiastical tithe be taken from the large tithe-collectors of this parish, who do not fulfill any of their obligations for maintenance of the church or relief of poor people, of whom they take no care and to whom they give no charity.

6. That byways and shortcuts be repaired and maintained at the expense of the proprietors of bordering lands, unless destitution prohibits said proprietors from doing so, in which case the community shall provide costs. . . .

8. That the Third Estate is not in any way obliged to use the mill and oven of the lords, it being understood that abuses are committed there, and proprietors will lose nothing by serving the public faithfully.

9. That aulnes, weights, and measures be uniform throughout the kingdom.

10. That dovecotes be destroyed, or reduced to the smallest possible number, and that it be ordered that those remaining shall be closed in such a way that pigeons may not leave during the times of planting and harvest.

11. That a new order and express prohibition be reiterated that beggars leave the parish.

12. That express prohibition be issued against all persons, regardless of condition, who would hunt with dogs before crops have been completely harvested, under pain of whatever fine it shall please the king to levy in this regard.

13. Finally, the undersigned parishioners once again have the honor of observing to His Majesty that by remedying the abuses described above, a tenth of their annual income will provide him with more than do all the taxes they pay today. By this means the government will save on the expenses of administration, no longer having clerks to pay, and the Third Estate, seeing taxes distributed equally among the three orders, will find its lot eased.

May the heavens deign to bless the projects and the charitable views of our great monarch, that his glory may be eternal like the vows of his faithful subjects.

B. List of Grievances for the Town of Vire (FEBRUARY 26, 1789)

List of grievances, complaints, and remonstrances of the community of inhabitants of the town of Vire, composed in the assembly held by the General Lieutenant of the *bailliage* of Vire, in the presence of the king's prosecutor and assisted by master Banse, head clerk of the court.

The Lieutenant General and the inhabitants decreed that their wishes were:

1. That in the assembly of the Estates General, opinions be counted by head and not by order and if pronouncements by order are decreed, one order cannot be bound by the votes of two others.

2. That only the assembled nation may consent to taxes, loans, and new offices, and no corporation, organization, nor even provincial estates will be allowed to represent the nation.

3. That, in keeping with his majesty's promise, the Estates General will assemble at fixed and determined periods, that taxes may only be consented to by the Estates until the period of their next meeting, and that each new assembly of estates will be preceded by a new choosing of deputies, so that no citizen can perpetually represent the nation. . . .

7. That all privileges and pecuniary exemptions be abolished, and taxes be collected without discrimination and in the same proportion from all orders within the province.

8. That, to facilitate commerce, tollgates be removed to the frontiers of the realm, that his majesty humbly be entreated to remedy the obstacles to commerce occasioned by differences in weights and measures, and to establish a uniform weight for all of the realm.

9. That the funds destined for charitable workshops be used on roads that run from villages to towns and not be turned to any other uses, and that byways henceforth become the charge of communities and not of the persons whose lands neighbor said byways.

10. That the right of *franc fief** be suppressed, as humiliating to the Third Estate.

11. That, at the same time, his majesty be humbly entreated to recall that decision, distressing to the order to which artisan and agriculturalist are born, which excludes from his majesty's service all citizens who cannot prove four degrees of nobility; that his majesty equally be entreated to bring about the reform of the sovereign court's abusive decisions whereby a gentleman is sought for an office which confers nobility before a candidate's merits are considered, in consequence of which merit will become sufficient grounds to enter the different estates.

12. That the liberty of citizens be protected, no *lettre de cachet* may be accorded except upon the demand of families appearing before the local judge; that the governors and commandants of the provinces may not, under any circumstances, restrict the liberty of citizens there residing without a preliminary hearing by a competent judge.

---

*Fee payable by commoners to the king for the right of holding a noble fief. The fee, equal to about one year's revenue, was due every twenty years.

13. That the king be humbly entreated to abolish the levying of militia as a burden upon communities which is contrary to citizens' liberty and the well-being of agriculture.

14. That his majesty be entreated not to give any exclusive right of conservation over woods and forests too far from his châteaux for his enjoyment, and that seigneurs and residents alike be permitted to hunt the wild beasts that destroy their harvests.

15. That it be permitted to freely take all the leavings of the sea, the cinders and ovens of the saltworks without being hindered by administrators of the salt tax.

16. That the venality of offices be abolished; that degrees of jurisdiction be diminished; that justice be free of charge; that civil and criminal edicts be reformed; that crime alone, and not the social standing of the criminal, shall determine the sentence, and that no citizen may, under the pretext of any privilege—even those attributed to the Châtelet—be brought before any other than his natural judge. . . .

20. That nobility no longer be a title inhering in the proprietorship of office, but that it be the reward for services rendered to the state. . . .

22. That his majesty be entreated to grant freedom of the press, the only means to propagate enlightenment among citizens; that he also be entreated to command that the clauses of the Edict of 1766 for the local authority of towns be executed quickly and return to their inhabitants the right he has just given to parish communities, to choose their own municipal officers.

That if the assembly does not now make any reclamation against the enormous mass of taxes of Normandy, it is because it hopes that the charitable opinions and justice which animate his majesty will lead him to establish, in the Estates General, a correct proportion for the fiscal contributions of different provinces. . . .

12. The Declaration of the National Assembly (June 17, 1789)

When the Estates General met at Versailles in May 1789, the Third Estate refused to organize itself without the promise that the three estates would deliberate and vote in common. Negotiations between the estates quickly reached a deadlock, which dragged on for several weeks. Finally, on June 10 the abbé Sieyès proposed and the Third Estate agreed to send a final appeal to the other two estates to join with it for common organization. During the next week, nineteen

Source: Gazette Nationale, ou Le Moniteur universel. Translated by Laura Mason.

deputies from the clergy joined the Third Estate, which on June 17 declared itself to be a National Assembly representing all of France.

THE DEAN OF THE ASSEMBLY: I will put to a vote the different motions concerning how the Assembly should constitute itself. Yesterday, each member was asked to sign the transcript of the deliberations; I take it upon myself to offer the Assembly a few thoughts on this proposal.

Signatures may weaken our resolution rather than strengthening it; because once the Assembly adopts the resolution it is, to all intents and purposes, accepted unanimously; whereas if signatures are not applied universally they reveal that the resolution was only partially accepted. What's more, signatures may become a bitter source of division among us, giving rise in some way to two parties within an Assembly whose union has, until now, been its greatest strength.

These thoughts are approved by the Assembly, and the request for signatures ceases.

The Assembly decrees that the deliberations will be signed only by the dean and the two secretaries.

The five motions to be deliberated are read. The first motion put to a vote is that of M. the abbé Sieyès; the other motions will be successively put to a vote if the first does not win an absolute majority.

M. the abbé Sieyès's motion is adopted by a majority of 491 voices against 90.

Consequently, the Assembly decrees that the following be drafted:

The Assembly, deliberating after the verification of credentials, recognizes that this Assembly is already composed of representatives sent directly by at least ninety-six one-hundredths of the nation.

Such a sizable deputation could not be rendered passive by the absence of deputies from a few *bailliages* or a few classes of citizens, because the absentees may not prevent those present from exercising the fullness of their rights, above all when the exercise of those rights is an imperious and pressing duty.

Moreover, because only verified representatives may assist in formulating the national will, and because all verified representatives should be in this Assembly, it is all the more essential to conclude the business that belongs to it and only to it, to interpret and set out the general will of the nation; between this Assembly and the throne there may exist no veto, no negative power.

Thus, the Assembly declares that the common work of national restoration can and must be initiated without delay by the deputies present, and that they must continue without interruption and without obstacle.

The name of National Assembly is the only name appropriate to the Assembly in the current state of affairs, because the members who constitute it are the only legitimately verified and publicly known representatives; because they have been directly dispatched by the near totality of the nation; and finally, because as representation is one and indivisible, no deputy, regardless of the order or community that has chosen him, has the right to exercise his functions separately from the present Assembly.

The Assembly will never lose the hope of uniting within its bosom all the deputies who are absent today; it will never cease calling them to the fulfillment of the duty imposed upon them, to contribute to the holding of the Estates General. At no matter what moment absentee deputies may present themselves during the session that is about to begin, the Assembly declares in advance that it will hasten to welcome and share with them, after verifying their credentials, the continuation of the great works that shall bring about the regeneration of France.

The National Assembly decrees that the grounds for this present deliberation will be drafted without delay, to be presented to the king and the nation.

13. The Tennis Court Oath (JUNE 20, 1789)

On June 19 the clergy voted by a narrow margin to join the new National Assembly. However, when deputies arrived at the meeting hall on June 20, they found the doors locked and guarded by soldiers, while posters nearby announced that the king would meet with them two days hence. Fearful that the king was about to dissolve the body of representatives, the deputies took over a nearby indoor tennis court and swore not to disperse until they had completed their work.

BAILLY: I do not need to tell you in what a grievous situation the Assembly finds itself; I propose that we deliberate on what action to take under such tumultuous circumstances.

M. Mounier offers an opinion, seconded by Messieurs Target, Chapelier, and Barnave; he points out how strange it is that the hall of the Estates General should be occupied by armed men; that no other locale has been offered to the National Assembly; that its president was not forewarned by other means than letters from the Marquis de Brezé, and the national representatives by public posters alone; that, finally, they were obliged to meet in the Tennis Court of Old Versailles street, so as not to interrupt their work; that wounded in their rights and their dignity, warned of the intensity of intrigue and determination with which the king pushed to disastrous measures, the representatives of the nation bind themselves to the public good and the interests of the fatherland with a solemn oath.

This proposal is approved by unanimous applause.

Source: Gazette Nationale, ou Le Moniteur universel. Translated by Laura Mason.

The Assembly quickly decrees the following:

The National Assembly, considering that it has been called to establish the constitution of the realm, to bring about the regeneration of public order, and to maintain the true principles of the monarchy, nothing may prevent it from continuing its deliberations in any place it is forced to establish itself and, finally, the National Assembly exists wherever its members are gathered;

Decrees that all members of this assembly immediately take a solemn oath never to separate, and to reassemble wherever circumstances require, until the constitution of the realm is drawn up and fixed upon solid foundations; and that said oath having been sworn, all members and each one individually confirm this unwavering resolution with his signature.

BAILLY: I demand that the secretaries and I swear the oath first; which they do immediately according to the following formula:

We swear never to separate ourselves from the National Assembly, and to reassemble wherever circumstances require, until the constitution of the realm is drawn up and fixed upon solid foundations.

All the members swear the same oath between the hands of the president.

14. Louis XVI at the Royal Session of the Estates General (JUNE 23, 1789)

When the king finally met with the deputies, he promised several reforms but showed himself committed to preserving the three orders. In light of the troops that surrounded the hall in which the royal session was held, his closing remarks may be understood as an overt threat.

The king's speech. Sirs, I believed I had done everything in my power for the good of my people when I resolved to assemble you, when I overcame all the difficulties that surrounded your convocation; when, one might well say, I exceeded the nation's wishes by demonstrating in advance what I wanted to do for its happiness.

It seemed that you had only to put the finishing touches on my work, and the nation impatiently awaited the moment that it would enjoy the prosperity brought about by the union between its sovereign's beneficent notions and the enlightened zeal of its representatives.

Source: Georges Lefebvre, ed., *Recueil de documents rélatifs aux séances des États-Généraux*, vol. 1, pt. II (Paris, 1962), pp. 274–283. Translated by Laura Mason.

The Estates General opened two months ago and it has not yet been able to agree on the preliminaries to its business. Perfect understanding should have arisen from love of the fatherland alone, and yet deadly division rouses alarm in every heart. I would like to think that the French have not changed but, to avoid reproaching any of you, I will take into consideration that the renewal of the Estates General after such a long time, the excitation which preceded it, and the aim of this convocation—so different from that which assembled your ancestors—must necessarily bring about opposition, debate, and excessive claims.

I owe it to the common good of my realm, I owe it to myself to bring an end to these deadly divisions; it is with this resolution, Sirs, that I gather you around me; it is as common father to all my subjects, as defender of the laws of my realm, that I come to remind you of the true spirit of the laws and to repress any attacks directed against them.

But, Sirs, having unequivocally determined the respective rights of each order, I will expect zeal for the fatherland from the first two orders, I will expect their commitment to my person, I will expect that with their knowledge of the pressing ills of the state, they will be the first to propose joining opinion with sentiment in matters of public good, which I consider necessary in the present crisis and which should bring about the health of the state.

The king's declaration concerning the present meeting of the Estates General.

Article 1: The king desires that the traditional distinction between the three orders of the state be preserved in its entirety, as fundamentally linked to the constitution of his realm; that the freely elected deputies of each of the three orders, forming three chambers, deliberating by order and, with the sovereign's approval, convening to deliberate in common, may alone be taken to constitute the body of representatives of the nation; consequently, the king declares null the proceedings adopted by deputies of the Third Estate on the seventeenth of this month, as well as any deliberations that might have followed, as illegal and unconstitutional.

Article 2: His majesty declares valid all credentials verified or to be verified in each chamber without opposition; his majesty orders that notice of verifications will be communicated between the orders. . . .

Article 3: The king overturns and annuls as unconstitutional, contrary to the letters of convocation, and opposed to the state's interests, the restrictions on credentials that inhibit the liberty of the deputies to the Estates General and so prevent them from adopting forms of procedure separately by order or in common according to the wishes of the three orders.

Article 4: If, contrary to the king's intentions, some deputies swore a reckless oath not to retreat from a particular form of deliberation, his majesty leaves it to their consciences to consider whether the proceedings that they are about to organize depart from the spirit or the letter of the commitment that they would have engaged. . . .

Article 6: His majesty declares that in subsequent meetings of the Estates General, he will not suffer *cahiers* or mandates to be considered imperative; they ought to be nothing more than simple instructions entrusted to the conscience and free opinion of the chosen deputies.

Article 7: His majesty having, for the good of the state, exhorted the three orders to meet together during this meeting of the Estates General solely to deliberate on matters of general usefulness, wants to make known his desires concerning the manner in which they may proceed.

Article 8: To be notably excepted from matters liable to be treated in common: all that regards the ancient and constitutional rights of the three orders; the form of constitution for subsequent Estates General; feudal and seigneurial property; the useful rights and honorific privileges of the first two orders.

Article 9: The specific agreement of the clergy will be necessary for all measures that affect religion, ecclesiastical discipline, the system of orders, and regular and secular corps.

Article 10: Deliberations on contested credentials that the united orders will undertake and which concerned parties may pursue in the Estates General, will be put to a plurality of votes. But if two thirds of any order shall vote against deliberation by the Assembly, the affair will be handed over to the king for his majesty to make a final ruling. . . .

Article 15: Good order, decency, and even free suffrage require his majesty to prohibit, as he does expressly, any person other than the members of the three orders composing the Estates General to attend proceedings, whether they be held in common or by order. . . .

The king's speech. I want as well, Sirs, to show you the various kindnesses I have bestowed upon my people. This is not done with the intent of circumscribing your zeal within the circle I am about to trace, because I will happily adopt all other plans for the public good proposed by the Estates General. I can say without illusion that no king has ever done so much for any nation; but what other nation could have better earned such treatment by its love than the French nation? I do not fear saying that those who hinder the accomplishment of my paternal intentions with excessive claims or by raising irrelevant difficulties will not deserve to be considered French.

Declaration of the king's intentions.

Article 1: No new tax shall be created and no current tax will be extended beyond the term set by law without consent of the nation's representatives.

Article 2: The new taxes to be established, or the current taxes to be extended will be imposed only for the period of time lasting until the next meeting of the Estates General.

Article 3: Because loans can become the occasion of higher taxes, none will be taken without consent of the Estates General with the exception, however, that in case of war or any other national emergency, the sovereign will be able to borrow immediately up to one hundred million. For it is the king's formal intention never to allow the safety of his Empire to become dependent upon any person. . . .

Article 5: The table of revenues and expenses will be made public annually according to the form proposed by the Estates General and approved by the king. . . .

Article 9: Once the formal arrangements announced by clergy and nobility to renounce their financial privileges have been fixed by their deliberations, the king intends to sanction them so that there will be no more privileges or distinctions in the payment of financial contributions.

Article 10: To sanction such an important arrangement, the king desires that the name of the *taille* be abolished in his realm, and that this tax be joined with the *vingtième* and all other land taxes, or that it be replaced in some manner, but always according to just and equal proportions, and without distinctions of state, standing, or birth. . . .

Article 12: All property, without exception, will be respected; his majesty expressly includes under the rubric of property: tithes, feudal rents, feudal and seigneurial rights and responsibilities and, in general, all useful or honorific rights and privileges attached to lands and feudal holdings, or belonging to persons. . . .

Article 15: Desiring to solidly and durably insure the personal liberty of all citizens, the king invites the Estates General to consider and propose to him means to abolish the orders known as *lettres de cachet* that preserve public safety, retain the precautions necessary to preserve family honor in certain cases, swiftly repress the beginnings of sedition, and guarantee the state against the consequences of criminal intelligence with foreign powers.

Article 16: The Estates General will examine and make known to his majesty the most suitable means to reconcile liberty of the press with the respect due to religion, morals, and the honor of citizens. . . .

Article 25: The Estates General will occupy themselves with the project that his majesty conceived long ago, to remove trade barriers to the frontiers of the realm so that the most perfect liberty may govern the internal circulation of national and foreign merchandise.

Article 26: His majesty desires that the unhappy effects of the salt tax and the significance of this revenue be carefully discussed and that, under any circumstance, a proposal be made at least to ease its collection. . . .

Article 28: According to wishes the king expressed in his declaration of last September 23, his majesty will examine all projects presented to him concerning the administration of justice, and the means to perfect civil and criminal laws with scrupulous attention. . . .

Article 30: His majesty desires that the use of the *corvée*, for the building and maintenance of roads, be entirely and permanently abolished in his realm. . . .

The king's speech. You came, Sirs, to hear the outcome of my arrangements and opinions which are consistent with my ardent desire to bring about the public good; if, by some destructive sentiment wholly foreign to my thinking, you abandon me in this fine enterprise, I alone will construct my people's ~~assert~~ good, I alone will consider myself their true representative, and knowing your ~~autonomy~~ *cahiers*, knowing the perfect accord that exists between the most general will of the nation and my charitable intentions, I will possess all the confidence that such perfect harmony should inspire and I will head toward my goal with all the courage and firmness that it should inspire.

Consider, Sirs, that none of your projects, none of your arrangements can have the force of law without my special approbation; I am the natural guarantor of your respective rights; all of the orders of the state may rely on my equitable impartiality. All defiance on your part will be gross injustice. It is I who have, until now, done everything for the happiness of my people and it is perhaps extraordinary that the sole ambition of a sovereign is that his subjects should finally cooperate to accept his charitable acts.

I order you, Sirs, to separate immediately and to return tomorrow morning to the rooms assigned to your order to resume meetings. In consequence, I order the grand master of ceremonies to prepare those rooms.

15. Abbé Sieyès, Speech After the Royal Session
(JUNE 23, 1789)

Having ordered the deputies to disperse, the king left the hall, followed by the nobles and most of the clergy. The Third Estate, however, refused to budge. Sieyès's speech is one of several that they heard that day. Members of the clergy and a substantial number of noble deputies joined them, and on June 27 the king capitulated and ordered the remaining deputies to join the new National Assembly.

Sirs, no matter how turbulent circumstances appear to be, we always have a guiding light. Let us ask ourselves what powers we exercise and what mission

Source: Archives parlementaires, vol. 8 (Paris, 1904), pp. 146–147. Translated by Laura Mason.

gathered us here from every point in France. Are we only proxies, only the king's officers? Then we should obey and withdraw. But if we are the people's envoys, let us fulfill our mission freely and courageously.

Is there one among us who would want to renounce the great confidence with which he is invested and return to his constituents to say, "I was afraid, you placed the destiny of France in hands that are too weak; send a man in my place who better deserves to represent you"?

We swore, sirs, and our oath will not be in vain, we swore to restore the French people to their rights. The authority that appointed you to this grand enterprise, the sole authority upon which we depend and which will know well how to defend us is surely far from crying out to us, "that is enough, stop." On the contrary, it pushes us forward and demands a new constitution from us. And who can create it without us? Who can create it if not us? Is there any power on earth that could strip you of the right to represent your constituents?

CHAPTER 3

The Emergence
of Popular Revolution

16. Rural Unrest

As news of events in Paris spread through the countryside, already restless because of worsening grain shortages, it set off panics that swept whole provinces. Hearing rumors that armed bandits were moving from village to village and that nobles were conspiring to resist the activities of the National Assembly, peasants in many parts of France armed themselves and attacked local châteaux to loot them and destroy records of feudal obligations. The following accounts describe two such uprisings in regions of France far removed from one another. The formation of urban militia described in the first account was a common response to local unrest.

A. Letter from the Commissioners of the Estates of Dauphiné to the Committee of Twelve (July 31, 1789)

Our province has been most violently agitated for the last several days; bourgeois militia have been formed in all the cities, towns, and villages because the fear of bandits has spread everywhere; the watch is carried out with care and all suspicious-looking persons are stopped.

Source: National Archives, D XXIXbis 1. Translated by Laura Mason.

An alliance from the side of the uncultivated lands has spread a general terror throughout the province. On Monday the 27th, a bandit no one knew came to announce to Aoste that the village of Morestel was being attacked and burned; at the same time, other bandits announced to Morestel that the village of Aoste was being looted and burned. The warning drew closer and closer, and the alarm was rung in all the villages; fear seized every heart and it was rumored that twenty thousand troops entered Dauphiné from the side of Bugey.

A letter written from Monferra to the lord of Voiron, giving him news of the arrival of these supposed twenty thousand men, was carried village to village and on to Grenoble, arriving there at eleven o'clock at night; it was supposed that it was only a couple of bandits chased from around Lyon by the city's troops, so it was possible to dispel the fright caused by this letter. But because the same warning had been given in every vicinity, even in St. Marcellin, all the people of the countryside quickly armed themselves with guns, pitchforks, and scythes, and ran to where it had been announced that the troops were to enter. Several couriers followed one another through the night to bring the same news to Grenoble.

The commission convened very early in the morning; the municipality of Grenoble joined them along with several notables, citizens, to deliberate on the means of defense against this supposed invasion; it was decided that it was necessary to create a state of preparedness and to beg the commander to obtain rifles; Mr. Dufort sadly agreed to allow arms to be placed in the people's hands; the conditions according to which they promised to return six thousand guns caused this abusive project to fail.

Tuesday was calm enough, thanks to the precautions of the village watch, which had sounded the alarm in the night, to announce that it was a false alert.

On Wednesday morning, the courier brought the most deplorable news that he had seen the château of Vaux ravaged by flames and still burning when he passed; the bandits had gone on to the château of Montferra, whose portal had already been destroyed; the people of the château handed over the wine cellar to the arsonists, who contented themselves with burning a businessman's house.

A troop of these bandits went to the château of Césarges, which they also wanted to burn; they were stopped by the same means used at Montferra; but they urged suspicion of the villagers of the plain, who were supposed to come to loot the following day; the event itself proved the truth of this advice; Césarges has been looted and stripped with the help of carts; everything was taken, right down to the hinges of the doors; there was money there that did not escape the thieves' foraging; the inhabitants of the neighboring village were themselves accomplices to the looting, mingling with the bandits; only some papers were saved.

The châteaux of Loras and Belaceuil were pillaged or burned as well; that of M. de Meyrieu at Verpillère was ruined; the furniture was broken or carried away but the fear of setting the village on fire saved the building from flames.

In light of this horrible disorder, the Parlement proposed to the Commission on the 29th to join with it . . . and to include some deputies from the municipality, to confer together on means to reestablish the public peace. . . .

Courier followed upon courier throughout the day of Thursday the 30th to bring news of châteaux that had been burned or ruined; the list is immense. . . .

All good citizens hastened to volunteer to stop the disorder. The committee requested M. de Durfort's troops; consequently, one hundred men of the Swiss regiment set out on the night of 30–31, as well as a similar number of bourgeois militia taken from the grenadiers and the chasseurs. These two companies were considerably augmented by young nobles and by the best bourgeois, who were put in step under the orders of M. de Frimont, who commands the detachment. . . .

Meanwhile, couriers have been dispatched to Vienne, Lyon, and Valence to bring troops of the artillery and to surround the bandits.

The city of Lyon, having taken the same precautions as those of Grenoble, sent two hundred bourgeois militia with troops in pursuit of these incendiary thieves; M. Reynaud, Major of Sonnenberg, in the detachment from Lyon, has just told M. de Durfort that thirteen of these bandits were killed, nineteen taken prisoner; they were taken to the prisons of Lyon; the provost conducted their trial there; they will be executed there or a reliable guard of troops will escort them. A consul of the community and residents of the area have been found among the convicts.

B. Letter from La Breaudière of Segondigny (Poitou) to the
Committee of Twelve (July 24, 1789)

I dare to believe that you will want to present this memoir to the king and all the noble delegates to the Estates General as soon as you receive it, in order to win help against atrocities that are being perpetrated, in the name of the Third Estate, against the persons and families of gentlemen taken from their lands and from the cities of this province by the vagrants and scoundrels who infest this canton.

Here, sirs, is the truthful account of what happened to my son and me yesterday evening, the 23d of this month: do not expect to find much organization of the details; I do not have the peace of mind necessary at the present moment to be concise in my narration; but I will be truthful without exaggerating.

On that morning, the subdelegate of La Châtaignevoye circulated a note to several neighboring parishes ordering all the inhabitants to come quickly and well armed to his town, to prevent the ruin and total destruction that, it was said, had been visited upon Cressuive and all the areas around Alentour by six or seven thousand English and Breton bandits.

An express dispatch from the syndic of Vernou brings this note to me in my bed very early in the morning; I dress quickly, run to Segondigny, where I am, to my misfortune, municipal syndic and president; the tocsin is rung quickly to convene the people without delay; I urge them to stand guard carefully to protect this little town from the fate that threatens. At this time I do what is being done in more than fifty villages of the canton: I promise to return at five o'clock in the evening to lead the people and conduct their defense at peril to my life. A worker from the Segondigny forest suggests that a warning be beaten to gather the workers of this forest, which is under cultivation, and join them with the parishioners. . . . Had I only suspected that this was the blackest treachery! I thank the worker for his good will and answer that he will be in charge of what he thinks necessary. Having taken these precautions which I thought wise, I returned home to prepare myself to get them at the appointed time. . . .

[. . . . A]t about 4:30, I hear the sound of the drum and some gunshots mingled with some sort of confused shouts; one of my sons and I run to Segondigny, believing for all the world that these were the enemies rumored since morning.

I leave it to you, sirs, to imagine our surprise upon walking through my door, to find [the forest] workers with white cockades on their hats and the Pidoux family in their midst, mother, father, and son who they had carried away from their house after insulting them a thousand times over and using violence to wrest money and wine; they now encircle us, cursing and saying in low voices, "Ah, ah! Monsieur the syndic, ah, ah!, monsieur the correspondent for the nobility, we have got you in our power"; then suddenly taking a very high tone, "Are you of the Third Estate?" Alone among sixty half-drunk madmen, it was quite necessary to reply, "Yes," and to shout "Long live the Third Estate." I believed, uselessly, that I could rid myself of such awkward company by this means, and that nothing more remained than to say, "Sirs, I thank you for your services, but they are no longer necessary because we have been given a false alarm; the bandits have gone. Nothing remains to be done but for each of you to return to work." "We do not leave you, sir, not this way," the mutineers replied. "We need money and do not think that our efforts will be wasted." "I do not have any on me," I retorted honestly, "why don't you ask for some at the house; besides, I find it very hard to pay for insults." Once again, I take advantage of their apparent calm to remind them that they run the risk of bringing very bad business upon themselves and I advise them to retreat peacefully. Labor lost! The plot was made in advance, as I learned this morning; they drag us to the city, we are escorted like criminals to the home of the fiscal prosecutor, a kind and honest man. In a moment his house is broken into; the room that we occupy is filled with half of these perverts; the others remain in the street to forbid us all means of retreat.

So, shut up without help from the residents, some of whom they communicated with and who they prohibited from coming to our assistance with threat of life and limb; it was necessary to listen to these traitors pronounce our death sentence, saying that they had orders to kill all gentlemen who refused to ally themselves with the Third Estate and, once rid of us, they were going to give the same treatment to Messieurs de la Boucheliève, La Roche Bochard, de la Milliancheve, and Gourjault, etc., our neighbors. Thus, it was necessary to don the cockade of the Third Estate. After having submitted, I thought there was nothing more to do than hand out some money to obtain our liberty. Alas! we were far from the denouement; the disaster was only being prepared. The leaders held council together in a kind of hall that adjoined our prison; . . . hardly had they rejoined their comrades when, in response to a very clear signal which I witnessed, one of these scoundrels, armed with an iron pitchfork, leaps at my throat saying, "Get out of here M. f——"; twenty others fall on me all at once to drag me outside, while the rest of those in the room pulled me in the opposite direction to make me stay; so I resembled a wretch who is being quartered. I struggle for more than a quarter of an hour between their hands to defend my gun, and I would have held out longer if, at that moment, I had not seen my dear child, weaker than I, between their hands and close to being torn to pieces by these madmen; his danger makes me tremble with horror and my strength abandons me; they finally seized this moment to take my arms, which were useless anyway since I was so crowded.

In this state of impotence, I no longer listened to anything but my despair, and seeing us lying cheek to cheek with a dozen guns and feeling iron pressed against my kidneys, I jump into the midst of the murderers, baring my chest and shouting at them in a solemn tone, "Strike, cowards and loathsome assassins . . . here is my heart . . . quench your rage with my blood . . . I will be avenged . . . but spare my son." You must understand, sirs, that in this moment of horror I had only two things in mind: recommending my soul to God and my revenge to my king.

This firm and decisive bearing (which this despicable horde doubtless did not expect) was our salvation; the salvation of my wife and daughters, of my hosts—bruised and bloodied although bourgeois—of my house, of theirs, and of the part of this little town that they boasted of reducing to ashes if anyone stirred to help us; this bearing, I say, which braved certain death, seemed momentarily to soften these fierce gangs and make their arms drop from their hands. They held a new council, the outcome of which was that for a second time we found ourselves with guns and pitchforks pressed against our chests as they shouted in an angry tone, "Give up, you are dead if you don't sign that you are of the Third Estate."

At the same moment, the only royal notary in the city, sieur Esquot, appeared, stamped paper in hand and radiating an insulting joy in spite of him-

self: he is the author (so it is said) of this insurrection prepared in advance . . .
and he tells me with a half honest, half mocking air, "Sir, I come from Niort;
the Third Estate there made all the gentlemen of the city pay amends; the only
one who refused has been torn to pieces at Mayeux." This brief exhortation
produced an effect in the souls of the conspirators that was, no doubt, pre-
meditated; the blackest fury sparkles in their eyes, a fearful clamor continues
to repeat, "Sign . . . sign, or we are going to pull out your heart and set fire to
this house." To avoid the final misfortunes, we had to resign ourselves and
sign, not without shaking with indignation, the renunciation of all financial
privileges and our consent to a single and uniform tax; as if the nobility had
not already done that (which unarguably proves that this banditry was exercised without the consent of the Third Estate).

Do not believe, sirs, that chance alone and the circumstances of the banditry which threatened us produced this scene of horrors. Those who carried
this out did not have the prudence to keep quiet: that very evening they announced, in the drunkenness of barbarous joy which the sieur Esquot shared,
that this had been planned more than fifteen days before and all that was
needed was a favorable opportunity to bring it to fruition; if the opportunity
had not appeared yesterday, they would have carried it out anyway. They justify themselves with a letter held by Talbot, a forest guard and their chief,
which charges them to run over the gentlemen of the countryside, mercilessly
slaughtering all who refuse to abdicate their privileges; to loot, to burn their
châteaux, promising not only that they will not be punished for these crimes,
but that they will be rewarded; . . .

Our situation, in short, is so ghastly that we are not allowed to communicate with our close relatives, our friends, and our neighbors, to leave our
houses for the most pressing business, nor to go from one city to another
without running the risk of being killed. The outrage of these anguished
circumstances seems to be the gift of the Third Estate or, rather, of the
scoundrels who claim to do its bidding. It is no longer safe to write, family secrets are violated, doors are forced, and disorder is at its height.

Here, sirs, is the summary and substance of what happened among the
mob yesterday, the 23d of this month, of which I have been witness and victim. I certify it on my honor and offer the most complete proof of it, assuming however that the fury of one party and the fear of the other does not
still every tongue. This is the deplorable state to which have been reduced
the gentlemen of this province, especially those who live on their lands; isolated, unable to help their cause because of their small number, without police or troops to defend them, without support of the government. Perhaps,
alas! at this moment I hold most dear, some must expiate by flame or the
killer's blade the crime of having persevered in firmest support of the
French empire, to which they seek to lend a hand as it crumbles everywhere.

Ah! that is the reward for so much blood spilled in combat for the glory
and prosperity of the monarch!

Join with us, sirs, we entreat you because you hold that which is most sacred; by your honor, which we all share; by your passionate desire to restore peace and concord to the bosom of our homeland that has been torn apart; and if this is not reason enough, by the disasters that harry us and which you will surely share. Place our sorrows in the breast of the one most just to consider them. Make our lamentations sound in the ears of the Estates General, even in the ears of the Third Estate (because we will never believe that the esteemed leaders of this body had anything to do with the abominable humiliations that are carried out in its name). Find prompt assistance for us that may calm our ceaseless anxiety; secure us against the destructive scourge of armed vagabonds; finally, save the honor of the fair sex, which is threatened with humiliation at any moment.

If we are left abject and at the pinnacle of the outrages we can no longer stand, we will be forced to seek asylum against proscription in another homeland.

To die for one's king, for one's country, for the just defense of the state, is a sacred duty; it is a glory that we know too well to leave it to another. But to die in degradation, in abandonment, at the hands of the filthiest wretches, is to reduce us to the most horrible despair; it is to tear our hearts out twice over.

17. M. the Duc d'Aiguillon, "Motion Concerning Individual Privileges and Feudal and Seigneurial Rights" (AUGUST 4, 1789)

Faced with news of the uprisings in the countryside, a collection of Breton deputies decided to propose that the Assembly abolish the remnants of feudalism, so satisfying the peasants and helping to restore order to the countryside. The Duke d'Aiguillon was a liberal noble, and his speech on August 4 was followed by an orgy of renunciation that lasted throughout the right, as nobles and clergy relinquished rights, prerogatives, and dues. By August 5, it seemed that the Assembly had indeed abolished feudalism. Although subsequent legislation detailed complex plans of compensation for many types of dues, all citizens of France were now equal before the law.

Sirs, there is no one who does not tremble before the dreadful scenes of which France is the theater. This popular ferment, which strengthened liberty when

Source: Archives parlementaires, vol. 8 (Paris, 1904), p. 344. Translated by Laura Mason.

guilty ministers were trying to rob us of it, is an obstacle to that same liberty now that the government's opinions seem to accord with our desires for the public good.

It is not bandits alone who, arms in hand, seek to enrich themselves amidst calamity: in several provinces, the people in general have formed a kind of league to destroy châteaux, lay waste to fields, and above all to seize *chartriers*, in which the titles to feudal properties are kept. They attempt finally to throw off a yoke that has weighed on them for so many centuries; and we must acknowledge, sirs, that this insurrection, although guilty (as are all violent attacks), may find excuse in the humiliations of which the people are victim. Admittedly, the owners of fiefs, of seigneurial lands, are rarely guilty of the excesses of which their vassals complain; but their business agents are often pitiless, and the unfortunate farmer, subject to the barbarous remains of the feudal laws that persist in France, groans under the servitude imposed upon him. We cannot deny that such rights are property, and that all property is sacred; but they are onerous for the people and everyone agrees that these rights impose continual troubles on them.

In this enlightened century in which wholesome philosophy has recovered its empire, during this fortunate era in which, united for the public good and free of personal interests, we set about regenerating the state, it seems to me, sirs, that before erecting the avidly desired constitution the nation awaits, we must, we must, I say, prove to all citizens that our aim and aspiration is to exceed their desires, to establish as quickly as possible this equality of rights which should exist between all men, and which alone can insure their liberty. I do not doubt that the owners of fiefs, the lords of lands, far from denying this truth, will be willing to sacrifice their rights to justice. They have already renounced their privileges, their financial exemptions; and we cannot, at this moment, request the pure and simple renunciation of their feudal rights.

These rights are their property. They constitute the only wealth of many individuals; and fairness forbids requiring any property to be relinquished without just indemnity being accorded to the proprietor who cedes the pleasure of his preference to the benefit of the public.

In keeping with these weighty considerations, sirs, and to make the people feel that you respond to their most cherished interests with skill and speed, I hope the National Assembly will decree that taxes shall be levied equally on all citizens, in proportion to their ability to pay, and that henceforth all feudal rights of fiefs and seigneurial lands may be purchased by the vassals of those same fiefs and lands, if they so desire; that settlements will be paid at a rate fixed by the Assembly. . . .

Accordingly, sirs, I have composed the following decree, which I have the honor to submit to your wisdom and which I pray you to take into consideration:

"The National Assembly, considering that the first and most sacred of its duties is to cede personal and particular interests to general utility;

"That taxes would be far less onerous for the people if they were shared equally among all citizens, according to their ability to pay;

"That justice requires that strict proportionality be observed:

"Decrees that corps, towns, communities, and individuals who have until now enjoyed individual privileges and personal exemptions will, in the future, contribute to all subsidies and public fees without distinction whether in the rate of taxes or the manner of their collection.

"The National Assembly considering moreover that feudal and seigneurial rights are also a kind of onerous tribute that harms agriculture and desolates the countryside;

"Unable, nonetheless, to deny that these rights are true property and that all property is sacred;

"Decrees that these rights will henceforth be purchasable if the debtor so desires, at the rate . . . judged equitable for each province by the National Assembly. . . .

"Finally, the National Assembly orders that all rights will be maintained and collected with exactitude as they have been in the past, until they have been reimbursed."

18. The Debate over the King's Veto

As the Assembly's constitutional committee considered the extent of royal power in the summer of 1789, a heated debate ensued between Monarchiens, who wished to give the king the power of an absolute veto, and those deputies who were suspicious of the conservative and antidemocratic tendencies of at least some of their opponents. In the first speech, Henri Grégoire vehemently opposes the absolute veto, insisting that only the people can be final judge. While some deputies, like Sieyès and the relatively unknown Maximilien Robespierre, opposed giving the king any voice whatsoever in legislation, Grégoire's views represented the compromise position that won the day. The Assembly voted by a large majority to grant the king a suspensive veto on September 15.

In the second speech, Monarchien Jean-Joseph Mounier suggests his admiration for the English model of politics by proposing that the democratically elected Assembly be balanced by an upper house of lifetime deputies and that the king be given an absolute veto. The Monarchiens lost on both counts. Mounier, who had led the revolutionary movement in his own province of Dauphiné in 1788, would leave the Assembly within weeks of giving this speech, critical of the events of the October Days and fearful of the influence of the Paris crowd. His speech on the veto, and his departure from the Assembly, suggest the limits of reform for some of the early revolutionaries.

A. Abbé Henri Grégoire, "Opinion . . . on the Royal Veto," at the Session of the National Assembly (SEPTEMBER 4, 1789)

Gentlemen,

In my opinion, the royal sanction is only an act by which the Prince declares that a given decree has emanated from the Legislature and which he promises to execute. His function amounts to promulgating the law.

By virtue of his rank, has he the right to participate in the legislative power? No, because he cannot have rights beyond those accorded him by the constituent power; consequently the king (I do not say the sovereign; henceforth this term designates the Nation), the king can only be an integral part of the legislature by the free concession of those from whom emanate all the rights of royalty . . . the People.

By partaking of this principle, the king cannot therefore refuse his consent to the Law; but, if one accounts for the influence of the passions, perhaps it is necessary to confer on him a prerogative which, being necessary for political tranquillity, is commensurate with the rigor of the principle I have just established. Thus, the royal veto can be envisaged only as an object of convenience and utility. The question then is reduced to knowing whether or not it is essential to national good to arm the king with an absolute or suspensive right to oppose law.

Charged by our mandates with rejuvenating the Constitution, or creating a new one from the debris of the old, we exercise at this moment the constituent power; thus, even when one accords to the Nation's august delegate the right to refuse law, his refusal can never be opposed to the Constitution.

I will attempt to prove, Gentlemen, that you have no right to accord the Prince an absolute veto; that, even if you had this right, you should not do so; and that it is in the Prince's interest not to have it.

1. You would exceed your powers in according him an indefinite veto; because you do not have the right to compromise or, even less, to alienate the liberty of your constituents; if the Nation's representatives and the king cannot agree on the acceptance or rejection of a decree, there is only one tribunal competent for judging in the last jurisdiction; this tribunal is that which creates kings, [the tribunal] of the People before which all individual interests disappear. Now, if the king had the absolute veto, he would be judge and litigant, and the national liberty could be in a struggle with despotism.

Besides, you cannot make an irrevocable pact for posterity, nor bind those who will succeed you, and you have scarcely more right over the liberty of future generations, than the power of past generations. Thus you would try

Source: Oeuvres de l'Abbé Grégoire, vol. 1 (Paris: KTO Press, 1977), pp. 51–61. Translated by Tracey Rizzo.

vainly to submit men of the future to the yoke of slavery; the People would always have the right to break the chains that you would have tried vexatiously to impose on them.

2. Had you the right to accord the Prince an indefinite veto, it would be impolitic to do so; for if the law is agreeable or indifferent to the king, he will approve it without difficulty, but then what does it serve him to say "I am opposed"? It would be, in this hypothetical [situation], only the illusory faculty to prevent someone from doing that which would be agreeable to him. Or the law will displease the Prince and then the will of the entire Nation will be sacrificed to the will of one man; will this lone man be less prone to error and corruption than twenty-four million of his compatriots? Prove to me that the king is, if not infallible, at least more enlightened than the totality of the People; guarantee me a constant succession of princes in whom ever-integral morals, ever-wise and moderate inclinations, will never be in collision with reason, that individual interest will never clash with national interest.

Unfortunately, kings are men; flattered by courtesans, and often escorted by lies, truth reaches their thrones only with difficulty. Unfortunately, kings, badly brought up for the most part, have tumultuous passions. One of the most deeply rooted in the human heart, one of the most ardent, is the thirst for power and the penchant for extending its empire. A king capable of dominating by the ascendancy of his genius, like Louis XIV, who did everything out of vanity, and who always put himself before his people; by virtue of an absolute veto, such a king will rapidly encroach upon legislative power by the facility of wielding the lever of executive power alone, which is always in operation. You will have a despot.

A feeble king will be subjugated by the agents of power, interested in invading the unlimited power of a master whom they have enslaved in order to reign in his name, and you will have then the most absurd veto, as well as the most formidable . . . that of the ministers. The king you have decorated with a fine title and the ministers he has honored with his confidence should doubtless reassure your own; but we lay the foundations of an edifice that will last for centuries. Our constitution, our legislation, should be independent of the moral qualities of the nation's leader; they should be as unassailable by a scoundrel, a Nero, that is to say, a Louis XI, as by a good Prince, a Henry IV, that is to say, a Louis XVI.

The partisans of an absolute veto give us efficient means to conquer the constant refusal of the royal sanction. These are popular insurrection, the ascendancy of opinion, a tax strike. What a conclusion! To want to raise a barrier only to enjoy the pleasure of destroying it by radical means!

Is the ascendancy of national opinion irresistible? Does not experience testify that tyrants of every century braved opinion and were deaf to the cries of reason?

Insurrection is opposing one misfortune to another; in forestalling evil, we will be exempted from remedying it.

The refusal to pay taxes will be a scourge which, as a counter-punch, strikes all citizens, and soon the body politic will be deprived of movement and life. Besides, would it not be illusory to say to the king, you have the right to accept or reject our laws, but if you refuse to grant our wishes, you will be forced by us to do so or dry up the public treasury?

It is incessantly repeated that our mandates demand a royal sanction. Have [its proponents] even defined those terms? Have they distinguished between the indefinite and suspensive vetoes? No, the right to establish the demarcation line between the authority conceded to the king and that reserved to the Nation is reserved to your wisdom.

It is incessantly objected that the king held a portion of the legislative authority formerly in France, and that [kings] do even now in most European governments. [Indeed], the King of England has the absolute veto. I am examining less what is done in other countries than what should be done. The history that is too often invoked is an arsenal where each takes arms from every fort, because it offers examples of every kind. The multiplicity of facts, instead of supporting a principle, often only indicates the violation of principles; and often one cites as exemplary that which should be considered abusive to reform.

3. It is in the king's interest to not have the absolute veto; for if the law is wise it will necessarily be to the advantage of the Prince, whose true happiness is inseparable from that of the Nation. If the law is bad, the king will incur no blame, and the Nation will be able to reflect on only itself for its error.

But a National Assembly can err. The prestige of eloquence, the effervescence of enthusiasm, or other causes can carry it too brusquely through an [issue] and divert it from its true objective; it is then that a limited opposition to the law can take place. This suspensive veto is only an appeal to the People, and the People, assured that it can pronounce definitively, will not be agitated; whereas the absolute veto [which] restrains and suffocates the national liberty under the scepter of despotism, can lead to insurrection.

Thus it is necessary to have a barrier against precipitous decisions, but this barrier should be neither insurmountable nor permanent; after a predetermined lapse of time, the obstacle posed by the Prince should be lifted by the will of the People.

There are even political circumstances in which the suspensive veto accorded to the Prince will menace national liberty. For example, in the interval between the current session and the next, will not the anti-Patriots whose party is dispersed yet not destroyed foment new troubles? They cabal in a base manner, that is to say, worthy of them, in an atrocious manner, that is to say, worthy of them. They buy corrupt men, subjugate the weak, lead the ignorant astray, and lead us perhaps into incalculable troubles for the extent and the duration.

In the hypothesis of the permanence and unity of the National Assembly, I opine for the suspensive veto, which being only an appeal to the People retains their right to it; but I am opposed with all my might to an absolute veto, which reduces the Nation to a subaltern role, whereas it is everything, and which becomes the most terrible arm of despotism.

B. Jean-Joseph Mounier, Speech on the Royal Sanction (SEPTEMBER 5, 1789)

... All that remains is to consider what influence the monarch ought to have on legislation.

The greatest care must be taken, regardless of the type of government, to prevent those who hold any authority from pursuing all their desires and establishing arbitrary power.

To accomplish this, the branches of government must be organized in such a way that they will never be united in the same hands. Despotism is found wherever government powers are united or confused. If policing and the administration of justice are guided by an arbitrary will, like that which is driven by passion or circumstance, then liberty does not exist. Government must be guided by preexisting laws, which have been prepared in a period of calm and after lengthy reflection.

If government powers are united, nothing restrains those who exercise them; they make laws according to their interests and give that respectable name to every whim; they make the execution of those laws retroactive and give them a sense that accords with their passions; they consider themselves the supreme and infallible arbiters of the destinies of their peers; but, if government powers are distinct, if insurmountable limits are opposed to their union, if legislative power is so constituted that those who exercise it must aspire to general happiness, if they are enlightened enough not to pass foolish laws, and if they cannot make hasty decisions, then the people will never be enslaved; only the salutary yoke of the law may exist.

That is the goal toward which those employed in organizing the government direct their efforts: separation of powers; but to remain separated, they must be secured from the attacks and reciprocal usurpations of one another.

There are a wealth of means available to secure the power vested in the representatives, and to prevent the monarch from making laws according to his will and so overturning the Constitution: the permanence of the legislative body; representatives' right of resistance; their exclusive right to propose laws; the free grant of taxes; the answerability of ministers; provincial administrations; municipalities; bourgeois militia; the freedom of the press.

Source: François Furet and Ran Halevi, eds., *Orateurs de la Révolution française* (Paris: Gallimard, 1989), pp. 890–907. Translated by Laura Mason.

Once all citizens have resolved to be free, once public spiritedness has penetrated every class, once the Constitution has become the elementary text for the education of youth, once preservation has been demanded of all groups and all individuals; what then, I ask you, is the ambition of a single man against such a generous nation?

But how, in turn, to secure executive power against the encroachments of the representatives? Without a doubt, if the representatives managed to seize the prerogatives of the throne, the people would tremble beneath the weight of tyranny in spite of free elections. No matter how great the wisdom of those who govern, their passions lead them astray when they are not dominated by precise rules and can do anything with impunity; even love of the public good becomes the source of the most disastrous errors.

It is, no doubt, useless to demonstrate that the executive power of a vast realm should enjoy great strength; such strength would be seen with envy or uneasiness by a people jealous of its liberty. Ambitious men and demagogues would impute fault to it and profit from every opportunity to weaken or destroy it. The usurpation of royal authority would bring the loss of public liberty as its consequence. Democracy is a foolish dream in a large state. Thrones lose authority only to give way to the degrading yoke of aristocracy; and feudal tyranny was established in France by the successive invasions of those who composed the general assemblies under the first and second dynasties of our kings; thus, defense of the crown's independence is defense of the people's liberty.

Therefore, we must give the greatest possible attention to the means by which we may secure executive power from all encroachments by the legislative power.

The most obvious means is to make the king an integral part of the legislative body and to require that the representatives' decisions be invested with the royal sanction in order to become laws. So it would be unnecessary to separate the powers entirely, to keep them forever distinct. The power to make the law should be and is, in fact, superior to the power to execute it. If the king were not part of the legislative body, if it were possible to make laws without his consent, then he would no longer enjoy sovereign power; he would be subordinate to the legislative body, which would then be able to dictate his absolute orders and successively annul all his prerogatives by means of its laws.

The monarch's authority would be protected by the Constitution in vain. The members of the legislative body, supreme judges and sole arbiters of their duties, would face no obstacle in transgressing the boundaries set them.

Therefore, to maintain the king's authority, no law may exist without royal sanction; this is not to say that all powers would be placed in the same hands, because the king would not be endowed with legislative and executive powers. Those powers would always remain distinct and separate because the king would not be able to make laws. He would hold a part of legislative authority only to preserve perpetually the separation of powers, to defend his prerogatives, and by that means to preserve the liberty of the people.

The question as to whether the royal sanction is necessary for all laws is therefore entirely independent of the other questions to which some have tried to subordinate it because, regardless of how the legislative body is composed, it will always be absolutely necessary to maintain separation of powers. Opinions now appear to be divided over the nature of the veto that the royal sanction should issue. Some want it to be unlimited; others only suspensive. This difference of opinion should yield to the following considerations.

The royal sanction can be nothing other than the king's consent to all legislative acts. Almost all of our electors believed that such consent was necessary. If the king could only suspend legislative acts then, clearly, it would no longer be possible to say that laws have royal sanction, and it would be necessary only to determine the period of time during which the king were able to suspend. The legislative body, by persisting in its resolutions, would thus make law without the consent of the prince. In such case, the royal sanction would no longer be necessary and the wishes of our electors, who wanted the king to share legislative power, would be entirely disappointed.

But can the simple ability to suspend the execution of a law inhibit the union of all powers into the hands of the representatives? Is it not obvious that as soon as the legislative body wanted to seize some portion of royal authority, the latter would be entirely defenseless?

It has been proposed that the king be given a suspensive right until new deputies arrive to make known their constituents' wishes, and it is maintained that once the wishes of the people, from whom sovereign power derives, are known, then obstacles should disappear. Certainly, the people's will is of compelling force; but the people cannot express its will through any means other than those that they themselves established when organizing the government, at least not so long as they have not judged the government oppressive and intended to abolish it; and will it not corrupt the government to unnecessarily elicit the will of the multitude when public happiness depends on that will being expressed by representatives and delegates?

It would be dangerous to remain silent at a moment when ideas about liberty are so often exaggerated and so remote from its true principles; government should be instituted for the happiness of all citizens and not in order to subordinate everything to the decisions of the masses. I rival the most democratically inclined in my respect for my peers and in my love of equality. I want fervently to see the dawning of the day when the personal liberty of the most obscure citizen will be as sacred as that of the wealthiest and most illustrious man; but I will always believe that, in order to be free and to save themselves from the dire consequences of intrigue, error, and haste, the people must confer the power to make and execute laws, and if they govern themselves they will lose their liberty and return to despotism or aristocratic rule after having experienced all the horrors of the cruelest anarchy. The people always have sufficient enlightenment to discern those who merit confidence; so they should freely choose men worthy of their votes and charge them to prepare laws and watch over the preservation of liberty; and these representatives, restored to the status of simple citizens after two or three years, should never forget the rights they possess; but the masses should not deliberate themselves.

How easy it would be for representatives, regularly seduced by projects for the public good, to orchestrate the resolutions adopted in different districts of the realm. Having exploited a royal prerogative, representatives could think it useful to their homeland to seize it, or to submit it to their continual vigilance or consent. Before long, they will have encouraged the same will in the voters. Has not experience taught us that when all citizens debate the public interest in a crowd, the debates are directed by the pressure of a few men who can fool the masses with the greatest ease and sway them to their own passions with the most ridiculous lies, making them adopt every opinion?

You have been told that popular assemblies never make bad laws; but among the ancient governments there was never a legislative Assembly to which all men were admitted indifferently; and yet how many tyrannical laws were the fruit of their deliberations! I will not cite examples here; those with only the slightest conception of history can recall such cases in great number. We know how the tribunes of Rome, Pisistratus, Pericles, and Alcibiades made themselves the masters of the people's deliberations; and we would certainly not include among the number of good laws those by which the Athenians divided up public funds, privileging circuses above the Republic's most basic necessities.

But, it is said that royal sanction may be necessary for the representatives' decisions but not for the nation that possesses sovereignty. Allow me, sirs, to expand on the consequences of such sophism.

I know that the principle of sovereignty resides in the nation; your declaration of rights contains this truth. But *being* the principle of sovereignty and *exercising* the principle of sovereignty are two very different things; and I will confidently defend the position that a nation which retains the exercise of sovereignty would be either very foolish or very unhappy. We should understand sovereignty to mean absolute and unlimited power. Thus, to say that a nation is sovereign, is to say that a nation has all powers; and certainly no one doubts that a nation can do whatever it likes, but it should want only that which affects its happiness; and since a nation is a collective body, it is itself prey to the clash of the claims and interests of those who compose it. It is torn by factions and subject to the empire of violence if it does not choose its leaders, if it does not organize its government and create a regular police force. And it can only organize this government by delegating authority. . . .

Others have said before me: how is it not possible to recognize that the royal sanction is almost always suspensive by nature, so long as it is not used to prohibit a constitutional prerogative? Either the proposed law is favorable to the monarch's power and so, whether the veto is absolute or suspensive, we well know that he will not use it to combat the law. Or the law is contrary to his power as defined by the Constitution, and so in defending his authority, the monarch defends the Constitution itself. Or the law concerns the general administration of the realm and does not touch his prerogatives, and so what motive would he have to stop a good law? Is it not evident that, on the contrary, the monarch has an interest in sanctioning the law if it is for the good of his people? Because who can deny that his happiness must increase in tandem with the growing prosperity of his empire?

But suppose that enemies of the public good persuade the monarch to refuse his sanction for a salutary law; if the law has nothing to do with his authority, then once its advantages are well known and clearly demonstrated, once the people's representatives have repeatedly persisted in the same resolution, I ask who can imagine a king and ministers capable of such rash foolishness as to continue to struggle against such overwhelmingly unequal forces. . . .

In finishing, sirs, allow me to return once more to that oft-repeated phrase: the general will. Allow me to observe that in no known government has the will of the masses been accepted as a sole guide. The people of the ancient republics were never subjected to a law that they did not want, but the people's every wish did not acquire the force of law. Rules were adopted to distinguish an arbitrary will or impassioned movement from a reflective will directed by the light of reason; and no one has ever suggested a better means to privilege reason than to require that resolutions pass various obstacles which, at the risk of stopping those that might be advantageous, more often stop those which could be harmful. . . .

Yes, sirs, it is a sacred duty for the Committee to tell you that it foresees the most harmful consequences if we establish a democratic regime by requiring the electors of every district of the realm to choose between the king and their representatives, or if we leave to new representatives the ability to destroy every obstacle to the separation of powers. The constant necessity of the royal sanction seems to the Committee to be a principle as respectable as that of the indivisibility of the crown. How could we subject public liberty to the risks of factions and intrigue and shape an arbitrary government for the French, all through the fear of depriving them of a few laws, as if all nations have not judged it reasonable and prudent to make no law without the consent of their magistrates! As if a new law were not often one more hindrance of independence! . . .

. . . How is it not possible to see that since the separation of powers is the foundation of liberty, we must insure that division and requiring the king's consent is a necessary means to do so. . . .

19. Women's March to Versailles

Tensions in Paris rose once more during the late summer and early fall as grain shortages drove up bread prices and word circulated that the king might use his veto power to halt passage of the August decrees. News that the king's guard had organized a drunken banquet and insulted the Revolution brought these simmering tensions to the point of explosion. On October 5, Parisian market women marched to Versailles, followed by Lafayette and the national guard, to demand bread from the king and ask for the punishment of those who had impugned the Revolution. When a crowd broke into the royal palace the following morning, Lafayette counseled the king to return to Paris with the women. On both days, the sequence of events suggests the degree to which established officials found themselves trying to catch up with popular initiative; this would become a familiar dynamic throughout the first half of the Revolution. The first account here was published by a participant in 1789; the second is drawn from an official inquest into the October Days that was held the following summer.

A. The Woman Cheret, *The Event of Paris and Versailles, by One of the Ladies Who Had the Honor to Be in the Deputation to the General Assembly* (1789)

About 8:30 in the morning, many women appeared at the city hall; some asked to speak to Messieurs Bailly and de la Fayette, to learn from them why it was so difficult to get bread and at such a high price; others wanted most absolutely for the king and queen to come to Paris and live in the Louvre where, the women said, they would be infinitely better off than at Versailles; finally, others demanded that those who had black cockades give them up immediately, that the Regiment of Flanders and the king's bodyguards be recalled, and that their majesties have no other guards than Parisian national soldiers. During this time, Messieurs de Gouvion, Major General Richard du Pin, second commandant of the volunteers of the Bastille, and Lefevre, distributor of powder, arms, and equipment, were in the greatest danger because the multitude, furious at not having found arms and ammunition, wanted to hang them, and it was only by some kind of miracle that they escaped. About noon or one o'clock, Monsieur the Marquis de la Fayette, who seemed to see nothing good in a trip to Versailles, finally came to believe that he must cede to the citizens' fervent wishes; Marie-Louise Lenoel, wife of Cheret, living in the rue Vaugirard, employed at that time in one of the most lucrative markets at Passy, abruptly leaves her virtuous mother, abandons the profits she is about to earn, mingles with the lady citizenesses going to Versailles, and flies away with them, under the supervision of sirs Hulin and Maillard, and other volunteers of the Bastille, those heroes who wanted to join to their laurels from July 14 the honor of again making the origin of the people's ills known to the National Assembly, knowledge without which great monarchs are worthless.

Source: Femme Cheret, Événement de Paris et de Versailles, par une des Dames qui a eu l'honneur d'être de la députation à l'Assemblée générale (Paris: Garnery & Volland, booksellers, [nd]). Bibliothèque Nationale: Lb39 7941. Translated by Laura Mason.

On October 5, 1789, the market women of Paris marched to Versailles to demand bread from the king and to protect him from the threat of counter-revolution. The following day, they would escort the entire royal family back to Paris. *(Musée Carnavalet, Paris/Jean-Loup Charmet)*

Arriving at daybreak, the citizenesses stopped to put themselves in order; at Sèvres, the men forced shopkeepers to sell them food, paying and returning to Versailles. On the road, two or three individuals, one of whom came on the king's behalf, were arrested, saw their black cockades torn, and were forced to join the line. When the women were about to enter their majesties' residence, the bourgeoisie of Versailles, the Flanders Regiment and the dragoons (we won't speak of the officers) clapped their hands, registered their satisfaction with shouts of joy, congratulated the women on their arrival, and begged them to work for the general good. Need anyone make such a request of French-born ladies who were led by the heroes of the Bastille? A few minutes later, about 4 o'clock, our citizenesses, led by sirs Hulin and Maillard, took the road to the National Assembly, where they had great difficulty entering. What an imposing sight for them! But at the same time, their appearance must have displeased certain members of a certain order, which would never have existed had our fathers been wise enough to understand that there having been only two kinds of people when the Franks invaded the Gauls, the victors who were nobles and the vanquished who were commoners, it is the greatest foolishness to admit among the representatives of a Nation like ours, men who only enjoy goods accorded to them by blind credulity. Be that as it may and in spite of the fearfulness that our good women friends spread among the sanctimonious churchmen, several of whom cleared out, the honorable members of the National Assembly, coming to understand that the women were absolutely committed to persist until there was something definite for always, accorded to our twelve deputies (1) a new prohibition against exporting grain;

(2) the promise that a tax of 24 livres would be levied on wheat, an honest price so that there can be enough bread, and bread at a price within reach of even the least comfortable citizens; (3) that meat would cost no more than 8 under the livre. At this juncture, it is said that the king's guard and the national soldiers amused themselves by firing at one another; it remains to be seen if the former distinguished themselves but the rumor is that we lost very few and that the king proved, on October 5, 1789, that he merits more than ever the title accorded him last June 17th, that of Restorer of the French Nation. Our citizenesses, clothed in glory, were returned by carriage, at his majesty's expense, to the city hall in Paris, where we welcomed them as liberators of the capital, their actions to forever ruin the present and future designs of the aristocracy.

B. Testimony of Master Jean-Louis Brousse des Faucherets (1790)

[Des Faucherets was forty-three years old, a lawyer for Parlement and the mayor's second-in-command at the department of public works. He lived on rue Paradis in the Marais. On October 6, having left City Hall to return home for a meal, des Faucherets returned at about 4:30 p.m.] . . . There he learned that Monsieur de la Fayette, constrained by the uncompromising will of the troops, had been obliged to march at their head to Versailles after having taken orders from the Commune of Paris, which charged him to do so; that then the Assembly of representatives gathered themselves in the great hall and, Monsieur the mayor having taken his place, the witness sat at the desk as his position of secretary required him to do; that time passed as they waited anxiously to receive deputations from the city districts who came to ask for news; that in order to be able to answer, they dispatched a first orderly; they were awaiting his return when, at about 11 o'clock at night, a woman appeared followed by a postilion of the mail; having climbed up on the desk, she announced that the people had arrived at Versailles, the bodyguard fired on them; that one of the bodyguard had been captured and she herself, assisted by a couple of other women, had hanged him from the gates of the château; that, anxious to bring news, she returned to Paris; that she had met a postilion, who was with her, and had forced him to give her his horse; this account increased the anxiety and deputations from the city districts grew in number; a new orderly was sent out to bring back more accurate details and to hasten the return of the first orderly; they were awaiting the first and second orderlies when, at about 3 o'clock in the morning, a band of women appeared, at the head of which was one named Magdeleine or Marguerite Chabry, called

---

Source: *Procédure criminelle instruite au Châtelet de Paris, sur la dénonciation des faits arrivés à Versailles dans la journée du 6 octobre 1789. Printed by Order of the National Assembly* (Paris: chez Baudouin, 1790). Translated by Laura Mason.

Louison, flowerseller in the neighborhood of the Palais royal, who gave an account of what the women who went to Versailles had done, and who added that after having won different decrees on grain from the National Assembly, she herself had a private audience with the king who, having sanctioned the said decrees, embraced her; that these decrees had been given to other women who, guided by master Maillard, volunteer of the Bastille, were about to arrive in carriages from the court, which had been ordered to bring them back to Paris; that, indeed, an hour later master Maillard and a dozen women arrived who brought the consignment of said decrees, the printing of which was immediately ordered; that all of this band, worn out with fatigue and hunger, requested food; all the bread and meat that could be had was gathered up and the women were served a meal that they shared among themselves in the room adjoining that of the Assembly. Curiosity having drawn the witness into this room, he saw the women seated around a table who, in the drunkenness of their joy, gave themselves over to the most scandalous remarks; having drawn close to one of them, whose face is not clear enough in his mind to describe, he heard her say quite clearly: "Oh! that little Marie-Antoinette, if we had caught her, we would have made her dance the dance that she deserves," and in response to the shock that he, the witness, evidenced at such talk, she added, "That is indeed what she deserves, because she alone is the cause of all the ills we suffer," after which he, the witness, returned to the Assembly hall where the representatives, uneasy and surprised to see that none of their couriers had returned, resolved to dispatch a third; the latter had no more success than the others, so requiring the dispatch of a fourth; they were awaiting the return of one of the four when they saw the arrival of Monsieur de Mousseaux, representative of the district of Saint Opportune and one of the four commissioners named by the Commune to accompany Monsieur de la Fayette to Versailles; he gave an account of all the events that he had witnessed and brought a letter from the commander-general, which announced the most complete peace; calmed by this happy news, the Assembly undertook to separate. . . .

TWO

From Liberal
to Republican Revolution
1789–1792

s the October Days receded into the past, many came to believe that the new nation's troubles were at an end, that the greatest task France now faced was to construct a new order. And, indeed, the deputies to the National Assembly had immersed themselves in drafting legislation that would institutionalize the liberal individualism of the Enlightenment. But the revolutionary road forward was by no means clear. The countryside remained uneasy as peasants and former seigneurs continued to dispute rights and dues, and as the new government struggled to impose order and revive tax collection. Of more long-range consequence were political differences that became increasingly sharp after the summer of 1790: differences over the status of the newly nationalized church, the king's loyalty to the Revolution, and whether to make war on threatening neighbors. The Assembly's decision to declare war only intensified existing tensions, and thus the nation would reach a new point of crisis by the middle of 1792. In the late summer of that year, Parisians and militants from the provinces took matters into their own hands by initiating a new revolution, the republican revolution of August 10. Few citizens would have time, however, to savor their changed political circumstances, for in addition to facing the weighty task of conducting a war, the nation had now to decide the fate of the king.

The Declaration of the Rights of Man *(Giraudon/Art Resource, New York)*

Creating a New France

Scarcely two months after declaring themselves representatives of the nation at large, the deputies of the National Assembly issued a statement of principle. Like Thomas Jefferson's "Declaration of Independence," drafted thirteen years earlier, the "Declaration of the Rights of Man and Citizen" enshrined Enlightenment notions of politics and individual liberties. "Man is born and remains free and equal in rights": in other words, all human beings have certain inalienable rights that precede the existence of government and which government must respect. All subsequent guarantees in the Declaration followed logically from this initial statement. Citizens may not be deprived of their rights to association, property, free expression. Laws may only prohibit what is harmful to society and no one may be compelled to do anything that the law does not expressly require. The citizenry is the source of the law and, consequently, public administrators are accountable to society.

There is much that will seem familiar to modern readers in the "Declaration of the Rights of Man." However, as the great French historian Georges Lefebvre pointed out, this document was important to contemporaries primarily for its negative value: it abolished the practices of the Old Regime and declared what society and politics would no longer be. The legislators of the National Assembly would have more difficulty in establishing what France ought to become. For, like the philosophes they so admired, these men were caught between the universal claims of the Enlightenment that they celebrated in the Declaration and much older social particularisms that had shaped every dimension of Old Regime life and which continued to shape how they themselves conceived of mankind. Ultimately, the revolutionaries of 1789 would fall far short of extending universal civil and political rights to all members of French society. But the National Assembly had forged a powerful weapon for struggle, for the "Declaration of the Rights of Man" laid the foundation upon which those who had been excluded from the social contract might base their demands for inclusion.

Religious minorities were the most successful in winning practical applications of the Declaration's guarantees. The article on freedom of conscience was quickly interpreted as promising full civil rights to French Protestants, who had already been granted limited rights by the 1787 Edict of Toleration. French Jews, on the other hand, were initially excluded from the protections implied by the article; Assembly legislators, like their Enlightenment predecessors, tended to regard Jews as resident foreigners—to whom they owed legal protection rather than civil rights—because they had different social customs and because many spoke Yiddish or wrote Hebrew rather than French. However, the diverse Jewish communities in the south, southwest, and east of France organized themselves and petitioned the Assembly steadily, finally winning full rights of citizenship late in 1791.

The free blacks and slaves of France's colonies would face far greater difficulties in their struggle to be included within the community protected by the Declaration. Although a number of Enlightenment authors had condemned slavery and the slave trade under the Old Regime, abolitionist sentiment was firmly opposed by the merchants and slave-holding colonists who were amassing huge fortunes in France's Caribbean colonies. These defenses of slavery survived the demise of the Old Regime and came to be associated with race when Vincent Ogé, a free black and slaveholder from Saint Domingue (now Haiti), demanded that the Assembly grant full political and civil rights to the free blacks of the colonies. Ogé had hoped to demonstrate to white planters that free blacks shared common interests with them, but the planters responded that the grant of rights to any persons of color would be an opening wedge for abolitionism. When the National Assembly acquiesced to the white planters, exempting the colonies from the constitution in March 1790 and threatening to prosecute anyone who organized resistance to slavery, Ogé raised a rebellion in Saint Domingue. Although he was defeated and executed within a few months, French troops were unable to restore calm to the island, for the slaves themselves rebelled shortly afterward, initiating a struggle for freedom that would last several years.

While Jews, free blacks, and slaves implicitly raised the question of who was a man, French women provoked legislators and citizens to consider whether "man" was a sex-specific being or an abstract category that included all human beings. Enlightenment authors had been particularly divided over women's status: while Jean-Jacques Rousseau sang the praises of the docile woman who confined herself to the home, the Marquis de Condorcet argued that women's status as human beings conferred on them the right to full citizenship as well as equal education and social conditions. Although the National Assembly never even considered allowing women to vote or hold office, many women took quite seriously the Revolution's promise of civil and political equality. Some, like the playwright Olympe de Gouges, called attention to the limits of the Revolution's universalistic promises, while others engaged in direct action through insurrection and political clubs.

As legislators and different constituencies within the new nation debated the extent and implications of constitutionalism, rural inhabitants conducted their own struggles over the shape of the new order. The promises made on the night of August 4 and the decrees issued during the subsequent week were meant to put an immediate end to rural disorder and violence by striking down feudalism and enacting a system of compensation. In truth, it would take years to dismantle the Old Regime in the countryside. Because of the confusing welter of dues and privileges that had existed throughout the country—some of which the Assembly considered property and so worthy of compensation, others of which were to be abandoned outright—peasants and former seigneurs faced an increasingly complex body of legislation that gave rise to as many disputes as it settled. The frustration created by detailed legislation was exacerbated during the early months of 1790 when former seigneurs attempted to capitalize on hesitation within the National Assembly by trying to recover rights they had lost the preceding summer. These efforts to revive dues and privileges provoked further local violence and a steady stream of complaints from affected peasants to their representatives in Paris.

All of these conflicts—over status, rights, and obligations—were difficult and, in some cases, violent. In a sense, they were the inevitable consequence of the ambitious social and political changes that revolutionaries initiated in a few short months. But they were arguments between groups who, for the most part, agreed on the fundamental principles that revolutionaries had claimed as their own. After the summer of 1790, however, new disagreements arose about the very nature of the Revolution, disagreements that not only heightened opposition but that divided revolutionaries among themselves. In particular, the revolutionary reform of the church, the king's flight in the summer of 1791, and the declaration of war in the spring of 1792 contributed to a process of radicalization that would finally generate another revolution in August 1792.

New Divisions

The future of the Catholic Church in France was called into question during the very first months of the Revolution: on the night of August 4, the National Assembly struck down the tithes, payments, and feudal dues that had helped to sustain parish priests, religious orders, and even the Holy See for generations; a few months later, the Assembly expropriated church lands. Without its traditional sources of revenue, the church became dependent on the government for support; the government, in nationalizing the church, could claim a direct interest in its organization. And so the Assembly embarked on a program of rationalization, the crowning achievement of which was the Civil Constitution of the Clergy, adopted in July 1790. The Assembly had already begun to pare away what it considered superfluous personnel by abolishing contemplative orders, leaving in place only those orders that engaged in such productive work as teaching or providing care for the sick and the poor. With the Civil Constitution, it declared the clergy salaried employees of the state, and announced its intention to reduce the number of dioceses and democratize clerical appointments, by allowing new curés and bishops to be elected by active citizens.

Although many clergy had long recognized the need for institutional reform of the church, the Civil Constitution drew increasingly vociferous criticism. Conservative Catholics were already alienated by the Assembly's grant of civil rights to Protestants and its refusal to declare Catholicism the state religion; now they condemned the suppression of dioceses and, in particular, the proposal to elect parish priests. Such elections, they argued, not only violated the traditional practices of the church hierarchy but, open to all active citizens, they potentially involved Protestants and Jews in the choosing of Catholic officials. Faced with growing opposition to the Civil Constitution, the Assembly forced the issue by decreeing, in November 1791, that all clergy—as government employees—must promptly swear a public oath of loyalty to the Constitution or face immediate dismissal. Attitudes toward the oath varied from region to region, but there was a sharp distinction between the responses of upper and lower clergy; although only seven bishops took the oath, slightly more than half of all French curés complied.

The debate over the Civil Constitution of the Clergy opened a new divide within France by tracing an opposition between revolution and Catholicism that would persist into the twentieth century. In many parts of the country, the debate would foster the belief that revolution and religion were fundamentally at odds, that citizens had to choose between them. In creating this sense of opposition, the conflict helped to create a popular base for counter-revolution, by driving citizens who might have accepted political reform to condemn, and even take up arms against, a revolution they feared would violate their fundamental beliefs.

As the rift over religion widened, Louis XVI created a new schism in the summer of 1791 by attempting to flee France. The king, a reluctant revolutionary at best, had seen his relations with Assembly and people deteriorate over the preceding year. As a devout Catholic, he became critical of the Civil Constitution of the Clergy after the Pope condemned it, and he was at odds with the Assembly over his refusal to endorse punitive decrees against émigrés. He reached his breaking point when, in the spring of 1791, crowds prevented the royal family from leaving Paris to celebrate Easter in the nearby city of Saint-Cloud. Convinced that he was being held prisoner, Louis began to plan his escape. On the night of June 20–21 the royal family slipped away from the Tuileries in a large carriage and headed toward the eastern border. After his arrest, the king would claim that he had wanted only to establish himself in the border town of Montmédy, to safely negotiate with revolutionaries in Paris. However, the Comte de Provence, the king's brother who reached safety in exile, claimed that Louis's true aspiration had been to emigrate and lead Austrian troops against his disobedient subjects. But the king's flight failed. Delays led to disorganization and Louis was finally recognized by a postman near the town of Varennes, who had seen his likeness on paper money. The entire royal family was arrested and returned to the capital.

Although Louis had dispelled any doubts about the reasons for his flight by leaving behind a letter that disavowed the Revolution, the National Assembly was unwilling to do without a king. Fearful of establishing a regency—a historically weak form of government—or a republic—which threatened to strengthen the political role of the populace—the Assembly circulated the fiction that the king had been kidnapped. Parisians gathered at the Champ de Mars a few days later to protest the king's reinstatement and the crowd soon became violent; the Assembly responded by sending in troops, who killed at least fifty people, and declaring martial law. The king was reinstated and he publicly accepted the Constitution the following September, but his flight and the subsequent events had lasting political consequences. By fleeing, Louis undermined his image as a monarch loyal to the Revolution; revolutionaries would henceforth have sound reasons to mistrust him. As well, he encouraged counter-revolution, for opponents within and outside France could and did claim that the king was being held captive by a Revolution of which he wanted no part. Finally, and perhaps most dangerously, revolutionaries themselves had been divided by the June events. Henceforth, there would be two visible parties of revolution: those who would cling to the constitutional monarchy as a bulwark against popular revolution and were willing to use military force to safeguard the status quo; and those who would press with growing insistence for a republic and were willing to call on the crowd to achieve it.

The king's frustrated attempt to flee also fueled what would become the final crisis of the constitutional monarchy: the move toward war. A growing community of émigrés (emigrants disgruntled with the Revolution) had stationed themselves just beyond the eastern border of France, where they raised armies and drilled soldiers under the benevolent eye of local German princes. The émigrés were a persistent source of uneasiness, and when the king's aborted flight encouraged several of Europe's crowned heads—among them, Marie Antoinette's brother, Leopold II of Austria—to threaten the citizens of France if they harmed Louis, it only heightened the national sense of danger. In the Jacobin Club in Paris, where radical politicians met to discuss current affairs, and within the Legislative Assembly itself, the deputy Brissot and his followers urged a declaration of war. War, they argued, would not simply protect the nation; it would force the Revolution's friends to declare themselves and would flush out traitors. Brissot's opponents, among them Maximilien Robespierre, replied that France was unprepared for such an act and they questioned whether the king's enthusiasm for war was not, in truth, fueled by his hope for a defeat and military coup. Brissot's position was strengthened, however, by the increasingly hostile stance of Austria and Prussia. War fever rose steadily, and when the new Austrian emperor began to mobilize troops in the early spring, the government needed no further provocation: France declared war in late April 1792.

The war was greeted with enormous enthusiasm—the energy of Rouget de Lisle's famous hymn, the "Marseillaise," conveys no small measure of contemporary feeling—and young men volunteered by the thousands. But the army had been badly disorganized by revolutionary reforms and the desertion of aristocratic officers, so French troops were plagued by defeat and desertion at the war's outset. In Paris the anxiety caused by defeat was intensified by renewed food shortages and the increasingly popular belief that the king was unwilling to prosecute the war with adequate vigor. On July 25 the Duke of Brunswick further heightened fear and uncertainty by issuing a decree on behalf of Austria and Prussia that made Paris directly responsible for the king's safety and promised "exemplary and . . . memorable vengeance" if any member of the royal family were harmed.

The Assembly responded to the Brunswick Manifesto by distributing arms and opening the National Guard to all citizens; the Paris sections began to demand the king's deposition. Finally, on August 10, Parisian artisans and shopkeepers—the sans-culottes who would play such an important part in revolutionary politics in the coming years—capitalized on the presence in the capital of provincial troops on their way to the front; they attacked the Tuileries palace itself. The royal family fled for safety to the Legislative Assembly but fighting continued: about six hundred of the king's guard and almost four hundred insurgents were killed in the bloodiest uprising that France had yet seen. The insurgents, at least, would be remembered as revolutionary heroes, for the Legislative Assembly acquiesced to the show of force. It suspended the king and called elections, in which all adult males would be eligible to vote, for a republican National Convention. The French monarchy had been swept away.

From Revolution to Republic

As had been the case during the summer of 1789, the Paris revolution of August 10 fostered disorder throughout the country. The new revolution had swept away

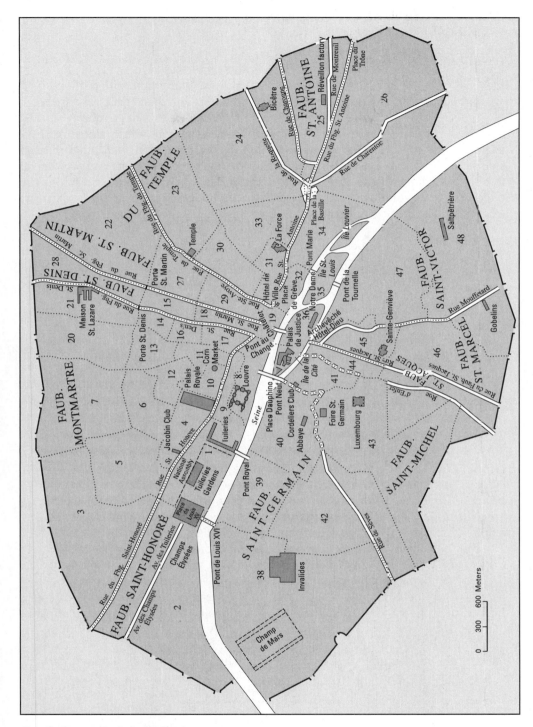

Revolutionary Paris in Sections

Detail of the principal streets, buildings, and traditional neighborhoods (faubourgs) of Paris, as well as the forty-eight electoral sections into which the city was divided in 1790. *(Source: George Rudé,* The Crowd in the French Revolution *[London: Oxford University Press, 1959]. Used by permission of Oxford University Press.)*

the king's veto against refractory priests—priests who refused to swear loyalty to the Civil Constitution—and so the battle against the church intensified; municipal and departmental officials imprisoned refractories and the Legislative Assembly ordered that all priests who refused to swear a new oath to liberty and equality be deported. But hostility did not focus on refractory priests alone; once again uncertainty produced fear, which, in turn, excited action. But rather than sharing rumors of anonymous bandits as they had in 1789, men and women throughout France began to speak of prison plots, worrying aloud that imprisoned counter-revolutionary suspects and simple thieves were awaiting a signal from abroad to break out and slaughter unsuspecting revolutionaries. And as municipal governments organized "domiciliary visits" for arms and suspect materials, they filled the prisons, so intensifying popular fears. It was under these circumstances that murders of priests and suspected counter-revolutionaries swept the countryside in the late summer; this wave of popular violence reached its peak with the Paris prison massacres of September.

The war had continued going badly even after the Revolution of August 10: the Prussians crossed the frontier in late August and quickly defeated the French fort at Longwy. At the beginning of September, Parisians learned that the fort at Verdun was under siege and possibly on the verge of surrender; if Verdun surrendered, no other stronghold stood between the Prussians and the capital. Fearful of the enemies before them and of those they believed to be among them, Parisians turned against the city's prisons. Setting up tribunals in prison courtyards, they marched out inmates for summary judgment: those found guilty were promptly executed, while those declared innocent were released and welcomed into the crowd. While the members of the Legislative Assembly, the Paris municipal government, and the Jacobin Club looked on, some eleven hundred to fourteen hundred people were killed in less than five days. The memory of the September massacres would be of profound importance to legislators, who would come to believe that if they were to keep the upper hand they must preempt popular violence by proving to the sans-culottes that they were doing everything possible to fight counter-revolution.

The Legislative Assembly dissolved itself on September 20, and the National Convention came to sit the following day. It was a young group—about two thirds of the deputies were under the age of forty-five—and as socially homogeneous as had been its predecessor; most of its members were lawyers, professionals, or property holders. Reflecting political rivalries that had emerged during the preceding year, two groups almost immediately began to compete for dominance within the Convention. The Girondins, so called because many of them hailed from the department of the Gironde, included among their number many of the Brissotins from the Legislative Assembly; the Montagnards (or Mountain, because they sat high in the back of the assembly hall) included the dynamic and enormously popular Georges-Jacques Danton as well as Maximilien Robespierre and Louis-Antoine Saint-Just, both of whom would eventually wield enormous power through the Committee of Public Safety. Although the two groups set out with a similar commitment to protecting property rights and restraining popular revolution, their rivalry led them to depict their opponents and then themselves as moving toward opposite ends of the political spectrum. The Girondins came to be known as economic liberals and secret friends of the king, while the Jacobins claimed to be increasingly staunch supporters of popular revolution in the form of sans-culotte activism.

Certainly, the most immediate piece of business before the Convention was to decide the king's fate. Few doubted that he was guilty of treason and the Convention voted by an overwhelming majority to condemn him. But having voted condemnation, the deputies proved more divided over punishment. The Girondins argued that the issue should be decided by a popular referendum, a gesture that their opponents reasonably claimed was an attempt to save the king's life. The Montagnards were deeply opposed, for they feared that a referendum would create chaos that could only serve counter-revolution. In the end, the Montagnards won the dispute over procedure, and the king's fate was decided by the members of the Convention alone; a slight majority approved the death penalty. Thus, on January 21, Louis XVI was taken to the Place de la Révolution and guillotined before an enormous crowd. Regicide—the murder of a king—was a radical act; it signaled to the French and to Europe at large that the Revolution had reached a point of no return.

chapter 4

LEGISLATING AN
ENLIGHTENED REGIME

20. National Assembly, Debate on Religious Freedom
(AUGUST 23, 1789)

The roots of this debate can be traced at least as far as the Edict of 1787, which granted certain civil rights to Protestants. However, because the edict did not entirely eliminate discrimination, Protestants and their defenders agitated for a comprehensive statement on religious toleration. By the time the Assembly deliberated on the Rights of Man in the summer of 1789, both sides had staked out positions. Opponents insisted that the special status of Catholicism as the official religion of the French state had to be protected, while Rabaut de Saint-Étienne, a Protestant, and the anticlerical Comte de Mirabeau insisted that privileging any religion threatened liberty. The noncommittal article 10 of the "Declaration of the Rights of Man and Citizen" was the outcome.

MAILLOT: Since religion is one of the principles associated with the rights of man, mention should be made of it in the declaration. If religion only consisted of the ceremonies of worship, it would undoubtedly be necessary to mention it only when drafting the Constitution. But religion is the most

---

Source: Archives parlementaires, vol. 8 (Paris, 1904). Translated by Tracey Rizzo.

solemn, august, and sacred of all laws; we address it in the declaration of rights. I propose the following article: "Since religion is the most sound of all political goods, no man should be disturbed in his religious opinions."

CLERMONT-LODÈVE: All the declarations that have been presented so far have discussed laws which assure the exercise of rights, and the force to protect them, but how can we forget for a moment the very sacred and solemn guarantee of religion? . . . Religion is the true guarantor of laws, without which I could never be safe enough against perfidy. Who would ensure my life against plots, my honor against calumny? . . . Without religion, all relations in society are severed; without it I am hardly the master of my person. All will come to share this point of view when each repeats what J.-J. Rousseau said himself: "Being merely myself, on what basis should I regulate my conduct?" In a word, without religion, it is useless to make laws or rules; living by chance is all that remains.

TALLEYRAND-PÉRIGORD: Religion, but which religion? Is it a question of every religion? But this is not precise. . . . The holy and sacred word of the Catholic religion should be pronounced in the Constitution; it is there that one will learn it is the only religion. . . .

THE PRESIDENT: It is decided that we will be occupied with the work of the Constitution. Article 18 of the declaration of rights becomes the object of discussion: "All citizens who do not challenge the dominant religion will not be disturbed in the exercise of worship."

CASTELLANE: [Renewed his motion so that it could be drafted thus:] "No man should be disturbed in his religious opinions, nor troubled in the exercise of his form of worship."

VICOMTE DE MIRABEAU: Would you wish, then, by permitting all religions, to make a circumstantial religion? Each one would choose a religion in accordance with his passions. The Turkish religion would become that of young men, the Jewish religion that of usurers, the religion of Brahma perhaps that of women.

Gentlemen, you have been told that man does not bring about religion in society. Certainly such a system is very strange. What is the sentiment of any man who contemplates nature, who raises his eyes to the heavens, and who meditates on his existence when he returns to himself? What is the first sentiment of he who meets his fellow in solitude? Do not both fall on their knees together and offer the tribute of their homages to the Creator? . . . I have not imagined that I could one day become the apostle of the religion I profess; I have not believed myself to be suited to theological discussions; I content myself to adore and to worship. Thus, I only support the first part of Mr. Castellane's motion.

COMTE DE MIRABEAU: Yesterday, I had the honor of submitting to you some reflections which tended to demonstrate that religion is a duty and not a right, and that the only thing appropriate to the declaration with which we are occupied is to forcefully pronounce on freedom of religion. . . .

We are permitted to form assemblies, circles, clubs, masonic lodges, every sort of society. The business of the police is to prevent these assemblies from disturbing public order. . . . To keep surveillance over any religion, even your own, so that it does not disturb the peace, that is your task, but you can do no more.

This so-called dominant religion is endlessly discussed: dominant! Gentlemen, I do not understand this word, and I need someone to define it for me.

Is it an oppressive religion of which you speak? But you have banished this word, and men who have assured the right of liberty do not assert that of oppression. Do you refer to the religion of the Prince? But the Prince does not have the right to dominate consciences or to regulate opinion. Is it the religion of the greatest number? But religion is an opinion; this or that religion is the result of this or that opinion. Opinions are not formed as the result of a vote; your thought belongs to you! It is independent, you can engage it.

Finally, an opinion which is that of the greatest number does not have the right to dominate. It is a tyrannical word which should be banished from our legislation, because if you use it in this case, you can use it in all. You will then have a dominant religion, a dominant philosophy, dominant systems. Only justice should dominate; it alone has the right to dominate each one, everything else is submitted to it. Now it is an evident right, already consecrated by you, to do anything that does not harm another.

RABAUT DE SAINT-ÉTIENNE: The honor which I share with you, gentlemen, to be a deputy of the nation and of this august assembly, gives me the right to speak in my turn, and to express my opinion on the question which occupies you. . . . But having the honor to speak to you, gentlemen, to ask you to include a certain and clearly enunciated principle in the declaration of rights, on which you can one day establish just laws pertaining to non-Catholics, I should first tell you their situation in France.

Non-Catholics (some of you, gentlemen, are perhaps unaware) received only that which could not be refused them from the Edict of November 1787. Yes, that which could not be refused them; I do not repeat this without some shame, but it is not a gratuitous indictment—these are the exact terms of the edict. This law, more famous than just, standardizes the forms for registering births, marriages, and deaths; it permits [Protestants] as a consequence to enjoy civil status and to practice their professions . . . and that is all.

Gentlemen, it is in eighteenth-century France that a maxim from barbarous times is maintained to divide a nation into a favored caste and a disgraced caste, and that one regards as progress an act of legislation which permitted French people, proscribed for one hundred years, to exercise their professions, that is to say to live, and which no longer deemed their children illegitimate. . . .

Protestants have done everything for the nation, and the nation treats them with ingratitude. They serve it as citizens; they are treated like outcasts. They serve men you have freed; they are treated as slaves. But finally, a French nation exists, and it is to her that I appeal on behalf of two million useful citizens who reclaim their French birthright today. I do her an injustice to think that she can pronounce the word intolerance; it is banished from our language, where it subsists only as one of those barbarous and outdated words which is no longer useful, because the idea it represents is destroyed. But, gentlemen, it is not even tolerance that I demand; it is liberty. Tolerance! Support! Pardon! Clemency! ideas supremely unjust toward dissidents in so much as it is true that difference of religion, difference of opinion is not a crime. . . .

Gentlemen, I therefore demand for French Protestants, for all the kingdom's non-Catholics, that which you demand for yourselves: liberty and equal rights. I demand it for those people torn from Asia [Jews], always errant, always proscribed, always persecuted for nearly eighteen centuries who adopt our morals and our customs. [I demand it], if, by our laws, they are assimilated with us. We ought not reproach [their] morality because it is the fruit of our barbarism and the humility to which we have unjustly condemned them. . . .

I conclude then, gentlemen, . . . that you should include in your declaration this article: "Every man is free in his opinions; every citizen has the right to freely practice his religion, and no one can be disturbed on account of his religion."

21. "Declaration of the Rights of Man and Citizen" (AUGUST 26, 1789)

Although it was officially in effect for only four years, this document has had a greater impact on world history than any other from the Revolution, influencing even the United Nations' Universal Declaration of Human Rights. An amalgam of Enlightenment political thought, which emphasized natural law, and Old Regime constitutionalism, the declaration guarantees rights to liberty, property, and freedom from oppression. Similar to its American predecessor, it also provides for a strict separation of powers. It was replaced by a new declaration in 1793.

Source: Frank Maloy Anderson, ed., *The Constitution and Other Select Documents Illustrative of the History of France, 1789–1907* (New York: Russell and Russell, 1908; reprinted 1967), pp. 59–61.

An officer of the National Guard takes an oath. *(Giraudon/Art Resource, New York)*

The Representatives of the French people, organized in National Assembly, considering that ignorance, forgetfulness, or contempt of the rights of man are the sole causes of public miseries and the corruption of governments, have resolved to set forth in a solemn declaration the natural, inalienable, and sacred rights of man, so that this declaration, being ever present to all members of the social body, may unceasingly remind them of their rights and duties; in order that the acts of the legislative power and those of the executive power may at each moment be compared with the aim of every political institution and thereby may be more respected; and in order that the demands of the citizens, grounded henceforth upon simple and incontestable principles, may always take the direction of maintaining the constitution and welfare of all.

In consequence, the National Assembly recognizes and declares, in the presence and under the auspices of the Supreme Being, the following rights of man and citizen.

1. Men are born free and remain equal in rights. Social distinctions can be based only on public utility.

2. The aim of every political association is the preservation of the natural and imprescriptible rights of man. These rights are liberty, property, security, and resistance to oppression.

3. The source of all sovereignty resides essentially in the nation: no body, no individual can exercise authority that does not proceed from it in plain terms.

4. Liberty consists in the power to do anything that does not injure others; accordingly, the exercise of the rights of each man has no limits except those that secure the enjoyment of these same rights to the other members of society. These limits can be determined only by law.

5. The law has only the right to forbid such actions as are injurious to society. Nothing can be forbidden that is not interdicted by the law, and no one can be constrained to do that which it does not order.

6. Law is the expression of the general will. All citizens have the right to take part personally, or by their representatives, in its formation. It must be the same for all, whether it protects or punishes. All citizens, being equal in its eyes, are equally eligible to all public dignities, places, and employments, according to their capacities, and without other distinction than that of their virtues and talents.

7. No man can be accused, arrested, or detained, except in the cases determined by the law and according to the forms it has prescribed. Those who procure, expedite, execute, or cause arbitrary orders to be executed, ought to be punished: but every citizen summoned or seized in virtue of the law ought to render instant obedience; he makes himself guilty by resistance.

8. The law ought only to establish penalties that are strict and obviously necessary, and no one can be punished except in virtue of a law established and promulgated prior to the offense and legally applied.

9. Every man being presumed innocent until he has been pronounced guilty, if it is thought indispensable to arrest him, all severity that may not be necessary to secure his person ought to be strictly suppressed by law.

10. No one should be disturbed on account of his opinion, even religious, provided their manifestation does not upset the public order established by law.

11. The free communication of ideas and opinions is one of the most precious of the rights of man; every citizen can then freely speak, write, and print, subject to responsibility for the abuse of this freedom in the cases determined by law.

12. The guarantee of the rights of man and citizen requires a public force; this force then is instituted for the advantage of all and not for the personal benefit of those to whom it is entrusted.

13. A general tax is indispensable for the maintenance of the public force and for the expenses of administration; it ought to be equally apportioned among all citizens according to their means.

14. All citizens have the right to ascertain, by themselves or by their representatives, the necessity of the public tax, to consent to it freely, to follow the employment of it, and to determine the quota, the assessment, the collection, and the duration of it.

15. Society has the right to call for an account of his administration by every public agent.

16. Any society in which the guarantee of the rights is not secured, or the separation of powers not determined, has no constitution at all.

17. Property being a sacred and inviolable right, no one can be deprived of it, unless a legally established public necessity evidently demands it, under the condition of a just and prior indemnity.

French Constitution

The National Assembly, wishing to establish the French constitution upon the principles which it has just recognized and declared, abolishes irrevocably the institutions that have injured liberty and the equality of rights.

There is no longer nobility, nor peerage, nor hereditary distinctions, nor distinctions of orders, nor feudal regime, nor patrimonial jurisdictions, nor any titles, denominations, or prerogatives derived therefrom, nor any order of chivalry, nor any corporations or decorations which demanded proof of nobility or that were grounded upon distinctions of birth, nor any superiority other than that of public officials in the exercise of their functions.

There is no longer sale or inheritance of any public office.

There is no longer for any part of the nation nor for any individual any privilege or exception to the law that is common to all Frenchmen.

There are no longer guilds, nor corporations of professions, arts, and crafts.

The law no longer recognizes religious vows, nor any other obligation which may be contrary to natural rights or the constitution.

22. Petition by the Jews Settled in France to the National Assembly Concerning the Postponement of December 24, 1789 (JANUARY 28, 1790)

Although the "Declaration of the Rights of Man" promised that "No one should be disturbed on account of his opinions, even religious," this was not considered applicable to Jews. The National Assembly undertook to debate the status of Jews separately the following December, only to postpone their decision. As the following petition suggests, the debate was not restricted to a simple question of determining abstract and universal rights; rather, deputies continued an Enlightenment debate about whether Jews had an ineradicably different character or were able to adopt French mores and habits. On the same day that this petition was delivered to the Assembly, it voted to restore certain prerevolutionary rights to the community of Sephardic Jews living in southwest France, rights from which the Ashkenazi Jews of eastern France were excluded. The National Assembly did not pass a decree conferring equal rights on all French Jews until September 27, 1791.

A great question is pending before the supreme tribunal of France: Will or will not the Jews be *citizens*?

This question has already been debated in the National Assembly and the speakers, whose intentions are equally patriotic, did not agree at the outcome of their debate.

Some wanted the Jews to be admitted to civil society.

Others argued that such admission would be dangerous.

A third opinion favored undertaking the complete improvement of the Jews' condition by means of gradual reform.

In the midst of these debates, the National Assembly thought it necessary to postpone the question; the decree of last December 24, regarding this postponement, is an act which is perhaps among those that most honor the prudence and wisdom of this assembly.

This postponement was based on the need to further clarify such an important question; to gather more certain information about what the Jews are and what they may be; to more precisely know what is favorable and what is disadvantageous to them; and finally to cultivate opinions by intensive discussion of a decree which, regardless of its outcome, will make decisive judgment of their future.

It has also been said that the postponement was based on the need to acquire exact knowledge of the true demands of the Jews; considering, it has

Source: *Adresses, mémoires et pétitions des Juifs, 1789–1794* (Paris: EDHIS, 1968). Translated by Laura Mason.

been added, the inconveniences of giving more extensive rights to this class of men than they desire.

But the National Assembly's decree cannot possibly be inspired by such a motive.

In the first place, the Jews' wishes are well known and completely unequivocal. They stated them clearly in their addresses of last August 26 and 31. The wishes of the Jews of Paris were repeated in a *new address* on December 24. They ask that all the shameful distinctions under which they have groaned to this day be abolished; that they be declared *citizens*.

Moreover, how could it be supposed that legislators, who trace all their principles to the immutable source of reason and justice, might want to abandon their regular practice and seek what they must do not in what should be, but in what is asked of them? If it were possible for the Jews to show or continue to show some heedlessness for the conquest of their rights because of the degradation to which they have been condemned, and if nevertheless these individuals could not remain in their current state without compromising the name of the French and fundamentally harming the interests of France; if it were demonstrated that the national regeneration which is almost accomplished could not survive alongside the distressing condition of the Jews; can we believe that the National Assembly would have the right to cede the public interest to thoughtless requests and that it would not, on the contrary, be its duty to raise up the men who wanted to remain degraded, compelling them to accept a destiny which is not theirs alone but that of all the French?

Therefore, it is not because they want precise knowledge of the Jews' demands that the question was postponed, but because it was deemed worthy of more careful scrutiny.

Moreover, the Jews' requests are, as we have said, well known, and we will repeat them here. They ask to be *citizens*. . . .

Let us begin with the principles which imperiously require that Jews be elevated to the status of *citizens*.

A first principle is that all men domiciled in an empire, living as subjects of that empire, should share equally in the same title and should enjoy the same rights. They should all have the title and possess the rights of *citizens*.

Because of their domicile and according to their quality as *subjects*, men contract the obligation to serve the homeland; truly they serve it; they contribute to the maintenance of the public weal: and public strength owes equal protection and an equal apportionment of benefits to all who assist in its creation. It would be a gross injustice if the public weal did not give returns of equal proportion to all from whom it received, if it favored some to the prejudice of others. These ideas do not need further development; they are patently obvious to all minds.

There now remains only one more thing to consider: are or are not the Jews who live in France *domiciled*? Do they or do they not live there as *subjects of France*?

Certainly, no one has ever thought to consider them *foreigners*; either because they would be wholly incapable of adopting another homeland; or because they are born, established, and have their families in France, either in certain towns or in the separate neighborhoods granted them; or finally because they pay all the taxes to which Frenchmen are subject, independently of all other taxes that they must still pay separately.

The Jews are not in any way *foreigners* in France. They are subjects of this empire; and consequently, they are and should be *citizens*. Because in a state of any sort there are only two classes of men: *citizens* and *foreigners*. Those who are not in the second class are in the first. Once more, Jews are thus and should be *citizens*.

In truth, they practice a religion disapproved by the religion dominant in France. But the time is past in which one could say that only the dominant religion gave right to advantages, prerogatives, and the lucrative and honorable employments of society. This maxim, worthy of the Inquisition, was opposed against the Protestants for a long time; and the Protestants had no civil status in France. Today, they have been restored to possession of that status; they are assimilated to Catholics in every regard; the intolerant maxim that we recall can no longer be opposed against them. Why continue to make the same argument against the Jews?

In general, civil rights are wholly independent of religious principles. And all men, no matter what religion they are, no matter the sect to which they belong or the worship they practice—as long as their worship, their sect, their religion does not offend the principles of a pure and strict morality—all such men, we say, who are equally able to serve the homeland, defend its interests, and contribute to its splendor should share equally in the title and rights of citizens.

What would be the results of the contrary system whereby the dominant religion alone, and other religions whose dogmas more or less approached that of the dominant, could confer this title and these rights? The result would be to establish the principle that strength should prevail over weakness, and the majority over the minority; whereas social rights must be measured and calculated by justice alone.

The result would be that in those countries where Catholicism is not the dominant religion, Catholics could legally be subject to all the injustices that now overwhelm the Jews.

The result would be that it would be permissible to assault or seduce conscience. You would assault conscience by using persecution to force individuals to forswear their religion; you would seduce it by offering greater advantages to the dominant religion than to their own. And you know that violence is no more permissible here than is seduction. You know that in matters of religion, man must subject his reason to evidence alone and not to force. You know that with force you will gain only hypocrites and apathetics, and such conquests will give religion more to complain of than to applaud. Finally, you know that the Jew is attached to his religion as you are to yours and that injustice is no more permissible against him than it would be against you; that conscience can receive inspiration from itself and from itself alone; that no being on earth has the right to compel conscience; and that only God may require men to account for their opinions of Him and for the ways in which they give homage. . . .

As well, the word *tolerance*, which seemed to be a word of humanity and reason after so many centuries and so many acts of *intolerance*, is not suited to a nation that seeks to establish its rights on the eternal foundation of justice. And America, to whom politics owes so many useful lessons, expelled that word from its code, as compromising individual liberty and sacrificing certain classes of men to others.

Because to tolerate is to accept that one has the right to prohibit; and the dominant religion which, unlike other religions, must have ministers devoted to the nation and worship paid for by it, does not have the right to prohibit another religion from humbly raising itself up alongside. But the necessary consequence of this principle is that if all religions have equal rights, it would be a contradiction to give one a right of preeminence over another in regard to the functions of citizens.

To be more firmly persuaded of this truth, one need only reflect on the nature of these functions. They consist in paying taxes to the state, which are the price of peace and public safety; in defending the homeland against internal divisions and external wars alike; in contributing talents, enlightenment, and virtues to the glory of the nation. But is it necessary to be of such and such a religion, to adopt or reject such and such a dogma in order to fulfill these obligations? When men are united for common defense and inspired with equal ardor for the public good, is one to ask whether they believe or not? In short, will anyone worry about the nature of their beliefs? Is not what they do more important than what they believe? From that moment, their religion, whatever it is, will be the measure of the rights that should be accorded them!

23. The National Assembly Decrees the Enfranchisement of Free Men of Color (MAY 15, 1791)

Upon passage of the "Declaration of the Rights of Man and Citizen," free citizens of color began to agitate for the application of the rights to themselves. In the fall of 1790 a rebellion of free blacks and mulattoes broke out in Saint Domingue, led by Vincent Ogé, while delegates like Raymond, in the document that follows, petitioned the Assembly. Paris responded with the following decree. However, the so-called May 15 decree only inflamed slaves' demands for freedom, and by August 1791 the slave rebellion had reached full force. Paris responded by rescinding this decree, thus illustrating the Assembly's vacillation and its terrible consequences. It did not unequivocally grant equality to free males of color until March 24, 1792.

Source: Archives parlementaires, vol. 26 (Paris, 1887), pp. 89, 97. Translated by Tracey Rizzo.

Mr. President,

Remaining to this day under the oppression of the white colonists, we dare hope that we do not ask the National Assembly in vain for the rights which it has declared belong to every man.

If our just protests, if the troubles, the calumnies that you have witnessed until today under the legislation of white colonists, and, finally, if the truths which we had the honor of presenting yesterday to the bar of the Assembly do not overcome the unjust pretensions of the white colonial legislators who want to [proceed] without our participation, we beg the Assembly not to jeopardize the little remaining liberty we have, that of being able to abandon the ground soaked with the blood of our brothers and of permitting us to flee the sharp knife of the laws they will prepare against us.

If the Assembly has decided to pass a law which lets our fate depend on twenty-nine whites, our decided enemies, we demand to add an amendment to the decree which would be rendered in this situation, that free men of color can emigrate with their fortunes so that they can be neither disturbed nor hindered by the whites.

Mr. President, this is the last recourse which remains for us to escape the vengeance of the white colonists who menace us for not having given up our claims to the rights which the National Assembly has declared belong to every man.

We are respectfully, etc.

Signed, Raymond.

PRESIDENT: The National Assembly decrees that the legislative corps will never deliberate on the political status of men of color who were not born of a free father and mother, unless it is the previous, free, and spontaneous wish of the colonies; the actually existing colonial assemblies will remain. But free men of color, born of a free father and mother, will be admitted into all future parochial and colonial assemblies if they otherwise possess the required qualities.

24. Olympe de Gouges, "Declaration of the Rights of Woman" (SEPTEMBER 14, 1791)

Olympe de Gouges (1748–1793) was a butcher's daughter from Montauban who managed to educate herself, move to Paris, and live by her pen. She wrote plays and treatises on many subjects, including the abolition of slavery as well as

Source: Olympe de Gouges, *Écrits politiques, 1788–1791* (Paris: Côte-femmes, 1993), pp. 204–210. Translated by Tracey Rizzo.

women's rights. Though her position on women's issues was quite radical, she remained a royalist, even going so far as to address her political writings to royal patrons, including the queen herself. This was the ostensible reason for de Gouges's execution in 1793, though her agitation on behalf of women's rights cannot have been irrelevant.

To the Queen

Madame,

Little skilled in the language appropriate to addressing royalty, I will not employ a courtesan's adulation to pay you homage with this unique work. Madame, my purpose is to speak to you frankly. I have not awaited the epoch of liberty to express myself thus; I displayed as much energy in a time when the blindness of despots punished such noble audacity.

When the whole empire accused you and held you responsible for its calamities, I alone in a time of trouble and storm, I alone had the strength to take up your defense. I have never been able to persuade myself that a princess raised in the midst of grandeur, had all the vices of baseness. . . .

Madame, may a nobler function [than plotting against the government] characterize you, excite your ambition, and fix your attention. It belongs to one whom chance has elevated to an eminent place to give weight to the progress of the Rights of Woman, and to hasten its success. If you were less well informed, Madame, I would fear that your individual interests would outweigh those of your sex. You love glory: consider, Madame, that the greatest crimes become immortal like the greatest virtues, but what a different fame in the annals of history. One is ceaselessly cited as an example, the other is eternally the execration of the human race.

It will never be a crime for you to work for the restoration of morals, to give to your sex all the credit it is due. This is not the work of one day, unfortunately for the new regime. This revolution will happen only when all women fathom the depth of their deplorable fate, and of the rights they have lost in society. Undertake, Madame, such a beautiful cause; defend this unfortunate sex and you will soon have one half the kingdom on your side, and at least one third of the other half.

Madame, with the deepest respect I am your most humble and obedient servant.

The Rights of Woman

Man, are you capable of being just? It is a woman who poses the question; at least you will not take away this right. Tell me, what has given you the sovereign empire to oppress my sex? Your strength? Your talents? Observe the Creator in his wisdom; look at nature in all her grandeur, with whom you seem to want to be in harmony, and give me, if you dare, an example of this tyrannical empire.*

Go back to the animals, consult the elements, study plants, finally cast a glance over all the modifications of organized matter, and submit to the evidence when I offer it to you; search, probe and distinguish, if you can, the sexes in the administration of nature. Everywhere you will find them mingled, everywhere they cooperate with a unity harmonious to the immortal masterpiece.

Man alone has dressed up this exception as a principle. Bizarre, blind, bloated with science and degenerated—in the century of light and wisdom—in the crassest ignorance, he wants to command as a despot this sex which has received all intellectual faculties; he pretends to enjoy the Revolution and reclaim his rights to equality only to say nothing more about it.

Declaration of the Rights of Woman and Citizen

Preamble

Mothers, daughters, sisters, representatives of the Nation, demand to be constituted into a national assembly. Considering that ignorance, forgetfulness, or scorn for the rights of woman are the sole causes of public misfortune and corrupt government, they have resolved to make a solemn declaration of the natural, inalienable, and sacred rights of woman in order that this declaration, perpetually before all members of society, will ceaselessly recall them to their rights and duties; in order that the powerful acts of women and the powerful acts of men can be compared at each instant with the purpose of every political institution, and so receive greater respect; so that the demands of female citizens, henceforth founded on simple and incontestable principles, are always directed toward the maintenance of the constitution, good morals, and the happiness of all.

Consequently, the sex that is superior in beauty as in the courage of maternal suffering recognizes and declares in the presence and under the auspices of the Supreme Being, the following rights of woman and of female citizens:

1. Woman is born free and lives equal to man in her rights. Social distinctions may be founded only upon common utility.

2. The purpose of any political association is the conservation of the natural and imprescriptible rights of woman and man; these rights are liberty, property, security, and above all resistance to oppression.

---

*From Paris to Peru, from Japan to Rome, the dumbest animal, in my view, is man. [Note in original.]

3. The principle of all sovereignty resides essentially in the Nation, which is nothing other than the union of woman and man: no body, no individual can exercise authority which does not emanate from it.

4. Liberty and justice consist in rendering all that belongs to others; thus the exercise of the natural rights of woman have only been limited by the perpetual tyranny that man opposes to them; these limits should be reformed by the laws of nature and reason.

5. The laws of nature and reason prohibit all actions harmful to society: anything that is not prohibited by these wise and divine laws cannot be prevented, and no one can be constrained to do that which they do not order.

6. The law should be the expression of the general will; all female and male citizens should concur personally, or by their representatives, in its formation; it should be the same for all: all female and male citizens, being equal in its eyes, should be equally admissible to every honor, position, and public employment, according to their capacities, and without any distinction other than those of their virtues and talents.

7. No woman is excepted; she is accused, arrested, and detained in cases determined by law. Women, like men, obey this rigorous law.

8. The law should only establish those penalties strictly and obviously necessary, and no one can be punished except by a law established and promulgated prior to the crime and legally applicable to women.

9. Any woman found guilty [is subject to] every rigor of the law.

10. No one should be troubled for holding basic opinions; woman has the right to mount the scaffold; she should equally have the right to mount the podium, provided that her demonstrations do not trouble the public order established by law.

11. The free communication of thoughts and opinions is one of the most precious rights of woman, since that liberty assures the legitimacy of children vis-à-vis their fathers. Every citizen should be able to say freely, "I am the mother of the child who belongs to you," without being forced by a barbarous prejudice to hide the truth; [an exception may be made] to respond to the abuse of this liberty in cases determined by law.

12. The guarantee of the rights of woman and citizen entails a major benefit; this guarantee should be instituted for the advantage of all, and not for the particular benefit of those to whom it is entrusted.

13. The contributions of woman and man to the support of the police and the expenses of administration are equal; she shares a part in all duties and diffi-

cult tasks; she should thus have the same share in the distribution of positions, employment, offices, honors, and jobs.

14. Female and male citizens have the right to verify themselves, or through their representatives, the necessity of the public contribution. Women can only join therein by their admission to an equal share not only of wealth but of public administration, and in the determination of the proportion, base, collection, and duration of the tax.

15. The mass of women, joined for tax purposes to men, has the right to demand an account of his administration from any public agent.

16. No society in which the guarantee of rights is not assured, nor the separation of powers determined, has a constitution; the constitution is null if the majority of individuals who constitute the Nation have not participated in drafting it.

17. Property belongs to both sexes whether united or separate; it is for everyone an inviolable and sacred right; no one can be deprived of it as it is the veritable patrimony of nature, unless public necessity, legally constituted, obviously needs it, and under the condition of a just and prior indemnity.

Postamble

Women, wake up; the tocsin of reason sounds throughout the universe; recognize your rights. The powerful empire of nature is no longer surrounded by prejudice, fanaticism, superstition, and lies. The flame of truth has dissipated all the clouds of folly and usurpation. Enslaved man has multiplied his forces, and he needs recourse to yours to break his chains. Having become free, he has become unjust toward his companion. O women, women, when will you cease to be blind? What are the advantages you have received from the Revolution? A more marked scorn, a more pronounced disdain. In the centuries of corruption you have reigned only over the weaknesses of men. Your empire is destroyed; what remains for you? . . .

Women have done more harm than good. Constraint and dissimulation have been their portion. That which force ravished from them ruse returned to them; they had recourse to all the resources of their charms, and the most irreproachable could not resist them. Poison and the sword were both subject to them; they commanded in crime as in virtue. The French government, above all, depended for centuries on the nocturnal administration of women; the cabinet kept no secret from their indiscretion; ambassadorial post, command, ministry, presidency, pontificate, cardinalate; finally anything which characterizes the stupidity of men, profane and sacred, all have been submitted to the cupidity and ambition of this sex, formerly contemptible yet respected, and since the Revolution respectable and scorned.

25. Maximilien Robespierre, "On the Abolition of the Death Penalty" (MAY 30, 1791)

The deputies to the National Assembly turned their attention to reforming almost every aspect of French society. In reforming the French system of justice, they did not only seek to answer demands made in *cahiers de doléances* and a multitude of pamphlets published since 1789; they attempted to give legislative expression to Enlightenment ideals and the new constitutionalism. In arguing for the abolition of the death penalty, Robespierre echoed the concerns of the philosophe Cesare Beccaria, who argued that torture and the death penalty must be replaced by just and moderate punishments that correct and deter rather than exact vengeance. Robespierre's was, however, a minority position, and the National Assembly kept the death penalty.

The news having reached Athens that some citizens had been condemned to death in the city of Argos, the Athenians ran to the temples and begged the gods to keep them from such cruel and destructive thoughts. I come to beg not gods but legislators, who should be the instruments and spokesmen by which the Divinity's eternal laws are dictated to man, to rid the French code of blood laws that command juridical murder and which repulse morals and their new constitution. I want to prove to them: (1) that the death penalty is fundamentally unjust; (2) that it is not the most effective of penalties, and that it increases crime far more than prevents it.

Outside of civil society, when a relentless enemy comes to attack my life, or when, twenty times repulsed, he returns again to lay waste to the field that I have cultivated with my hands, either I must perish or I must kill him because I can only oppose my own strength against his, and the law of natural defense vindicates and approves me. But within society, when the force of all is armed against one, what principles of justice can justify their putting the one to death? What necessity can pardon that? A victor who kills his captive enemies is called barbaric! A man who slaughters a child that he could disarm and punish seems a monster! A criminal condemned by society is nothing more to it than a vanquished and powerless enemy; he is weaker before society than is a child before a grown man.

Hence, in the eyes of truth and justice, these scenes of death that it orders with so much ceremony are nothing more than cowardly murders, crimes committed solemnly not by individuals but with legal forms by whole nations. No matter how cruel, how excessive these laws, marvel at them no more. They are the work of a few tyrants; they are the chains with which they

Source: Henry Morse Stephens, *Principal Speeches of the Statesmen and Orators of the French Revolution* (Oxford: Clarendon Press, 1892), pp. 299–304. Translated by Laura Mason.

prostrate the human race; the arms with which they subjugate *i* written in blood. "It is not permitted to put a Roman citizen to was the law passed by the people; but Sylla conquered and said: took up arms against me deserve death." Octavius and his partners in crime ratified this law.

Under Tiberius, to have praised Brutus was a crime worthy of death. Caligula condemned to death those who were so sacrilegious as to undress before an image of the Emperor. Once tyranny had invented crimes of lèse-majesté, whether the actions were modest or heroic, who would have dared think that they could merit a penalty less severe than death without himself becoming guilty of lèse-majesté?

Once fanaticism, born from the monstrous union of ignorance and despotism, invented in its turn crimes of divine lèse-majesté, once it imagined in its delirium to avenge God himself, was it not necessary that it offer up blood as well and, at the very least, place those who claimed to be in his image at the level of monsters?

The partisans of this ancient and barbarous routine say the death penalty is necessary; without it, there would be no such powerful brake on crime. Who told you that? Have you calculated all the means by which penal laws may act on human senses? Alas! how much physical and moral pain may man endure before dying!

The desire to live gives way to pride, the most imperious of passions that hold sway over men's hearts; the most terrible of all penalties for the social man is shame, the overwhelming testimony of public loathing. When the legislator can strike citizens in so many places and in so many ways, why would he believe himself reduced to relying on the death penalty? Punishment is not created to torment the guilty, but to prevent crime through the fear of incurring it.

The legislator who prefers death and horrible penalties to the gentler means that are within his power outrages public delicacy, dulls the moral sentiments of the people he governs like an unskillful teacher who exhausts and debases the soul of his student with the frequent use of cruel punishments; in the end, he weakens and saps the means to govern by wanting to exercise them with greater force.

The legislator who institutes this penalty rejects the salutary principle that the most effective means to repress crime is to shape penalties to the character of the different passions that produce it and, in a word, to punish the passions themselves. Such a legislator confuses all ideas, he disturbs all relationships and openly thwarts the goal of all penal laws.

The death penalty is necessary, you say? If so, why have several societies had the sense to refuse it? By what fateful coincidence were these people the wisest, the happiest, and the freest? If the death penalty is most effective at preventing serious crimes, then crime should be most rare in societies that have adopted and used it freely. But it is exactly the reverse. Look at Japan; nowhere is execution and torture more freely used; nowhere are crimes so common and so abominable. One could say that the Japanese want to fight bitterly, using barbaric laws that dishonor and annoy them. Did the Greek republics, in which punishment was moderated and the death penalty either extremely rare or wholly unknown, have more crimes or fewer virtues than those countries governed by blood laws? Do you believe that Rome was sullied by greater infamy when, in its days of glory, the law of Portia had abolished the harsh penalties passed by kings and decemvirs, than it was under Sylla, who restored those laws, or the emperors who carried their severity to an excess that equaled their infamous tyranny? Has Russia been overturned since the despot who governs it suppressed the death penalty altogether, as if he wanted to expiate the crime of holding millions of men under the yoke of tyranny with this humanitarian and philosophical act?

Listen to the voice of justice and reason; it calls out to us that human judgment is never so certain that a society can put to death a man condemned by other men who are subject to error. Were you to imagine the most perfect judicial order, were you to find the most enlightened judges with the greatest integrity, there will always remain some room for error or for prevention. Why prohibit the means to repair them? Why condemn to impotence the helping hand that reaches out to oppressed innocence? What matter these sterile regrets, these illusory reparations that you accord to an empty shadow, to inanimate ash? They are sad testimony to the barbaric rashness of your penal laws. Deprive man of the possibility of expiating his offense by repentance or virtuous acts, pitilessly shut him off from all return to virtue, to self-esteem, hasten to send him down, in a word, to the tomb that is still covered over with the recent blemish of his crime is, to my eyes, the most horrible refinement of cruelty.

The legislator's first duty is to shape and preserve public morals, the source of all liberty, the source of all social happiness; when he turns aside from this general aim to pursue a particular end, he commits the coarsest and the most harmful of errors.

It is necessary then that laws always offer to a people the purest model of justice and reason. If the powerful severity and moderate coolness that should characterize them are replaced with anger and vengeance, they will spill blood that they could have spared and which they have no right to shed; if they exhibit cruel scenes and corpses murdered by torture before the eyes of the people, they will distort notions of justice and injustice in the hearts of citizens, they will nourish prejudices in the bosom of society that will produce others in their turn. Man is no longer such a sacred object for man; there is a less capacious idea of his dignity when public authority makes light of his life. The idea of murder inspires far less dread when the law itself offers the example and spectacle of it; the horror of crime diminishes as soon as it is punished by yet another crime. Be wary of confusing efficacious penalties with excess severity; one is wholly opposed to the other. Everything favors moderate laws; everything conspires against cruel laws.

It has been observed that crimes were more rare and penal laws less harsh in free countries; all minds hold fast to this idea. Free countries are those in which the rights of man are respected and where, consequently, laws are just. Wherever laws offend humanity with excessive severity, there is proof that the dignity of man is unknown, that the dignity of the citizen does not exist; there is proof that the legislator is nothing more than a master who commands his slaves, and who punishes them pitilessly according to his fancy. I conclude that the death penalty should be abolished.

26. Discussion of the Le Chapelier Law (JUNE 13, 1791)

On March 2, 1791, the Assembly abolished guilds as part of its ongoing assault on privilege. The rhetoric that subordinated particular interest to the general will was applied to forms of association among workers more broadly in June. Defining workers' organizations as self-interested, the Assembly voted to forbid all such organizations, in a move that some historians believe demonstrates the bourgeois or capitalist orientation of the revolutionary leadership. It must be noted, however, that associations of capitalists were also forbidden.

LE CHAPELIER: Gentlemen, I demand all your attention be focused on that which I am about to submit to you. I come from the Committee of the Constitution to report an infringement of the constitutional principles which suppress corporations, an infringement which greatly threatens public order.

Several individuals have attempted to re-create forbidden corporations in the form of assemblies of trades and work which have named presidents, secretaries, syndics, and other officers. The purpose of these assemblies, which have proliferated in the realm and which have already established correspondences between them—this correspondence is proven by this verifiable copy of a letter received by the municipality of Orléans—the purpose of these assemblies, I say, is to force the entrepreneurs of work, formerly known as masters, to raise a day's wages; to prevent individual workers and others employed in their workshops from concluding amiable agreements; to make them formally acknowledge the obligation to submit themselves to the value of the day's work fixed by the assembly and other rules that they are permitted to make. Violence is even used to enforce these rules; workers are forced to strike even if they are content with the salary they receive. [The assemblies] want to depopulate the workshops, and already several workshops have been overturned and different disorders committed.

Source: Archives parlementaires, vol. 27 (Paris, 1887), pp. 210–212. Translated by Tracey Rizzo.

The first workers who assembled obtained permission to do so from the municipality of Paris. The municipality seems to have made a mistake in this matter. Undoubtedly, all citizens must be permitted to assemble; but citizens of certain professions should not be permitted to organize on the basis of their so-called common interests. Corporations no longer exist in the state; there is nothing more than the particular interest of individuals and the general interest. No one is permitted to inspire an intermediate interest in citizens, to separate them from the public good by a spirit of corporation.

The assemblies in question have presented special motives in order to obtain the authorization of the municipality. They describe themselves as destined to provide aid to sick or unemployed workers of the same profession; these cases of aid appear useful, but make no mistake about this assertion. It is up to the nation, and to public officials operating in its name, to furnish work to those whose existence depends on it and to aid the infirm. These particular distributions of aid, when they are not made dangerous by poor administration, tend at the very minimum to revive corporations. They require frequent meetings of individuals from the same profession, the nomination of syndics and other officers, the formation of rules, and the exclusion of those who do not submit to those rules; it is thus that privileges, masters, etc. are reborn.

Your committee believed that it was urgent to prevent the spread of this disorder. These unfortunate societies have been succeeded in Paris by another society which is established under the name, society of duties. Those who did not accord to the duties and rules of this society have been harassed in every manner. We have every reason to believe that the institution of these assemblies has been encouraged in the workers less for the purpose of raising a day's wages for work than for the secret purpose of fomenting trouble.

It is therefore necessary to reassert the principle that only free conventions between one individual and another can fix the work day for each worker; it is then up to the worker to maintain the convention he has made with his employer. Without examining what the salary of a day's work should reasonably be, I avow only that it should be a little higher than it is presently. (Murmurs) What I say is true: in a free nation wages should be considerable enough that the wage earner can achieve a condition which is above the absolute dependence that produces the privation of basic needs, and which is nearly that of slavery. Also, English workers are paid more than the French.

I said thus, that, without fixing here the exact value of a day's labor, a value which should depend on conventions freely concluded between individuals, the Committee of the Constitution thought it indispensable to submit to you a draft of the following decree, whose object is equally to prevent coalitions that workers form for raising wages for a day's work and those that entrepreneurs form for lowering them.

Here is the draft of the decree:

1. The prohibition of every type of corporation of citizens of the same trade and profession is one of the fundamental bases of the French Constitution; it

is forbidden to reestablish them in practice under any pretext and any form whatsoever.

2. Citizens of the same trade or profession, entrepreneurs, those who have open shops, workers in whatever trade, cannot, even when assembled, name presidents, secretaries, or syndics, keep registers, pass decrees or minutes, or form rules based on their so-called common interests.

3. It is forbidden for any administrative or municipal corps to receive any address or petition in the name of a trade or profession, to make any response to them, and they are enjoined to declare null any deliberations which were taken in this manner, and to carefully watch those who either attempt to follow up or execute it.

4. If, against the principles of liberty and the Constitution, citizens of the same profession, trade, and craft resolve or conclude agreements among themselves to collectively refuse the aid of their industry or labor or to accord it only at a fixed wage, whether the agreement be accompanied by oath or not, it will be declared unconstitutional, in contempt of the "Declaration of the Rights of Man," and null and void: the administrative and municipal corps are charged to declare this to them. The authors, chiefs, and instigators who provoked, directed, or presided over them will be brought before the police tribunal at the request of the procurer of the commune, condemned to 500 livres amends each, suspended from the exercise of the rights of active citizenship for one year, and barred from primary assemblies.

5. All administrative and municipal corps and their members are prohibited from responding in their own names to, or employing, admitting, or tolerating one to admit to work in their professions or in any public works, those entrepreneurs, workers, and artisans who provoke or sign deliberations or conventions, unless they have retracted or disavowed them, of their own accord, before the police tribunal.

6. If these deliberations or conventions, posters posted, letters circulated, contain any threats against entrepreneurs, workers, artisans, or foreign apprentices who come to work in this place, or against those who are contented with a lower salary, all authors, instigators, and signatories of the written acts will be fined an amend of 1000 livres and three months' prison.

7. Those who use threats or violence against workers, using the liberty accorded by the constitutional laws on work and industry, will be pursued by criminal proceedings and punished according to the rigor of the laws, as disturbers of public order.

8. All groups composed of or created by artisans, workers, apprentices, or laborers which oppose the free exercise of industry and labor belonging to any sort of person, any terms established by mutual agreement or the action of the police and execution of judgments rendered in these matters, as well as

bidding and the public adjudication of various enterprises, will be charged with seditious assembly; as such, they will be dispersed by the police according to the requirements of the law, which have been made known to them, and the authors, chiefs, and instigators of such assemblies, and all who have committed acts of violence will be punished according to the full rigor of the law.

27. "Insurrection of the Blacks in Our Colonies," *Paris Revolutions* (OCTOBER 29 TO NOVEMBER 5, 1791)

Parisians were generally sympathetic to islanders who demanded liberty, including free men of color and slaves. Vincent Ogé, later martyred, was one of the first to make this demand. Free men of color did win their rights from the Assembly in May 1791, but although the Assembly discussed the question of slavery, it would not legislate on it. The author here reports the events of summer and fall 1791: the outbreak of a large-scale slave rebellion on Saint Domingue in August, and the subsequent retrenchment by the government, which revoked the May decree in September.

Brave and unfortunate Ogé! Your blood will not have run on the scaffold for nothing! Your atrocious torture has not been lost on your brothers! There are among us those who will inscribe their names on the list of peoples who firmly want their freedom at whatever price. They will have it, despite the revocation of the decree of May 15 [1791]; and this revocation itself, which raised the status of thirty thousand men of color to the shock of thirty thousand creoles, served only to provoke insurrection and hasten the independence of five hundred thousand black men. But perhaps it will cost the lives of those thirty thousand creoles, and will cost us the loss of our colonies. So what! Since we are obliged to these horrible calculations, so what! Perish! Yes, perish thirty thousand whites engorged with gold, vices, and prejudices. Better than our thirty thousand mulattoes, for whom our constitution will do everything, as much as for all estimable citizens. Better than five hundred thousand blacks all disposed to become men, excepting their color. There is nothing to balance; the laws of justice go before those of commercial convenience, and our interests after those of the human race outraged for so long by the conduct of whites toward brown and black men.

Source: "Révolutions de Paris," no. 121 (Oct. 29–Nov. 5, 1791), pp. 215–221, in Yves Benot, *La Révolution française et la fin des colonies* (Paris: Éditions la Découverte, 1988), pp. 243–248. Translated by Tracey Rizzo.

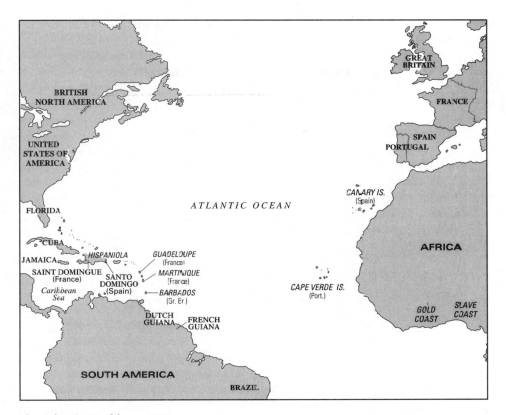

The Atlantic World, ca. 1791
The French colony of Saint Domingue was one of several European colonies in the eighteenth-century Atlantic region.

Without losing time to verify the news from Saint Domingue,* there can be no doubt a revolution in miniature, similar to our own, has broken out there. The white aristocratic revolt has provoked the vengeance of blacks and mulattoes for a long time.

Have not America's colored men reclaimed their rights, following the example of the French people? Why call a "revolt" in the islands that which is called "insurrection" in Paris? Either we are rebels in Paris or they in Saint Domingue are only the oppressed who overthrow the yoke: the same causes should yield the same results. . . .

---

*Far from confirming the news, missives to the National Assembly from the ship captains and merchants of The Hague render [news] still more dubious, and only announce [an opportunity for] slandering the Friends of the Blacks, and a double speculation which raises the prices of overseas commodities found in our ports. [Note in original.]

That which we have done for the continent, the islanders of color are proposing to try today, and they should succeed. They have on their side climate, numbers, strength, and still more motives than we. What! Thirty thousand proprietors refuse rights to active citizens because they are not white! What! Twenty-five thousand creoles, the whip raised, march ahead and work five hundred thousand men like beasts of burden because they are black; they sell them, buy them, brand their faces or shoulders like vile livestock; they mutilate them and put them in chains; they exhaust them with work or let them expire under the lash of the whip. The farmer in our countryside treats his farm animals more humanely. They choose among these unfortunate creatures the lightest or the youngest women to satisfy the master's caprices; and their children serve as the playthings of the master's heir and are martyrs to him.

And twenty-five thousand individuals, enervated by debauchery and idleness, firmly believe that the Creator put them here below to be served by five hundred thousand of their fellows who differ from them only in the skin! And twenty-five thousand creoles, more stupefied by their shameful vices than are five hundred thousand unfortunates by an excess of fatigue and the number of blows they suffer, can think that such a regime is completely natural, legal, and should subsist a long time! They hope to transfer this monstrous heritage to their nephews, and that the latter will imitate their ancestors with impunity; and they launch the loudest cries at the smallest complaints of their slaves, in view of their chains bathed in sweat and tinged with blood! The proclamation of the rights of man excites the bile of the planter who no longer has any principles of compassion. And egotistical infamy dares to claim the rights of property when one of his slaves breaks the yoke and heads for the mountains where the love of *liberty* attracts them! And because the man of color could say the word *liberty* when passing by the Negroes' quarters, it is necessary that all of armed France cross the seas quickly to fire on naked, defenseless men, exhausted from want, and in whom there hardly remains enough strength to shout from one ear to another: "And we too are born to be free!"

In this state of things, what should the mother country do? With whom will she side over all this vague and alarming noise? Is the insurrection at Saint Domingue well proven? Before responding to this question, and without referring it to the legislative corps, here you have, at the first news, the executive power deciding to send six thousand foot soldiers. Is this very hasty measure even legal? Right? Six thousand troops at the command of M. Blanchelande! This action is too precipitous not to be suspect. . . .

Go over to the Negroes' camp: Brothers! With outstretched hands our representatives say we are white like your oppressors, but we flatter ourselves to have nothing in common with them except skin color. Like you in Saint Domingue, we have risen up in France, and it was among us that was heard the first cry for liberty which rang out to your shores drenched in your sweat and tinged with your blood. You have perhaps heard that we come to you with cannon, bayonets, and soldiers; but the cannons and soldiers are for you, if the creoles' artillery is against you. You demand to be free; this is just. But be as generous as we have been in France. What can twenty-five thousand whites do who have arms, yet do not know how to serve, against five hundred thousand Negroes accustomed to the hardest work? Let your enemies live, after rendering them unable to harm you; and instead of ravaging their fine plantations, and your work, conserve them to cultivate them for your benefit, directed by your neighbors the mulattoes; let your tyrants depart as long as they take their gold and their vices with them; let them stay if they want to; five hundred thousand well-unified men can withstand several individuals, enslaved to their passions and their luxury. Preserve the remains of your chains to demonstrate to your children that, thanks to your courage, they were born free, and thus owe you their lives twice over. Brothers! remember that you have good friends across the seas, who at the first signal want to share with you their enlightenment and all the benefits of civilization hereafter better ordered.

28. Pierre François Gossin, "Report," and "Decree on the Transfer of Voltaire's Remains to Sainte-Geneviève" (MARCH 1791)

By decree of the National Assembly, the church of Sainte-Geneviève became the Pantheon on April 4, 1791. In this former holy place would come to rest the remains of France's men of genius, first of whom was Voltaire. As an exemplary philosophe, Voltaire had special significance for revolutionaries, for his tireless fight against religious intolerance, his criticism of absolutism, and his admiration for British representative institutions had inspired a generation of young men who sought to establish their reputations as champions of justice, intellectual freedom, and secular reform. To remedy the Old Regime's historic ingratitude, the Assembly sought to honor Voltaire at last. In an act meant to symbolize the continuity between Enlightenment and Revolution, some two hundred thousand people gathered on July 11 for an elaborate ceremony that returned Voltaire to the city of his birth.

Source: "Décret sur la translation des cendres de Voltaire à Sainte-Geneviève, précédés du Rapport fait par M. Gossin, au nom du Comité de la constitution" (Paris, 1791). In Emory University Library Special Collections. Translated by Tracey Rizzo.

Report

Sirs,

Since May 30, 1778, burial honors have been denied Voltaire. In acquitting ourselves toward him who prepared men for toleration and liberty, we ought to establish this same day as one of national recognition;

Gentlemen, philosophy and justice claim Voltaire, whose memory was nearly proscribed by persecuting fanaticism, for the epoch of their triumph.

Voltaire's remains, which were rejected by the capital, have been collected in the Church of the Abbey of Sellières; the sale of this burial place excited the zeal of the municipality of Paris, which has reclaimed the possession of these precious remains.

Shortly [afterward], the cities of Troyes and Romilly wanted them, and one of them determined that [the remains] should be shared; it is thus that in Italy two cities have disputed the spirit of a celebrated poet.

You have ordered your Committee of the Constitution to report on the petition of the Paris municipality; its object is that Voltaire, who was born and who died within these walls, should be transferred from the Church of Romilly, where he is presently buried, to the monument destined by a grateful country to receive the remains of great men.

The title "great" has been given to Voltaire by a Europe in awe. [Since he is] dead, every nation has consecrated him thus, and when all his detractors have perished, his memory will become immortal.

Voltaire created a monument which remains among the greatest of good deeds, as among the most sublime productions of genius; Voltaire crushed fanaticism, denounced errors, until then idolized by our antique institutions; he tore away the veils which covered every tyranny; before the French Constitution [was written] he said: "Whoever serves his country well has no need of ancestors." The serfs of Mont Jura have witnessed the burning of old trees you uprooted. He cried vengeance for Sirven and Calas, killed in the name of justice; he cried vengeance for the whole human race, even before you effaced from our sanguinary codes the laws which have burned celebrated victims.

The Nation admitted the outrage done this great man; the Nation will repair it; and the French, now free, confer "liberator of thought" on one of the founders of their liberty, an honor he has received from them.

Decree

Having heard the report from the Committee of the Constitution, the National Assembly decrees that François-Marie Arouet de Voltaire is worthy of receiving the honors conferred on Great Men; in consequence, his remains will be transferred from the Church at Romilly to that of Sainte-Geneviève in Paris.

The assembly charges the director of the department of this city to execute this present decree.

CHAPTER 5

REVOLUTION IN THE COUNTRYSIDE

29. The Continuing Contest over Seigneurial Rights

Disorder in the countryside did not begin with the "Great Fear" nor did it end with the August decrees. Because of grain shortages and the hopes raised by the calling of the Estates General, rural unrest and resistance to the payment of dues emerged as early as the spring of 1788. The August decrees did not put an end to these tensions, because many of their articles seemed ambiguous and because most of the reforms promised would require further legislation to become enforceable. The following documents illustrate two of the many hundreds of contests over seigneurial rights that were fought throughout France in 1789–1790. The first traces a dispute whose origins date to well before the opening of the Revolution, while the second seeks to clarify the intent of the Assembly's legislation.

A. Petition from Inhabitants of the Somme to the National Assembly Concerning Seigneurial Rights and Taxes (Received by the National Assembly on December 31, 1789)

Our lords,

Filled with the most respectful confidence in your decrees, in the wisdom that dictates them, as we are in your equity, the inhabitants, corps, and communi-

---

Source: National Archives, D XIV 10. Translated by Laura Mason.

ties of the parishes of Mailly, Rayneval, Thory, Louvrechy, Sauvillé-Mongival, in the generality of Amiens, the *élection* of Montdidier, undersigned, have the honor to very humbly represent to you:

That last April 23 they had the honor to submit, by deputation, a petition containing their just complaints concerning the humiliations they have long suffered at the hands of M. the duke of Mailly, their seigneur, to M. the director-general of finance with the plea to submit it to your august Assembly.

This petition has been unsuccessful until the present moment; the requests that the declarants made there have only become more urgent, now that taxes are going to be adjusted to each property; your decrees, our lords, encourage the declarants to appeal to you again; their painful situation imposes an imperious duty upon them because without your powerful help they will remain eternally bound beneath the yoke of the arbitrary despotism that you are about to destroy; they confidently dare to entreat your help.

Facts

The late M. the maréchal de Mailly, for his pleasure and personal convenience, had roads and avenues opened which go from one village to another across the properties of the declarants, without regard for their vigorous complaints or rather those of their ancestors; in addition to the considerable profit that M. the duke of Mailly has already made from the sale of twenty-four hundred of their trees, the same avenues are still shaded by more than fifteen thousand others, such as elms (these are in the greatest number), cherry trees, apple trees, etc. which shelter the neighboring soil and place it beyond cultivation. These trees even extend over the public squares of the parishes, alongside the houses of residents, whose roofs they dirty and damage because they are no more than two feet from the walls.

The communities have sounded their cries of oppression in vain each time; M. the maréchal and, following his example, M. the duke were perpetually deaf to their voices and insensitive to their sorrows. The ancestors of the declarants long ago took their complaints to M. Chauvelin, at the time Intendant of the generality of Picardy; this magistrate, convinced of the legitimacy of their complaints, sent Master Darquet to the area and, in light of his report, the plantings were acknowledged to be unjust and harmful. But to keep them, M. the maréchal invented a means of seduction; it was agreed that he would tear down one tree between every two that were standing; for those that remained, it was agreed that M. the maréchal would pay the communities a compensation double that of the damage each tree was estimated to have caused, so that if the damage was estimated at five sous for each tree, he would pay ten sous and always proportionally half above the evaluation; finally, in conclusion of this agreement it was decreed that the remaining trees

NUIT DU 4 AU 5 AOÛT 1789
OU LE DÉLIRE PATRIOTIQUE.

The common man destroys the trappings of feudalism. *(Giraudon/Art Resource, New York)*

could not, in the future, be of a distance any less than forty feet one from the other.

Alas! what could timid vassals oppose against the power of a seigneur in those times? Be that as it may, M. the maréchal in no way carried out the conditions that he had agreed to, and the agreement, in which he had involved the credibility of M. the Intendant, remained so impotent and disrespected that, twenty years later, the trees that were their object have doubled in number; and so it is that M. the duke of Mailly freely enjoys the usurpation of more than twenty arpents* from the communities named above, a usurpation that is ruinous for most of the true proprietors but which brings not only pleasure to M. the duke but a profit that is all the greater and more significant because he has the trees chopped down when there is a market for them; he is so convinced of his right to make perpetual use of the trees in this way that by means of a circular and a bailiff's proclamation of last October 26, he prohibited any of his vassals from interfering with this enjoyment which he claims as his own by a system of pretended possession for several years; but this possession belonged to the ancestors of the declarants from time immemorial until M. de

---

*Unit of measure equal to about an acre.

Mailly, sheltered by his power, and then his son in succession appropriated it by force.

Moreover, how could he thus claim to keep it with no title other than that of usurpation and at a time when the assembled nation is returning the enjoyment of their natural rights to each of its subjects? The title of the declarants is certainly unvarying and M. the duke of Mailly should be deprived of his; he owes more, he owes a sizable compensation because it is certified that he deprived his unhappy vassals of many years of harvests, of a value of more than forty thousand livres, especially in recent years, as much by the planting that he has had done on their lands as by the game that he kept there at the cost of their seed. At this very moment, the game is so numerous that it eats the grain as soon as it appears on the ground, so much so that it seems that the fields have been harvested by fire. The vassals are menaced with court proceedings; they cannot destroy this voracious game, which is sheltered by a large number of enclosures and sheds once it has ravaged their fields. And yet, such is the terrible situation of the vassals of M. the duke of Mailly.

But should he have the cruel power to continue to keep these miserable shelters for game when they have been destroyed everywhere else, when the *cahiers* of three governments—Peronne, Montdidier, and Roys—in which the declarants themselves were included, *cahiers* composed by Master le Vasseur, himself the agent of M. the duke, asked for the destruction of both kinds of plantings, whether trees or cover for game. This destruction would, moreover, seem all the more just because more than two thousand arpents of woods still serve as a retreat for this game, true destroyers of the existence of these unhappy vassals whose misery is horrible.

Under such circumstances, our lords, the above-named communities very humbly beg the august National Assembly to undertake to have the petition containing their complaints and grievances, which they gave to M. the director-general of finance last April 23, shown to them and to do justice to it as well as to the present petition, by commanding that the plantings in question as well as the enclosures and sheds that serve as shelter for game will be destroyed promptly by M. the duke of Mailly as harmful, and in case of his failure to do so that the supplicants will be and remain authorized to do so at his cost, so that each proprietor will be equally authorized according to the terms of the national decree to hunt and kill the destructive game on his personal property, the only means by which to place one and another in the position to pay the tax that is to be divided among each of their lands according to the orders that have been received from Messieurs the municipal officers and that, in addition, M. the duke of Mailly will be held responsible to them for estimated damages owed them as much for the aforementioned plantings, which deprived them of the enjoyment of the lands that they have so long shaded, as for the devastation caused by his game, especially during the past year and this one.

The supplicants unite their voices with those of all good Frenchmen for the glory and prosperity of the magnificent works of the august National Assembly.

B. Letter from the Community of Marnay (Haute Saône) to the National Assembly Concerning Rights to Waterways (APRIL 15, 1790)

The constitution of France, be it civil or ecclesiastic, has been decreed, sanctioned, and completed. Different laws and decrees have issued from it to become its ornament, support, and stability.

With all of these laws and decrees, no one can or should be ignorant of his duty, which illustrates, illuminates everything, making clear the path that each should follow. However, there remains a point regarding rivers on which the august Assembly contented itself with saying only that no one may appropriate waterways. In several communities traversed by non-navigable rivers, there are former seigneurs who accorded themselves exclusive rights to fishing which they want to enjoy today as they did in the past, in the persons of their tenants and estate agents, even though no concessions have been made to them on this matter.

Therefore, it seems very important that it please the august Assembly to issue an explanatory decree on this matter, to make known whether fishing rights belong to former seigneurs or to communities.

These assertions are indisputable, because some time after the rise in water that took place last winter, a resident of Marnay, in the former province of Franche Comté, who holds a meadow close to the Lougnon river which traverses this region, fished a pond which is in that meadow and forms a part of it. The fishers to whom the former seigneur alienated his alleged right to the river had him summoned before the cantonal justice of the peace for damages; in vain were the laws on this subject cited, the rights of property entreated; in spite of everything this judge condemned him to pay six livres and costs; all this proves quite obviously that this judge thinks the river still belongs to the former seigneurs, that the seigneurs alone have the exclusive right to fishing the river and even the ponds, although this right was overturned in principle along with other feudal rights.

Therefore, to avoid all differences that may arise, it is of the utmost importance that the august Assembly deign to issue a decree on this matter and, in those cases in which it believes that waterways, as part of the region's territory, belong to communities rather than former seigneurs, that it declare that

---

Source: National Archives, D XIV 10. Translated by Laura Mason.

the communities may enjoy the right to fish in common or may alienate it for profit. . . .

Signed by Moreau, prosecutor for Marnay.

30. Petition from the Residents of Roscoff (Finistère) to the National Assembly Concerning the High Price of Bread (JANUARY 1790)

In August 1789 the National Assembly enacted a long-held wish of eighteenth-century Physiocrats by decreeing free trade in grain. The decree was, however, neither popular nor easily enforceable; the majority of French citizens still believed that the government was obliged to insure the community's subsistence. Furthermore, shortages were rarely seen as the result of impersonal market forces or administrative shortcomings, but as a consequence of hoarding by peasants or speculators. The following document illuminates a problem that was to plague revolutionaries for years as communities competed to acquire grain at a fair price or keep what they had produced.

The residents of Roscoff, deeply moved by the approach of the happiness that your vast works will allow them and all of France to enjoy, offer you their recognition of so many good deeds and dare to hope that you will deign to welcome favorably the complaints that misery drags from them. Filled with respect and admiration for the decrees of the august Assembly of the nation, they swore to protect it even at the cost of their lives. Their submissiveness and their virtues, which distinguish them from those surly bandits who spread desolation through most of our provinces, should also distinguish them before the fathers of the homeland who, once enslaved, have been freed by their efforts.

The city of Roscoff is an attractive seaport situated one league from St. Pol de Léon, its bishopric; populated by sailors, this place is not very agricultural, the meager quantity of prime necessities collected there are not sufficient for the people's subsistence throughout the year; consequently, they are forced to go each week to the market of St. Pol to seek a kilo of grain, and the unfortunate man often has the sorrow of returning without provisions because the market being poorly stocked, competition not having been estab-

---

Source: National Archives, D XXIXbis 3. Translated by Laura Mason.

lished there, his resources not allowing him to reach the price fixed by the salesman, he has no other option but to parcel out his money and take recourse to the arbitrary tax of the baker, who sells him bread at four sous and more per pound.*

This tenacity on the part of the cultivators who supply the market of St. Pol de Léon has been felt with particular keenness since your decree on the free circulation of grain throughout France; assured of the enormous profit that monopolists offer them and certain of selling from their homes without moving, they only bring to market what will exonerate them in the eyes of their fellow citizens, whom they starve with the protection of the law.

The sudden rise of grain prices from thirty-two to forty-five livres per three hundred thirty livres is proof of what we have just asserted; such a high price scarcely four months into the year predicts the most alarming misery for all people.

The city and the port of Brest . . . have so much felt how little lower Léon could spare its grain that, without prejudice to the multitude of soldiers and workers who populate this canton, it passed a law not to requisition grain from the countryside within ten leagues of the city.

And yet, in spite of the evidence, in spite of the disadvantages of depleting such a small canton too hastily, large numbers of ships appear daily and are immediately filled.

The cultivator, assured of his subsistence, unconcerned by the awful prospects of his wretched neighbor, only considers the large profit that the monopolist offers him.

What amazes us and what should surprise all of France is that these cargo ships have Bordeaux as their destination, which is in truth a vast city, but one whose population is smaller than that of Paris; but if one calculated the prodigious quantity of grain dispatched to this city, it would perhaps surpass consumption in the capital.

However, we dare not believe that the city of Bordeaux, filled with brave and honest citizens, sows alarm, desolation, and perhaps famine, the most terrible scourge, through a large part of the Breton coasts by speculation which is unseasonal and terribly inopportune.

All these reasons, our lords, dictated by misery and approaching need, make us hope that our groans will be heard and that the Assembly of the nation, always intent on the good of all, will deign to suspend the execution of its decree regarding the circulation of grain along the coasts neighboring Roscoff, which is to say, in this region of Brest. It is the wish of a multitude of seamen who, having already shed their blood for the glory of the fatherland, wish only to conserve it that they might yet defend the fatherland.

---

*Lower Brittany is perhaps the only region where the sale of bread is not submitted to a tax and a weight regulated by the police. [Note in original.]

31. Remarks on the Dialect and Mores of the People of the Countryside in the Department of Lot-et-Garonne, Sent by the Society of Friends of the Constitution of Agen to the Abbé Grégoire (1791)

In 1790 the abbé Grégoire prepared a questionnaire on dialects and the mores of the peasantry, which he had published and circulated among friends, colleagues, and local chapters of the Society of Friends of the Constitution. Most explicitly, Grégoire asked about local idioms that legislators hoped to replace with French which, they believed, would facilitate administration and the promulgation of laws, and help to eradicate prejudice and superstition. But Grégoire looked further, asking as well about education and the degree to which the peasantry had assimilated revolutionary ideas. The respondents to the questionnaire included local clergy, members of political clubs, and urban savants; in other words, the learned men of the locale. Thus, we must remember that responses were not transparent reflections of country life; rather, they are accounts produced by men who were themselves actively negotiating their relationships to local people and the acquisition or possession of learning.

QUESTIONS: Is use of the French language universal in your region? Are one or several dialects spoken? Does this dialect have an ancient and known origin? . . .

ANSWER: The French language has, in recent times, become more popular and more widely used in our regions, but its use must become universal. Dialect is customarily spoken in all the villages and in the countryside, and we can maintain without fear of being mistaken that French is only spoken in circles that pride themselves on being cultivated. From which it results that only a very small number use French. We can even add that the Garonne, which divides our department from south to north, creates room by its division for two entirely different dialects. On the right bank, the language, soft and easy, seems to take its pronunciation, its compound phrases, and its frequent diminutives entirely from the Italian language. On the opposite bank, to the contrary, above all when one has moved three or four leagues to the south, the dialect, crude and full of breaks, seems to borrow and draw its harshness and its pronunciation from Spanish. . . .

Our dialect thus seems to have the same origin as Italian and Spanish, which did not really become languages until they were codified by good au-

Source: Lettres à Grégoire sur la Patois de France, 1790–1794. Avec une introduction et des notes par A. Gazier (Paris, 1880; Geneva: Slatkine, 1969), pp. 107–122. Translated by Laura Mason.

thors. But I would almost dare to maintain that these two languages sooner find their origins in our idiom than vice versa. Even our French language seems to owe much to our idiom. In the learned research that has been done by our troubadours, one can see that Provençal, Languedocien, and Gascon, which do not differ much among themselves, were the languages of our first poets. . . .

QUESTIONS: Are there often several words to designate the same thing? Among what occupations does the dialect seem to be most common? Are there many words to express nuances of ideas and intellectual objects?

ANSWER: The language of our region seems richest for representing rustic work and the occupations of the pastoral and rural life; but, often limited by the needs of laborers, which are only those of nature, there are not many words to express the same things; but the language of action almost always supplements the poverty of our idiom. Led by palpable ideas to abstract notions, our farmers, endowed with vivid imaginations, often employ this last resource to make themselves heard. Desire, refusal, disgust, hatred, aversion, anger, etc. are expressed by rapid movements of the arms, the head, and the whole body, according to whether the speaker feels more or less keenly. Nevertheless, our lingo does not fail to have a certain richness for describing lively and tender passions, such as paternal and filial affection, friendship, love, etc.; but as the ideas and expressions for rendering them are also in direct ratio to knowledge and enlightenment, and in general those who ordinarily speak dialect are little enlightened, we can affirm that there are few words to express the same ideas and the same intellectual objects; but we also have bold metaphors, which are almost always very expressive and very apt.

QUESTIONS: Are there many words contrary to modesty? What may one infer from them concerning the purity or corruption of morals? Are there many curses or expressions particular to great gestures of anger? Are there many locutions in dialect that are very vigorous and even absent from our French idiom?

ANSWER: Words contrary to modesty do not appear to have flourished in our dialect or in our countryside. Morals there were even quite innocent and pure; but, since commerce and luxury have drawn the sons of our laborers into numerous workshops, they have carried back the corruption of the big cities. Militia released from their service and, especially in the past seventeen or eighteen years, the need to scatter several regiments throughout the region because of epizootic disease have completely spoiled the simple morals of our farmers. Nonetheless, as the character here is more mild than brusque, more gentle than violent, there are no strong and forceful expressions in their language to express violent passions. There is no comparison between our residents and those of Provence. . . .

QUESTIONS: Does the writing of this dialect have features and letters other than those in French? Does this dialect vary much from village to village?

What is its territorial reach? Do people know how to express themselves in French? Is preaching done in dialect? Has this practice ceased?

ANSWER: There is no difference in the writing or the letters; they are entirely the same. Our dialect varies from village to village, and I am convinced that a careful observer could detect nuances at the distance of less than a league; but these differences are all the more perceptible when there is a river to cross. Dialect is, as we have already had occasion to say, the ordinary language of our village and our countryside; there are but very few people who express themselves otherwise; one is even obliged to so express oneself in order to be heard by those who live with us and who serve us. It would be difficult to establish precisely the territorial reach of this dialect, but we can affirm that a man born in this country will easily hear Provençal and Languedocien; and if the first lingo is harder and more rough, the second is gentler and more pleasant. . . . There are very few people of the countryside who speak and understand French; accordingly one is obliged to give sermons, instructions, and catechism in dialect. . . .

QUESTIONS: Do you have many proverbs that are particular to your region? What is the influence of dialect on morals, and vice versa? Is the dialect close to French? Since when? What would be the political importance of destroying this dialect? What would be the means?

ANSWER: Our dialect has an infinite number of proverbs that are unique to it; they even vary from village to village, like the language. Most of them are related to the time for sowing, for pruning the vines, and the repertoire of these maxims is found only in the memories of our farmer forefathers, who transmit them to their children, and those to the grandchildren, etc. All have great confidence in these proverbs, and experience very often proves that they are the fruit of observation and prudence. What's more, most of them are found in the Latin authors who wrote on agriculture in ancient times, such as Varron, Columelle, Pliny, etc.

While language sometimes influences morals, the influence of morals upon language was, in this region, much more straightforward. Thus, we believe that one ought sooner to seek the purity or corruption of morals in the influence of climate, commerce, luxury, and wealth. Morals here did not lose their ancient simplicity until our artificial needs called so many inhabitants into the cities, from which they periodically returned, to change the language and morals while increasing industry. How true it is that fatal experience proves every day that man only polishes his language and way of life at the expense of his simplicity and innocence! The morals of our forefathers were simple like their dialect, which seems made to depict simplicity and goodheartedness. Accordingly, religious and political [idealism] might possibly have wished to leave them their simple and natural virtues before this grievous change was implemented; but now ignorance, joined to corruption, would be the father of all ills. Therefore, it would doubtless be useful to procure means of instruction for all of them; the ignorant and corrupt heart needs a brake, and this brake is found only in the knowledge of religion and laws. It would thus be necessary to increase the number of public schools in our countryside, to place masters at their head who are enlightened and without prejudice, to give them simple works that are within reach of their students. The elementary works must contain clear and easy knowledge of natural history, of legislation, of the rights of man and citizen. Above all, morals and religion, which alone can act as a brake on a corrupt heart and create happiness for all, must not be neglected there. We must observe, in passing, that we find the situation very poorly suited to favor such establishments in this region, because our houses, scattered through the countryside, only form very scarcely populated villages; other regions, on the contrary, seem better to lend themselves, because the county seats of the parishes ordinarily form quite sizable hamlets.

QUESTIONS: Is teaching done in French in the schools of the countryside? Are the books uniform? Is each village provided with a school master? What is taught in these schools? Do curés and vicars oversee them? Do they have an assortment of books to lend? Is there a taste for reading?

ANSWER: There is absolutely no uniformity in the manner of teaching. The school masters, in the villages that have them (for there are very few), teach reading in French and in Latin; but, in general, they all have a mania for beginning with the latter language; so that education in our countryside is almost reduced to making the students able to assist their pastors, on feast days and Sundays, in singing praise of God in a tongue they don't understand. Most of our villages, too small, as we have observed, to have recourse to a school master, are wholly without instruction or only have the instruction of their curés who, it is true, distinguish themselves by the zeal and attentiveness with which they teach the villagers of their duties toward God and their fellows; but, as they can scarcely assemble other than feast days and Sundays, for very little time, they are still, for the most part, given over to the most abysmal ignorance: not knowing how to read, they would know nothing of the taste for reading; and if they know how to spell out a few words, they only have the *Hours* of the diocese between their hands. . . .

QUESTIONS: Are there many prejudices? Of what sort? Have the people become more enlightened in the past twenty years? Are their morals more degenerate? Are their religious principles weakened? What are the causes and what would be the remedies of these ills?

ANSWER: Prejudice, the sad fruit of ignorance and superstition, still holds absolute sway in our countryside. In general, our farmers believe in magic, ghosts, sorcerers, werewolves, seers, fortune-tellers, etc. We had a very striking example before our very eyes fourteen or sixteen years ago; it occurred in the town and surrounding region of Condom when M. Vic d'Azir, the celebrated academician, was sent by the government to remedy, if possible, the terrible devastation that epizootic disease was wreaking on the countryside. We saw our laborers, even several of those who prided themselves on being educated, abandon this scholar to follow a so-called seer who pretended to master this harmful malady by means of some prayers, some plants, and some drugs. It must be admitted as well that the ridiculous custom once practiced in most dioceses, and for less than thirty years in that of Auch, has contributed in no small way to perpetuating this stupid gullibility. I myself recall having heard, not twenty years ago, a formula found in some ancient rituals from a good, gullible curé of the latter diocese before the parish mass; it was this: "Sorcerers and sorceresses, seers and seeresses, leave the church before the Holy Sacrifice of the Mass begins!" What is most remarkable, is that one often saw people leaving, believing themselves sorcerers or, what is more likely, to impress that belief more easily on these good people. Nonetheless, it is true that we have noticed, for some time, that people are becoming less gullible; nevertheless, it is to be hoped that this lack of belief will not be pushed too far. Men always take things to extremes. It also seems that, during this period, morals have become more corrupt and religious principles have weakened. Since we have already suggested the means that naturally offer themselves to remedy these ills, we will content ourselves with adding that it will not be easy to completely eradicate prejudices, which have put down very deep roots. We must expect success from education and from time. It will take several generations before they can achieve their ends. . . .

QUESTIONS: What moral effects has the Revolution produced on [the people]? Does one often find patriotism among them, or simply affection inspired by personal interest? Are ecclesiastics and former nobles exposed to the crude insults and abuses of the country people, to the despotism of the municipalities, etc.?

ANSWER: The Revolution does not yet seem to have effected great change in the behavior or opinions of our farmers; but the abolition of the *dîme** and of several feudal rights seems to have powerfully excited affections in them that are naturally inspired by personal interest. A few, led astray at first by people with bad intentions, were even carried to excesses suggested by greed and need in those unhappy years. But these mistakes were only temporary; as soon as the good people recognized their faults, they hastened to disavow them and return to their duties, and those who had tried to lead them astray had nothing but shame and the remorse of having formulated such a criminal

---

*The *dîme* was the church's most important source of income under the Old Regime; it was a tax that was levied on all crops and livestock, regardless of their owner's estate.

plot. Nonetheless, I would not want to maintain that their patriotism is quite purified. If they have it, it is wholly founded, as among most ignorant and coarse people, on greed and personal interest. One could even say that, in general, they refuse to pay feudal rights that were not suppressed and which the National Assembly only declared to be purchasable. Nonetheless, in spite of the recent troubles in the department of Lot, our countryside has been very calm, and in our cantons we have not heard that ecclesiastics and former nobles are exposed to the insults and abuses of our laborers, still less to the despotism of mayors and municipalities. . . .

NEW TENSIONS

32. The Municipal Council Versus the Society of Friends of the Constitution of Tours (NOVEMBER 1790)

The collapse of the royal bureaucracy in the summer of 1790 gave unprecedented autonomy to towns and cities throughout France at the same time that it bequeathed to them a ready pool of skilled administrators. Thus, municipalities often found themselves governed by the same kinds of elites, sometimes the very same men, who had dominated local politics during the Old Regime. But new organizations and new institutions were also emerging. The Society of Friends of the Constitution, or Jacobins, had affiliated clubs throughout France, whose members corresponded with the National Assembly and the mother club in Paris while working locally to promote revolutionary enthusiasm, educate their members, and oppose counter-revolutionary writings. These documents sketch tensions over local government and revolutionary goals that were emerging throughout France in 1790-1791.

Minutes of the Municipal Council of Tours, November 3, 1790

Today, Wednesday, November 3, 1790, eight o'clock at night, the municipal council of Tours is assembled in its regular meeting place. . . . Delegates of the military council of the citizens' guard of this city entered, and . . . Master

---

Source: National Archives, D XXIXbis 14. Translated by Laura Mason.

Cartier [lieutenant colonel of the citizens' guard] speaks, saying that they come to denounce to the municipal council a printed tract which has the title *To the true French* and the expressions of which are incendiary, tending to excite the French people to counter-revolution; this printed tract they left on the desk, a specimen of three small pages without the printer's name, but at the bottom of which are written these words: "I certify having printed said document given to me by Father Dupré, signed Legier . . . "; the said delegates added that the military council has received information that persuades it that it is, indeed, said Father Dupré, canon of the former chapter of Saint Gatien of this city, who is the author of the tract or it was at least he who delivered it for printing. . . .

The witnesses having withdrawn, said printed tract was read in the presence of the deputy prosecutor of the commune; . . . the municipal council formally acknowledged the complaint he lodged against the principal authors, adherents, and accomplices of said tract; it orders that he will be informed, at the town prosecutor's request, of the outcome of the above-mentioned deeds, that the order will be given to summon witnesses; it orders as well that a copy of said tract, described above, will remain attached to the present papers after having been signed and initialed *ne variateur* by M. Valette, the president.

The municipal body appointed M. Aubry, one of its members, as commissioner to deliver the aforementioned commission, hear witnesses and undertake the other acts of information that may follow.

Excerpt from the Register of the Deliberations of the Municipal Council of the City of Tours, November 3, 1790

The general council of the commune deliberating on important matters, several deputations from the military council arrived one after another to announce deliberations undertaken concerning the doors of the monasteries of Saint Gatien and of Saint Martin, and concerning a printed tract that was denounced.

The notables withdrew, having observed that this involved police matters not relevant to them.

The company having gathered in the municipal council chambers, the new deputations followed to announce that in order to find the author of the tract which Master Légier, who is a member of the military council and who was interrogated by it, acknowledged printing, the council gathered information and had different individuals appear to give depositions.

The delegates read the interrogation of Master Légier and the depositions of witnesses, which they did not want to leave on the desk and which indicate that Master Dupré, canon of Saint Gatien, is the author of the document. They requested that the military council be authorized to send commissioners to seize the papers of Master Dupré. They announced that the military council would not rest, even if it had to remain throughout the night, until the municipal council had issued a definitive resolution. . . .

[T]he municipal council deliberated on the matter and, considering the sensation that this tract has made, it decreed by a majority that it will proceed directly to the complaint that the deputy prosecutor of the commune wants to lodge; that there are no grounds to adopt the request made concerning the papers of Master Dupré, the pieces that have been read make sufficiently clear that Master Dupré had the document in question printed. A search of his papers can only seek actions about which there has been neither denunciation, complaint, nor information. Such searches have never been authorized by vague and indeterminate suspicions.

Having brought in the last deputation, . . . the council informed it of the action that it had taken, and considering that it is 9:30 in the evening, they postponed until the following day the procedures to be undertaken; the delegates declared that they would inform the National Assembly of all that the military council had done. It was decreed that while waiting for the proceedings to be sent, a copy of the present deliberations would be addressed to our deputies.

Excerpt from the Register of the Deliberations of the Municipal Council of the City of Tours, November 4, 1790

In light of the denunciation made to the municipal council by the Society of Friends of the Constitution, regarding the actions and speeches that several officers of the Regiment of Anjou, most notably the nephew of M. the commander, allowed themselves to make and which are likely to provoke turmoil in this city; considering the importance of anticipating the terrible consequences of such conduct; and considering that M. the commander ought to take the most effective measures to suppress such activity and prevent its repetition, the council decreed that it would write to M. the commander of Anjou. We informed him that the possible consequences of the deeds which had been denounced imposed upon us the duty to tell him that such deeds must be firmly repressed, and perhaps the expedient of absenting his nephew for some time would be infinitely useful; moreover, we record the present letter in our registers so that subsequent episodes could not be imputed to us. Upon receipt of this letter the commander, who was keenly affected by the present letter in our registers and by the conduct of the denounced officers, loudly attested to his most acute and sincere pain, and replied by giving assurance that the acts and speeches in question were as opposed to the thinking of the corps he commands as they are to himself in particular; that he had forbidden monsieur his nephew to go to the café Louis XVI: and that upon receiving a reprimand, the latter had given his word of honor to be more circumspect in the future and not to allow himself comments which could be considered blameworthy. Upon this reply the municipal council decreed . . . that the denunciations, letter and reply would be and would remain certified by today's deliberation.

Letter from the Society of Friends of the Constitution, Established in Tours and Affiliated with Paris, to the Municipal Officers of the City of Tours, November 8, the Year Two of Liberty [1790]

Neither obstacles nor disgrace will slow the zeal of the Society of the Constitution.

When a tract entitled *To the true French* was denounced to you, when the national guard identified the author and vendor of this seditious lampoon, you could have, with a single word, secured the person of Master Gosselin Dupré, former canon, and prevented removal of his papers, so putting the courts in a position to seize the thread of a conspiracy that threatens liberty and public tranquillity.

But you chose to look on this affair with a more tranquil eye. The abbot Dupré escaped and it is likely that his papers have disappeared. The National Assembly will judge if our zeal has been excessive.

Be that as it may, the public prosecutor of the commune of Lineray has just demonstrated that even if villages are less educated than cities, they are no less patriotic; he had the abbot Dupré arrested and taken to Amboise. A deputation from Amboise informed you of the arrest, and prompted your meeting this morning.

We have been informed that you engaged in some kind of proceeding, following the denunciation by the military council, that you issued some decree against Master Dupré and took the moderate action of requesting the national guard to conduct M. Dupré to its buildings in Tours.

We cannot anticipate how you meant to follow up this affair; but we must dutifully and honestly tell you what we have done and what we have yet to do. All of our transcripts and petitions have been addressed to the National Assembly, we have advised it of the arrest which occupied you this morning, and we will inform it regularly of subsequent activity.

You have not been able to issue decrees based on our denunciation; the right to police does not in any way entail the right to conduct criminal trials nor to issue decrees; you should only receive our information and order the commune's prosecutor to lodge a complaint and give information before the ordinary court. You could have, perhaps you should have, arrested the abbot Dupré immediately, secured him to hand over to judges within twenty-four hours, and informed the National Assembly of this. And if you had done so, we would not regret the loss of papers whose examination might have prevented great misfortune.

But if, after the municipality of Delimoray has had the abbot Dupré arrested because of the public outcry, you allow yourselves to release him, you will make yourselves personally responsible for the inevitable consequences of this affair.

The abbot Dupré is accused of a crime of lèse-nation [treason]. His crime is obviously connected to a conspiracy that has already been uncovered in several departments, and the abbot Dupré can give information that the committee of investigations needs; moreover, it is not for you to rule on an accusation of this sort; it is the National Assembly's right to pronounce; and we declare to you that our denunciation and the denunciation by the national guard council have brought the affair to the National Assembly's attention.

Therefore, we demand either that M. the abbot Dupré be sent immediately to Paris under good and sure guard with the instructions that you have been given, or that he be placed in his house, to remain there under arrest until the National Assembly has decreed his fate.

Letter from the Society of Friends of the Constitution, Established in Tours and Affiliated with Paris, to the Committee of Investigations of the National Assembly, November 8, the Year Two of Liberty [1790]

The present situation of the city of Tours and its environs must hold the attention of the Friends of the Constitution. We have regularly observed different movements and, above all, during the past month we have noticed a coalition between priests, former nobles, and the other enemies of the Revolution. We even believe that these movements are associated with a universal conspiracy, and that they have much in common with events in Béfort and Jalès.

We have made some useful discoveries in concert with the council of the national guard. Everything is recorded in the transcripts that have been sent to M. the President of the National Assembly and to the Society of Friends of the Constitution, sitting at the Jacobins in Paris.

We are monitoring our searches; we will scrupulously forward the results to you. But we do not believe we should postpone informing you of news that has been given to us and which is the main object of our investigation.

Priests and former nobles speak out loudly against the Constitution. The word "counter-revolution" is mingled amidst all they say. Some former nobles who, until now, wore the mask of patriotism, have recently adopted an aristocratic tone. Some departed recently and everything leads us to believe that it is for a rendezvous in Paris or its vicinity. Indeed, the road from Tours to Paris, which passes by way of Vendôme, is visibly busier than ever although it is not yet finished. (The city of Vendôme is entirely given over to aristocracy.) The hatters are suspected of having received a commission for a large number of hats which are said to be destined for persons of consideration. It is also said that the recruiters have already formed a sizable troop.

You can count on our vigilance, Gentlemen; but we cannot let you ignore that the Friends of the Constitution can expect nothing from the municipality of Tours. Its conduct has, until now, made good citizens moan and we are certain that our work will not be supported. We would be happy if it were not cut short.

Our denunciation against the officers of the regiment of Anjou had no effect. The same is true of the denunciation we made against M. Dupré, canon of Saint Gatien and former secretary of M. de Couzie, bishop. He escaped because of the negligence, if not to say the activity of the municipality, whose aristocratic principles have been visible under every circumstance.

Your very humble and very obedient servants, the Friends of the Constitution of Tours

P.S.: We learned that Father Dupré was arrested by the national guard of Amboise, that the municipality of Tours wants him released, that the commander of the national guard of Tours has just gone to the town hall to enumerate the dangers of this release. Several suspect ecclesiastics are leaving this city. The Society of Friends of the Constitution and each of its members have been threatened. It would perhaps be desirable to transfer this matter to a court other than that of Tours.

From the Society of Friends of the Constitution, Established in Tours and Affiliated with Paris, to the Municipal Officers of the City of Tours, Received November 11, 1790

Live Free or Die

Denunciation and Petition of the Society of Friends of the Constitution of Tours

To the gentlemen, municipal officers of the city of Tours,

The Society of Friends of the Constitution is devoted to the propagation of true principles and maintaining public order. In accordance with its founding principles, it must watch all movements.

It has learned that different denunciations have been made to you because your duty is to act and properly direct the power confided in you by the Constitution. The denunciations have remained impotent and the society sees with horror that the silence you kept only encouraged the Revolution's enemies.

You cannot be ignorant of the new storms that are forming over our heads; or, if you are, then the society must inform you of them. A coalition has recently established itself in the very heart of this city, and the Constitution is threatened by men the nation appointed to defend it. Delays in the collection of taxes and in the sale of national lands are a real calamity, and such delays are the clear outcome of intrigues by the multitude whose personal interests are harmed by the Revolution. For a long time, good citizens have been made uneasy by nighttime gatherings, and no one has tried to disperse these assemblies. Seditious writings against the Constitution have been circulated, and no one has deigned to seek out the authors. Ministers refuse to read the decrees of the National Assembly from the pulpit, they provoke civil war by audaciously preaching against the Constitution, and no one raises his voice to remind them of their duty.

This impunity can only intensify disorder and, indeed, the evil has now reached its zenith; the society denounces this recent incident to you. M. Dufour, officer of the Regiment of Anjou and nephew of M. Dausault, lieutenant colonel of this regiment, makes seditious statements, daily and in public places, which tend to provoke a general uprising. On Monday, November 1, All Saints' Day, before noon, several officers entered the café Louis XVI in the rue Royale, which is owned by M. Falaise; they behaved in the most indecent way by singing, dancing, and shouting, "Long live the king, long live the queen, we support them," and afterward Master Dufour, one of them, sang in a high voice, "Ah, ça ira, string up the democrats." A few days ago, the same person said "that aristocratic blood had flowed long enough; that now democratic blood must flow in great waves." Several citizens were present and have made declarations to that effect.

The activities that have stirred up the city of Tours and its environs for several months are indisputably similar to events which recently took place in the city of Béfort; happily, the conspiracy of Béfort was discovered and the authors arrested, a decree of the National Assembly ordered that they would be taken to prisons for criminals guilty of lèse-nation; the moment has finally come when the law unfurls its force and this is the moment when political bodies must intensify their zeal and vigilance. . . .

The society flatters itself that you will attend to the dangers that threaten the homeland. By doing so, you will deserve the suffrage of all good citizens and especially that of the National Assembly, to which the present address will be sent on the day following the society's decree. . . .

33. The Debate over the Civil Constitution of the Clergy

The section of the August decrees that eliminated the tithe and nationalized church lands stripped the church of its resources and paved the way for the transformation of Catholic clergy into paid employees of the state. Because the nation would henceforth provide financial support for the church, the Constituent Assembly claimed the right to participate in ecclesiastical organization. Thus, the Civil Constitution of the Clergy (decreed in July 1790) set clerical salaries, rationalized the distribution of bishops and parish priests, and made clerics electable officials. Although the Pope was silent at first (he would later condemn the Civil Constitution), the conservative press and a large number of bishops in France quickly attacked it. The first selection was penned by a bishop whose seat had been suppressed by rationalization.

As debate intensified over the Civil Constitution of the Clergy, the Assembly decided to require all clergy to publicly swear an oath of loyalty to the Constitution or face immediate dismissal. To a certain extent, acceptance or rejection of the oath traced social tensions that were inherent within the former First Estate: lower clergy were far more likely to accept the oath than were the wealthy and

La lecture d'un second bref du Pape signé Royou ayant indigné plusieurs esprits une société patriotique à fait faire un mannequin representant le Pape qui sur le requisitoire d'un des membres a été brulé ainsi que les ouvrages de l'abbé Royou.

Members of a Parisian patriotic society burn the pope in effigy after he has issued a bull condemning the Civil Constitution of the Clergy (May 4, 1791). *(From* Révolutions de Paris, *volume 10. Courtesy Harvard University)* powerful bishops. Beyond this, however, the decision to take the oath was shaped by a variety of factors, ranging from individual notions of the Revolution's goals and the nature of religious office to regional variations in language, religious practice, and economic structures. The second selection is one parish priest's explanation of why he has chosen to swear the oath.

A. Warning from Monsieur the Archbishop of Vienne, to the Secular and Regular Clergy, and to the Faithful of His Diocese (NOVEMBER 11, 1790)

Charles-François, by the grace of God and of the holy, apostolic seat, archbishop of Vienne, primate of primates of the Gauls, to the secular and regular clergy, and to all the faithful of our diocese, hail and blessings in the name of our Lord, Jesus Christ.

The last pastoral letter we addressed to you, our very dear brothers, has become the occasion of various writings which do not spare us. A few of them assert that, by sending this letter to messieurs the curés, we invited them to incite the people to rebel against the state and the law; we will omit the rest. Certainly our first duty when we were put to this test, and thanks be to heaven we did not forget it, our first duty was to *pray for those who treated us in this way,** and at the same time to bless and thank our beloved Master, who by his great goodness shares some of his humiliation with us. . . . But what do we say to you, our beloved faithful? We will recall to you the words of the apostle of the Thessalonians, already cited in this same letter, and *we exhort you not to let yourselves be shaken by the persecutions that come upon us; because you should know that we are fated for them,*† and that they are the prerogative of the honorable functions that our Lord has charged us to fulfill on your behalf. Pastors and flock, let us entrust ourselves to His promises, and let us hope that it will please Him to bestow special blessings on the works best marked by the sign of the cross.

Great care and diligence have been taken to prevent the communication of our instructions, above all to prevent their being read in the churches. These careful precautions, this affected forgetfulness of normal considera-

---

*Matt. 5.44.

†I Thess. 3.3.

Source: Augustin Barruel, *Collection ecclésiastique* (Paris: chez Crapart, 1791–1793), pp. 508–533. Translated by Laura Mason.

tions, so much zeal, so many movements to muzzle the truth and hold it captive, have in many places contributed in no small way to calling more attention to it; and for its minister this is the right place to say: *Regardless of intent and regardless of what it may cost me, so long as the truth is advertised, nothing else will matter, there I find, there I will always find my joy.** . . .

Without abandoning our principles or the mood we exhibit, we will deliver very important warnings, made necessary by the circumstances in which we find ourselves.

Laws have been published which, under the name of decrees concerning the Civil Constitution of the Clergy, would overturn the constitutive principles of the church and which could not be executed without rendering France schismatic and costing it the inestimable treasure of faith. Issued by a purely civil authority, the laws rule on subjects reserved by J.C. for spiritual authority, whose exercise is independent of all other; they even undertake to change what was regulated by immutable decrees. They would take from the sovereign Pontiff, visible head of the universal church, the finest rights assured to him by those whose vicar he is here below: they would leave nothing whole in the hierarchy, and in place of the divinely established episcopal government they would substitute a presbyterian government that will remain subject to the multitude of laity; and you would see, our beloved faithful, as if by the first efforts of these strange powers, the sudden destruction of the seat of Vienne and sixty others, which is to say almost half of the dioceses of France; the creation of several others by the simple will of men; new divisions and new circumscriptions for all the rest, and a similar upheaval among the ecclesiastical provinces. . . . So much more destruction, so many more innovations, while awaiting those that have been announced and so many more undertakings, especially for the parishes! Let us all hope, our beloved faithful, for our Lord's singular mercy for this nation that He has so often favored. Let us hope that in a state renowned, until now, for its devotion to the Christian and catholic faith, laws which would become so disastrous will soon be revoked. . . .

Salvation is found only in the unity of the church and in faithfulness, as much in believing and professing what the church teaches as in respecting and practicing what it prescribes. Nothing, therefore, is more important than knowing its teaching and precepts well, and because all are not called indiscriminately to regulate religious and universal belief within its bosom, nor to command, it is no less necessary to have sound ideas concerning its governance.

J.C. Himself is the author of this government; and it pleased Him to reduce its entire economy to episcopal authority. [. . . W]e must carefully observe that the bishops are here called to govern the church; that *they are appointed by the Holy Spirit Himself to govern it.* Their power must not, then, limit itself to delivering authentic decisions, and to pronouncing infallible

---

*Phil. 1.18.

judgments on faith and morals. No, they will also be invested with supreme authority to regulate hierarchical functions, to make laws for discipline, to maintain those laws, sometimes to change them, more often to offer dispensations from them. And in this venerable council of Jerusalem, which will serve as a model for all others from century to century; when the apostles who established the canons there said, *It seemed good to the Holy Spirit and to us,** did they found a discipline to be repealed under their successors?

Nonetheless, our beloved faithful, to preserve unity we must set apart from the successors of the apostles, the successor of the head of the apostles, the successor of Peter, the vicar of J.C. If the bishops are the pastors of the people, he is the pastor of the people and of the bishops. His seat will always be the center of catholic communion for all that concerns faith, the regulation of morals, and the authority of spiritual legislation. . . . This primacy of the Roman pontiff, this universal primacy, not only of honor but of the true jurisdiction over all pastors, as over all of the flock, is a fundamental part of the divine constitution of the church;† it is manifest that no authority on earth could prevent its exercise; it is manifest that to try to do so, and to interfere with the necessary relationship between members and leader, would be to desire to destroy the ties of unity. . . .

According to the different principles established or recalled, we would fail our principal obligations to God in a fundamental way, our sacred engagements that He required us to contract on your behalf, our beloved faithful, and what we owe ourselves if, at the present juncture, we were to authorize by silence or otherwise, what is called the new organization of the clergy. Since it is well known that the plan was submitted for the examination of the supreme pontiff, and even that an assembly was assigned to proceed with this discussion, our respect for the head of the church imposed upon us the requirement of awaiting his response; but the publication of decrees and the use to which they have already been put did not allow us to delay any further.

In thus sincerely renewing our profession of a complete and constant obedience to the civil government for that which is within its domain, we must cry out against the serious attacks on spiritual authority, and above all against that which most directly concerns our archiepiscopal seat. If it could be suppressed, at least it would be by a decree that adheres to the forms of ecclesiastical power: it is by the same power that the hierarchical functions of all the dioceses of France, like those of the rest of the church, should be regulated.

Thus, in accordance with our conscience, invoking the saintly name of God, and after having conferred with our venerable presbytery, we solemnly protest against the pretended suppression of the archbishopric of Vienne:

---

*Acts 15.28.

†*Cens. de Fac. an. 1542, in art. 23 Lath.* Non modo ovium, sed et pastorum tu unus omnium Pastor. *S. Bern. de consid. lib.* 2, c. 8.

protestation that will serve as necessary for all other benefices said also to be extinguished in the diocese. . . .

We protest at the same time, and for the same reasons, the pretended divisions of our diocese into different portions, to join and attribute to several neighboring dioceses; declaring null and even schismatic every act of jurisdiction, whether ordinary or delegated, that is undertaken on our territory by virtue of civil and political dispositions, without the intervention of the proper authority.

And seeing that the magistrates who would believe they must enforce execution of the decrees we protest here are, for the most part, members of our diocese; and that we have charge of their souls; addressing ourselves to God on their behalf, we exhort them not to sacrifice eternal interests to a few temporal pretensions, but to remember well that they and we will soon be called before the same tribunal, to be judged without appeal on our respective duties.

For the rest, we persist in the sentiment of unreserved submission to the decisions, and the most respectful deference to the regulations, even provisional, which may issue from the saintly apostolic seat.

Henceforth addressing ourselves to those who share the sacred ministry with us in requisite subordination and whose sublime dignity, fundamentally associated with our own, would be degraded or rather abolished if placed in dependence upon temporal authority; we urge them to remember these elementary truths, and even to expand upon them according to utility and the needs of the faithful people entrusted to them. . . .

B. Minutes of the Swearing of the Oath by Jean-Baptiste Petitjean, Curé of Epineuil, Department of the Cher (JANUARY 1791)

Today, January 23, 1791, in conformity with the law passed in Paris on December 26, 1790: the decree of the National Assembly, dated November 27 of that year, asserts in article 1: Bishops, former archbishops, and parish priests continuing in employ, will be required, if they have not already done so, to pledge the oath to which they were made liable . . . , concerning the Civil Constitution of the Clergy. Consequently and by virtue of the latter decree, they will swear to watch carefully over the faithful of the diocese or parish confided to them, to be faithful to the Nation, the law, and the king, and to uphold, with all their power, the Constitution issued by the National Assembly and accepted by the king. Master Jean-Baptiste Petitjean, curé of Epineuil, swore the oath purely and simply at the conclusion of the parish mass, in the

---

Source: National Archives, F19 414. Translated by Laura Mason.

presence of the regional council of the commune and all the faithful; and said Master Petitjean having immediately explained the motives that impelled him to swear this oath, he requested that they be included in the minutes and they were as follows.

It is through love, duty, and religion that I have sworn the oath required by law, which is in conformity with the principles and sentiments that have always been engraved in my mind and in my heart. What can this oath contain that is opposed to religion? Does it tend to the destruction of faith or of morals? It is primarily related to the Civil Constitution of the Clergy: but this Constitution touches neither our dogmas, nor our mysteries, nor our sacraments, nor our evangelical ethic, nor the institution of sacred ministers, nor the teaching that belongs to their ministry, nothing of this sacred trust given by J.C. to the priests that he created is thereby violated by sacrilegious enterprise; its religious edifice remains intact and respected there. We will always have the same altars, the same sacrifice, the same sacrificers, the same sacraments, the same faith, the same ethic, the same teachers. The National Assembly in no way usurped the censor, which it left in hands exclusively honored by J.C.

What claim then can justify refusing to swear an oath required of us, ecclesiastical public functionaries, by law and which does not in any way damage the foundation of the religion? The Civil Constitution of the Clergy, it is said, destroys the clergy's power; this law steals their goods; it alters the territorial demarcations of the particular jurisdictions of its members; it destroys the ancient hierarchy and organizes a new one in its place which is completely unknown to Christianity.

The clergy is stripped of its goods. . . . But an ecclesiastic is only the enjoyer of a portion of those goods, and not the owner . . . even the corps itself does not have proprietorship of these goods, or else its proprietorship is only tenuous. Each corps within a state owes its institution to the sovereign, he created it, he may destroy it; and once the corps is suppressed, what becomes of the supposed proprietorship? A political society which recognizes that it owes a livelihood to the public functionaries of the religion it professes may acquit its debt either directly by itself, or indirectly through individuals by virtue of formal or tacit permission which accords them the power to sustain religious ministers with settlements from their landed properties. But the latter solution imposes too heavily on the sovereign not to remain always within its authority. Abolish this authority and the clergy would become the sole, or at least the most important, proprietor within the state, and if the clergy were to hold the territory, what would prevent it from quickly suppressing the state? The priesthood would overrun the empire, but the kingdom of J.C. is not of this world, not here below. No, priests, whether considered individually or collectively, have no right of property and even less right still to sovereignty over territories. Perhaps the name, functionaries of the religion, entitles them to a salary, but it is indisputably the sovereign's right to pay them from landed wealth or otherwise as it judges most fitting, according to time and circumstances.

The boundaries of ecclesiastical territories are being changed. . . . The clergy who have nothing other in exclusivity than a spiritual jurisdiction claim territorial jurisdiction; this is a contradiction. . . . Go forth, preach my doctrine throughout the world, that is the mission of Christ and the basis of the power of the Apostles. J.C. did not allocate a particular territory to each apostle; he did not demarcate borders or bishops or priests. From whence come these demarcations then? Having the power to preach throughout the world, will priests divide it up and jointly agree to hold unlimited power over certain cantons, in which each will exercise his power exclusive of all others . . . and will the people be subject to these exclusive authorities? Will they receive, from someone other than themselves, the law which requires them to confide in this minister rather than another? And will the sovereign count for nothing in such divisions of its territory? Will the demarcations be traced independently of it? Will the sovereign suffer with impunity that control will be exercised over the lands it rules? The clergy exists for the people, not the people for the clergy. Parishes being established by guaranties, dioceses can only be the result of the sovereign's will, according to the anterior or posterior wishes of the citizens included within these diverse territories. The priest tendering a purely spiritual power and the peoples submitting themselves neighborhood by neighborhood, some to Paul and some to Apollo, have in this way established . . . , if I may say so, the spiritual and fundamentally unlimited jurisdiction of Paul and of Apollo. But if the sovereign made or had to make territorial demarcations regarding the provenance of the spiritual jurisdiction, who may oppose its right to change these demarcations, to reduce or adjust the number of priests and bishops according to its will?

Finally, a hundred new hierarchies, entirely unknown to Christians, have been erected on the ruins of the ancient hierarchy. This reproach concerns especially the law that requires ceasing to depend on the Pope in matters concerning the system of clergy and people. I will say only one thing about this. The entire corpus of ecclesiastical history makes clear that each church governed itself, independently of Rome, during the first centuries of Christianity. It is true that Rome is the center of Christianity but by this title the church was never owed, and is still not owed, any other expressions than those of unity of faith and communion to sustain its leader, which is at the same time communion to sustain the universal church.

Thus, far from overstepping its domain through the Civil Constitution of the Clergy, the National Assembly has only recovered its inalienable rights over temporal power which were usurped. Its decrees only support the first canons; they affirm the fundamental truth that the distinctive character of the two powers is that one is entirely spiritual, the other entirely temporal. Immortal glory, then, to this illustrious Assembly for having returned the church to its original institutions, for having purified the clergy of human passions that damage the virtues whose brilliance should characterize it. Immortal glory to this august assembly for having carried out a reform that the faithful and the saintly fathers hoped for throughout ten centuries, a reform which so many councils tried uselessly to accomplish, and which the gallican church could not carry out. The church, restored in all of its purity, springs forth again, as though once more from the hands of its divine founder; by means of these practices we see a revival of the morals of the first age of Christianity, and an eternal flourishing of the faith and piety of pastors and people. There, messieurs, are the enlightened and reasonable motives on which are based the obligation by which I believed myself bound to swear the oath that you have just heard. Praise God and sing the *Te Deum.*

34. "Declaration of the King Addressed to All the French About His Flight from Paris" (June 21, 1791)

The spectacular late-night escape of the royal family from the Tuileries Palace on June 20, 1791, signified a major turning point in the Revolution. Above all, it revealed the extent of the king's estrangement from the Revolution's goals; his superfluity, if not treachery, was becoming increasingly apparent even to himself, as his words here indicate. Dressed as a commoner, the king was recognized and detained by a postmaster at the border town of Varennes within a day of his departure from Paris. This episode, more than any event which had so far occurred in the course of the Revolution, severely compromised the majesty of the crown.

To the French People

As long as the king could hope to see the kingdom's order and happiness restored by the means employed by the National Assembly and by his residence next to this Assembly in the capital city, no personal sacrifice mattered to him. If this hope had been fulfilled, he would not even have contested the deprivation of his liberty occasioned by the denial of an absolute veto without which all of his efforts since October 1789 have been null and void. But today, when the sole recompense of so many sacrifices is to see the kingdom destroyed, all powers disregarded, all property violated, personal safety endangered everywhere, crimes unpunished, and complete anarchy establishing itself above the law, and when the semblance of authority given him by the new Constitution is insufficient to repair a single one of the evils afflicting the realm: the king, after having solemnly protested all the acts emanating from him during his captivity, believes it his duty to place before the eyes of the

Source: Archives parlementaires, vol. 27 (Paris, 1887), pp. 378–383. Translated by Tracey Rizzo.

French and of all the universe the picture of his conduct, and of that of the government which has been established in the kingdom. . . .

It should be remembered that when the Estates General, calling itself the National Assembly, began to occupy itself with the kingdom's Constitution, there were movements in Paris designed to make the deputies neglect one of the principal clauses contained in their *cahiers*, namely that *the making of the laws should be in concert with the king*. These movements were undertaken in the provinces, too, where factions had the cunning to have memoirs sent to the Assembly. Despite this clause, the Assembly put the king outside the Constitution by refusing him the right to grant or withhold his sanction to articles which it regards as constitutional, in reserving for itself the right to include in that category those which it determines appropriate; and in restricting to [articles] regarded as purely legislative the royal prerogative to a right of suspension up to the third legislature; a right purely illusory as so many examples prove only too well.

What remains to the king other than a vain semblance of royalty? He has been given twenty-five millions for the expenses of the civil list; but the splendor of the household he must maintain to do honor to the dignity of the French crown . . . must absorb all of it.

He has been left the usufruct of some of the crown's domains, with several formalities obstructing their use. These domains are only a small portion of those that kings have possessed since ancient times, and of the patrimonies which his majesty's ancestors united to the crown. One is not afraid to put forth that, if all these lands were joined together, they would exceed by much the sums allocated for the maintenance of the king and his family, and then it would cost the people nothing for this portion.

A matter difficult for the king to discuss is the attention paid to the separation, in financial and all other arrangements, between services rendered to the king personally and [those rendered] to the state, as if these objects were not truly inseparable and the services rendered to the person of the king were not also those [rendered to] the state. . . .

The king does not think it is possible to govern a kingdom of such great extent and importance as France by the means established by the National Assembly, as they currently exist. By according to all decrees, without distinction, a sanction that he well knows could not be refused, his majesty was thus motivated by the desire to avoid all discussion, which experience had taught him to be useless at best; what is more, he feared that it would only be thought that he wanted to retard or undermine the National Assembly's work, in whose success the Nation took so great an interest. He put his confidence in the wise men of the Assembly who recognized that it is easier to destroy a government than to reconstruct one on totally different bases. Several times when they announced the revision of decrees, they believed it necessary to marshall armed forces, essential to any government; they also recognized the utility of inspiring [confidence] in this government and its laws, which must assure the prosperity and status of everyone, a confidence which would bring back into the kingdom all those citizens forced to expatriate due to discontent in some, or fear for their lives and property in the majority.

But the more one sees the Assembly approaching the end of its work, the more one sees the wise men discredited, the more dispositions increase daily which could render the conduct of government difficult if not impossible, and inspire mistrust and disfavor. Other regulations have only augmented disquiet and embittered discontent instead of applying healing balm to the wounds that still bleed in several provinces. The spirit of the clubs dominates and pervades everything; the thousand slanderous and incendiary newspapers and pamphlets, which are distributed daily, are merely their echoes, and they prepare minds to be led in the manner they want. Never has the National Assembly dared to remedy this license, so much estranged from true liberty; it has lost credit and even the force it would need to retrace its steps and change that which appears in need of correction. One can see what is to be expected from the clubs, from the spirit which reigns in them and the manner in which they are seizing the leadership of the new assemblies; and if they show any inclination to revise anything, it is to destroy the remnants of royalty and to establish a metaphysical and philosophical government impossible to put into practice.

Frenchmen, is it for this that you sent your representatives to the National Assembly? Do you desire that the anarchy and despotism of the clubs replace the monarchical government under which the nation has prospered for fourteen hundred years? Do you desire to see your king overwhelmed with insults and deprived of his liberty when his only occupation is to establish yours?

Love for its kings is one of the virtues of the French, and his majesty has personally received marks [of this affection] too touching ever to be forgotten. The rebels know well that as long as this love persists, their work can never be achieved; they know as well that in order to weaken it, it was necessary, if possible, to destroy the respect that has always accompanied it: this is the source of the outrages the king has received and of all the ills he has suffered for the past two years. His majesty would not describe these painful scenes here if he did not want to make known to his faithful subjects the spirit of these rebels who tear their country's bosom while feigning to desire its regeneration. . . .

After all these facts and the impossibility the king found himself in to do good and prevent the evil which is committed, is it surprising that the king sought to recover his liberty and to get himself and his family to safety?

Frenchmen, and above all Parisians, you inhabitants of a city which his majesty's ancestors were pleased to call the good city of Paris, disabuse yourselves of the suggestions and lies of your false friends; return to your king; he will always be your father, your best friend. What pleasure will he not have in forgetting all his personal injuries, and in being returned among you, while the Constitution, which he will have accepted freely, will cause our holy religion to be respected, the government to be established on a firm foundation

and useful in its actions, the property and the status of each one no longer to
be troubled, the laws no longer to be disobeyed with impunity, and finally liberty to be established on firm and immovable foundations.

35. Anonymous, "The Queen's Farewells to Her Darlings of Both Sexes" (1792)

A Mr. Bernelot, of the National Guard, allegedly "found" this letter from the
queen after her arrest. Its authorship is not known. This pornographic pamphlet
was one among many that circulated against the queen throughout these years.
Between 1789 and 1792 as many as two hundred differently titled licentious pamphlets and books were printed. By 1793, Marie Antoinette was a regular target.

It is therefore infamy which the wrath of the gods never pardons.
    Good God! who from your celestial throne looks with an indulgent eye
upon the crimes of your rebellious children; you, whose son died for our sins
and cannot return to earth, sacrifice me in his place to atone a third time for
the errors of my ungrateful and guilty people toward him You whose just and
holy spirit does not govern the so-called National Assembly, which, not satisfied with continuing to overrun my property with the payments it exacts, ravages the law by its profane decrees and overturns your religion, temples, and
altars, in company with obstinate demons.
    It is with a just submission and a salutary confidence that I address my
wishes to you for being avenged after my death. I leave you this precious care,
and without any frivolous superstition I leave this earth with sadness for my
children who cherish me, but with no regrets for my subjects.
    God! Before my soul is enveloped in the profound shadows of death, per-
mit me one more time to retrace for my enfeebled thinking the memories of
my delicious years.
    Oh Trianon! Former place of repose so dear to my heart, what have I
done to be torn from your seductive enticements? Enchanting luxury, delicious garden, what has become of you since my cruel captivity? . . .
    Oh sweet nights, which brought so much happiness! Oh the pleasant days
of lovers, who so often enveloped my soul in your mysterious pleasures, alas!
You are no more, your reign over my heart is like that over my throne. They

Source: Hector Fleischmann, ed., *Les pamphlets libertins contre Marie-Antoinette* (Paris: Publications
modernes, 1908), pp. 311–315. Translated by Tracey Rizzo.

are both plunged into the abyss, from whence they come out only to be in horror of humanity.

Polignac, Lamotte, d'Oliva, Sophrosie, d'Arcourt, Fromenville, Julie, Bonnemot, and C., where are you? What has become of you since my cruel fall? What is this ingratitude which has caused you to abandon me in my time of trouble? Why do you flee far from me? Are you unaware that your sincere friend Antoinette will soon see the end of her life's course, formerly so brilliant and so happy? Alas! You will never see again that which your light fingers have made expire a thousand times in a most happy lethargy, and which your tender cares recalled to life by an overflow of pleasure.

Come back, charming Artois, lovable and delicious prince, even in your impotence. You who so often plunged into my amorous heart with a hundred vigorous thrusts, your flesh inflamed, its soft rubbing drowning out our tender sighs, and intoxicating our souls in a divine delirium.

Oh delicious Coigny, you who with your refined measures satisfied my burning desires so well in an indefatigable intoxication, you are surely not insensible to my cruel destiny.

Oh Rohan, vigorous cardinal, Hercules of my burning and ferocious passion, you no longer exhaust your existence to satisfy my heart. I die regretting you.

And you, poor Calonne, you whose pleasures blunted with time, unfortunately your friend can no longer give you the marks of her affection in exchange for financial intrigues which enabled me to conceal how my heart's thirst for gold was quenched.

Goodbye poor Lafayette, you no longer have the hope of a great happiness, you must be content to have pressed this plump white hand to the place where your heart should be.

Oh charms of my life! your possession was a crime in the eyes of a people who, far from being submissive, seem to want to augment my pains still more, a people whom I abhor, who have deservedly attracted my implacable hatred, and whose temerity I will sooner or later punish. Farewell all my pleasures. Farewell to hunting, to immense forests that I so often traversed; the echoes of your hills recall my misfortunes to all of France. They teach that it is this ferocious people who have wrenched me away from your agreeable womb, to lead me as a captive to a lugubrious palace, surrounded by crime.

Finally, you, cherished husband, you will no longer have the pleasure of pouring for your adorable wife the divine nectar of Bacchus; she will no longer force you to leave your reason at the bottom of a bottle of bliss, she will no longer drain your vital energies, only to hasten to lose them elsewhere; she will no longer surprise your candor; finally your brow will unfortunately bear the laurels which are destined to it.

This manuscript was actually found in the gallery of St-Cloud, and I believed I could prove my patriotism by publishing it.

Bernelot

CHAPTER 7

WAR AND A NEW REVOLUTION

36. Manon Roland on the Meetings of the Girondins in Her Home (1793)

Manon Roland (1754–1793) exemplified many of the contradictions of Enlighten-ment and early revolutionary womanhood. Imbued with both a love of the clas-sics and a dedication to Rousseauian virtue, Roland became a facilitator of liberal political discussion. Married to a man who occupied important posts in the new government, she found herself at the center of the most hotly debated questions of the day. Contented to remain within the confines of domesticity, she explains here how she used it to her advantage. Eventually her Girondist views and associations won her the disfavor of the Jacobins, and she was guillotined in October 1793.

Roland had to discuss matters with which he was charged [as Interior Secre-tary] with the deputies. I was elegantly lodged in an agreeable neighborhood and at a moderate distance from different people; I lived well at home, as is my custom. I hardly ever received indifferent people there, having always kept the company of enlightened individuals who associated with my hus-band for cabinet duties or compatibility of tastes. It was decided that the deputies who had customarily gathered in conference would come to my house four times a week, after the session of the Assembly and before that of

Source: Paul de Roux, ed., *Mémoires de Madame Roland* (Paris: Mercure de France, 1966), pp. 126–137. Translated by Tracey Rizzo.

the Jacobins. Pétion, Buzot, Robespierre constituted the core of this small committee, along with Brissot and Clavière. Louis Noailles, Volfius, Antoine the younger, and several others joined us frequently. There were examined the state of affairs: that which the Assembly convened to do, how one could propose it, the people's interests, court happenings, individual tactics. These conferences interested me a lot, and so as not to miss them, I never deviated from the role appropriate to my sex.

Seated near the window, before a small table on which were books, study aids, and dainty handiwork, I plied the needle or wrote letters while they talked. I preferred to write because this made me appear more indifferent to things and made them indifferent to me as well. I could do more than one thing at a time and the rhythm of letter writing permitted me to keep up my correspondence while paying attention to everything except what I was writing. It seems to me that I am three: I divide my attention in two like a material object, and I consider and direct the work of the two parts as if I am a third party. I remember one day when these gentlemen made a lot of noise, finding themselves of diverse opinions. Remarking on the rapidity of my writing, Clavière said pleasantly enough that only the head of a woman could stand this, and yet this was astonishing to him. "What would you say," I asked him, smiling, "if I repeated to you all the reasons you are about to give?" Except for the customary compliments I paid the gentlemen at their arrival and departure, I never permitted myself to say a word, though I often needed to bite my lips to prevent myself. If anyone addressed me directly, it was after the circle had broken and all deliberation was ended. Rest, water, and sugar were the only refreshments they found at my home, and I announced that it was all that seemed appropriate to offer men who came to talk after leaving the table. I have often reflected, particularly during this period, how the sage Pythagoras had profoundly considered the effect of silence and with what reason he required it of his disciples.

To hold one's tongue when one is alone is not an amazing feat, but to steadfastly remain silent in the middle of men who speak of matters which interest you, to repress flashes of insight when you notice a contradiction, to hold back intermediate ideas which escape the discussants and in the absence of which they conclude badly or are not heard, to measure like that the logic of each one while always controlling oneself, is a great means of acquiring penetration and rectitude, of perfecting intelligence and enhancing the strength of character.

The habit of this practice, the study of history, the taste for philosophy (the hungry soul's comfort) could only make me love political schemes. Not the cabinet's petty intrigue whose affairs are decorated by such a lofty name; not the sterile skill of the novelist who makes gossip triumph and amuses only scoundrels; but politics considered as the art of governing men and of organizing their happiness in society. No one speaks less of it than I, because the discussion little suits women. Those women who do discuss affairs of state seem to always sound like yesterday's newspapers. Yet no subject to my mind is more worthy of contemplation. Sometimes I permit myself to speak of it with my friends; I let the others chat. I amuse myself enough with certain old men who fancy themselves to instruct anyone to whom they speak and who could see me often without fearing that I am capable of anything more than sewing a shirt or adding up numbers.

I was not always content with the committee; it is not that the meetings always seemed useless to me, for many good things were said, but they didn't resolve anything, or rather they did it rarely or badly. It facilitated the communication of ideas and new opinions, but it hardly ever decided on measures. These conferences were very apt to excite in each member a deeper meditation on matters with which they should be occupied, but they hardly provided legislators the means to pass a good decree. I have nevertheless seen some proposed, of which two or three were realized. The French scarcely know how to deliberate—a certain lightheartedness leads them from one matter to the next without proceeding in an orderly fashion, or conducting an in-depth analysis of each one. They do not know how to listen; the one who speaks always abounds in his meaning and is occupied more with developing his next thought than with responding to the other's. Their attention is easily exhausted, the desire to laugh is awakened by a word, and a pleasantry reverses all logic.

National Assembly, Jacobins, minor committees have all furnished me with these conclusions. Such people are not solemn enough to be free; as long as one gives them flowery chains they will be the first to play with them. But the moment I speak of is already long gone. The national character has changed much in a year, and if misery may compel us to be serious it is accompanied by a ferocity whose consequences are not susceptible to ordinary comprehension. Anticipate nothing during these times.

37. The Debate over the Declaration of War

The debate over whether or not to enter war was one of the most divisive in the Assembly. It divided Jacobins from Girondins, and more particularly Robespierre from Brissot. Robespierre suspected that war would threaten the fragile successes of the Revolution, and alleged that counter-revolutionary interests were behind war mongering. In his speech against war, he urges his colleagues not to rally the people behind the cause of war, but to warn it against political dissimulation. He thus offers an interesting cautionary note about the ubiquitously invoked "people."

Jacques-Pierre Brissot (1754–1793) was a left-wing journalist before the outbreak of the Revolution, who founded one of the earliest revolutionary newspapers, *French Patriot*. He is also known for founding the Society of Friends of the Blacks. After his election to the legislative assembly in 1791, he gathered about him a coterie in the Jacobin Club known as the Brissotins. The question of war was one of the first major issues to divide them from Robespierre and other Jacobins. The speech printed here was published as a pamphlet by the club in January 1792.

Parisian municipal officers visit each neighborhood of the city to proclaim "the Fatherland endangered" (July 22, 1792). *(From* Révolutions de Paris, *volume 16. Courtesy Harvard University)*

A. Maximilien Robespierre, Discourse on War Delivered to the Jacobin Club (JANUARY 2 AND 11, 1792)

Do we make war or do we make peace? Do we attack our enemies or wait for them to attack us in our homes? I believe that this articulation does not present the question in all its relations and in every extent. What position should the Nation and its representatives take regarding our internal and external enemies, under the circumstances in which we find ourselves? This is the perspective from which we ought to consider [the question] if we mean to encompass everything and discuss it with all the precision it requires. What matters most of all, what will be the fruit of our efforts, is to clarify to the Nation its true interests and those of its enemies; it is not to deprive liberty of its

---

Source: Henry Morse Stephens, ed., *The Principal Speeches of the Statesmen and Orators of the French Revolution, 1789–1795*, vol. 2 (Oxford: Clarendon Press, 1892), pp. 304–332. Translated by Tracey Rizzo.

last resource by sidetracking public opinion in these critical circumstances. I will attempt to achieve this object by responding principally to the opinion of M. Brissot. . . .

No one doubts today that a powerful and dangerous coalition exists against equality and the principles of our liberty; everyone knows that the coalition which puts sacrilegious hands on the foundation of the Constitution is actively occupied with the means of achieving its objective, that it dominates the court, that it controls the ministers; you are agreed that it had the goal of further extending ministerial power, and of aristocratizing the national representation; you have urged us to believe that the ministers and the court have nothing in common with it; in this regard, you have skewed the positive assertions of several orators and of general opinion; you have contented yourselves with allegations that the conspirators could not extinguish liberty. Are you unaware that it is these conspirators who bring misfortunes to the people? Are you unaware that the conspirators, backed by the forces and treasury of the government, are not neglected? That you yourselves formerly passed a law to hotly pursue one faction of those who are in question here? Are you unaware that, since the departure of the king [for Varennes], about which the mystery is beginning to lift, they have had the power to roll back the Revolution, and to commit with impunity the most blameworthy attacks against liberty? That thus so much indulgence or protection came from you suddenly? . . .

. . . The most extravagant idea that can be born in a politician's head is to believe that it suffices for a Nation to enter armed amongst a foreign people to make them adopt its laws and its constitution. No one loves armed missionaries; and the first counsel that nature and prudence give is to repulse them as enemies. I have said that such an invasion would awaken the memory of the conflagration of the Palatinate and the last wars more easily than it would plant the seed of constitutional ideas, because the mass of people in these lands know the facts of our Constitution better. The accounts of enlightened men misrepresent everything that we know of the awe in which they held our Constitution and our armies. Before the effects of our Revolution can be perceptible to foreign nations, it is necessary that they be consolidated. To desire to give them liberty before having conquered it ourselves is to assure simultaneously our servitude and that of the whole world. It is an exaggerated and absurd idea to think that the moment a people is given a constitution, all others will respond at that exact instant to the signal. Would the example of America, which you have cited, have sufficed to break our chains if the time and coincidence of fortunate circumstances had not imperceptibly led to this Revolution? The Declaration of Rights is not sunlight, which illuminates every man at the same time; it is not the sword, which strikes every throne at the same time. It is easier to write on paper or to engrave in bronze than to establish in the hearts of men these sacred characters effaced by ignorance, passion, and despotism. What can I say? Are they not misunderstood everyday, trampled underfoot, ignored even by those who have promulgated them? Is the equality of rights elsewhere than in our constitutional charter? Is not the hideous head of despotism, of aristocracy, raised again and resuscitated in new forms? Does it not still repress powerlessness, virtue, and innocence in the name of laws and of liberty itself? Does not the Constitution, as the daughter of the Declaration of Rights, bear a strong resemblance to her mother? What can I say? Once radiating a celestial beauty, does this virgin still resemble herself? Has she not come out battered and soiled by the impure hands of this coalition who trouble and tyrannize France today, and who is only lacking the adoption of the perfidious measures to consummate their fatal projects which I combat at this very moment? How can you believe then that they will perform the miracles that they have not yet been able to perform at the very moment that our internal enemies have designated for war? . . .

Favorable movements are those which are directed against tyrants, as in the American insurrection, or that of July 14; but war on the outside, provoked, and directed by the government in the circumstances we are in, is a nonsensical movement, a crisis which can lead the body politic to death. Such a war can only sidetrack public opinion, create diversion from the justified anxiety of the nation, and prevent a favorable crisis to which the outrages of the enemies of liberty would [eventually] lead. It is for these reasons that I have described the disadvantages of war. . . .

The real way to manifest one's respect for the people is not to deaden it by boasting of its power and liberty, but by defending it, by warning it against its own failings; for even the people has them. "People" is in this sense a very dangerous word. No one has given us a better idea of the people than Rousseau because no one loved them more: "The people tends always to the good, but it does not always see it." To complete the theory of the principles of government it will suffice to add: the people's mandatories often see the good, but they do not always want it. The people want the good because public well-being is its interest, because good laws are its safeguard; its mandatories do not always want it because they develop an interest separate from that of [the people], and because they want to turn the authority it has confided in them to the profit of their arrogance. Read what Rousseau has written on representative government and you will judge if the people can remain inactive with impunity. However, the people sense more vividly and see more clearly all that derives from the first principles of justice and humanity than the majority of those who are separate from it; and its common sense in this regard is often superior to the wit of clever men; but it has not the same aptitude to disentangle the twists and turns of the artificial politics [that clever men] employ to deceive and to serve themselves, and its natural goodness disposes it to be the dupe of political charlatans. Those of them among us know this well and profit from it. . . .

Therefore I calmly and sadly sum up. I have proven that war in the hands of the executive power is only a means to subvert the Constitution, only the climax of a profound conspiracy hatched to destroy liberty. Favoring this project of war, under any pretext whatsoever, is thus to badly serve the cause of liberty. All the patriotism of the world, all the commonplaces of politics and morality do not change the nature of things, nor the inevitable result of the steps proposed. To preach confidence in the intentions of the executive power, to justify his agents, to call public favor on the generals, to represent defiance as a frightful state of affairs or as a means to disturb the harmony of the two powers and public order, is therefore to deny liberty its last resource, the vigilance and energy of the nation. I had to combat this system; I have done it; I have not wanted to be harmful to anyone; I have wanted to serve my country by refuting a dangerous opinion; I would have opposed it even had it been proposed by the being who is dearest to me. . . .

B. J.-P. Brissot, "Third Discourse on the Necessity of War," Delivered to the Jacobin Club (JANUARY 20, 1792)

Gentlemen,

I turn now to the arguments which Maximilien Robespierre has made against me in this tribunal and which I have not yet refuted.

The question which divides us can be reduced to very simple terms, and I echo those of my adversary exactly: "What position should we take in the circumstances we are in?"

To determine this position, it is necessary to know these circumstances. For, if we are in belligerent, hostile circumstances then I do not say it is necessary to attack but to defend ourselves; and since in defending ourselves, it is better to make our enemy's country the theater of war than our own, it is therefore necessary to hasten to carry [the war] beyond the Rhine.

Will anyone dare deny these hostile circumstances? Will anyone deny that the emigrants succeeded in gathering forces at Worms, at Coblenz, in arming them, in provisioning them? Does anyone deny that they threatened us with future invasion? Does anyone deny that the electors [of the Holy Roman Empire] not only granted them asylum, but also considerable aid, which they accepted, moreover, from various princes who have an interest in maintaining the fire of discord in the bosom of France?

Consequently, does it not become absolutely necessary that France deploy its forces and threaten to crush its imprudent neighbors in turn, in order to stop these gathering [forces], these menaces, these impending hostilities? . . .

What does one say to this pressing dilemma? The French court wants war and it is necessary to be wary of its secret intentions.

Source: J.-P. Brissot, "Troisième discours de J.-P. Brissot, Député, sur la nécessité de la guerre" (Paris: Société des amis de la constitution, 1792), pp. 1–18. Translated by Tracey Rizzo.

And I say, gentlemen, I say the court does not want war. I said it on the same day of December 14 when the king gave his famous speech; all that display did not seduce me. I foresaw from then on that there would be no proposition of war on January 15. I have persisted in my prediction although all the ministers seem to have been told to blow the war trumpet, and my prediction was verified; for, you have seen, gentlemen, the minister of foreign affairs brings you calming letters which announce the elector's submission. You have seen him publish a proclamation which makes manifest his fears of unexpected aggression. You have heard him preach peace in his last speech.

A new strategy, someone cries; the court always wants war, but it changes tactics the better to make you adopt it.

But this strategy would be useless and even stupid; for if the court wants war why doesn't the king propose it to the National Assembly? . . .

I have already asked you, gentlemen, what do the petty calculations of a few individuals matter to a great nation? What does it matter to know what they do or do not want? To know all the strands of the intrigues which brew in their chambers, all the passions of the scoundrels or corrupt women who direct them? A great nation should have only two great objectives before its eyes, principles and force.

However, I should respond to an objection which has been made to me.

If the courts of France and Vienna, someone said to me, do not want war at the present, it is because they are not prepared; they only want it in the spring. I agree, but what can we conclude from this? *That it is necessary to make war now.* We are sure of success in being the first to attack; all the advantages await us on enemy territory; all the disasters will follow us in our homes. Furthermore, gentlemen, all that can be said on this question can be reduced to this threefold perspective: either the Emperor [of Austria] wants war, or he only wants it in the spring, or he does not want it at all.

If he wants it, it is necessary to prevent him [from being the first to attack]; if he only wants it next spring, it is still necessary to hasten to prevent him; if he does not want it at all, it is necessary to force him to give us all the satisfaction which can dissipate our uneasiness and put us within reach of terminating this arms race by declaring war on him. Therefore, in each case, war is necessary.

It is obvious now that we are not free to want or not to want war. It is not belligerence on our part, for we are being attacked; our security is in danger if the coalition comes into existence, and if it does not it is still causing us costly disquiet. . . .

Certainly the fears that some have of the executive power are well founded; they stem from its nature, its formation. The people do not have control over the ministry, and it was truly criminal of those who revised the Constitution to have deprived the people of its influence in this regard; in this case they sowed anarchy and distrust.

However, the Constitution is sworn; it is necessary to obey it: it puts the direction of the army in the king's hands. It should remain there, but all his actions [must] be surveyed and publicized. . . .

If I am deceived on the question of war, it is at least with a clear conscience. [If I err] I will have thus paid tribute to human fragility; but I declare that before venturing my opinion, I took every precaution to prevent error, followed events steadfastly . . . and reassured myself in seeing that the most celebrated men and the best patriots shared my opinion. If M. Robespierre does not tremble to be alone in his, how will I be timid in supporting mine on foundations so well proven?

Events come to my aid, the electors have yielded, the emperor will yield, I dare predict; thus we would do well to deploy a great force in order to compel him to recognize our rights and to deprive the malcontents of this support. . . .

38. The "Marseillaise" (August 1792)

The lyrics to the "Marseillaise" were penned by Rouget de Lisle, an infantry captain stationed in Alsace. Rouget reputedly wrote what he called the "War Song for the Army of the Rhine" in a single night in April, after receiving news of the French declaration of war. Composed in the spring, the song did not become popular in Paris until the late summer, when radical *fédérés* arrived from Marseilles, bringing the tune with them. The participation of the *fédérés* in the Revolution of August 10, their reputations as committed revolutionaries, and their energetic singing helped to insure that the song which became the anthem of the new republic was named after their home city. Under the Empire, government officials would consider the song uncomfortably revolutionary, and it was banned outright during the Restoration. It reappeared, however, during the revolutionary moments of 1830, 1848, and 1870–1871, and was restored to its place as the national anthem of France in 1879.

Paris Chronicle (August 29, 1792)

War song: At present, people in all of the theaters are requesting the song "Forward, Children of the Fatherland." The words are by Monsieur Rouget, the captain of genius stationed at Huningue. The tune was composed by a

Source: Chronique de Paris, August 29, 1792; Laura Mason, *Singing the French Revolution: Popular Culture and Politics, 1787–1799* (Ithaca, N.Y.: Cornell University Press, 1996). Copyright © 1996 by Cornell University. Used by permission of the publisher, Cornell University Press.

German for the army of Biron; it has a character that is both touching and warlike. The *fédérés* were the ones who brought it from Marseilles, where it was very much in fashion. They sing it with great unity and the moment when, shaking their hats and rattling their sabers, they shout all at once: "To arms, citizens!" truly makes one shiver. They sang this martial tune in all the villages they passed through, and in this way these new bards inspired civic and combative feeling in the countryside. They often sing in the Palais-royal, and sometimes in the theaters between the acts. Here are the words. . . .

Forward, children of the homeland!
The day of glory is upon us;
Against us, the bloody standard
Of tyranny is raised.
Do you hear these ferocious soldiers *Austrians*
Bellowing in the fields?
They come into your very midst
To slaughter your sons, your wives!
To arms, citizens, form your battalions,
March on, march on, that impure
Blood will water our furrows.

What do they want, this horde of slaves,
Of traitors, of conspiratorial kings?
For whom are these vile fetters,
These irons so long prepared?

French people! For us, ah what outrage!
What transports they should excite!
Is it us that they dare to consider
Returning to ancient slavery?
To arms . . . [etc.]

What! these foreign troops *Austrians*
Would lay down the law in our homes!
What! these mercenary phalanxes
Would bring down our proud warriors!
Great God! by means of shackled hands
Our heads would bend beneath the yoke!
Vile despots would become
The masters of our destinies!
To arms . . . [etc.]

Quake tyrants! and you traitors
The disgrace of all parties;
Quake! your patricidal projects
Will at last receive their due,
All are soldiers to battle you;

If they fall, our young heroes,
The earth will produce new ones
Ready to fight against you.
To arms . . . [etc.]

French people! as magnanimous warriors
Hold or rein in your blows;
Spare these sad victims
Who regretfully arm themselves against us.
But these bloodthirsty despots!
But the accomplices of Bouillé,
All these pitiless tigers
Rending their mother's breast!
To arms . . . [etc.]

Sacred love of the homeland,
Guide us, sustain our avenging arms
Liberty, beloved Liberty!
Fight alongside your defenders
Beneath our banners to which Victory
Runs in answer to your manly tone:
That your expiring enemies
Will see your triumph and our glory.
To arms . . . [etc.]

39. The Brunswick Manifesto (July 25, 1792)

In April 1792, France declared war on Austria and its ally, Prussia. In spite of an overwhelming enthusiasm for war, French armies initially did quite badly. By mid-July the Assembly would decree a national state of emergency as radicals evermore vocally accused the king of treasonous disregard for winning the war. In that same month, the commander of the Austrian and Prussian allied troops, the Duke of Brunswick, issued the following declaration. Within weeks of the manifesto's publication in France, the fate of king and Revolution was sealed: the Tuileries palace was invaded and the monarchy overthrown on August 10.

Source: Frank Maloy Anderson, ed., *The Constitution and Other Select Documents Illustrative of the History of France, 1789–1907* (New York: Russell and Russell, 1908; reprinted 1967), pp. 119–122.

[On behalf of] their Majesties, the Emperor and the King of Prussia who have committed to me the command of the united armies which they caused to assemble on the frontiers of France, I wish to announce to the inhabitants of this kingdom the motives which have determined the measures of the two sovereigns and the intentions which guide them.

After having arbitrarily suppressed the rights and possessions of the German princes in Alsace and Lorraine, disturbed and overthrown good order and legitimate government in the interior; exercised outrages and brutalities against the sacred person of the king and his august family which are carried on and renewed daily; those who have usurped the reins of the administration have at last completed their work by declaring an unjust war against His Majesty the Emperor and by attacking his provinces situated in the Low Countries. Some of the possessions of the Germanic Empire have been enveloped in this oppression, and several others have only escaped the same danger by yielding to the imperious threats of the dominant party and its emissaries.

His Majesty the King of Prussia, united with his Imperial Majesty by the bonds of a strict defensive alliance and himself the preponderant member of the Germanic body, could not excuse himself from marching to the help of his ally and co-state; and it is under this double relationship that he takes up the defense of this monarch and of Germany.

To these great interests is added another aim equally important and very dear to the hearts of the two sovereigns; it is to put an end to the anarchy in the interior of France, to stop attacks against the throne and altar, to reestablish legal power, to restore to the king the security and liberty of which he is deprived, and to put him in a position to exercise the legitimate authority which is his due.

Convinced that the sound part of the French nation abhors the excesses of a faction which dominates it, and that the greatest number of the inhabitants look forward with impatience to the moment of relief to declare themselves openly against the odious enterprises of their oppressors, His Majesty the Emperor and His Majesty the King of Prussia call upon them and invite them to return without delay to the ways of reason, justice, order, and peace. It is in accordance with these views that I, the undersigned, the General, commanding in chief the two armies, declare:

1. That, drawn into the present war by irresistible circumstances, the two allied courts propose to themselves no other aim than the welfare of France and have no intention of enriching themselves by conquests;

2. That they do not intend to meddle with the internal government of France, but merely wish to deliver the king, the queen, and the royal family from their captivity, and to procure for His Most Christian Majesty the necessary security that he may make, without danger or hindrance, the conventions he shall deem suitable and may work for the welfare of his subjects, according to his promises and as far as it shall depend upon him;

3. That the combined armies will protect the towns, boroughs, and villages and the persons and goods of those who shall submit to the king and who

shall cooperate in the immediate reestablishment of order and of the police in the whole of France;

4. That the national guard will be called upon to watch provisionally over the peace of the towns and country districts, the security of the persons and goods of all Frenchmen, until the arrival of the troops of their Imperial and Royal Majesties, or until otherwise ordered, under pain of being personally responsible; that on the contrary, those of the national guard who fight against the troops of the two allied courts, and who shall be taken with arms in their hands, will be treated as enemies and punished as rebels to their king and disturbers of the public peace;

5. That the generals, officers, under-officers, and troops of the French line are likewise summoned to return to their former fidelity and submit themselves at once to the king, their legitimate sovereign;

6. That the members of the departments, districts, and municipalities shall likewise answer with their heads and their goods for all offenses, fires, murders, pillaging, and acts of violence that they shall allow to be committed, or which they have not manifestly exerted themselves to prevent within their territory; that they shall likewise be required to continue their functions provisionally, until His Most Christian Majesty, being once more at liberty, may have provided for them subsequently or until it shall have been otherwise ordained in his name in the meantime;

7. That the inhabitants of the towns, boroughs, and villages who may dare to defend themselves against the troops of their Imperial and Royal Majesties and fire on them either in the open country, or through the windows, doors, and openings of their houses, shall be punished immediately according to the strictness of the law of war, and their houses destroyed or burned. On the contrary, all the inhabitants of the said towns, boroughs, and villages who shall submit to their king, opening their doors to the troops of their Majesties, shall at once be placed under their immediate protection; their persons, property, and effects shall be under the protection of the laws, and the general security of all and each of them shall be provided for;

8. The city of Paris and all its inhabitants without distinction shall be required to submit at once and without delay to the king, to put that prince in full and perfect liberty, and to assure him as well as the other royal personages the inviolability and respect which the law of nations and men requires of subjects toward their sovereigns; their Imperial and Royal Majesties declare personally responsible with their lives for all events, to be tried by military law and without hope of pardon, all the members of the National Assembly, of the department, district, municipality, and national guard of Paris, the justices of the peace and all others that shall be concerned; their said Majesties also declare on their honor and their word as Emperor and King, that if the château of the Tuileries be entered by force or attacked, if the least violence or outrage be offered to their Majesties, the king, queen, and royal family, if their

preservation and their liberty be not immediately provided for, they will exact an exemplary and ever-memorable vengeance, by delivering the city of Paris over to a military execution and to complete ruin, and the rebels guilty of these outrages to the punishments they shall have deserved. Their Imperial and Royal Majesties, on the contrary, promise the inhabitants of Paris to employ their good offices with His Most Christian Majesty to obtain pardon for their misdeeds and errors, and to take the most vigorous measures to assure their lives and property, if they obey promptly and exactly all the above-mentioned orders.

Finally, their Majesties being able to recognize as laws in France only those which shall emanate from the king, in the enjoyment of a perfect liberty, protest beforehand against the authenticity of any declarations which may be made in the name of His Most Christian Majesty, so long as his sacred person, that of the queen, and those of the royal family shall not be really in security, for effecting of which their Imperial and Royal Majesties beg His Most Christian Majesty to appoint the city in his kingdom nearest the frontiers, to which he would prefer to retire with the queen and his family under good and sufficient escort, which will be furnished him for this purpose, so that His Most Christian Majesty may in all security summon such ministers and councilors as he may see fit, hold such meetings as he deems best, provide for the reestablishment of good order and regulate the administration of his kingdom.

Finally, I declare and bind myself, moreover, in my own private name and in my above capacity, to cause the troops entrusted to my command to observe a good and exact discipline, promising to treat with kindness and moderation all well-intentioned subjects who show themselves peaceful and submissive, and only to use force against those who shall make themselves guilty of resistance and ill will.

It is for these reasons that I call upon and exhort all the inhabitants of the kingdom in the strongest and most urgent manner not to oppose the march and the operations of the troops which I command, but rather to grant them everywhere a free passage and with every good will to aid and assist as circumstances require.

40. Deposing the King

The Brunswick Manifesto, published on July 25, 1792, threatened an invasion of France and total destruction of Paris in the name of Louis XVI, and sealed the fate of the king. No one could continue to doubt his hostility to the Revolution. While

Source: J. M. Roberts and R. C. Cobb, eds. *French Revolution Documents*, vol. 1 (New York: Barnes & Noble, 1966), pp. 507–513. Translated by Tracey Rizzo.

the Assembly deliberated, the people of Paris took matters into their own hands, as these two documents show. The first, reflecting the views of forty-seven of the forty-eight Paris sections, denounces Louis's treason and demands his removal. The second is the response of the Assembly to the popular uprising of August 10; it formally deposes the king.

A. Petition from the Paris Sections to the National Assembly Demanding the Suspension of the King (AUGUST 3, 1792)

Legislators, it is when the fatherland is in danger that all its children ought to press around it; and never has so great a peril threatened the fatherland. The commune of Paris sends us to you; we come to bring the opinion of an immense city into the sanctuary of the laws. Filled with respect for the Nation's representatives, filled with confidence in their courageous patriotism, [Paris] has not despaired of public safety; but it believes that to cure the ills of France it is necessary to attack them in their source and not lose a moment. It is with grief that it denounces, through our agency, the head of the executive power to you. Without doubt, the people have the right to be indignant with him; but the language of anger does not befit brave men. Compelled by Louis XVI to accuse him before you and before all of France, we shall accuse him without bitterness as without pusillanimous deference. It is no longer time to listen to that protracted indulgence which befits generous peoples, but which encourages kings to perjury; and the most respectable passions must be silent when the salvation of the State is in question.

We shall not retrace for you the entire conduct of Louis XVI since the first days of the Revolution, his sanguinary projects against the city of Paris, his predilection for nobles and priests, the aversion he exhibited for the body of the people, the National Constituent Assembly, which was outraged by court valets, encircled by men of arms, wandering in the midst of a royal city and finding an asylum only in a tennis court. We shall not retrace for you the oaths he violated so many times, the protestations incessantly renewed and incessantly contradicted by actions, up to the moment when a perfidious flight opened the citizens' eyes, blinded by the fanaticism of slavery. We shall leave aside everything that is covered by the people's pardon; but to forgive is not to forget. Besides, we would forget these delinquencies in vain; they will soil the pages of history, and posterity will remember them. . . .

Armed enemies threaten our territory abroad. Two despots publish a manifesto against the French nation that is as insolent as it is absurd. French parricides, led by the king's brothers, kinsmen, and allies, prepare to rend the bosom of their fatherland. Already the enemy at our frontiers places executioners opposite our warriors. And it is to avenge Louis XVI that the national sovereignty is impudently outraged; it is to avenge Louis XVI that the tyrants have renewed the wish of Caligula, and that they would wish to destroy all the citizens of France with a single blow!

The flattering promises of a minister have led to a declaration of war, and we have commenced it with incomplete armies destitute of everything. . . .

The head of the executive power is the first link in the chain of counter-revolution. . . . Far from putting himself in opposition against our domestic and foreign enemies by a formal act, his conduct is a formal and perpetual act of disobedience to the Constitution. As long as we shall have such a king, liberty cannot grow strong; and we are determined to remain free. From a remnant of indulgence, we might have desired the authority to ask you for the suspension of Louis XVI as long as the danger to the fatherland shall exist; but the Constitution precludes that. Louis XVI invokes the Constitution incessantly; we invoke it in our turn and ask for his suspension.

Since it is very doubtful whether the Nation can have confidence in the present dynasty, we ask that the ministers may provisionally exercise the executive power once [he is suspended] until the will of the people, our sovereign and yours, is legally pronounced in a National Convention as soon as the security of the State permits it. The ministers [are] jointly responsible, selected by the National Assembly, but outside of its own body, according to the constitutional law, and selected by the open vote of free men. Meanwhile, let our enemies, whoever they may be, arrange themselves beyond our frontiers; let scoundrels and perjurers abandon the soil of our liberty; let three hundred thousand slaves advance; they will find before them tens of millions of free men, as ready for death as for victory, fighting for equality, for the paternal home, for their wives, their children, and the elderly. Let each of us be soldiers in turn; and if it is necessary to have the honor of dying for the fatherland, let each of us make his memory illustrious by the death of a slave or a tyrant before yielding the last breath.

B. Decree of the National Assembly for Suspending the King (August 10, 1792)

The National Assembly, considering that the dangers to the fatherland have reached their height;

That it is the most sacred duty of the legislative body to employ all means to save it;

That it is impossible to find it remedied, unless they occupy themselves with removing the source of its evils;

Considering that these evils spring principally from the suspicions which the head of the executive power's conduct has inspired, in a war undertaken in his name against the Constitution and the national independence;

That these suspicions have provoked a desire tending to the revocation of the authority delegated to Louis XVI from different parts of the kingdom;

Considering, nevertheless, that the legislative body ought not to wish to aggrandize itself by any usurpation; that in the extraordinary circumstances in which unforeseen events have placed it, it cannot reconcile what it owes to its unshaken fidelity to the Constitution with its firm resolve to be buried under the ruins of the temple of liberty rather than to let it perish, except by taking recourse to the sovereignty of the people and by taking at the same time indispensable precautions so that this recourse may not be rendered illusory by treason; [the legislative body] decrees as follows:

1. The French people are invited to form a national convention; tomorrow, the extraordinary commission shall present a proposal to indicate the method and the time of this convention.

2. The head of the executive power is provisionally suspended from his functions until the national convention has pronounced upon the measures which it believes ought to be adopted to assure the sovereignty of the people and the reign of liberty and equality.

3. The extraordinary commission shall present a method for organizing a new ministry within a day; the ministers currently in service shall provisionally continue the exercise of their functions.

4. The extraordinary commission shall likewise present, within a day, a proposal for a decree upon the selection of a governor for the royal prince.

5. Payment of the king's salary will remain suspended until the decision of the national convention. The extraordinary commission shall present, within twenty-four hours, a proposal for a decree upon the stipend to be granted to the king during his suspension.

6. The registers of the annual salary shall be deposited in the office of the National Assembly, after having been numbered and attested by two commissioners of the Assembly who shall repair for that purpose to the intendant of the annual salary.

7. The king and his family shall reside within the precincts of the legislative body until calm may be reestablished in Paris.

8. The department shall give orders to prepare accommodation at the Luxembourg for them within a day, where they shall be put under the custody of the citizens and the law.

9. Every public functionary, every soldier, every officer, of whatever rank he may be, and general of an army, who shall abandon his post in these days of alarm is declared infamous and traitorous to the fatherland.

10. The department and the municipality of Paris shall cause the present decree to be immediately and solemnly proclaimed.

11. It shall be sent by special couriers to the eighty-three departments, which shall be required to cause it to reach the municipalities of their jurisdiction within twenty-four hours, in order to be proclaimed with the same solemnity.

41. The September Massacres (September 1792)

When news reached Paris on September 2 that Verdun had fallen, the citizens of the city panicked; no other fortress stood between invading Prussian troops and the capital. Convinced that the city's overfilled prisons held the "enemy within," Parisians invaded them, set up popular tribunals, and promptly executed every man and woman that the self-appointed judges condemned. Neither the Paris Commune nor the Assembly attempted to stop the violence, and some eleven hundred to fourteen hundred people were killed in five days. This account is taken from a newspaper that was sympathetic to the Parisian revolutionaries who were responsible for the September massacres.

The People's Justice

Sunday, September 3, at about 2:00 in the afternoon, the alarm cannon of the Pont Neuf sounded three rounds; the tocsin was sounded, and drums beat the call to arms in all the Paris sections.

What happened? the citizens asked themselves as they came out of their houses. Has Verdun been taken over? Are the enemies at Chalons? Will they be at our doors tomorrow?

Verdun is not taken, at least not the citadel. Chalons is perhaps threatened by the presence of Prussian troops, the enemy from the north is not at our doors; but we have one in our midst, whose diabolical expression will shine forth to-morrow night. Before facing the enemies from outside, let us foil the terrible plot of the villains who, perhaps tonight, will burn Paris after having pillaged it.

And, in truth, the prisons overflowed with people; new prisons were being built which, at the rate the tribunals are working, would soon be insufficient. Unfortunate family men, made unable to acquit the sacred debt of their children's milk by the harshness of the times, find themselves crowded pell-mell with the villains and accomplices of the riot of August 10; with priests deciding, for the first time in their lives, to speak according to their consciences; with trouble-making prelates and counter-revolutionaries stirring up the poorly quenched fires of religious and royalist fanaticism in their former dioceses; with military officers who are revealing to the enemy the easiest entrances to their fatherland; with a bunch of gaming-house henchmen and counterfeiters of assignats, banking their fortunes on the ruin of morals and national credit.

One of these wretches, condemned to ten years in irons and tied to the stake of ignominy in the place de Grève on the first Saturday of September,

Source: Révolutions de Paris, no. 165 (September 1–8, 1792). Translated by Laura Mason.

had the audacity to insult the French people and to shout out from the very scaffold: "Long live the king, long live the queen, long live M. Lafayette, f—— the nation!" The commune's prosecutor heard him and returned him to the judges, who sent him to the guillotine on Sunday morning. Here is the terrible conspiracy that this criminal, ready for his punishment, revealed as though to avenge himself with threats only too well founded and, what's more, supported by several depositions given in the sections.

About the middle of the following night, a signal would be given for all the prisons in Paris to open at once; the prisoners were to be armed as they left, with the guns and other murderous instruments that we gave aristocrats time to hide by publishing the news of domiciliary visits several days in advance; the cells of La Force were stocked with munitions to this end. . . .

These hordes of freed devils, swelled by all the aristocrats hidden in the backs of their villas since St. Laurent, commanded by the treacherous officers sent to the Abbaye prison, would begin by overrunning the principal posts and their cannons, seizing sentinels and patrols, the majority of whom were without bullets because of an incredible lack of foresight by the sections, and setting fire to five or six neighborhoods at once, to create a necessary diversion from the grand project of rescuing Louis XVI and his family. . . . An army of royalists that would spring up from beneath the paving stones, would protect the prince's hasty escape and his rendezvous with Brunswick, Frederick, and Francis; magistrates and the most patriotic of the legislators would probably be slaughtered, if it were possible to do so without running too great a risk of stirring up the people.

The success of such a brazen stroke would, of course, be uncertain. But the commotion that it would stir, even in failing, could cause the greatest disorder and favor the invasion of the frontier at all points. The people who, like God, see everything and are everywhere, and without whose permission nothing happens here below, no sooner had knowledge of this infernal conspiracy than they took the most extreme but only appropriate course of action to prevent the atrocities being prepared for them and to show themselves merciless toward those who had no mercy for them. They chose their moment well; they knew that with the first bad news from the frontier, the Paris elite would leave their homes for the scene of danger. From that moment, this city, stripped of its principal forces and reduced to its pikes, would appear as a great battlefield abandoned to pillage.

The clear instincts of the people frustrated all of these measures. According to a surveillance decree, all of the city's barriers were left open Sunday morning. At 3 o'clock, the sounding of the alarm cannon had them closed. Many people had profited from them throughout the morning. The dawdlers were arrested; several carriages were obliged to turn back and driven to the committee of the Quatre-Nations section. Of the twenty-one persons that they carried, three were slaughtered en route because of evidence that was more than suspect. Of the eighteen remaining, fourteen suffered the same punishment on the very steps of the room in which they were first interrogated. . . .

This first execution, carried out in the courtyard of the committee, was only a prelude. Nearby the prison held the very guilty who might perhaps have been saved by formalities or other considerations. The people wanted to judge for themselves the substance of the proceedings, and at the same time to guard against the plot revealed that morning by the guillotined man. Twelve commissioners were quickly named and immediately placed at the booking window of the prison. By the will of the people and in the name of the Nation, open up for us; it was opened. Bring us the justices of the peace who are here, let men such as Montmorin, Thiéry, the bishop of Chartres, etc. appear. The above-named prisoners appeared; pass by, they were told, to go to the Conciergerie; that was their death sentence. (At the Conciergerie, the criminals were told: pass by to go to the prison of the Abbaye.) They went out, after having left their jewels and other objects of value in the hands of the prison guard. The people awaited them at the door, to sacrifice them to public condemnation. The execution completed, they shouted "Long live the Nation," as if to make known that a free people, like the human body, owes its political health to the amputation of its gangrenous limbs. Blood ran and each of those who carried weapons seemed to compete for the honor of contributing to this great act of justice. The bodies were already piling up in the courtyard of the Abbaye when a deputation from the legislature, seconded by another from the municipality, rushed in to lecture the multitude, to inspire in them some feeling of pity and a little confidence in the magistrates and judges of their choosing. A man came out of the crowd and stood before them, carrying an iron spear, blood from which ran over his hands. "This blood," he told them, "is that of Montmorin and company; we are at our post, return to yours; if all those we appointed to administer justice had done their duty, we would not be here; we are doing their labor and we are on the job; the more guilty people we kill, the more we win."

The deputies, amongst whom was Chabot, could not gain any concession; the impure blood of traitors to the homeland did not cease flowing. . . .

The people, who had placed one of its tribunals of last resort at the very foot of the great stairway of the former palace of justice, exercised the same virtues and vengeance there; the stones of the courtyard were bathed with blood, the heaped-up bodies offered the terrible image of a slaughterhouse of men. Throughout an entire day, from Sunday to Monday, death sentences were passed, and the sentences carried out as soon as they had been passed; but the most rigorous equity was observed among a thousand barbarous acts; it was a duty to consult the prison registers; and the same arms that mercilessly struck off the head of the bandit, the murderer, the forger, the traitor to the homeland, opened fraternally to embrace the debtor of good faith set free. Upon his exit from prison, he was lavished with assistance, given something to eat, and all that was demanded in return for such care was a shout of "Long live the Nation.". . .

The people are human, but without weakness; wherever they detect crime, they throw themselves upon it without regard for the age, sex, or condition of the guilty. They demanded an eye for an eye from the shopkeeper of the Palais-Royal, indignant to find that this woman whose heinous crime was already several years old, was still in the prisons of the Conciergerie. Judges! All the blood spilled on September 2 and 3 should redound to you. It was your criminal slowness that took the people to extremes for which you alone should be held responsible. The impatient people seized the sword of justice from your hands, where it has too long been idle, and did your job. If a few innocents perished, no one should be accused but you, and your conscience should be your first executioner. . . .

[. . . S]ome would like the people to restrain its rage at the very moment that it recovers all its energy! Can one make such a demand, above all under present circumstances? The *Bulletin of the War* informed the people that the Austrian soldiers cut the ears off every municipal officer they can catch and ruthlessly nail them to the tops of their heads; and it would be inexcusable if the people, at this moment of open war, allowed themselves to retaliate! The people still know that in several Parisian villas, those of aristocrats who have not been able to escape since the affair of the 10th, they kill time with a little mahogany guillotine that they bring to the table with dessert; one after another they place several dolls in it whose heads have been made to resemble those of our best magistrates or representatives, and which in falling allow a red liquor like blood to flow out of the body, which is really a bottle. All those present, especially the women, hasten to dip their handkerchiefs in this blood, which turns out to be a very agreeable ambergris-scented water that they inhale with delight, as they wait to make the blood of patriots flow in waves for real. And no one wants to draw a curtain over the details of the people's vengeance, who are not ignorant of what awaits them if they fall once more under the yoke of the aristocracy! . . .

42. Speeches on the Trial of the King

To put the king on trial and execute him was not merely to attack the man; it was to fundamentally challenge the very institution of the monarchy. That this was so would help to explain why several hundred of the Convention's deputies delivered speeches, published pamphlets, or had their opinions on this subject entered into the official record during the two months that preceded the Convention's vote, of January 15, 1793, on whether to execute the king. The following are excerpts from speeches that represented two dominant kinds of arguments. In the first, C.-F.-G. Morrison makes a defense of sacred kingship that Louis's own lawyers would use at his trial in December. So much did Morrison believe in the king's inviolability that he abstained from voting in January,

Source: Michael Walzer, ed., *Regicide and Revolution: Speeches at the Trial of Louis XVI*, trans. Marian Rothstein (Cambridge: Cambridge University Press, 1974), pp. 110–120, 139–158. Reprinted with permission of the publisher.

although he knew this meant one less vote for the king's life. The text by the Marquis de Condorcet, which was published rather than spoken, reflects the position of the Girondins. Like Robespierre in 1791, Condorcet was opposed to the death penalty; unlike Robespierre, he hewed to that principle even when he believed the king guilty of treason, arguing that Louis should be subject to the "gravest penalty in the penal code short of death."

A. Speech by Charles-François-Gabriel Morrison (NOVEMBER 13, 1792)

Citizens, since we have before us a question of the gravest importance, a question which touches the essence of polity as well as the principles of justice, any decision we make ought to follow only after the fullest discussion. And if among the speakers there is one who presents an opinion at variance with the majority, it is precisely he to whom we should listen with the greatest attention. Error is often useful to make the truth more clearly felt. It is the shadow in a painting which defines the forms.

Citizens, I invoke these truths on my own behalf. My opinion appears isolated. It is in opposition to that of the majority of delegates. But in this assembly, the love of approbation must yield to duty; in this assembly, too, my very errors may have their use. I beg of you then, in the name of France, hear me out in silence, however shocking some of my reflections may appear.

Citizens, like you I am overcome with the greatest indignation when I consider the many crimes, the atrocities, with which Louis XVI is stained. My first and doubtless most natural impulse is to see this bloody monster expiate his crimes by the cruelest torments that can be devised. I know that he has earned them all. Yet I must deny my impulse; before this tribunal, representing a free people who seeks happiness and prosperity in acts that are just, in acts that are humane, generous, and kind, because only through such acts can happiness be found. I must deny my impulse, and heed instead the voice of reason, consult the spirit and the disposition of our law, seek only the interest of my fellow citizens, for that alone must be the single goal of all our deliberations.

Your legislative committee, of which I have the good fortune of being a member, has proposed for discussion three questions: Can the king be judged? By whom ought he to be judged? In what way may he be judged? Without departing from the principal object of our present discussion, citizens, I would like to propose to you another series of questions, a series of which only the first is to be found among those proposed by your committee.

Can Louis XVI be judged? Is it in the interest of the Republic that he be judged? Do we not have the right to take, with respect to him, measures for the general safety? Finally, what ought these measures to be?

I will undertake to discuss in succession each of these questions: and if the Convention finds itself in accord with me, it will not entertain the report of the committee, but will adopt the measures I propose. In general terms, that is the end I seek.

Can Louis XVI be judged? Citizens, I approach this question among a people exercising, without constraint, the plenitude of its sovereignty. I have no intention of contesting their rights; I shall always respect them. But these rights have limits, limits all the more sacred in that nature herself has fixed them for the happiness of the entire human race.

Citizens, we all come into the world susceptible to diverse passions which act upon us, often in opposition to one another. We should be continually agitated and continually unhappy did we not have the power to resist some of these passions, and rather to give ourselves over to those which will lead us most surely toward our happiness.

We have this power and yet to exercise it we must sometimes compel ourselves to consider before we act. What is true for each man is true for the nation as a whole. To determine a course of action, we must do more than ask if we have the power to carry it out. Sometimes we must resist our most natural impulses and suspend all action the better to weigh the consequences. If these few mild precautions are taken, our judgment always has a faithful governor, benevolent acts lead to personal happiness; just acts alone can bring honor and prosperity to nations.

Thus a sovereign people has no other rule than its supreme will. Yet as the will of any people must be that it flourish, and as nothing save justice can promote this end, its rights and its powers have as their limits such duties as justice dictates. Citizens, it is by these principles that I will be guided in examining whether Louis XVI can be judged.

I know well that kings, as they were first conceived, were no more than delegates of the people; that their function, their duty, was to execute the general will and to guide it for public prosperity by all the means at their disposal. He among them who was guilty of treason or of some other crime was, in fact, answerable for it. This is clear, as in their original societies men could seek only their mutual advantage, and it was certainly in the interest of all to punish the traitor and the miscreant.

Yet this right to judge kings, irrevocable from its source in the sovereignty of peoples, may nevertheless receive modifications in the manner of its exercise. For example, a nation might establish by a precise article of its social contract that despite its inalienable right to pronounce sentence, given a crime and a conviction, the accused person will not be judged, will not be sentenced, unless before his crime there existed a statute which he has contravened. Thus our neighbors, the English, have for many years acquitted their criminals in those cases provided for by statute law. Thus, since the establishment of juries among us, the greatest scoundrel would be acquitted if our penal code had no statute which could be applied to him.

I would go further, for it is a consequence of my principles that a nation, be it by superstition, ignorance, or reasons of interest well or ill considered, can declare a magistrate inviolate; that is, he cannot be indicted while in office, and if he commit any crime, he can suffer no punishment but discharge.

I fully agree of course that such a declaration can bind only a people who wish to hold to it. To claim the contrary would be to challenge the sovereignty of the people. That, I repeat, has not been my intention. Yet when a nation has promulgated a law, although it be a bad law, although that nation have the right to change the law at will, nevertheless, that changed law cannot have a retroactive effect, and the previous law must apply to all events which took place while it was still in force. One cannot dispute this truth without doing injury to the most basic principles of justice, principles sacred to all orderly nations, principles unknown only to tyrants.

Let us return to Louis XVI. In order to judge him according to our institutions, there must be a statute which can be applied to him. Yet no such law exists. The penal code, which takes precedence over all previous criminal law, decrees that those who betray their country be put to death. It is evident that Louis XVI has betrayed his country; he has been guilty of the most horrid perfidy; again and again he has forsworn himself; his aim was to enslave us beneath the yoke of despotism; he caused part of Europe to rise against us; he delivered up our positions and those of our brothers; he sacrificed our bravest defenders; he sought everywhere to create anarchy and disorder; he sent the coin of France to her armed and united enemies; he ordered the slaughter of thousands of citizens who committed no crime against him but that of loving liberty and their country. The blood of these unhappy victims still runs warm in the streets; they call upon all France to avenge them. But here we are religiously ruled by law; coolly, as impassive judges, we consult our penal code. Well, that penal code has no provision which may be applied to Louis XVI, since when he committed his crimes there was a written law which carried an express exception in his favor; I refer to the Constitution.

Citizens, when I open that work, a work that is without question disorderly and unreasonable, a work that contradicts the first principles of social order, but nevertheless, a work which governed us all at the time when these crimes which we now lament took place among us, I find within it these articles:

The person of the king is inviolable and sacred.

If the king put himself at the head of an army, and direct the forces of it against the nation, or if he do not oppose, by a formal act, any such enterprise undertaken in his name, he shall be held to have abdicated.

After abdication, express or legal, the king shall be in the class of citizens, and may be accused and tried like them, for acts posterior to his abdication.

The person of the king is inviolable and sacred. That inviolability was, we were told, introduced only in the interest of the people, and not as a privilege for the king. And no doubt, this was the purpose, as the interest of the people is the sole purpose of all social institutions. But the king found advantages for himself as well, just as magistrates find some little advantage in the exercise of the functions with which they are entrusted. Surely no one would seek to deny so self-evident a proposition.

The king, you will reply, was inviolable only by virtue of the Constitution; the Constitution is no more and his inviolability has ceased with it.

Citizens, here I must remind you of a truth without which we would have been plunged long since into all the horrors of anarchy; laws that have not been abrogated by other laws continue to exist, and every citizen is obliged to obey them, for his own good and for the good of all. What holds true for laws in general is true for the Constitution. With the exception of those portions which have been negated by laws or acts posterior to it, such as the elimination of the monarchy and the establishment of the Republic, the Constitution stands.

Yet I will concede that the Constitution no longer exists. But, I ask, should a law which existed at the time of a crime, and which established a penalty for it, be ignored when the punishment for that crime is later deliberated, even if that law has been abolished in the interim? I cannot believe that anyone acquainted with the first principles of equity would dare answer this question in the affirmative.

What! You will reply, Louis XVI constantly violated the Constitution; by all possible means he sought to destroy it and with it the liberty which should have followed from it. And now you wish to permit him to take advantage of that same Constitution which he himself never sincerely adopted!

Yes, citizens, yes. That is what I propose. The Constitution was the law of my country without the consent of the king; it was law by the will of the sovereign, the people, who swore to maintain it until such time as, by the exercise of their sovereign powers, they might make laws in greater harmony with their love of liberty and equality. Yes, if I broke the laws of the land, albeit I had never approved them, I ought nonetheless to suffer punishment according to those laws. And if they contained some clause favorable to my position, I would have the right to ask for that benefit, to ask it of the sovereign, which would have no right to refuse, since my right sprang only from its supreme will, a will which it can change only for the future. Fortunately these maxims are incontestable. Fortunately for us, we practice them daily.

Finally, you will say to me that the Constitution declared inviolability only for those acts which were essential to monarchy, and for which ministers were, in fact, responsible. Citizens, I hope you will accept my response to this objection.

The king was only, so to speak, the head of his council; everything was done in his name, yet he answered for nothing, since the ministers, his subalterns, were independently responsible, each for his own department. Thus he could not be punished for his exercise of executive power, since, as I have said, his agents were in fact the ones responsible.

Yet he could commit crimes which were independent of his position as the foremost public official. Like any other citizen, he could form an alliance with the enemies of his country, furnish them aid, send them the coin of the realm. He could place himself at the head of an army; he could cause the slaughter of his fellow citizens; he could, in other words, like any other corrupt and evil man, attempt to commit all those crimes of which he stands accused. Therefore the sovereign people which is always the arbiter of justice did not wish that he escape punishment, nor that his inviolability should protect him, since for these crimes there was no other responsible agent, there was no one to pay the penalty to society or to offer society any satisfaction.

Yet by formulating its supreme will into statute, the people determined what punishment would be inflicted upon him, and that punishment was merely the forfeit of his throne, a punishment which it judged to be perhaps more rigorous a penalty for a despot than all those now meted out by our penal code. If some still doubt these truths, these doubts can be easily allayed by the text of the Constitution itself. Here it is: "After abdication, express or legal, the king shall be in the class of citizens, and may be accused and tried like them, for acts posterior to his abdication." The proposition is evident. Citizens, that was the will of the sovereign. We must now reverently respect that will.

You say, we cannot avoid passing judgment on Louis XVI because our mission demands it absolutely. You are mistaken, citizens, you do not have before you now the task of judging Louis XVI. I call my conscience to witness, I call upon all my colleagues in the legislature, I call upon all the citizens of the Republic.

Louis XVI would have overwhelmed us with the weight of his perfidy. That liberty of which we were the trustees was, perhaps, about to slip from our hands, had the throne of Louis XVI existed for an instant longer. We had an obligation to overthrow it, but there . . . our powers stopped. And if the welfare of the nation was, for a single instant, our supreme law, if that law, the first among all, gave us duties as well as rights, we ought to have stopped when we had taken such measures as were necessary to preserve the general safety and our liberty.

Our powers ceased when the king was king no longer. If Louis XVI committed perfidious crimes, he merited, a thousand times over, he merited the forfeit of his throne, which was the penalty set by the Constitution. That penalty should have been pronounced against him in a regular and legal manner. I repeat, our powers had ceased to exist. We had only one course of action: to call upon the people, to call together a National Convention. And we do so.

The National Convention was formed. It had been formed to pronounce upon that forfeiture, to write a new constitution, to make new laws of governance, and during that time, to conduct the government in the most advantageous possible way.

The National Convention, therefore, was called to pass upon the deposition of Louis XVI; but convinced with reason that the existence of liberty and public prosperity is not compatible with the existence of a king, the Convention abolished the monarchy. From that moment, Louis had ceased to be king in law. From that moment, there were no more kings, and I fervently hope that they will never, never again defile the soil of the French Republic.

I recognize that the foundation of the Republic and the suppression of monarchy are in no way a statutory judgment against Louis XVI, and are in no way a punishment directed against him as a man. A sovereign people can change the form of its government at will. It can dethrone its kings, even though they be guilty of no crime. But here, the National Convention, charged with the question whether Louis XVI had been deposed, has nothing more to decide since, by his de facto deposition, he has already undergone the only punishment determined for those crimes which he committed while he was yet king.

And if the National Convention did have the mission of making further judgment on Louis XVI, I maintain that that mission could not be fulfilled, since a judgment within the social order can consist only in the application of a preexisting law. And as there is no further preexisting law which might be applied to Louis XVI, there may now be no further sentence passed against him. I believe I have demonstrated these propositions. There is no law which can be applied to Louis XVI. . . .

B. Speech by the Marquis de Condorcet (December 3, 1792)

In a case where an entire nation has been wronged and is at once prosecutor and judge, it is the opinion of mankind, the opinion of posterity, to which that nation is accountable. It must be able to declare: all the general principles of jurisprudence recognized by enlightened men in all lands have been respected. It must be able to defy the blindest partiality to cite a violation of the slightest rule of equity; and when that nation judges a king, then kings themselves, in their inmost hearts, must feel moved to approve the judgment.

It is important to the happiness of mankind that the conduct of France toward the man it too long called its king should be the final step in curing other nations of whatever superstition in favor of monarchy may remain among them. Above all, we should beware lest we increase that superstition among those still ruled by it. All nations do not recognize the eternal truths, the unshakable foundation of the French Republic; and whereas our philosophers and our soldiers spread them to foreign nations; whereas tyranny trembles as much before our maxims as before our armies, we would be imprudent to surprise, to frighten perhaps, by the boldness of our actions, those whom we may cause to respect severe but impartial equity. Thus, it is to the laws of universal justice, common to all constitutions, unalterable in the midst of clashing opinions and the revolutions of empires, that we must submit our decisions.

Can the former king be judged?

An action can be grounds for legitimate punishment only if a previous law defined that action expressly as a crime; and it can be punished only with a penalty which likewise was prescribed by a previous law. This is an axiom of humanity and justice.

If, however, the law failed to distinguish in the list of crimes those which circumstances made more heinous, one ought not to conclude that the law wished to exempt them from punishment, but only that the aggravating circumstances did not seem to require the prescription of a specific penalty. The laws of Solon include none against parricide. Shall we conclude that the monster who was guilty of this crime was intended to remain unpunished? No, surely he was to be punished as for a murder.

If, then, the laws of France say nothing specifically about a king who conspired against the people, although he be much more guilty than a citizen, it does not follow that he should be spared, but only that those who wrote the laws did not wish to distinguish him from other conspirators. <u>He should be judged then by the usual law, if another law did not specifically exclude him.</u>

Was such an exclusion expressed by the Constitution? Citizens, if such an impunity had been made law, if the Constituent Assembly had committed such a crime against humanity, if the nation had been weak enough to accept that dishonorable law by its silence, by the election of representatives, by the oaths which were demanded of them, then, as a friend of justice, as a friend of liberty, I would say: "The king cannot be judged and punished."

But that scandalous impunity was never enacted.

Two articles make this clear. In one, the person of the king is declared inviolable and sacred. The other declared that for all crimes committed after his legal abdication, he would be judged like other citizens. . . .

The word "inviolable" is not defined by the Constitution, as it is applied to the king; but it is defined elsewhere, as it applies to the representatives of the people.

Their inviolability entails two conditions, quite distinct, and both applicable to the king. The first is that they might not be made to suffer for what they did or said as representatives, and as soon as there was a king established by the Constitution he must necessarily have shared in this kind of inviolability.

This prerogative, extended to all the king's executive acts, posed dangers which that of the deputies did not. Thus the king was required to have these acts validated by the signature of a minister responsible for their legitimacy. The Nation was not without checks, and if it had not all those which might be demanded by the principles of justice rigorously applied, at least it had all those compatible with the existence of so bizarre an institution as monarchy.

Thus, all that the king did as the repository of national power cannot be imputed to him. But he is accused by common report of crimes foreign to his royal duties. It was not as king that he paid for libels to ruin the credit of the Nation, that he sent subsidies to the enemies of France, that, in concert with his brothers, he formed a league with the enemies of the Nation; it was not asking that, in despite of the laws which he himself had approved, he armed foreign troops against the citizens of France.

The other condition of the inviolability of the deputies was that they could not be prosecuted except by decree of the legislature. Thus when the Constituent Assembly discussed the question of the inviolability of the king, this point was mentioned, and with reason, for by the very nature and importance of his functions, he could not be answerable before a tribunal on the summons of those public officials whose conduct he was to oversee. It was shown that the man who had the authority to suspend the formation of laws, the head of the executive, the head of the army and the navy, should not be exposed to the risk of being stopped from these great tasks by the will of a particular tribunal. With the same success, the arguments used to exempt the deputies from the common order of judicial prosecutions were used in his favor.

It is true that the course of justice, should a deputy be prosecuted, was described and that no one dared do the same for the king. But the base maxim, that a king who was an incendiary, an assassin, a parricide, should remain unpunished, never stained the laws of a France already more than half free. Do you believe that if such a servile principle had been inserted into the text of the Constitution, the Nation would have consented to adopt, or at least to try, the Constitution and to regard it as a binding law? Would we have dared show it to the world as a Constitution less disfigured by gross violations of natural law than those of the greater part of the nations of the earth?

Some will reply that the inviolability of a king should be complete, since he could have no impartial judge. This is to argue that the magnitude of the crime should become a title to impunity; that crimes against the safety of an entire people should have been placed beyond the reach of the law. Thus, the leader of any conspiracy which had imperiled nation and liberty could say to the people: "You cannot judge me, for I have wronged you all; there is no one among you whom I have not caused to fear for his rights, for his property, for his life." And since each man regains his individual right to see to his safety as soon as the law ceases to protect it, this refinement of justice would become the signal for disorder and arbitrary vengeance.

Some will mention, as a proof of that absolute impunity, the article by which the king, in the case of legal abdication, is to be judged for his subse quent crimes like any other citizen. But for crimes subsequent to the period of their duties, the inviolable deputies are also judged like other citizens.

The inviolability of the king and of the deputies, expressed by the same word, should be understood in the same way; with this difference alone, that the Constitution prescribed for the latter the way in which they were to be judged, whereas in reference to the king it remains silent. This silence alone was doubtless enough to awaken the indignation of men who cherished in their hearts the sentiment of liberty and equality.

Thus, the impunity of the king was not decreed by the Constitution. Yet that document did not set forth the way in which he was to be judged. It enacted that if he ceased to be king, he would, for his subsequent crimes, be prosecuted and judged like any other citizen; but it decided nothing as to how he might be judged or prosecuted for his prior crimes.

Here I could end my examination of the articles of the Constitution. . . .

I shall reply, however, to an indirect consequence of the Constitution, by which some have been struck. The Constitution provides that upon certain offenses committed by the king, his abdication is presumed. For the crimes subsequent to his abdication, it treats him as a citizen. Therefore intention was, in the case of those other offenses, to subject him only to the loss of his throne, which from that point became the only punishment he might suffer.

An examination of the actions which would provoke the loss of the throne suffices to make us feel the weakness of such an argument.

Indeed, they are all necessarily public actions for which a judicial inquiry would be useless if the general safety permitted the least exception to the principle of submitting all accusations to the same rules of judgment. Moreover, among those very acts, some could be considered not to be true crimes except by the later conduct of the king; others could be prosecuted only in an illusory manner.

Thus, for example, if revoking his oath, if obstinately remaining outside the territorial limits of France, he became guilty by the sole assertion that he retained his right to the throne, one might suppose that guilt would cease were he to submit to the legal abdication decreed by the Constitution. One might almost consider from the same point of view, his failure to oppose by an official decree any enterprises undertaken in his name.

Finally, in the event that the king might be at the head of an enemy army, the law treating him for his crimes after abdication like any other citizen could not without absurdity be viewed as an amnesty for all that might have preceded that act of overt rebellion—for the crime, that is, of having incited civil war. Why then were the legislators silent? Doubtless they felt that the king was then in a state of open war, and that he could be prosecuted only after having been vanquished while persisting in his rebellion, only after having added new crimes to those which had called for his abdication.

It is impossible to understand these laws any other way. Indeed, how could the same men who would have punished a willful absence by abdication have wished to see plots for proscription and assassination go unpunished? How would they have punished the retraction of an oath more severely than the violation of that same oath by acts of treason or tyranny? How could failure to resist by a formal decree have seemed more criminal than an ostentatious resistance, belied by perfidious connivance with those same enemies against whom he pretended hostility?

Is it not more natural to think that the writers of the Constitution were content to mark a legal proceeding for cases so plain as to render useless a judicial investigation, and that they left to be determined by circumstances those which would have demanded such an investigation? Doubtless they believed that it would be difficult to plan in advance a form proper to such unforeseen and extraordinary events as must necessarily precede the trial of a king. Is it not enough to be obliged to accuse the majority of the Assembly of timidity and reticence, that Assembly whose wisdom and courage have so just a claim to the gratitude of the Nation? How, on the face of it, could we consider that body guilty of having so openly contradicted the same Declaration of Rights that it regarded as its first title to fame? Why, given two ways of regarding the question, should we choose that which assumes in the work of these same men, proclaimed by them on the same day, so shocking a contradiction?

Finally, a man cannot demand favorable conditions for a contract which he did not carry out, or which he openly breached. For example, a debtor whose creditor promised to take no action against him on condition that the debtor give him a house, fully furnished, could legitimately be prosecuted if, following that agreement, he had removed a portion of the furnishing. Why, then, might the members of the Constituent Assembly not have believed that the king, in violating the conditions of the Constitution, lost the right to counter judicial prosecutions with that inviolability which he held from the Constitution alone? that he might be judged for the crime of violation of the Constitution by virtue of the principles of common law, and that an explicit statement was not required?

How, moreover, could the Constituent Assembly have set down in the Constitution the method by which the king was to be judged? The legislature, in accord with the spirit of the Constitution, could not have the power to accuse him. To whom could that power belong? To the Nation alone, and thence to the representatives which it named to the Convention. It would therefore have been necessary that the Constitution indicate to the National Assemblies precisely the same plan of conduct that the Assembly of 1792 followed on August 10. And if one recalls with what timid circumspection the Constituent Assembly spoke of the inalienable right of the people to change its constitutional laws, one will be less astonished to see that the Assembly has not dared facilitate the exercise of this power by placing in the Constitution a means by which, in the case of serious accusations brought against the king by the citizens, the legislature might call a National Convention.

It has been said that Louis XVI ought not to be judged, for, if he had not counted on an absolute inviolability, he would perhaps have refused the crown. What! He would have refused the crown if he had not been told: You may commit any crime with impunity, you may even betray, for the second time, that people which has given you the throne in recompense for the first betrayal? Yet did Louis XVI, already declared inviolable, and in the same terms, before the first violation of his oath, believe that he was beyond judgment when he was brought back from Varennes? And did Louis XVI not know that his base servants, despite all their vileness and all their power, could not bring about the adoption of this article, so clear and so simple, nay, they could not even cause it to be proposed: "The king, whatever crime he may commit, shall never be punished therefor, other than by deposition?" How then could he have believed that such was the sense of the articles of the Constitution, since the framers of that document would not even suffer this sense to be brought directly before them? How could he find an assurance of absolute impunity in the distressing silence which met his greatest efforts?

It is time to teach kings that the silence of the laws about their crimes is the ill consequence of their power, and not the will of reason or equity. . . . .

L'idole Renversée

PART

THREE

The Republican Crisis
1793–1795

he rifts that had emerged among French men and women during the liberal phase of the Revolution did not vanish with the execution of the king. They continued to multiply and intensify, plunging the nation into a period of profound crisis that would last until the inauguration of the Directory late in 1795. The nature and outcome of these conflicts should remind us that the 1790s were not revolutionary simply because the subjects of an ancient monarchy had replaced their king with a republic. They were revolutionary because so many men and women throughout France and her colonies mobilized themselves, to become involved in political, social, and cultural projects that promoted a dizzying array of programs for the future. Not surprisingly, many of these programs were in direct competition with one another; not only did revolutionaries disagree among themselves about what direction the Revolution should take but, as well, there remained many citizens of the new republic who hoped to turn back the clock altogether, to restore the Old Regime. The National Convention and its agents would come to confront this crisis first by fighting those it deemed counter-revolutionary and then by silencing revolutionary voices that questioned or criticized its increasingly single-minded vision of the nation. This strategy may have unified and saved the republic, but at terrible cost. For once the crisis of the Terror was ended, renewed conflict over the future of the republic became mingled with the burden of putting its short past to rest.

Destruction of the Symbols of Royalty *(Photo Bulloz)*

Centrifugal Forces

During the first half of 1793, the crises that the new republic had to face multiplied at an alarming rate. Worse still, the nation was not simply facing foreign threats; it was being torn apart from within.

By the beginning of February 1793, France was at war on every border. To meet this challenge, the National Convention voted a levy of three hundred thousand men. When the demand for conscripts reached the Vendée, in western France, however, it fed internal war by touching off an explosion of rural resentment. To the peasants of the poor and relatively isolated areas of western France, the Revolution seemed only to benefit urban bourgeois, upon whom it conferred municipal offices and the opportunity to buy church lands even as it took first the peasants' priests and then their king. When those same urban bourgeois appeared in the countryside—now clad as the National Guard—to commandeer local sons for revolutionary armies, they were met with popular insurrection. Young men across the countryside took up royalist cockades, armed themselves, and appealed to local nobles to join them as they gathered into small guerrilla bands; they would constitute an armed force of some thirty to forty-five thousand strong by late spring. By early summer, the rebels had overrun several towns and laid siege to the city of Nantes, engaging in an unnervingly successful counter-revolutionary movement that drew badly needed troops away from the republic's frontier.

As counter-revolution was organized in the west, what came to be known as Federalist revolts emerged in southern France. There, citizens who had welcomed the declaration of the republic and accepted the execution of the king rebelled against local radicals and what they considered the political extremism and tyranny of the capital. The first city to witness such a revolt was Marseilles, in late April, but the most spectacular and threatening municipal rebellion took place in Lyons, the second largest city in France. Jacobins had dominated the municipal government of Lyons since November 1792, under the leadership of an incendiary and mentally unstable manufacturer named Joseph Chalier. By the spring of 1793, the municipality was unable to ensure cheap or abundant provisioning because of the disruption of regular trade and lack of funds, and it dealt with the crisis by threatening violence against local elites and jailing political opponents. When crowds of women took provisioning into their own hands and ransacked the army's well-stocked warehouses, the Convention's local representative ordered troops to march on the city. Fearing that a military presence would only strengthen the Jacobins' hand and provoke a massacre, the city overthrew the municipal government at the end of May. Although the new government proclaimed its loyalty to the republic, the Convention declared Lyons in revolt and began to mass troops around it in midsummer.

Meanwhile, revolution and war continued to trouble the French colony of Saint Domingue. The slave uprising of 1791 had quickly turned into a full-scale insurrection. Island slaveholders demanded armed support but, to their dismay, the French troops that arrived in the fall of 1792 were commanded by an ardent abolitionist named L. F. Sonthonax. Sonthonax allied himself with the insurgents, who seized and sacked the principal city of Le Cap in the summer of 1793. The slaves' de facto seizure of their freedom and Sonthonax's provisional declaration

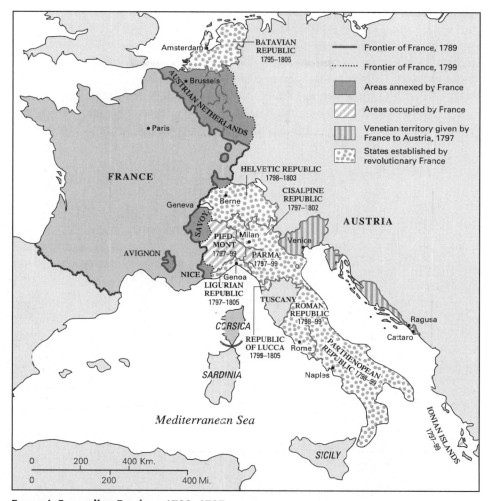

France's Expanding Borders, 1789–1797
Revolutionary governments under the Directory and under Napoleon spread
revolutionary ideas along with military might. *(Source: The Times Atlas of World History, 4th
ed. © HarperCollins Publishers Ltd., 1993. Reproduced by permission.)*

of it (confirmed by the National Convention in 1794) might have restored peace to
the island. However, England and Spain now entered the conflict. Claiming an interest in rescuing white colonists, but more probably hoping to annex the once-
profitable sugar colony, both sent armed expeditions to invade Saint Domingue in
1793 and prolong what had already become an extremely violent conflict.

Facing war, rebellion, and counter-revolution, the Convention had also to
confront the activist population of Paris. Parisians had been vital participants in
the Revolution since 1789, and the continuing problem of food shortage combined with their involvement in a singularly new kind of politics to radicalize them

quickly. Their most visible spokesmen were sans-culottes, independent artisans and shopkeepers who shared a common belief in the importance of economic independence, the exercise of direct democracy through insurrection or referenda, and the political value of education. Although the sans-culottes celebrated the condition and rights of workingmen, women's activism was of equal importance in advancing the struggle for affordable food and popular representation.

In addition to rioting and petitioning, some of these men and women attended sectional assemblies and radical political clubs—like those of the Cordeliers and the Jacobins—which provided arenas for political education, discussion, and organization. And after Claire Lacombe and Pauline Léon founded the Society of Revolutionary Republican Women in May 1793, women could hold political offices as well as attend meetings. Newspapers like Jean-Paul Marat's *The People's Friend* and Jacques-René Hébert's *Father Duchesne* also served as important means of information and organization because both journalists editorialized heavily and explicitly addressed the issues that were of greatest concern to working people.

Parisian activism had ebbed and flowed since 1789, but it reached new heights after the August revolution. As inflation drove bread prices higher in the winter of 1792–1793, crowds and deputations to the Convention began to demand that the government set maximum prices on bread and institute harsh penalties against grain hoarders. The ensuing debate among the legislators contributed to the declining Parisian popularity of the Girondins, who were increasingly characterized as the sole proponents of a free market and as the enemies of the sans-culottes. Although the Convention agreed to pass a partial maximum on grain prices in early May, the Girondins' reputation continued to decline. At the end of the month, crowds surrounded the legislative halls and, to the deep misgivings of many of the deputies there, forced them to expel the Girondins. But the expulsion solved nothing; rather, it aggravated Federalism in the south by reinforcing the conviction that radicals in the capital were dominating politics and tyrannizing the countryside.

As we have seen, the Federalist and counter-revolutionary crises continued to deepen throughout the summer, and so crowds again surrounded the Convention in early September to demand more vigorous prosecution of the war, the provisioning of the capital, and the elimination of counter-revolutionary suspects. The Convention responded with decrees that would be among the foundations of the Terror. This episode marked both the zenith of popular activism and influence, and the beginning of its official containment.

The Restoration of Order

The crisis reached a height in midsummer 1793, but the men of the National Convention had not waited that long to take action. In April they had created the Committee of Public Safety, a watchdog committee that was granted ever-greater powers until it became, in effect if not in name, the executive power of the nation. The committee's activities were seconded by those of the Revolutionary Tribunal, an extraordinary court whose sentences could not be appealed, and the

Committee of General Security, which oversaw policing and tried to follow shifts in public opinion. Novel legislation was not long in fol owing. In July the Convention suspended the new constitution and declared an indefinite state of emergency. In August, turning their attention to the demands of the war, the deputies voted a mass levy to mobilize the nation: young, single men were called into the army, while those left behind—women, children, old or married men—were to devote their efforts to producing munitions and other supplies. But the most extensive series of emergency decrees came in the wake of the insurrection of September 4 and 5. Bowing once more to pressure from the sans-culottes, the deputies declared that "terror is the order of the day": in rapid succession, they decreed a law on suspects—which immeasurably broadened the definition of counter-revolutionary activity and allowed suspects to be jailed indefinitely—a maximum on wages and prices, and the creation of a revolutionary army to scour the countryside for grain hoarders.

The extraordinary measures were successful and the tide began to turn in the late summer and fall. In the west, troops halted the progress of the Vendée rebels and began to drive them back beyond the Loire River. In the south, republican troops defeated first the insurgents of Marseilles and ther, after a long and bitter siege, those of Lyons. The war at the frontier was fought more slowly, but French armies drove the allied powers beyond their borders by the end of 1793. In the Caribbean, the black leader Toussaint l'Ouverture would not join French republican forces until May 1794, when he received word that the Convention had finally abolished slavery. After that, however, Toussaint's presence and the strength of numbers he brought with him would be decisive, permitting the French to repel the armies of Spain and discourage those of England.

But the deputies to the Convention and, in particular, the members of the Committee of Public Safety sought more than military victory. They arrayed themselves in battle against the decentralization of power which, they believed, had given birth to the crises they faced, and so they sought to contain all who competed with the National Convention for political power or initiative. Parisian sans-culottes and activist women fell quickly before this impulse. The September insurrection marked the beginning of the containment of the sans-culottes as the Convention restricted sectional assembly meetings and encouraged wider participation to dilute the influence of radicals by offering to pay poor attendees. Within a few weeks, the police had harassed the sans-culottes' most vocal and radical allies—the *enragés*—into silence. October—the month of the Convention's greatest domestic military victories—witnessed the settling of old scores and the imposition of still greater public order in Paris: the Revolutionary Tribunal sent the Girondins and the queen to the guillotine, and the Convention banned women's political clubs, rhetorically banishing women to the household.

We have focused thus far on efforts to save the republic from the crises it faced in 1793–1794, but the citizens of France were not merely reacting to external forces. They were also trying to bring into being a new political culture that would purge the habits of the Old Regime from people's minds, replacing them with new models of behavior, new signs and symbols, even new kinds of religion. Thus, citizens in the marketplace were able to purchase songs, theatrical plays, and novels that celebrated republican virtues; they could adorn their homes with dinner plates that commemorated the war or playing cards that replaced kings, queens, and jacks with famous deputies. Friends and strangers alike replaced the formal and hierarchical "vous" (you) with the familiar "tu," and "Monsieur" and "Madame" gave way to "citizen" and "citizeness." The Convention, trying simultaneously to de-Christianize and rationalize French culture, introduced a revolutionary calendar, the months of which had poetic names that evoked the seasons and were composed of three ten-day periods. Décadi, or the tenth day, replaced Sundays, and celebrations of republican martyrs and a deist Supreme Being took the place of traditional Christian holidays.

These innovations were not the superficial trappings of a citizenry trying to keep up with the times; rather, they were believed to serve profoundly serious ends by providing republican instruction at every moment. Meanwhile, legislators reached still deeper into society. The legislative assembly's legalization of divorce and abolition of primogeniture created the potential for fundamental change in the ways that women and men negotiated power in the household. In the Convention, Saint-Just set his sights on reshaping the economy by redistributing the property of landholders who had been condemned as counter-revolutionaries, and Robespierre hoped to reshape man himself by fostering republican virtues that would recall those of the ancient republics.

By the beginning of 1794, the republic had begun to overcome the crises that threatened it, but the members of the Committee of Public Safety had become obsessed with centralizing their power and imposing order. More extraordinary measures were instituted. In the spring, the committee struck left—executing the sans-culottes' spokesman, Hébert, for having tried to extend the Revolution too far—and then right—sending Danton and his allies to the guillotine for reputedly trying to hold the Revolution back. Violations of legislative immunity and the subversion of regular judicial procedure were formalized by the law of 22 Prairial (June 10, 1794). Executions reached new highs in Paris: some thirteen hundred people were guillotined in the capital during the next six weeks. By the end of the Terror, about forty thousand people throughout France would die by execution or while suffering imprisonment.

As the Terror reached its high point, discontent began to coalesce. Deputies in the Convention, who had voted to renew the membership of the Committee of Public Safety every month for almost a year, began to complain of Robespierre's aspirations to power. The members of the committees, thrown together without relief and with little sleep for months, began to fight among themselves. And so it was that when Robespierre climbed to the podium of the Convention to announce a new conspiracy against the Revolution and to threaten a new purge in midsummer, he could not rally his listeners to him. Rather, on the following day—9 Thermidor (July 27)—the Convention voted his arrest, along with that of Saint-Just and several other members of the Committee of Public Safety. Robespierre's allies in the Jacobin Club tried to excite a sans-culottes insurrection on his behalf but the Paris populace, discouraged by months of constraint and arrests, responded apathetically. Robespierre, Saint-Just, and about eighty others were sent to the guillotine on the following day.

The Thermidoran Reaction

The arrest of Robespierre and his closest allies on 9 Thermidor would prove to mark the end of the Terror, but that can only be seen retrospectively. At the time, many observers believed that the Convention—having rid itself of yet another enemy—would continue business as usual. Political change emerged slowly and haphazardly, in part because so many members of the Convention had been implicated in the Terror: deputies had colluded both actively—by passing legislation or serving as representatives in the provinces—and passively—by renewing the standing membership of the Committee of Public Safety each month. Now they, in company with the nation at large, faced new and difficult questions. Who would be held responsible for the past? How could old scores be settled? And, most critical of all, what was to become of the republic?

The most immediate signs of a shift in the Convention's policies were a sharp drop in executions and the release of hundreds of people who had been imprisoned under the conditions of the law on suspects: in August thirty-five hundred people were set free in Paris alone. Within weeks, bands of young men who called themselves "gilded youth"—they were freed prisoners, sons of shopkeepers, draft dodgers—began to appear in different parts of the city, to "cleanse" Paris of signs of the Terror. They browbeat café owners into taking less radical names for their establishments, smashed busts of Marat, and hounded actors once known as Jacobins by bellowing the reactionary anthem "The People's Awakening." Although the "gilded youth" were initially a relatively isolated minority, the broader public began to share their opinions when they learned of atrocities in the west: in the fall, for instance, the deputy Carrier was charged with having executed counter-revolutionaries in Nantes by piling them onto barges, which he sank in the Loire River. When the revelations set off riots against the Jacobin Club, the Convention responded by closing down the club's meeting hall and effectively disbanding the Jacobins.

The swing to the right in public opinion was paralleled by the Convention's efforts to free itself of its reputation as the protector of working people. The Convention encouraged the purging of sans-culottes from offices in the sectional assemblies and, in a more far-reaching and debilitating gesture, it repealed the maximum. Wages continued to stagnate but inflation sent prices skyrocketing at the very moment that the freezing of the Seine hampered the transport of grain and firewood: working people starved or committed suicide out of despair while the well-to-do—prosperous and feeling themselves newly free—flaunted their wealth in theaters and cafés.

When the worst of the season had passed, working people did as they had done so many times since 1789; they turned out in crowds to demand that the Convention attend to their concerns, by insuring regular and affordable provisions. The first such popular insurrection, on 12 and 13 Germinal (April 1 and 2, 1795), failed to produce any long-term changes, so the crowds returned at the beginning of Prairial (May 20–23). This would prove to be the last great popular insurrection of the Revolution. The National Convention drove the petitioners from their halls and then called on the National Guard and "gilded youth" to subdue working-class neighborhoods. After three days of street fighting, the authorities could declare an unqualified victory as suspected agitators were executed and the populace disarmed.

And yet, the violence of the Thermidoran reaction in Paris—however damaging to the bodies and spirits of the sans-culottes—was relatively minor compared to that of the "White Terror" in southern France. There, former terrorists faced reprisals that ranged in severity from shunning to assassination. Some of the cities that had participated in the failed municipal revolts of 1793—Marseilles, Lyons, Aix—witnessed the purging of municipal administrations and rioting. Most brutal, however, were the prison massacres that took place throughout the region as the desire for revenge mingled with popular fears of attack (now from Jacobins rather than "aristocrats") like those that had produced the prison massacres of September 1792. Over the next three years, some two thousand southerners would be killed as part of a prolonged cycle of violence and retribution.

As private citizens settled old scores and debated their relationship to past and future, the Convention too faced the question of whither the Revolution. The possibility of putting the child Louis XVII on the throne died with the boy, and his uncle's statements upon declaring himself Louis XVIII made clear that there would be no compromise between royalism and revolution. Nor did the deputies believe it possible to simply restore the constitution of 1793: in particular, they were anxious to exclude common people—whom they held responsible for the dictatorship of the preceding year—from politics. In the end, the deputies of the National Convention drafted a new and far more conservative constitution. But they would only go so far: fearing a purge of republicans, they added a clause requiring that at least two thirds of their number be elected to the new government. The Paris sections, now dominated by "gilded youth" and quasiroyalists, responded with insurrection. No longer willing or able to call out the sans-culottes in their defense, the Convention deputies turned to the army. Troops commanded by the young Napoleon Bonaparte easily defeated the uprising with, in Napoleon's famous words, "a whiff of grapeshot." The deputies had saved the republic, but they did so by turning to the very man who would bring it down only four years later.

POPULAR MOVEMENTS
BEYOND THE CONVENTION

43. Definitions of the Sans-Culotte, the Moderate, and the Aristocrat (APRIL–MAY 1793)

The name "sans-culotte" means, literally, "without breeches"; in other words, it referred to those who wore the long trousers of the workingman. Historically, the sans-culottes were popular activists in Paris who exercised power through neighborhood, or sectional, assemblies and by joining insurgent crowds at moments of crisis. While spokesmen tended to represent the sans-culottes as all the working poor of Paris, their leaders were primarily skilled artisans and shopkeepers. In the following selections, an anonymous writer defines the sans-culotte and his enemies; note the tendency to conflate political opinions with social status.

A. Response to the Impertinent Question, But What Is a Sans-Culotte?

A sans-culotte, sirs, you Rogues? It is a being who always goes about on foot, who has no millions, as you would like to have, no châteaux, no valets to serve

Source: Albert Soboul and Walter Markov, *Die sansculotten von Paris* (Berlin: Akademie-Verlag, 1957), pp. 2–4. Translated by Laura Mason.

him, and who is housed simply with his wife and children, if he has them, on the fourth or fifth floor.

He is useful, because he knows how to work a field, how to forge, saw, file, roof, make shoes, and spill his blood to the very last drop for the good of the Republic.

And because he works, one is sure not to see his face in the Café de Chartres, nor in the dives where there is conspiring or gaming, nor in the Theater of the Nation when *Friend of the Laws* is being performed, nor in the Vaudeville Theater at a performance of *Chaste Suzanne*, nor in the reading rooms where for two sols, which are so precious, they offer Gorsas's filth along with the *Chronicle* and the *French Patriot*.

In the evening, he goes to his section, not powdered, perfumed, and outfitted in the hope of attracting the attention of all the citizenesses in the stands, but rather to support the good motions with all his energy, and to crush those that come from the abominable faction of the statesmen.

For the rest, a sans-culotte always has his saber with the razor's edge, to cut off the ears of all the malefactors. Sometimes he walks with his pike; but at the first sound of the drum, he can be seen leaving for the Vendée, for the army of the Alps, or for the army of the North. . . .

B. Definition of the Moderate, the *Feuillant*, the Aristocrat (in short, of that class of citizens from whom should be taken the million that must be raised from throughout the Republic)

The aristocrat is he who, out of scorn or indifference, is not inscribed in the register of the National Guard and has not sworn the civic oath. . . . He who by his conduct, his activities, his speech, his writings, and his associations gives proof of how much he misses the Old Regime and disapproves of the Revolution in all ways. He who by his conduct makes people presume that he would send money to the émigrés or join the enemy army; that, finally, he only lacks the ability to do one and the opportunity to do the other. He who forever despairs of the Revolution's triumph. He who announces news that is distressing and known to be false. He who, because of false economies, leaves his lands uncultivated without wanting to give them by halves nor consolidate them nor sell them at their just price. He who did not buy national property although he had the occasion and means to do so. And, above all, he who announced that he did not dare to buy it; and counseled others not to do this civic act. He who, having the ability and the occasion, did not provide work for workers and day laborers at a good wage relative to the cost of goods. He who did not take out subscriptions for volunteers and, above all, he who has never given according to his ability to do so. He who, out of aristocratic feeling, does not frequent priests who have taken the oath [to the Civil Constitution of the Clergy] and, above all, he who counsels others not to do so. He

"The People, Eater of Kings": The artist envisions a statue "to be placed at the most important points of [France's] frontiers." *(From* Révolutions de Paris, *volume 20. Courtesy Harvard University)*

who has not improved the condition of indigent and patriotic humanity, although notoriously able to do so. He who, out of spitefulness, does not wear a cockade of three thumbs' width; he who bought other than the national outfit, and, above all, he who does not glory in the title and the headgear of the sans-culottes. *doesnt work vicious*

44. Address by the Sans-Culottes Section to the National Convention (SEPTEMBER 2, 1793)

Sans-culottes did not reject the principle of private property but neither were they proponents of the free market. Rather, they urged the government to regulate the economy and so help them to create an egalitarian society purged of the terrible gap between rich and poor; a society in which every citizen would have

Source: Albert Soboul and Walter Markov, *Die sansculotten von Paris* (Berlin: Akademie-Verlag, 1957), pp. 136–140. Translated by Laura Mason.

the right to a decent existence, public relief if necessary, and education. Here we see sans-culottes applying their general principles to the very specific problems of inflation and grain shortages that had plagued France throughout the spring and summer of 1793.

People's proxies,

How long will you suffer royalism, ambition, egoism, intrigue, and avarice, in alliance with fanaticism to hand over our frontiers to tyranny and carry death and destruction everywhere? Monopolists to spread famine throughout the Republic in the guilty hope of making patriots cut one another's throats and reestablishing the throne over their bloody corpses with the help of foreign despots? Make haste, time is growing short. . . . The universe is watching you, humanity reproaches you for the ills that desolate the French Republic; and posterity will blacken your names forever in the centuries to come if you do not bring remedy quickly. . . . Make haste, people's proxies, to chase away the armies of all the former nobles, priests, parlementarians, and financiers of all judicial and administrative functions; to permanently fix the prices of essential goods, raw materials, salaries for work, profits of industry and commerce; you have the right and the power. . . . What's that! aristocrats, royalists, moderates, and intriguers tell you that this is an attack on property, that property should be sacred and inviolable. . . . Indeed; but do they not know, these villains, do they not know that property is limited only by the extent of physical needs? Do they not know that no one has the right to do what may harm another? What is more harmful than the arbitrary power to put a price on goods that seven eighths of the citizenry cannot afford? . . . Finally, do they not know that each person who makes up the Republic should use his intelligence and strength for her benefit, spill his blood to the last drop for her: in return, the Republic should assure the means for each of them to acquire the essential goods without which they cannot preserve their lives. . . .

Have we not, you say, passed a terrible law against monopolists? People's proxies, do not deceive yourselves. . . . This decree, by forcing all those who have considerable amounts of essentials to declare them, favors monopolists more than it destroys monopoly; because it places all their merchandise under the Nation's protection and allows them to sell it at whatever price it pleases their greed to set. Consequently, the general assembly of the sans-culottes section, considering that it is the duty of all citizens to propose measures which appear to be most suitable for restoring abundance and public tranquillity, determine to request that the Convention decree:

1. That former nobles may neither exercise any military function nor hold any public employment, of whatever nature it might be; that former parlementarians, financiers, and priests be dismissed from all administrative or judicial functions;

2. That the prices of all essential goods be permanently fixed according to their prices in the years called former years, from 1789 through 1790, and in proportion to their different quality;

3. That raw materials be fixed at such a price that the profits of industry, salaries from work, and profits from commerce. which were moderated by the law, will allow the industrious man, the worker, and the tradesman to acquire not only the things necessary and indispensable for existence, but as well that which may add to their enjoyment of it;

4. That all farmers who did not harvest because of some complication be indemnified from the public treasury;

5. That a sufficient sum be allocated to each department to make the prices of essential goods the same for every member of the French Republic;

6. That the sums allocated to the departments be used to eliminate the inequality created by the prices of foodstuffs and essential goods, and the prices of transport throughout the French Republic which ought to bring the same advantages to each of its children;

7. That leases be canceled and restored to the same price at which they were during the common years that you choose to permanently fix the maximum prices of foodstuffs and essential goods;

8. That a maximum on fortunes be set;

9. That a single individual may possess only one maximum;

10. That no one may hold more lands than is necessary for a predetermined number of plows;

11. That a single citizen may hold no more than one workshop, one boutique;

12. That all those who have merchandise or lands in their names be recognized as proprietors.

The sans-culottes section believes that these measures will restore abundance and tranquillity, gradually eliminate the inequalities of fortune that are too great, and increase the number of proprietors.

45. Jean-Paul Marat, *The People's Friend*
   (JUNE 23, 1793)

Jean-Paul Marat began to publish his influential newspaper, *L'Ami du peuple*, in 1789. He used its pages to champion the cause of the poor and to urge revolutionary activism. Although he favored a dictatorship during the early years of the

Source: L'Ami du peuple, no. 224 (June 23, 1793); A. Vermorel, ed., *Oeuvres de J. P. Marat* (Paris: Décembre-Alonnier, 1869). Translated by Laura Mason.

Revolution, Marat came to be a vocal proponent of direct democracy, which would allow all (male) citizens to shape legislation through electoral assemblies and insurrection. Marat's popularity among Parisians is attested to by the fact that he was elected to represent them as a deputy to the National Convention. Marat was assassinated in July 1793 by Charlotte Corday, a young woman who held the journalist responsible for the fall of the Girondins. Immediately upon his death, he became the object of a popular and patriotic cult.

Means to Ward off Danger and Remedy the Ills of the Fatherland

The fatherland has fallen prey all at once to the horrors of external war, the horrors of civil war, the disasters of poverty, and the fear of famine: it will not give way beneath the weight of these ills; its resources are boundless if we know how to use them. *Poor administration*

In the current state of things, the most pressing danger is that of seeing new departments follow the example of the departments of the Eure, Calvados, and Jura, in other words, seeing the enemies of liberty raise the standard of revolt against the Convention. Taking vigorous measures against the rebel chiefs, as the Convention did, enlightening all citizens with a good review of the causes of the latest insurrection in Paris, and presenting the new project of the Constitution to the entire Republic are the most efficacious means to prevent this calamity and to rally the children of the fatherland around its altars.

The most formidable dangers that threaten the fatherland come next from the civil war that has broken out in several departments. The only effective means to cut down all the counter-revolutionaries in revolt with a single blow is to recall the unfaithful troops sent against the rebels, after having arrested their leaders, to discharge suspect generals and to require all citizens in the eight or ten contiguous departments to arm themselves with pitchforks, scythes, pikes, guns, and sabres, to take provisions for eight days, to join the troops sent against the rebels, and to fall upon them all at once and crush them without mercy, as did the courageous sans-culottes of Cantal.

The goods of the principal rebels should be offered in recompense and divided among all those who joined this salutary expedition.

Once the internal rebellion has been smothered, the external war will be a mere game; the united powers, deprived of their support in the heart of the state, will themselves be the ones who demand peace.

While awaiting that, we must put ourselves in the position to repulse them vigorously.

Placing the department of war in able and certain hands, discharging generals who cannot be depended upon, curbing those who seek independence, and holding to a defensive system are indispensable measures.

Sad experience proved that, regardless of talents and the desire to do good, the ministry of war is too great a burden for a single man, especially now that the Republic has eleven standing armies and simple signatures take eight hours.

It was therefore necessary to consider dividing the ministry between several ministers, appointing each to supervise an army or form an administrative council. The second task differs from the first in name only because, to avoid hampering or intersecting one another, these ministers must organize their campaigns as would the members of an administrative council. Consequently, that is the only road to follow if we want the engine to function. The difficulty lies in finding enlightened, active, and honest subjects, now that despotism has corrupted all men of talent who wanted to sell themselves.

The reform of the generals will be easier, because nobles, their protégés, and their servants who were at the head of our armies are, in spite of what is said, the most ignorant of our general officers. ← aristocrats

At present, one of the most threatening dangers among the evils that afflict our fatherland, and one whose consequences would be irreparable, is the despair into which monopolists' rapaciousness and merchants' greed is pushing the people, who will soon find themselves unable to afford the exorbitant prices of essential goods if the Convention does not immediately take effective measures to bring prices down. "What did the Revolution bring us?" he will say, trembling, "better despotism with all its abuses."

To provoke the return of the Old Regime, some shrewd rascal need only show him the comparative prices of goods under despotism and under the Republic. Republic must rise above old Regime

Even these measures will not be sufficient to restore order and solidity to the Revolution if, renouncing at least these false maxims of unlimited freedom of opinion and the press, the villains who serve the counter-revolution with voices and pens have not been ruthlessly dealt with. If freedom of opinion must be unlimited, it is to serve the fatherland and not to do away with it. *free press to honor land* Everything that favors good should be legal, nothing that favors evil should be legal: the patriotic party must destroy the enemy faction or be destroyed. Therefore, no mercy for paid libelists who slander the Revolution, who defame the activities of constituted authorities faithful to the fatherland, who pervert public opinion! Let their presses be broken and let them be shut up in prison.

For the same reasons, let the post be inspected and do not permit any dangerous writings to circulate. *dangerous writings*

Until now, we have held disastrous principles in this regard and our police have been worthy of the Petites-Maisons. In what country of the world is a reckless person who disturbs the established order spared reprimand and punishment, and why should we not do the same to establish the reign of justice that despots do to destroy it?

During the four years that we have spoken of liberty, we have not yet had the slightest notion of it. Learn then, pitiless essayists, that liberty is not for idiots, nor for the violent, nor for the spiteful, but for good men who do not want to abuse it. One might as well demand liberty for thieves hiding out in the woods as for enemies of the fatherland standing at the tribune or sitting in robes. Only fools and traitors could deny these truths.

46. Jacques-René Hébert, *Le Père Duchesne*

Although Jacques-René Hébert was born to a modest bourgeois family and received a traditional education in Latin and classics, one of the distinctive features of his newspaper, *Le Père Duchesne*, was its reliance on what Hébert believed to be the rough-and-ready language of the sans-culottes. Hébert used this "popular" language to express radical opinions and to offer rather vague political solutions. (He believed, for example, that "good laws, unity, and peace" would bring an end to high prices and shortages.) After Marat's assassination, Hébert came to the fore as the journalist claiming to speak to and for the people. He was arrested and executed in March 1794.

Father Duchesne's great anger against the rich who want to starve the people by hoarding grain and goods. His good advice to the Convention, that it should raise an army of ten thousand sans-culottes in each department to force the big farmers to bring grain out of their granaries where it is getting moldy, and to bring sugar and soap into the sunlight from the hoarders hiding it underground, to sell it later for its weight in gold.

Bread, fuck, that's the word of the day; the sans-culottes don't want the riches of the gods of the earth; they don't give a damn about their palaces, their cooks, their carriages, their horses, their lackeys; happiness doesn't exist in all that crap but in work and virtue. The sans-culottes don't know and don't want anything else; but the sans-culottes need bread. The earth was made for all living beings, and from the ant to the proud insect who calls himself man, each must take his subsistence from this common mother. I know that the big always want to eat the little: wolves devour sheep, the eagle tears at the entrails of the timid turtledove; man, for his part, destroys everything, devastates everything, eats everything within reach. There is no animal on two feet who has not eaten thousands of other animals in his life. Lions, which we consider to be ferocious beasts, tigers, which we can't speak of without trembling, are a thousand times less cruel and less ravenous than are we; these monsters, so savage and so bloodthirsty, at least respect their fellow creatures, and they don't eat one another; but men have no crueler enemies than themselves; they betray one another, they insult one another, they devour one another, they create all kinds of ways to hurt and destroy one another; nonetheless, they boast of being nature's masterwork and the image of the divinity. Oh fuck, what blasphemy! It's absolutely clear that the world would no longer exist if its author were as wicked and cruel as man.

French none

Source: *Le Père Duchesne*, no. 273 (n.d.), in Jacques-René Hébert, *Le Père Duchesne, 1790–1794* (Paris: EDHIS, 1969). Translated by Laura Mason.

Where does your ill humor come from, old fool? What evil befell you, happy stove merchant? You, who usually laughs at the stupidity of others and who is never so funny as when you want to get angry, what's bugging you today? What did you step in? Do you think you're better than your fellows, you who speak with such contempt? I don't scorn them, dammit, I pity them. What else, when I see Europe bloodied and in flames; when I hear the cannon roar from North to South; when I see cities ablaze, the countryside ravaged, the earth covered with bodies, don't I have a reason to be distressed; when I seek the cause of all this chaos and I think that a half dozen imbeciles called kings or emperors brought about all these ills, I change my name, I break my pipe, I pull the hair from my moustache, I beat everything around me and, in my black humor, I don't even spare my poor Jacqueline. I argue with her over nothing, I look for quarrels on the head of a pin: in a word, I'm the most sullen guy in the Republic.

What gets me even more heated up, dammit, is to see the French at cats and dogs and tearing out each other's eyes, instead of standing hand-to-hand to chase away the villains who are making war against them. The rich think ~rich people~ only of their interests; they are the Republic's greatest enemy; they despise the Revolution because it has established liberty and equality; they want, for better or worse, to take the place of the great men, to make laws for us and to oppress the sans-culottes; they heap up coin upon coin; their basements are filled with our banknotes that they tucked away; each day they build their fortunes on public ruin; they hoard all the foodstuffs; they glory in giving us a bad time, and in reducing us to the most horrible poverty if we don't restore the monarchy. The sons-of-bitches hold all goods in their hands, keeping them out of circulation, and they don't bring any grain out of their storehouses until it is rotten; even then they won't let us have it at any price less than its weight in gold. ~blames Bread Prices on nobles~

Fuck, we've got to finish this off. A mass levy has been proposed to the sans-culottes; that's well done; but it's not against the Prussians, Austrians, or Spanish that they should march. We have seven hundred thousand good rascals who are armed, who would know how to rout the worthless slaves fighting for the tyrants and make them eat our dust. Our armies need only be delivered from the riff-raff of the Old Regime, from all the aristocratic whippersnappers who poisoned them; commanded, as I have never stopped demanding, by good old veterans, I guarantee their success. We have domestic enemies a thousand times more formidable, and we will never rest as long as they exist. So then, dammit, since they want to have all the republicans march at once, it should only be against the traitors, conspirators, monopolists who disturb and undermine us from within. War to the death against all rogues. It won't be long if we are led well. Let regiments of ten thousand sans-culottes be formed in each department. It would not be extremely expensive to arm and equip them. Their duties would not be difficult. First, have them make a few promenades through the countryside to take account of the harvests of the big farmers; after having left a year's provisions in each canton, let the remainder of the harvest be paid for by the public treasury and transported to a common storehouse in each department. Dammit, that's how the armies and the big towns will find their sustenance, and when the year is good and the harvest can feed all the inhabitants of the Republic for three years, there will be a reserve in case of shortage.

After this campaign, which will restore order and calm all anxiety, our patriots will make similar visits to the monopolists of Marseilles, Lyons, Bordeaux, Nantes, Rouen. Their shops will be emptied out, the sugar and soap mildewing in the basements of these bloody bastards who hoarded it up will be brought out into the air. They will be forced to sell it so the abundance of products will bring prices down, and things will work out, dammit.

Oh yeah, the rich only oppress us because we want it. Fuck yes, when we decide to give the smallest sign of life, all those sharks of bankers, sharks of merchants will have to give up. They monopolized our means of support, let's monopolize the muscle to force them to give it back, and they must give way to force and, above all, to the law. The merchant must live from his labor, nothing is more just; but he should not grow fat on the blood of unfortunates. Existence is the first property; and everyone must eat, no matter what the price. Hunger brings the wolf out of the woods. Shudder then, bastard bloodsuckers of the people, you wanted to reduce us to despair. You flattered yourselves that the sans-culottes would fall at your feet to beg you for a miserable scrap of bread, you lied to yourselves. The same muscle that pickled the throne of the jackass Capet will fall on you. You won't screw around with the Convention's decrees anymore, you won't insult public poverty anymore. The people, your master, won't lie down much longer. You have reduced them to despair; they will strike back; tremble, dammit.

47. Petition from the Revolutionary Republican Women to the National Convention on the Leadership of the Armies and the Law of Suspects (AUGUST 1793)

Although Parisiennes had earlier tried to create revolutionary women's groups, it was only with the founding of the Society for Revolutionary Republican Women in early 1793 that a political club exclusively for women came into existence.

Source: Women in Revolutionary Paris. Selected documents translated with notes and commentary by Darline Gay Levy, Harriet Branson Applewhite, and Mary Durham Johnson (Urbana: University of Illinois Press, 1979), pp. 172–174. Copyright 1979 by the Board of Trustees of the University of Illinois. Used with permission of the University of Illinois Press.

During its brief tenure, from February to October 1793, the society responded to the current of events and made demands that soon placed it to the political left of the Jacobins and the Convention. Although the women sided with the Jacobins in their struggle against the Girondins during the spring of 1793, they later accused the new leadership of the Convention (the Mountain) of excessive moderation. As the following selection makes clear, the goals of the women in the society were similar to those of Parisian sans-culottes.

Legislators:

Justly indignant at the numerous lies coming from the Ministry, notably from the Ministry of the Interior, whose minister got away with abandoning his post by resigning from it, we come to demand that you execute the constitutional laws; we were not the first to accept this Constitution just to have anarchy and the reign of intriguers continue without end. The calculated war has lasted long enough; it is time at last that the children of liberty be sacrificed for their Fatherland and not to the ambition and pride of a pile of scoundrels who lead our armies. Show, by dismissing all nobles, that their defenders are not among you; above all, hasten to prove to all of France that the envoys of a great people have not been made to come at great expense from all corners of the Republic simply to enjoy a pathetic scene at the Champ de Mars. Show us that this Constitution, which we believed we should accept, exists and should make for our happiness; for it is not sufficient to tell people that their happiness is in the offing—they must experience its effects, and the experience of four years of misfortune has taught people to distrust the beautiful promises that are ceaselessly being made. People are indignant that men gorged on their gold and fattened on the purest of their blood preach sobriety and patience to them.

Believe us, Legislators, four years of misfortunes have taught us enough to know how to discern ambition even under the mask of patriotism; we no longer believe in the virtue of these men who are reduced to praising themselves; finally, more than words are necessary if we are to believe that ambition does not rule your committees; organize the government according to the Constitution. In vain are we told that France will be lost by this measure; she could not be lost if responsibility were no longer an empty word, or if the lying minister knew for certain that he would carry his head to the scaffold. Finally, we see only the loss of intriguers in a country where the laws are strictly observed. Do you want us to believe that the enemies of the Fatherland have no obliging defenders in your midst? Ruin all the nobles without exception; if there are any of good faith among them, they will give proof of it by voluntarily sacrificing themselves to the good fortune of their Fatherland; do not fear to disorganize the army; the more talent a general has,

nobles do not have to lead armies

the worse his intentions, and the more urgent it is to replace him; do not do injustice to patriots by believing there are no men among them worthy of commanding our armies; take some of these brave soldiers whose talent and merit have been sacrificed to the ambition and pride of the formerly privileged caste.

If under the rule of despotism crime obtains preference, virtues should have it under the rule of liberty. You have passed a decree under which all suspects are to be arrested, but I ask you—isn't this law ridiculous when it is the suspects themselves who are to execute it? Oh, Legislators, thus are the people toyed with; see this equality which was to have been the foundation of their happiness; there is the recompense for the incalculable troubles they have so patiently suffered. No, it will not be said that the people, reduced to despair, were obliged to do justice themselves; you are going to give it to them by ruining all guilty administrators and by creating extraordinary tribunals in sufficient number so that patriots will say, as they leave for the front: "We are calm about the fate of our wives and children; we have seen all internal conspirators perish under the sword of the law." Decree these great measures and the general mobilization—you will have saved the Fatherland.

radical

48. Toussaint L'Ouverture

Pierre Dominique Toussaint L'Ouverture (1746–1803) was a literate house slave in Saint Domingue (see the map on page 121). Inspired by events in France, Toussaint organized widespread discontent among Saint Domingue's four hundred thousand slaves into the only successful slave rebellion in history. Although the Convention abolished slavery in 1794, bloody conflicts on the island persisted, in large part because of military intervention by the Spanish and the British. Toussaint was arrested by Napoleon in 1802; he died in France in solitary confinement without seeing his country achieve independence, which it did in 1804, when it became Haiti. In the first two selections, Toussaint rallies his followers to the cause of liberty. In the third, he explains why he accepted arms from the Spanish.

Source: George F. Tyson, Jr., ed. and trans., *Toussaint L'Ouverture* (Englewood Cliffs, N.J.: Prentice-Hall, 1973), pp. 29–30. Copyright © 1973 by Prentice-Hall, Inc. Reprinted with permission of Simon & Schuster.

A. Proclamation to the Slaves of Saint Domingue
(AUGUST 25, 1793)

Having been the first to champion your cause, it is my duty to continue to labor for it. I cannot permit another to rob me of the initiative. Since I have begun, I will know how to conclude. Join me and you will enjoy the rights of freemen sooner than any other way. Neither whites nor mulattoes have formulated my plans; it is to the Supreme Being alone that I owe my inspiration. We have begun, we have carried on, we will know how to reach the goal.

B. Proclamation of August 29, 1793

Brothers and Friends:

I am Toussaint L'Ouverture. My name is perhaps known to you. I have undertaken to avenge you. I want liberty and equality to reign throughout Saint Domingue. I am working towards that end. Come and join me, brothers, and combat by our side for the same cause.

C. Letter to General Laveaux (MAY 18, 1794)

It is true, General, that I had been deceived by the enemies of the Republic; but what man can pride himself on avoiding all the traps of wickedness? In truth, I fell into their snares, but not without knowing the reason. You must recall the advances I had made to you before the disasters at Le Cap, in which I stated that my only goal was to unite us in the struggle against the enemies of France.

Unhappily for everyone, the means of reconciliation that I proposed—the recognition of the liberty of the blacks and a general amnesty—were rejected. My heart bled, and I shed tears over the unfortunate fate of my country, perceiving the misfortunes that must follow. I wasn't mistaken: fatal experience proved the reality of my predictions. Meanwhile, the Spanish offered their protection to me and to all those who would fight with me for the cause of their kings, and having always fought in order to have liberty I accepted their offers, seeing myself abandoned by my brothers the French. But a later experience opened my eyes to these perfidious protectors, and having understood their villainous deceit, I saw clearly that they intended to make us slaughter one another in order to diminish our numbers so as to overwhelm the survivors and reenslave them. No, they will never attain their infamous objective, and we will avenge ourselves in our turn upon these contemptible beings. Therefore, let us unite forever and, forgetting the past, occupy ourselves hereafter only with exterminating our enemies and avenging ourselves, in particular, on our perfidious neighbors.

49. Anonymous, "Freedom of the Negroes" (1794)

This song dates from the winter of 1794, when news arrived in Saint Domingue that the National Convention had finally abolished slavery.

Did you know republicans
What was the fate of the negro?
That a wise decree reintegrated him
Among the rank of humans;
He was a slave at birth,
Punished by death for a mere gesture . . .
Even his child was sold.
Sugar was stained with his blood,
Kindly spare me all the rest . . . (bis)

Real executioners, debased by gold,
Promising to loosen his chains
Made inhuman attempts
To tighten them even more.
But against their diabolical plots
Nature protests
And two peoples, breaking their shackles
Despite the distance of the seas
End up agreeing about all else. (bis)

When they thought it best
To be born on your heated soil
Sugar cane and coffee
Chose neither master nor manager.
This mine is in your field,
And today nobody challenges it.
The harder you toil to win it
Surely the fairer it is
That the net yield remains with you. (bis)

Americans, equality
Proclaims you today our brothers.
You had the same inherited
Rights to freedom.
You are black, but common sense
Thrusts aside a fatal prejudice . . .

Source: Jean Copans, *The French Revolution and the Black People of and from Africa* (Nairobi: Maendelo House, 1989), p. 2. Reprinted with permission of the author.

Would you be less interesting
In the eyes of white republicans?
Color goes, and man remains! (bis)

50. Creole of Saint Domingue, *My Odyssey: Experiences of a Young Refugee from Two Revolutions* (1793)

Althéa de Puech Parham, a niece of the author six generations removed, published these private letters in 1959. Known only as "Creole of Saint Domingue," the author was a young man when he wrote them. Like many sons of the plantation aristocracy in the Caribbean, he was sent to Paris to be educated, only to return to his homeland of Saint Domingue when the Revolution began. Having witnessed the upheavals there, he fled, as did some twenty-five thousand other exiles. He wrote this letter to a college friend in May 1793. Here he places the blame for the Revolution squarely on the shoulders of philosophes in general and abolitionists in particular.

Now I will speak to you of the government of the Negroes before the insurrection. I will tell you of the conditions among these men who have done us so much harm, of these unchained tigers whose roots in barbarism cause Nature to shudder.

You will see how much one must beware of the lying declamations of those egoistic pedants who, from the depths of their libraries, judge everything by hearsay, and make a pretense of feeling compassion for some unfortunates whom they have never seen or known, so they may claim the right to lodge complaint against those people whom they do see daily. If you know any of these gentlemen, remember to tell them that I do not believe as they do; theirs is an irremediable crime, and they do not overwhelm me with all the sonorous and high-sounding words of four or five syllables which they can find in the dictionary.

Comfortably dressed in cottons from our isles,
Their houses furnished with our beautiful mahogany,
Treating their delicate tastes
With our coffee and chocolates,
With honey from our delicious roses;
Requesting each day from our happy clime,
Our dyes, our fruits, our drugs, our spices,

Source: Creole of Saint-Domingue, *My Odyssey: Experiences of a Young Refugee from Two Revolutions*, ed. Althéa de Puech Parham (Baton Rouge: Louisiana State Univ. Press, 1959), pp. 40–44.

And our most humble products.
"No slaves!" they say to us.
There should be none, as who of us is unaware?
But whilst an evil to which we are accustomed,
An evil that extends from princes to subjects,
From our ancestors to us, from West to East,
For an evil whose harm is fraught with blessings,
Their doubtful remedy is cruel in its results.
Is it not better, for the present,
To lament, but endure in peace?
"But no," they coldly cry in fury.
"The African must be free and the master die!"
Which they have done their best to bring about.
Well, compassionate friends of the African races,
Come here and look over our productive plains
Whose treasures, before, were carefully gathered
For commerce to disperse
To faraway shores.
What spectacle greets your eyes?
Bloody cadavers in frightful heaps;
Scattered ruins; sanctuaries burned;
And mortals once happy,
Whom today misery has overpowered.
Good God! And why all this horror
That suddenly arms an uncouth mob
With steel and the power to kill?
Why? For an imaginary benefit
Of which they prait [sic], for promises of bliss,
When their design is only to mislead the populace;
For the empty project, so often aborted,
Of establishing upon the earth
A Perfect Society, a Heaven
Which no people are yet capable
Of enduring or possessing.
Imbeciles! For a word you slaughter
Your brothers, your compatriots,
And even those friends, the foreign helots
Whom you feign to protect!

Those unfortunates! What were the conditions in their own barbaric countries from which they came? The picture made by all the voyagers is frightful. Transported to us, they became happier than the peasants of any nation; and not one regretted leaving his savage country. In self-concern alone, if not in humanity, was it not sufficient incentive for the colonist to take good care of his workers who cost him much, that they rendered so much profit when they were healthy, and that they became so expensive when they were ill.

Those whippings of which one hears were always applied by one of their own comrades who had the talent of making more noise than pain, and only for faults which were punished much more severely elsewhere. This method of chastisement was adopted because the African, barely civilized, is considered a child and must be treated as such. He came from under the whip less marked, less humiliated, and less punished than our comrade D. ever was that certain day when, despite his eighteen years, our professor had him so nicely thrown out by the school porter. It is also that the skin of D., like that of any other European, is made of a different piece of cloth from that of which it pleased Nature to fabricate the hindquarters of the Africans, and it is this fact that these Philosophers have not realized.

"But these poor Negroes," they say, "work from morn till night." For my own part, I have never known a country where those that haven't a farthing to their names are not obliged to work from morn till night, and often from night to morn. The majority of human beings are unfortunately compelled to earn a living by the sweat of their brows.

Fortunate, then, are those whom Fate has thrown
Among the ranks of mortals condemned to work;
And regulated by the grace of a wise economy,
To work according to their strength and capacity;
Who, three times a day, in a comfortable place
Are reunited to their families around an abundant table;
Who, when the sun surrenders to the quiet night,
These tired ones can, until the morrow,
Be free from care and have their needed rest,
Which love alone has the right to disturb;
Who, when perchance misfortune does arrive,
Do not die without help upon a bed of misery,
But have the kind care of the healer's art
About the couch when suffering reigns;
And when age weighs upon their whitened heads
Reducing them from strength to weakness,
Who can, in the bosom of peace, await the moment
That Heaven has marked for their lives to end.

Such was the existence of the Negro in the Colony of Saint Domingue. The laws made for their safety were very severe. No doubt with us, as elsewhere, some individuals infringed the laws; but all the French are not villains because France produces types such as Partouchen, Mandrin, Desrus, etc.; so, like these great criminals, the bad colonists were not always punished, the reason being a simple one; which is that in these islands, as upon the continent or in America, riches unfortunately have often the craft to throw a golden blindfold over the eyes of Justice. Besides, it is seldom that a colonist of Saint Domingue can be shown culpable of these pretended crimes that are believed to be common among us, and when they were committed, it was always done by a European, a Philosopher upon arrival but a cruel Master two months later! The Creole makes a point of honor of being gentle and indulgent.

But if our slaves were so well treated, why did they revolt? One must ask those composers of phrases who have inundated our country with their incendiary writings; those stupid innovators who brought turmoil to France and killed their king; those Whites of Europe who were found at the head of the insurgents; those idiots who thought that the destruction of commerce would usher in a counter-revolution and who needed an army to sustain their new rights. One must take into account the jealousy, the Machiavellism of a rival nation, etc. One must find the reason, at last, in the character of all the ignorant populace, principally in the Negroes, like machines which can easier be made to start than to stop! These are the causes which started, accelerated, and prolonged the revolt, and destroyed the most beautiful country upon the earth.

51. Ronchet, "Address from the Provisional Municipality to the National Convention, in the Name of Liberty, Equality, and the One and Indivisible Republic" (AUGUST 2, 1793)

Federalism was one of the first major challenges to the unity of the new Republic: it emerged to counter the Jacobin domination of the central government and proposed a decentralized federal system of administration that would allow more autonomy to provincial governments. The hotbed of the Federalist revolt, Lyons, incurred the wrath of the Convention in the summer of 1793, when it rebelled against its Jacobin municipality. Lyonnais resistance was short-lived, however, because neither Lyons nor any other Federalist city was able to raise adequate defenses against the Convention. When Lyons was defeated in October, the Convention ordered that its name be changed to "Liberated City" and that a plaque be erected which proclaimed: "Lyons made war on Liberty; Lyons no longer exists."

Source: "Adresse de la municipalité provisoire à la convention nationale" (Lyons: Aimé Vatar-Delaroche, 1793). Bibliothèque de la ville de Lyons. Translated by Tracey Rizzo.

Citizen Representatives!

Attending to the happiness of twenty-four million Frenchmen, will you refuse to hear the voice of a great city that will speak the language of truth and reason to you through the mouthpiece of its provisional magistrates? What! Calumny, the most atrocious lies, and the discourse of several scoundrels, already proscribed by opinion and soon to be extinguished by the law, have the sole privilege of being the only ones believed today, while we who are animated and electrified by a holy and sincere love of the laws, of order, of equality, of liberty, are we to be ignored unceasingly?

Representatives! we are men, we are Frenchmen; from this double title we have the right to demand that you hear us, and we dare to hope you will listen.

What have we done? Of what are we accused?

To begin with, we have been insurgent since May 29, but it is against anarchy and oppression that we have risen up en masse. Arbitrary imprisonment, outrageous harassment, insulting threats, perverse tribunals, dishonest magistrates, attacks on liberty, assassinations, massacres, capricious taxes: here you have the grievances which have preoccupied the political machinery of Lyons for a long time, and particularly the municipal regime.

A monstrous association of immoral, unprincipled, and shameless men coolly calculate the renewal, within our walls, of the bloody and abominable scenes that dishonored Paris in the too awful September days. Citizens illegally organized a bloody tribunal; monsters tranquilly drew up the list of the proscribed, preached agrarian law, and raised an army loyal only to them: here are our enemies against whom we defend our lives and our property. What are our crimes thus far? On what basis are founded the reproaches heaped upon us thus far? Unjust attack! What man would not defend himself?

But in using a legitimate defense, will the citizens of Lyons give themselves over to an excess of vengeance and abuse of their victory?

No! Content to have triumphed, they have respected their assassins, though keeping their swords at the ready. To attest to this, they call upon public knowledge, on the word of their own enemies who yet live, even on the testimony of representatives Gauthier and Nioche. There is more: excepting those whom public opinion has designated as the most guilty, all others who served the party and the projects of the suspended municipality are free, and indulgence has already shaded their crimes with profound forgetfulness. Would they have done as much? They who have inhumanely massacred a portion of the prisoners they have taken from us, against the policy of military men; they who have announced the massacre of sixteen thousand proprietary citizens; they who commanded the pillage of the national armory several days before, making a pretext of conscripting foreign forces, only to make them serve their abominable designs?

But we continue. The department suspended the municipality: Nioche and Gauthier adopted this measure: the presidents and secretaries of the sections were called to provisionally replace its functions.

The consent of the city confirms this choice. Liberty, equality, and the one and indivisible Republic is the hope of their hearts as it is the sole basis for their administration. Demand to see their registers, order the communication of their deliberations, examine all their decrees, and you will have complete proof of the truth of what we say.

Meanwhile, the representatives of the army of the Alps wrote, beginning the negotiations: "ten thousand guns, the liberty of prisoners, the extradition of all objects designated for the armies of the frontier." These were their demands. The last was too much, since nothing had been decreed about that which was destined for the army. If the supplies have not arrived there, Crancé, Albitte, and Gauthier should respond, as they gave the order to Carteau to return everything to Valence and Saint-Esprit, despite the disputations of the Pyrenees department and the repeated requisitions of Rouyer, Brunel, d'Esper, and Prosjean.

As for the ten thousand guns, and the release of the prisoners, will our personal safety leave us only one day to discuss such propositions? We regard these as nonavenues as well.

Ignorant of all principles and in violation of every law, our enemies commit a crime in identifying us as rebels and insurgents, and in publishing that "Lyons is the beginning of a new Vendée, it has harbored the white cockade, it has proclaimed Louis XVII the king, it rouses forces against the Convention, it has ignored decrees and authority, it has chopped down the liberty tree, and it has demanded the reestablishment of the Old Regime."

So many words, so many lies. The Lyonnais do not want a king. The Lyonnais have no other cockade than the tricolor. The Lyonnais rally and have always rallied to the Convention. Far from imitating the Vendée rebels, the Lyonnais abhor the Old Regime, and take force and measures only against anarchy, and to defend their property and their lives, not to march against Paris and the Convention. Finally, the liberty tree stands tall; it is the object of our veneration, the testament to our faith, the sign of our cult, of our holy idolatry. One hundred and fifty thousand souls attest to these facts, and the affirmation of one hundred and fifty thousand souls should certainly carry more weight than the enemy's dagger, which seeks only to oppress us.

If for an instant the integrity of the national representation has been discussed, the motives and necessity of the disastrous events of May 31, June 1, and June 2 [the insurrection against and purge of the Girondins in Paris] should be considered.

Calculate with impartiality the impressions [these events] produced, and judge then, with as much honesty as good faith, if it were probable that free men who came two days before to crush anarchy, had not seriously occupied themselves with it. However, what has been the result of [our] meditations? Unanimous acceptance of the constitutional act, general rallying behind the Convention as the center of unity, and, at the same time, a measure of vigorous resistance to the execution of the decrees against the city of Lyons that have astonished religion and justice.

What more can we, what more should we do, citizen representatives? Natural law and social and political laws are the compass and course we have followed.

And furthermore, we stand accused, lies are heaped upon lies, calumny upon calumny. To all [the lies] already denounced is added that our so-called resistance to oppression is only a revolt in combination with Marseilles, Bordeaux, with Pitt, Dumouriez, and Cobourg, with all the enemies of the Republic! Carrying calumny to delirium, they allege that we have received, by route of Geneva, four million in gold to aid us in our liberticidal projects; that we have written to all the administrations, to all the generals, to all the armies in order to lead them into what they call our conspiracy; that we have sent two thousand passports to émigrés in Switzerland so that they can return to France; finally, that we share intelligence with the Kings of Sardinia and Spain, and with Condé, to deliver the city of Lyons to them where they will place the throne of the counter-revolution.

The honest man, the true patriot, the sincere republican, how can he respond to such absurdities? They can provoke nothing more than a scornful smile; they do not have even the feeble power to render our hearts indignant. What! the people of the Rhône and the Loire, the city of Lyons, receive four million in gold from Geneva to resist oppression! But we do not have need of it; our own resources more than suffice to spare us the debasement of a request or a less than honorable acceptance.

Spain, the Piedmont, the traitor Condé connive with us! But our brothers in arms combat these powers, and we will all march against them if we must.

Passports to the émigrés! But every day we chase them from our territory, according to the law; every day we seek them out, and unceasingly provoke the surveillance of good citizens, and the denunciations of good patriots against them.

Invitations to armies, to generals, to administrations to enter into revolt! But all our writings, all our addresses, all our letters are printed and public; one can read them, and one will see our principles and our conduct.

Pitt, Dumouriez, Cobourg, Bordeaux, Marseilles are in intelligence with us! The first three are enemies of the Republic; they are consequently those of the Lyonnais. As for Marseilles and Bordeaux, they have received no support or aid from us, but we owe it to truth to point out that those cities want liberty, equality, and the one and indivisible Republic as much as we do, and that we fraternize with these two great cities on these terms.

Thus, citizen representatives, the truth; this is what we oppose to the calumny disseminated, placarded, and peddled in every corner of the Republic against the department of the Rhône and the Loire and particularly against the city of Lyons.

Could we have enlightened your religion and encouraged you to most promptly recall the decrees you hurled against this city! No sentiment of weakness counsels us in demanding this act of justice of you. No, citizen representatives, pusillanimity cannot be found in the hearts of generals, who fighting under the aegis of the law, make you remember that the dearest interests can in several days, in several hours, be confided to their courage, their energy.

Youth, numerous, disciplined, and full of ardor; experienced men, if instructed, know to calculate the chance of danger and the ease of victory in advance, the immense resources of every type, the justice of our cause, natural law, the promulgation of the rights of man, there you have all that militates in our favor. Join to these the probability that our neighbors do not want to fight us, that French do not want to murder French, and see then if, in asking you to retract the decrees against Lyons, we let ourselves be influenced by fear and cowardice.

It is humanity, nature, and fraternity alone which make their preponderant and sacred voices heard here; it is their names that we speak, citizen representatives. It is in their names that we entreat you to refrain from substituting the result of some particular passions for measures that prudence, wisdom, and reflection alone should counsel.

Upon completion of your political career, do you want to return to the general class of simple citizens covered in the blood of the French departments you roused against the French citizens of Lyons? How will you account for this spectacle? Why do you make of yourselves an eternal model of remorse, sadness, anxiety?

Citizens! France, Europe, posterity watches; you will be called to their tribunals one day. What a terrible judgment for the representatives of twenty-four million souls! What reproaches if, charged with the most important of missions, you do not elevate yourselves above particular interests, above the pettiness of individual passions, to soar on the wings of philosophy, magnanimity, humanity, of every moral and political virtue, toward the goal that the French nation has indicated to you, its splendor, its glory, its perfect happiness!

Cheers and fraternity.

52. Memoirs Concerning the Vendée War

The Vendée war of 1793–1796 was the longest and bloodiest conflict in the Revolution, resulting in some two hundred thousand casualties. Rebels in this region of France initially reacted against mass conscription ordered by the Convention in March, but the war quickly became a rallying point for counter-revolutionaries who defended king and priests. The following two selections offer different perspectives on the conflict. The first is written by the sister-in-law of a leading gen-

Source: Claude Petitfrère, ed., *La Vendée et les Vendéens* (Paris: Gallimard/Julliard, 1981), pp. 22–26. Translated by Tracey Rizzo.

eral on the side of the Vendeans. The second, from the perspective of government forces, describes the guerrilla tactics of the Vendeans.

A. Memoir of Madame de Sapinaud (1824)

The Vendée war began on March 5, 1793. Peasants revolted on the side of la Buffelière; they were then dispersed in neighboring parishes, and came upon M. Sapinaud de Bois-Huguet, better known under the name of la Verrie. "We take you," they told him, "for our general and you will march at the head of us." Sapinaud tried to make them envision the misfortunes they would attract to themselves and to the Vendée. "Friends," he told them, "it is like hurling a clay pot against an iron cauldron. What will we do? One lone department against twenty-two! We will be crushed. It is not for myself that I speak; I have been horrified by life since I witnessed all the crimes perpetrated by barbarians against our forsaken country, and I would prefer to perish leading you, in combat for my God and my king, than to be led to a prison like all my contemporaries. Believe me, return to your homes, and do not destroy yourselves uselessly." These brave peasants, far from surrendering to his rationale, argued that they could never submit themselves to a government which had cast out their priests, and imprisoned their king. "We have been deceived," they said. "Why send us these constitutional priests? These are not the priests who have attended our fathers on their deathbeds, and we do not want them to baptize our infants." My brother-in-law did not know what course to take; he hesitated to deliver these good peasants and expose himself to a death which seemed certain to him. Finally, seeing their obstinacy, he ended up giving in, taking charge of them, and departing that same day for Les Herbiers. The peasants of Gaubretière joined them. Passing the château of Sourdy, they forced Sapinaud de La Rairie to march under the command of his uncle.

B. Memoir of General Turreau (1795)

Favored by all the accidents of nature, the brigands have a particular tactic which they know how to apply perfectly to their position and to local circumstances. Assured of the superiority which their manner of attacking gives them, they never let themselves be anticipated: they do battle only when and where they want. Their skill in the use of firearms is that of no known people; neither warrior nor tactician fires more gunpowder than the hunter of Loroux and the poacher of the bocage. Their attack is a terrible eruption, sudden, nearly always unexpected, because it is very difficult in the Vendée to recognize much, to be aware of much, and consequently to be guaranteed a surprise. Their battle formation is in the form of a crescent, and their arrow-shaped flanks are composed of their best sharpshooters, of soldiers who do not fire a shot without aiming first, and who hardly ever miss a target given a reasonable distance. You are crushed before even realizing you are under a mass of fire, such that our ordnance does not achieve an effect which can be compared to it. They do not wait for a command to fire; they do not know the [organized] fire of battalion, of file, or of platoon; and yet that which they make you suffer is as copious, as unflagging, and above all much more fatal than ours. If you resist their violent attack, it is rare that the rebels dispute your victory, but you get little fruit from it because they retreat so rapidly that it is very difficult to reach them, especially since the terrain hardly ever permits the use of cavalry. They disperse themselves; they escape from you across fields, woods, bush, knowing all the trails, byways, gorges, knowing all the obstacles which oppose their flight and the means to avoid them. If you are obliged to cede to their attack, you have as much difficulty operating your own retreat as they have the facility to flee you when they are defeated. As conquerors, they encircle you, cut you to bits; they pursue you with a fury, a relentlessness, an inconceivable velocity. They rush in the attack—in victory as in defeat; but they do not fire any less often for that. They load their arms while marching, even while running, and this constant state of mobility causes their fusillade to lose nothing of its vivacity and precision.

CHAPTER 9

LEGISLATING THE TERROR

53. Constitution of the Year I (JUNE 24, 1793)

Because of the emergency situation of 1793–1794, this constitution was never put into practice. However, it is worthy of study because it reveals the ideals of the men of the National Convention and because its differences from the Constitution of 1789 suggest how much changed during the first four years of the Revolution. This declaration addresses more social issues; note especially the right to be free from servitude (18), the right to welfare (21) and to education (22). It also includes more belligerent clauses (27 and 35) protecting the right to insurrection.

Declaration of Rights of Man and Citizen

1. The aim of society is the common welfare. Government is instituted to guarantee to man the enjoyment of his natural and imprescriptible rights.
2. These rights are equality, liberty, security, and property.
3. All men are equal by nature and before the law.
4. Law is the free and solemn expression of the general will; it is the same for all, whether it protects or punishes; it can command only what is just and useful to society; it can forbid only what is injurious to it.

Source: Frank Maloy Anderson, ed., *The Constitution and Other Select Documents Illustrative of the History of France, 1789–1907* (New York: Russell and Russell, 1908; reprinted 1967), pp. 171–174.

5. All citizens are equally eligible to public employments. Free peoples know no other grounds for preference in their elections than virtue and talent.

6. Liberty is the power that belongs to man to do whatever is not injurious to the rights of others; it has nature for its principle, justice for its rule, law for its defense; its moral limit is this maxim: Do not do to another that which you do not wish should be done to you.

7. The right to express one's thoughts and opinions by means of the press, or in any other manner, the right to assemble peaceably, the free pursuit of religion, cannot be forbidden. The necessity of enunciating these rights supposes either the presence or the fresh recollection of despotism.

8. Security consists in the protection afforded by society to each of its members for the preservation of his person, his rights, and his property.

9. The law ought to protect public and personal liberty against the oppression of those who govern.

10. No one ought to be accused, arrested, or detained, except in cases determined by law and according to the forms it has prescribed. Any citizen summoned or seized by the authority of the law, ought to obey immediately; he makes himself guilty by resistance.

11. Any act done against man outside of the cases and without the forms that the law determines is arbitrary and tyrannical; the one against whom it may be intended to be executed by violence has the right to repel it by force.

12. Those who may incite, expedite, subscribe to, execute or cause to be executed arbitrary legal instruments are guilty and ought to be punished.

13. Every man being presumed innocent until he has been pronounced guilty, if it is thought indispensable to arrest him, all severity that may not be necessary to secure his person ought to be strictly repressed by law.

14. No one ought to be tried or punished except after having been heard or legally summoned, and except in virtue of a law promulgated prior to the offense. The law which would punish offenses before it existed would be a tyranny: the retroactive effect given to the law would be a crime.

15. The law ought to impose only penalties that are strictly and obviously necessary: the punishments ought to be proportionate to the offense and useful to society.

16. The right of property is that which belongs to every citizen to enjoy, and to dispose at his pleasure of his goods, income, and of the fruits of his labor and skill.

17. No kind of labor, tillage, or commerce can be forbidden to the skill of the citizens.

18. Every man can contract his services and his time, but he cannot sell himself nor be sold: his person is not an alienable property. The law knows of no such thing as the status of servant; there can exist only a contract for

This drawing shows an allegorical representation of Liberty, one of many similar illustrations produced during the Revolution. *(Musée de la Révolution Française, Vizille. Cliché: P. Fillioley)*

services and compensation between the man who works and the one who employs him.

19. No one can be deprived of the least proportion of his property without his consent, unless a legally established public necessity requires it, and upon condition of a just and prior compensation.

20. No tax can be imposed except for the general advantage. All citizens have the right to participate in the establishment of taxes, to watch over the employment of them, and to cause account of them to be given.

21. Public relief is a sacred debt. Society owes maintenance to unfortunate citizens, either in procuring work for them or in providing the means of existence for those who are unable to labor.

22. Education is needed by all. Society ought to favor with all its power the advancement of public reason and to put education at the door of every citizen.

23. The social guarantee consists in the action of all to secure to each the enjoyment and maintenance of his rights; this guarantee rests upon the national sovereignty.

24. It cannot exist if the limits of public functions are not clearly determined by law and if the responsibility of all the functionaries is not secured.

25. The sovereignty resides in the people; it is one and indivisible, imprescriptible, and inalienable.

26. No portion of the people can exercise the power of the entire people; but each section of the sovereign, in assembly, ought to enjoy the right to express its will with entire freedom.

27. Let any person who may usurp the sovereignty be instantly put to death by free men.

28. A people has always the right to review, to reform, and to alter its constitution. One generation cannot subject to its law the future generations.

29. Each citizen has an equal right to participate in the formation of the law and in the selection of his mandatories or agents.

30. Public functions are necessarily temporary; they cannot be considered as distinctions or rewards, but as duties.

31. The offenses of the representatives of the people and of its agents ought never to go unpunished. No one has the right to claim for himself more inviolability than other citizens.

32. The right to present petitions to the depositories of the public authority cannot in any case be forbidden, suspended, nor limited.

33. Resistance to oppression is the consequence of the other rights of man.

34. There is oppression against the social body when a single one of its members is oppressed: there is oppression against each member when the social body is oppressed.

35. When the government violates the rights of the people, insurrection is for the people and for each portion of the people the most sacred of rights and the most indispensable of duties.

Constitutional Act of the Republic

1. The French republic is one and indivisible. . . .

Of the Conditions of Citizenship

4. Every man born and living in France fully twenty-one years of age;

    Every foreigner fully twenty-one years of age, who, domiciled in France for one year, lives there by his own labor, or acquires property, or marries a French woman, or adopts a child, or supports an aged man;

    Finally, every foreigner who shall be thought by the legislative body to have deserved well of humanity, is admitted to the exercise of the rights of French citizenship.

5. The exercise of citizenship is lost: by naturalization in a foreign country; by the acceptance of employments or favors proceeding from a nonpopular government; by condemnation to ignominious or afflictive penalties until rehabilitation.

6. The exercise of the rights of citizenship is suspended: by the condition of accusation; by a judicial order for contempt of court until the order is abrogated.

54. Instituting the Terror (SEPTEMBER 5, 1793)

The Revolution reached its crisis during the summer of 1793 as France faced inflation, food shortages, civil war, and military defeat. Radical journalists and deputies called for more stringent measures against speculators and hoarders, and although the Convention declared a mass levy on August 23, sectional militants wanted a broader policy of national enlistment. It is against this background that Jacobins and members of the Paris Commune allied themselves with Parisians demonstrating for bread on September 4. On September 5, the demonstrators marched to the Convention and demanded that it adopt decrees to address popular concerns. While the days of September 4 and 5 appear to have been a sans-culottes' victory, they also mark the beginning of the movement's decline: Danton's proposal that sectional assemblies be restricted to two meetings per week and that the poor be paid for attendance would dilute the activism and militance that had been the source of sectional strength until that point.

Business of the National Convention (September 5, 1793)

The President announces that a large number of citizens of Paris ask to march through the hall and have their deputation present a petition to him.

Source: Archives parlementaires, vol. 73 (Paris, 1908), pp. 411–418. Translated by Laura Mason.

The deputation enters: the mayor and several municipal officers at its head. . . .

CHAUMETTE [the city prosecutor]: Legislators, the huge assembly of citizens gathered yesterday and today in front of and inside the city hall have only one wish and a deputation brings it to you; it is this: "Subsistence, and the force of the law to obtain it." Therefore, we are charged to request that you create the revolutionary army you already decreed and which was aborted by the intrigues and fears of the guilty. (*Unanimous applause, repeated several times*) That this army form its nucleus in Paris quite soon and that, in each department it traverses, the army be enlarged by all men who want a Republic, one and indivisible; that this army be followed by an incorruptible and formidable tribunal and by the fatal instrument that strikes down plots and ends their authors' days with a single blow; that the army be charged with forcing avarice and greed to give up the riches of the earth, inexhaustible nurse to all its children; that the army carry these words on its banners, which will be the motto for all time: "Peace to men of good will, war against agents of famine, protection of the weak; war against tyrants, justice, no oppression." Finally, let this army be so composed that it can leave sufficient forces in every town to repress the malevolent.

Legislators, you declared that France was revolutionary until its independence was assured; that decree must not be in vain. Hercules is ready; put the club in his strong hands, and soon the earth and liberty will be purged of all the criminals with which they are infested. The fatherland will breathe easy. The subsistence of the people will be guaranteed. . . .

BILLAUD-VARENNE [moves]: There will be a revolutionary army and the minister of war will forthwith be required to present the plan of its organization. . . .

(*Danton appears at the podium. The applause of the Assembly and of the citizenry accompanies him and prevents him from speaking for a few moments.*)

DANTON: I think, as do several members, especially Billaud-Varenne (*applause*), that it is necessary to know how to profit from the sublime vigor of the people who crowd around us. I know that when the people demonstrates its needs, when it offers to march against its enemies, we must take no measures other than those which it offers itself; because the national genius has dictated them. I believe it would be beneficial for the Committee [of Public Safety] to make its report, to plan and propose means of execution; but I also see no inconvenience in immediately decreeing a revolutionary army. (*Applause*) Let us broaden these measures, if need be.

You come to proclaim before all of France that she is still truly in revolution, in active revolution; well good! This revolution must be consummated; do not be afraid of activity that might provoke counter-revolutionaries in Paris. Doubtless, counter-revolutionaries would like to extinguish the flame of liberty in the hearth where it burns most brightly; but the great mass of true patriots, of sans-culottes who have struck down their enemies a hundred times over, still exists; they are ready to move forward: know how to lead them and they will astonish yet again and thwart all plots. A revolutionary army is not enough; be revolutionary yourselves. Remember that industrious men who live by the sweat of their brows cannot go into the sections; that intrigue can take hold of the sections only in the absence of true patriots. Therefore, decree that there will be great assemblies in the sections twice a week, that the man of the people who attends these political assemblies will have just remuneration for the time that they take away from his work. (*Applause*)

Moreover, we do well to announce to our enemies that we intend to be constantly and entirely on guard against them. You have decreed that thirty million will be put at the disposition of the minister of war for the manufacture of arms; decree that such manufacture will not cease until the nation has given a rifle to each citizen. Announce the firm resolution to have as many rifles and almost as many cannons as there are sans-culottes. (*Applause*) Announce that it is the Republic which places a rifle in the citizen's hand; that it says to him: "The fatherland entrusts you with this arm for its defense; you will bring it forth each month and whenever required to do so by the national authority." That a rifle is the most sacred thing among us; that a man sooner lose his life than his rifle. (*Applause*) Therefore, I ask that you decree at least one hundred million for the production of arms of all types, because if we had arms, we would all march. It is the need for arms that enchains us. The endangered fatherland will never want for citizens. (*Same applause*)

But there remains the punishment of the domestic enemies you hold, and of those you have yet to capture. The revolutionary tribunal must be divided into a large enough number of sections . . . so that each day an aristocrat, a villain pays for his crimes with his head. (*Applause*)

Therefore I ask:

1. That Billaud's motion be put to a vote;
2. That it also be decreed that the Paris sections hold extraordinary assemblies on Sundays and Thursdays, and that every citizen participating in these assemblies who wants to claim an indemnity will, according to his needs, receive one of forty sous per assembly;
3. That the Convention decree that it will place one hundred million at the disposition of the minister of war for the manufacture of arms, and particularly of rifles; that these extraordinary factories receive all necessary encouragements and additions, and that they do not cease work until France has given a rifle to each good citizen.

Finally, I ask that a report be given on the means to increase the revolutionary tribunal's activity. That the people see its enemies fall; that it see the Convention attending to its needs. The people are great and they give you remarkable proof of that at this very moment, for although having suffered from an artificial famine plotted to drive them to counter-revolution, they knew that they would suffer for their cause and, even under the heel of despotism, that they would exterminate all governments. (*Applause*)

Such is the character of the French, enlightened by four years of revolution.

Homage to you, sublime people! You join perseverance with greatness; you desire liberty relentlessly; you fast for liberty, you will get it. We march with you; your enemies will be confounded; you will be free.

(*Universal applause rings in all parts of the hall; cries of "Long live the Republic" are heard several times. All the citizens who fill the hall and the stands are moved to stand; some raising their hands in the air; others shaking their hats; the enthusiasm appears to be universal.*)

Danton's three motions are passed.

(*New acclamations are heard. The hall rings with shouts of "Long live the Republic!"*)

BILLAUD-VARENNE: I ask, first, that an amendment be added to the decree just passed that the payment of forty sous per day, accorded to poor citizens, be acquitted by the rich, and that we invite the other cities of the Republic to do the same. . . .

My second motion is to arrest all counter-revolutionaries and suspect men from this day forward; and in order to execute this measure, I ask for the repeal of the counter-revolutionary measure which forbids public functionaries, under penalty of death, to make domiciliary visits and arrests at night. . . . We must search out our enemies in their lairs. Night and day hardly suffice to arrest them. I request a repeal of the decree. (*Applause*) I ask that the same measures be extended to all the communes of the Republic, and that every noble and every priest who is not residing in his municipality upon receipt of the decree, be considered suspect.

BASIRE: I would like to speak to that. . . . I do not want to fight the motion (*great silence*) but to comment on it. We have already decreed the arrest of suspects repeatedly; but these measures could never be entirely carried out; they were only momentarily useful because of the terror they inspired in aristocrats that we were unable to seize. But these decrees remained either incomplete or they were aborted, for a very important reason; the word "suspects" was poorly interpreted. People believed that it meant only nobles and priests, but they were mistaken. I have a few comments on this, and I ask that the word "suspects" be defined.

In the first place, almost all the youth from the former class of nobles have emigrated; no one remains except children, old people, and women who tend the wealth and pass money to others. The youths who remain offer the touching sight of patriotism; they serve the fatherland (*a few murmurs are heard*); there are even a few in this assembly. Almost all the priests were deported. (*Murmurs*) . . . Why have all of your measures failed to produce any results? Because you have restricted them to these sorts of people. You have very dangerous men in the sections, I swear it, renegades who have long been ranting for a revolution in the sections; you had *feuillants,* you had Brissotins, you still have hypocrites; and I ask you whether all of these men were nobles. No, there were not even two nobles among them. Who then are the people amongst whom are found the second group of suspects? Shopkeepers, large traders, speculators, former prosecutors, bailiffs, insolent servants, *intendants*, and businessmen (*applause*), the independently wealthy, quibblers by inclination, profession, education . . . (*the same applause*).

All of them are naturally greater enemies of liberty than the very ones of whom we spoke earlier. It is because of our mistaken manner of seeing men that we have only pursued nobles until now, leaving agitators and ranters in the sections who stir up the people and who are the source of our ills, of the phony shortages that we feel. These people are very difficult to define. . . .

I ask, as a first measure, that a more categorical definition be given of what is meant by "suspect." (*Murmurs*)

SEVERAL VOICES: That has been done.

BASIRE: It would be easy for me to shout out oratory against the enemies of the people; but we must seize and strangle them, rather than amusing ourselves by shouting against them.

Let us then truly occupy ourselves not with rantings, but with the means to achieve those ends. These means, which I know after two years' work with the Paris police, are

1. That the general council of the commune examine the situation of the revolutionary committees and that it be authorized to name replacements to office for those who are not patriots;
2. That the revolutionary committees prepare lists of suspects tomorrow;
3. That, the day after tomorrow, these lists be taken to the Committee of General Security of the Convention, which will propose measures for these suspects on the following day. . . .

BASIRE: A true security police, on which we can really count, must be organized in Paris. But there will never be an active and complete security police in Paris as long as it is concentrated in a single corps, because a single administration cannot know all the suspects scattered and hidden throughout this great city. The police will not truly exist until each section is assured of a patriotic revolutionary committee, which has the mandate to bring in suspects, the mandate to arrest, the right to make domiciliary visits and to disarm, and which can act by itself without recourse to central authority: because revolutionary committees must currently have recourse to the intervention of police commissioners. Moreover, I note that it would be dangerous to allow one section to make revolution in another; that could antagonize the citizens; create patriotic committees, they will do the rest. . . .

THE PRESIDENT [of the Convention]: I announce that the Committee of Public Safety has decreed several measures that accord with the ones being discussed. I will invite Barère to make his report.

A MEMBER [of the Convention]: We must suspend deliberations.

SEVERAL VOICES: No! no!

BILLAUD-VARENNE: There is one measure to take which need not pass through the committee's net, a measure that is the necessary consequence of those you have already decreed; it concerns the revolutionary committees. The Convention has already recognized the need to provide a salary to citizens with little wealth who attend the general assemblies of the sections that will take place twice weekly. I ask that the members of the revolutionary committees, who give all their time and watchfulness to public service, receive an indemnity, and that this indemnity be fixed at the same rate paid to electors.
    This motion is decreed.

BILLAUD-VARENNE: Finally, I ask that to complete these measures, the Convention order, in conformity with Basire's speech, the purification of the revolutionary committees. There are infinitely suspect men within these committees. There are priests there who carry their fanaticism everywhere. It is time to expel all these hypocrites who only set their sights on those seats out of ambition and hatred.

THE PRESIDENT: Barère made the motion:

1. That the general council of the commune be charged with examining the lists of the revolutionary councils, and be authorized to name replacements to office for everyone or for that part of them whom it knows to be without civic feeling;

2. That these committees, so reorganized, be charged to proceed immediately with the arrest and disarming of all suspects;

3. That, consequently, it be given full powers in this regard to act without the intervention of any authority whatsoever. I put these motions to a vote.

    The motions, so stated, are unanimously decreed.

55. Law on Suspects (SEPTEMBER 17, 1793)

The law on suspects complemented and completed the decrees passed by the Convention on September 5. Although laws had been passed against particular categories of enemy—refractory priests, émigrés, speculators—no legal defini-

Source: Frank Maloy Anderson, ed., *The Constitution and Other Select Documents of the History of France, 1789–1907* (New York: Russell & Russell, 1908; reprinted 1967), pp. 186–187.

tion of the counter-revolutionary "suspect" had yet been developed. This law legalized the work of local committees of surveillance, but its vague definitions suggest the breadth of revolutionaries' fears.

The Law on Suspects

1. Immediately after the publication of the present decree, all suspect persons who are in the territory of the Republic and who are still at liberty shall be placed under arrest.

2. The following are considered suspect persons: first, those who by their conduct, their connections, their remarks, or their writings show themselves the partisans of tyranny or federalism and the enemies of liberty; second, those who cannot, in the manner prescribed by the decree of March 21 last, justify their means of existence and the performance of their civic duties; third, those who have been refused certificates of good citizenship; fourth, public functionaries suspended or removed from their functions by the National Convention or its commissioners and not reinstated, especially those who have been or shall be removed by virtue of the decree of August 14; fifth, those of the former nobles, all of the husbands, wives, fathers, mothers, sons or daughters, brothers or sisters, and agents of the émigrés who have not constantly manifested their attachment to the Revolution; sixth, those who have emigrated from France between July 1, 1789, and the publication of the decree of March 30–April 8, 1792, although they may have returned to France within the period fixed by that decree or earlier.

3. The committees of surveillance established according to the decree of March 21 last, or those which have been substituted for them, either by the orders of the representatives of the people sent with the armies and into the departments, or in virtue of special decrees of the National Convention, are charged to prepare, each in its district, the list of suspect persons, to issue warrants of arrest against them, and to have seals put upon their papers. The commanders of the public force to whom these warrants shall be delivered shall be required to put them into execution immediately, under penalty of removal.

4. The members of the committee cannot order the arrest of any person without being seven in number and having an absolute majority of votes.

5. The persons arrested as suspects shall first be conveyed to the jail or the place of their confinement; in default of jails, they shall be kept from view in their respective dwellings.

6. Within eight days they shall be transferred to the national building, which the administrations of the department shall be required to designate and cause to be prepared for that purpose immediately upon receipt of the present decree.

7. The prisoners can cause to be transferred to these buildings the movables which are of absolute necessity to them; they shall remain there under guard until the peace.

8. The expenses of custody shall be at the charge of the prisoners and shall be divided among them equally: this custody shall be confided preferably to the fathers of families and the parents of citizens who are or shall go to the frontiers. The salary for it is fixed for each man of the guard at the value of a day and a half of labor.

9. The committee of surveillance shall, without delay, send the list of the persons whom they have caused to be arrested to the Committee of General Security of the National Convention, with the reason for their arrest and the papers which have been seized with them as suspect persons.

10. The civil and criminal tribunals can, if there is need, cause to be arrested and sent into the above-mentioned jails persons accused of offenses in respect of which it may have been declared that there was no ground for accusation, or who may have been acquitted of the accusations brought against them.

56. The National Convention Outlaws Women's Clubs and Popular Societies (OCTOBER 30, 1793)

Just as the September decrees marked the height of the political power of sans-culottes and the Paris sections, they also marked that of the Society of Revolutionary Republican Women. Almost immediately, members of the Mountain and of the Jacobin Club began to denounce the society for exciting seditious behavior. Meanwhile, market women who opposed price controls and the society's insistence that all women wear cockades criticized the society and then engaged in street battles with its members. At the end of October, the women of the Paris markets turned to the National Convention to demand that it abolish the Society of Revolutionary Republican Women, whose members, they claimed, threatened their profits and their persons. The Convention, already in the process of consolidating its power and trying to undermine democratic agitation, responded quickly.

Source: Women in Revolutionary Paris. Selected documents translated with notes and commentary by Darline Gay Levy, Harriet Branson Applewhite, and Mary Durham Johnson (Urbana: University of Illinois Press, 1979), pp. 213–217. Copyright 1979 by the Board of Trustees of the University of Illinois. Used with permission of the University of Illinois Press.

National Convention; Moise Bayle, Presiding; Session of 9 Brumaire

AMAR, for the Committee of General Security: Citizens, your committee has been working without respite on means of warding off the consequences of disorders which broke out the day before yesterday in Paris at the Marché des Innocents, near Saint-Eustache. It [the committee] spent the night receiving deputations, listening to various reports which were made to it, and taking measures to maintain public order. Several women, calling themselves Jacobines, from an allegedly revolutionary society, were going about in the morning, in the market and under the ossuaries of Les Innocents, in pantaloons and red bonnets. They intended to force other *citoyennes* to wear the same costume; several [of the latter] testified that they had been insulted by them. A mob of nearly six thousand women gathered. All the women were in agreement that violence and threats would not make them dress in a costume [which] they respected but which they believed was intended for man; they would obey laws passed by the legislators and acts of the people's magistrates, but they would not give in to the wishes and caprices of a hundred lazy and suspect women. They all cried out, "Vive la république, une et indivisible!"

Municipal officers and members of the revolutionary committee of the Section du Contrat Social quieted people down and dispersed the mobs. In the evening the same disturbance broke out with greater violence. A brawl started. Several self-proclaimed Revolutionary Women were roughed up. Some members of the crowd indulged themselves in acts of violence towards them which decency ought to have proscribed. Several remarks reported to your committee show that this disturbance can be attributed only to a plot by enemies of the state. Several of these self-proclaimed Revolutionary Women may have been led astray by an excess of patriotism, but others, doubtless, were motivated only by malevolence.

Right now, when Brissot and his accomplices are being judged, they want to work up some disorders in Paris, as was the case whenever you [the Convention] were about to consider some important matter and when it was a question of taking measures useful for the fatherland.

The Section des Marchés, informed of these events, drew up a resolution in which it informs your committee that it believes several malevolent persons have put on the mask of an exaggerated patriotism to foment disturbances in the section and a kind of counter-revolution in Paris. This section requests that it be illegal to hinder anyone's freedom of dress and that popular societies of women be strictly prohibited, at least during the Revolution.

The committee thought it should carry its investigation further. It raised the following questions: (1) Is it permissible for citizens or for an individual society to force other citizens to do what the law does not prescribe? (2) Should meetings of women gathered together in popular societies in Paris be allowed? Don't the disorders already occasioned by these societies argue against tolerating their existence any longer?

Naturally, these questions are complicated, and their resolution must be preceded by two more general questions, which are (1) Can women exercise political rights and take an active part in affairs of government? (2) Can they deliberate together in political associations or popular societies?

With respect to these two questions, the committee decided in the negative. Time does not allow for the full development to which these major questions—and the first, above all—lend themselves. We are going to put forward a few ideas which may shed light on them [these questions]. In your wisdom you will know how to submit them to thorough examination.

1. Should women exercise political rights and meddle in affairs of government? To govern is to rule the commonwealth by laws, the preparation of which demands extensive knowledge, unlimited attention and devotion, a strict immovability, and self-abnegation; again, to govern is to direct and ceaselessly to correct the action of constituted authorities. Are women capable of these cares and of the qualities they call for? In general, we can answer, no. Very few examples would contradict this evaluation.

The citizen's political rights are to debate and to have resolutions drawn up, by means of comparative deliberations, that relate to the interest of the state, and to resist oppression. Do women have the moral and physical strength which the exercise of one and the other of these rights calls for? Universal opinion rejects this idea.

2. Should women meet in political associations? The goal of popular associations is this: to unveil the maneuvers of enemies of the commonwealth; to exercise surveillance both over citizens as individuals and over public functionaries—even over the legislative body; to excite the zeal of one and the other by the example of republican virtues; to shed light by public and in-depth discussion concerning the lack of reform of political laws. Can women devote themselves to these useful and difficult functions? No, because they would be obliged to sacrifice the more important cares to which nature calls them. The private functions for which women are destined by their very nature are related to the general order of society; this social order results from the differences between man and woman. Each sex is called to the kind of occupation which is fitting for it; its action is circumscribed within this circle which it cannot break through, because nature, which has imposed these limits on man, commands imperiously and receives no law.

Man is strong, born with great energy, audacity, and courage; he braves perils [and] the intemperance of seasons because of his constitution; he resists all the elements, he is fit for agriculture, commerce, navigation, voyages, war—everything that calls for force, intelligence, capability, so in the same way, he alone seems to be equipped for profound and serious thinking which calls for great intellectual effort and long studies which it is not granted to women to pursue.

What character is suitable for woman? Morals and even nature have assigned her functions to her. To begin educating men, to prepare children's minds and hearts for public virtues, to direct them early in life towards the good, to elevate their souls, to educate them in the political cult of liberty;

such are their functions, after household cares. Woman is naturally destined to make virtue loved. When they have fulfilled all these obligations, they will have deserved well of the fatherland. Doubtless they must educate themselves in the principles of liberty in order to make their children cherish it; they can attend the deliberations of the sections [and] discussions of the popular societies, but as they are made for softening the morals of man, should they take an active part in discussions the passion of which is incompatible with the softness and moderation which are the charm of their sex?

We must say that this question is related essentially to morals, and without morals, no Republic. Does the honesty of woman allow her to display herself in public and to struggle against men? To argue in full view of a public about questions on which the salvation of the Republic depends? In general, women are ill suited for elevated thoughts and serious meditations, and if, among ancient peoples, their natural timidity and modesty did not allow them to appear outside their families, then in the French Republic do you want them to be seen coming into the gallery to political assemblies as men do? Abandoning both reserve—source of all the virtues of their sex—and the care of their family?

They have more than one alternative way of rendering service to the fatherland; they can enlighten their husbands, communicating precious reflections, the fruit of the quiet of a sedentary life, [and] work to fortify their love of country by means of everything which intimate love gives them in the way of empire. And the man, enlightened by peaceful family discussions in the midst of his household, will bring back into society the useful ideas imparted to him by an honest woman. We believe, therefore, that a woman should not leave her family to meddle in affairs of government.

There is another sense in which women's associations seem dangerous. If we consider that the political education of man is at its beginning, that all its principles are not developed, and that we are still stammering the word "liberty," then how much more reasonable is it for women, whose moral education is almost nil, to be less enlightened concerning principles? Their presence in popular societies, therefore, would give an active role in government to people more exposed to error and seduction. Let us add that women are disposed by their organization to an overexcitation which would be deadly in public affairs and that interests of state would soon be sacrificed to everything which ardor in passions can generate in the way of error and disorder. Delivered over to the heat of public debate, they would teach their children not love of country but hatreds and suspicions.

We believe, therefore, and without any doubt you will think as we do, that it is not possible for women to exercise political rights. You will destroy these alleged popular societies of women which the aristocracy would want to set up to put them [women] at odds with men, to divide the latter by forcing them to take sides in these quarrels, and to stir up disorder.

CHARLIER: Notwithstanding the objections just cited, I do not know on what principle one could lean in taking away women's rights to assemble peaceably. (*Murmurs*) Unless you are going to question whether women are part of the human species, can you take away from them this right which is common to every thinking being? When a popular society is negligent with respect to general order, to laws, then the members, accused of the offense, or the entire association, if it has made itself guilty, will be pursued by the police. And you have examples of the dissolution of several societies which had been taken over by the aristocracy. But may fear of a few abuses to which an institution is susceptible not force you to destroy the institution itself? For what institution is exempt from inconveniences?

BAZIRE: There is not anyone who does not sense the danger of abandoning to the police the surveillance and the overseeing of the popular societies. Thus, this remedy, which is itself an abuse, should not be cited against the all too real drawbacks of women's societies. Here is how the suspension of these societies can be justified. You declared yourselves a revolutionary government; in this capacity you can take all measures dictated by the public safety. For a brief period you have thrown a veil over principles out of fear that they might be abused to lead us into counter-revolution. Therefore, it is only a question of knowing whether women's societies are dangerous. Experience has shown these past days how deadly they are to the public peace. That granted, let no one say anything more to me about principles. I ask that in a revolutionary spirit and by way of a measure of public security these associations be prohibited, at least during the Revolution.

The decree proposed by Amar is adopted in these terms:
The National Convention, after having heard the report of its Committee of General Security, decrees:
Article 1: Clubs and popular societies of women, whatever name they are known under, are prohibited. [Article] 2: All sessions of popular societies must be public.

57. Georges-Jacques Danton, "Concerning Arbitrary Measures and Arrests" (JANUARY 23, 1794)

The movement of the Indulgents emerged in the late fall of 1793. Believing that the Terror had gone far enough, they argued that government and revolutionary committees had become tyrannical and they attacked the efforts of the popular radical Hébert to intensify the Terror. Georges-Jacques Danton, one of the Convention's most dramatic orators, was sympathetic to some of the Indulgents' criticisms and he too made a number of speeches which, like the selection here, favored restoring regular legal and civil procedure. The arrest and execution of

Source: Henry Morse Stephens, ed., *Speeches of the Statesmen and Orators of the French Revolution, 1789–1795*, vol. 2 (Oxford: Clarendon Press, 1892), pp. 275–276. Translated by Laura Mason.

the radical Hébertists in March did not, however, mark the end of the Terror. Fearful of Danton's critical influence within the Convention, the Committee of Public Safety had him arrested and executed the following month.

I am opposed to the sort of distinction, the privilege which seems to have been accorded to Desmoulins's father-in-law. I want the Convention to attend only to general business. If you want a report on this citizen, there must be reports for all the others as well. I raise my voice against the priority they try to give him, to their own prejudice. Moreover, it raises the question of whether the Committee of General Security is not so overburdened that it can hardly find time to occupy itself with individual claims.

A revolution is not made geometrically. Good citizens who suffer for liberty should console themselves with this great and sublime lesson. No one asked for revolutionary committees more than I, it was upon my proposal that they were established. You wanted to create a sort of patriotic dictatorship, by the citizens most devoted to liberty over those who had made themselves suspect. The committees were created at a time when federalism was prevailing. They were necessary then; although it is still necessary to maintain them in all their strength; but be wary of the two shores upon which we could wreck ourselves. If we were to do too much for justice, we might give ourselves over to moderation, and arm our enemies. Justice must be rendered in such a way that it will not weaken the strictness of our measures.

When a revolution moves toward its conclusion, even though it is consolidated, when the Republic wins its victories and conquers its enemies, a crowd of late-coming and freshly minted patriots emerges; struggles, passions, prejudices, and particular hatreds emerge and often the true, constant patriots are crushed by the newcomers. But where the outcome is general measures in favor of liberty, let us be wary of condemning them. Better to exaggerate liberty and the Revolution than to give our enemies the slightest hope of turning back. Is this nation not very powerful? Does it not have the right as well as the strength to enhance its measures against aristocrats and to dispel the errors raised against the enemies of the fatherland? If the Convention does not hasten to do justice to a citizen at the very moment it is able to do so without damaging the public good, it violates that citizen's rights.

My colleague's claim is just in itself, but it elicits a decree unworthy of you. If we accord privilege, it should be to those citizens who do not have resources of wealth or acquaintance with members of the Convention amidst their unhappiness; the unhappy, the needy must be aided first. I ask that the Convention consider the means that will allow it to do justice to all the victims of arbitrary measures and arrest without impairing the activity of the revolutionary government. I will be careful not to prescribe the means here. I ask that this question be sent for consideration to the Committee of General Security, which will consult with the Committee of Public Safety; that the

Convention make a report to the National Convention, to be followed by a wide-ranging and penetrating discussion; because all of the Convention's discussions have the triumph of reason and liberty as their outcome.

The Convention only succeeded because it was of the people; it will remain of the people; it will ceaselessly seek out and abide by public opinion; it is this opinion that should determine all laws that you proclaim. In deepening these questions, you will, I hope, obtain results that will satisfy justice and humanity.

58. Bertrand Barère, on Behalf of the Committee of Public Safety, Report to the National Convention on the Maximum (FEBRUARY 22, 1794)

Bowing to pressure from Parisian sans-culottes, the Montagnards became advocates of price controls in the spring of 1793. In March they promoted and won a maximum price on bread. In September the Convention extended the maximum to a broad range of goods defined as necessities, badly disrupting prices and supplies in the process and encouraging the development of a black market. Here Bertrand Barère (1755–1841) justifies the maximum, which had become extremely unpopular, before proposing amendments that would extend and stabilize the controlled economy in France. In the process, he assures the people that the maximum can be a powerful instrument of the Revolution and admonishes the citizens to do their part.

Citizens,

The law of the Maximum was a trap set for the Convention by the Republic's enemies; it is a gift from London, but its counter-revolutionary origin is forgotten. Like those hard-working scientists who know how to extract poison from even the most subtle of beneficial remedies, the Convention will finally obtain all the advantages the people ceaselessly demand from this law of the Maximum. . . .

Thus the Convention decreed a supplement to the law of the Maximum on 11 Brumaire, on the recommendation of the Committee of Public Safety. [The law] had been improvised by malevolence and crime; it was improved by your patriotism and enlightenment. . . .

Source: "Rapport fait au nom du Comité de salut public par Barère, sur l'exécution du Décret du 11 brumaire, et sur la publication des tableaux du 'maximum' des denrées et marchandises soumises à la loi du 'maximum' " (Paris, March 1794). Bibliothèque Nationale, 8° Le38 705. Translated by Tracey Rizzo.

It is not enough to vanquish the armies of kings, to destroy tyranny, to strike down the aristocracy, to divide riches, to demolish great fortunes; it is still necessary to make popular laws, improve the condition of every citizen, augment agriculture, revive industry, democratize commerce, honor work (which is the true and indestructible wealth of nations), favor the useful worker, and offer abundance to need without lavishness, waste, exaggeration, or violence.

Basic needs and the sudden and disproportionate variation in the cost and availability of life's necessities are the causes of the greatest commotion in republics; they are a double-edged sword in the hands of the ambitious and the scheming. How many tyrants have pacified people by distributing storehouses of grain and silver! How many wretched ministers have fomented revolutions with ringleaders on the basis of needs they created themselves! How many methods of despotism do not stem from these fake shortages, these monopolies secretly accumulated, these cries of artificial need! . . .

Thrift is the virtue of a free people. Daily sacrifices are the portion of those who fight for their rights. "Liberty and potatoes! Liberty and yams!" a free Negro from Saint Domingue, who now is a member of the Convention, said vigorously a few days ago. Well! Do you think the Republican from Europe does not have the same courage as the free man from Africa? And do you believe that we who planted the first liberty tree cannot do and say as the Blacks of America who received this gift [from us] of our holy love for humanity? . . .

Let us be closer to nature. Do not order these ridiculous and impious feasts; do not imitate priests or kings. Chase out the ones and beat the others by voluntarily imposing necessary deprivation and tolerable sacrifices. Let useless and expensive festivals disappear; let aristocratic parasites cease to consume a month's worth of food in one day; and let the rich stop insulting the people by covering their tables with superfluous dishes and a spread which serves only vanity or intemperance. Armies should not be denied toasts of liberty, and civic meals presented in friendship require neither luxury nor the squandering of resources. . . .

Our fathers, we ourselves, have fasted for a holy day, for a tenth-century monk, or for a sacerdotal hoax. Let us fast instead for liberty. It is much holier than all religious institutions. Practice thrift for a while; let us voluntarily impose a civic frugality to sustain our rights. . . .

We had a monarchical system of commerce; it aspired only to riches, it had no country. Monarchy has no need of virtue. A republican system of commerce is necessary for us, that is to say, a commerce which prefers its country to all others, a commerce with moderate profits and virtues. Republics have no other solid foundation. . . .

The work of the commission for subsistence and provisions comes to present to you, to shed light, to put within reach of all citizens that which only a few know; it will stimulate industry, reproach the manufacturer of consumer goods, and moderate the usury and profits of the businessman and the man of industry.

The consumer will no longer buy merchandise which has passed through five or six miserly hands, that is to say, from those who sponge off them.

People will no longer buy things which have waited in the shops of the greedy man or of the heartless speculator until his avarice indicates the most advantageous moment to be sold. Needs will no longer be spied upon only to be arbitrarily imposed by commerce.

This class of speculators, whose enormous profits were useless to the manufacturer who did not sell higher, and which weighs uniquely on the consumer, will finally be forced to renounce its parasitic role and its devouring inclinations. Or, to summarize, fraternity will be established between aid and need, between the producer and the consumer.

We have chased out bankers who situated themselves between man and the divinity, the banker who placed himself between administrators and administrated, the banker who insinuated himself between the state's creditor and the republic's debtor. Let us also diminish then the number of these bankers who are mixed up in commerce and who have only multiplied public misery one hundredfold by extending the ladder of intermediaries between the people who buy and the producer who sells. . . .

The secret of commerce will be known. The operations of industry will be divulged, the manipulation of all matters will see the light of day, all profits moderated, all interests and vices balanced, every crime, every abuse against the life of the people and the needs of the Republic denounced and punished.

Today you take a great step in political economy; you will spread knowledge of the nation's work; you bring light to all the operations of commerce and industry.

After long labors, naturalists and doctors have made the tables of mortality for the human species; you have in two months made the tables of life for the people.

No nation possesses a similar work. Kings will well beware of commanding it, still less of revealing it. But a popular government should commence with the amelioration of the condition of its citizens by a work of this type.

It was worthy of the French Republic to prove to all nations that the people are happy, and that republican government is established in good faith, without aristocracy, without charlatanism, and without consulting the calculations and intrigues of personal interest. . . .

59. Law of 22 Prairial Year II (JUNE 10, 1794)

With the passage of the law of 22 Prairial, the Terror reached the moment of its greatest intensity. In introducing the law on behalf of the Committee of Public Safety, the deputy Georges Couthon argued that patriots had nothing to fear from

Source: Frank Maloy Anderson, ed., *The Constitution and Other Select Documents from the History of France, 1789–1907* (New York: Russell & Russell, 1908; reprinted 1967), pp. 154–157.

patriotic judges, that legal forms were the tricks of deceptive lawyers, and that written records and oral testimony were not reliable proof because they could be falsified. In short, Couthon proposed sweeping away regular judicial procedure as he broadened the category of capital offenses. For the next two months, until 9 Thermidor, executions rose dramatically, especially in the capital: 1,515 people were executed in Paris during June and July.

1. The revolutionary tribunal shall have a president and four vice-presidents, one public accuser, four substitutes for the public accuser, and twelve judges.

2. The jurors shall be fifty in number.

3. The different functions shall be discharged by the citizens whose names follow: . . . The revolutionary tribunal shall divide itself into sections composed of twelve members, to wit: three judges and nine jurors, which jurors cannot give judgment at a number less than that of seven.

4. The revolutionary tribunal is instituted in order to punish the enemies of the people.

5. The enemies of the people are those who seek to destroy public liberty, either by force or by artifice.

6. Those are reputed enemies of the people who have promoted the reestablishment of royalty or sought to depreciate or dissolve the National Convention and the revolutionary and republican government of which it is the center.

Those who have betrayed the Republic in the command of places and armies, or in any other military function; carried on correspondence with the enemies of the Republic; labored to make the supplies or the service of the armies fail;

Those who have sought to impede the supplies for Paris or to cause scarcity within the Republic;

Those who have seconded the projects of the enemies of France, either in aiding the withdrawal and impunity of conspirators and the aristocracy, or in persecuting and calumniating patriotism, or in corrupting the servants of the people, or in abusing the principles of the Revolution, the laws, or the measures of the government, by false and perfidious applications;

Those who have deceived the people or the representatives of the people in order to lead them into operations contrary to the interests of liberty;

Those who have sought to promote discouragement, in order to favor the enterprises of the tyrants leagued against the Republic;

Those who have spread false news in order to divide or disturb the people;

Those who have sought to mislead opinion and to prevent the instruction of the people, to deprave morals and corrupt the public conscience, to impair the energy and the purity of the revolutionary and republican principles, either by stopping the progress of them, or by counter-revolutionary or insidious writings, or by any other machination;

Contractors whose bad faith compromises the safety of the Republic, and the wasters of the public fortune, other than those included in the provisions of the law of 7 Frimaire;

Those who, being charged with public functions, abuse them in order to serve the enemies of the Revolution, to distress the patriots or to oppress the people;

Finally, all those who are designated in the preceding laws concerning the punishment of the conspirators and counter-revolutionaries, and who, whatever the means or the appearances with which they cover themselves, have attacked the liberty, unity, and security of the Republic, or labored to prevent the strengthening of them.

7. The penalty provided for all offenses, the jurisdiction of which belongs to the revolutionary tribunal, is death.

8. The proof necessary to convict the enemies of the people is every kind of evidence, either material or moral or verbal or written, which can naturally secure the approval of every just and reasonable spirit; the rule of judgment is the conscience of the jurors enlightened by love of the fatherland; their aim, the triumph of the Republic and the ruin of its enemies; the procedure, the simple means which good sense dictates in order to come to the knowledge of the truth, in the forms which the law determines.

It is confined to the following points:

9. Every citizen has the right to seize conspirators and counter-revolutionaries and to arraign them before magistrates. He is required to denounce them when he knows of them.

10. Nobody can arraign a person before the revolutionary tribunal, except the National Convention, the Committee of Public Safety, the Committee of General Security, the representatives of the people who are commissioners of the Convention, and the public accuser of the revolutionary tribunal.

11. The constituted authorities in general cannot exercise this right without having notified the Committee of Public Safety and the Committee of General Security and obtained their authorization.

12. The accused shall be examined in public session: the formality of the secret examination which precedes is suppressed as superfluous; it shall occur only under special circumstances in which it shall be judged useful for a knowledge of the truth.

13. If proofs exist, either material or moral, independently of the testified proof, there shall be no further hearing of testimony, unless that formality appears necessary, either to discover the accomplices or for other important considerations of public interest.

14. In a case in which there shall be occasion for this proof, the public accuser shall cause witnesses to be summoned who can show the way to justice, without distinction of witnesses for or against.

15. All the proceedings shall be conducted in public and no written deposition shall be received, unless the witnesses are so situated that they cannot be brought before the tribunal, and in that case an express authorization of the Committees of Public Safety and General Security shall be necessary.

16. The law gives sworn patriots to calumniated patriots for counsel; it does not grant them to conspirators.

17. The pleadings finished, the jurors shall formulate their verdicts and the judges shall pronounce the penalty in the manner determined by the laws.

The president shall propound the question with lucidity, precision, and simplicity. If it was presented in an equivocal or inexact manner, the jury may ask that it be propounded in another manner.

18. The public accuser may not on his own authority discharge a prisoner bound over to the tribunal nor one whom he shall have caused to be arraigned there; in a case in which there is no matter for an accusation before the tribunal, he shall make a written report of it, with a statement of the reasons, to the chamber of the council, which shall pronounce. But no prisoner may be discharged from trial before the decision of the chamber has been communicated to the Committees of Public Safety and General Security, who shall examine it.

19. A double register shall be kept of persons arraigned before the revolutionary tribunal, one for the public accuser and the other for the tribunal, upon which shall be enrolled all the prisoners, according as they shall be arraigned.

20. The Convention modifies all those provisions of the preceding laws which may not be in agreement with the present law and does not intend that the laws concerning the organization of the ordinary tribunals should apply to the crimes of counter-revolution and to the action of the revolutionary tribunal.

21. The report of the committee shall be joined to the present decree as instruction.

10

REVOLUTION IN SOCIETY AND CULTURE

60. Anonymous, "Reflections of a Good Citizen in Favor of Divorce" (1789?)

Divorce was prohibited in France as long as marriage was governed by canon law. Although legal separations were available, they did not enable estranged spouses to remarry. Proponents of divorce made their case loud and clear throughout the eighteenth century, and they reached a crescendo in the early years of the Revolution. With the desacralization of marriage, the state was empowered to make—or break—marriages. Petitions, such as this one, would ultimately influence the Assembly to legalize divorce in 1792.

"As much as the knot of will and affection is despised and slackened that of constraint is narrowed." (Montaigne 2 V. C. 5.)

Source: Anonymous, "Réflexions d'un bon citoyen en faveur du divorce" (Paris, 1789, according to Roderick Phillips). Bibliothèque Nationale, Rz 2969. Translated by Tracey Rizzo.

To the gentlemen of the National Assembly, on the establishment of Divorce.
Sirs,

The whole of humanity comes to reclaim your justice in favor of the thousands of unhappy spouses who linger in badly made and often despised marriages. Victims of cupidity, ambition, caprice, and the tyranny of their parents can only be reproached for their submission and obedience: will you permit that a misfortune without remedy become a horrible punishment? Break, sirs, break the detested vows, contrary to natural law, to good morals, to propagation, to individual happiness, familial peace, and the true spirit of religion.

State of the Question

In reclaiming divorce, we are far from wanting to favor fickle, inconstant, or libertine tastes where the exchange of pleasures would play more a part than solid reasons. We intend to speak here of legal divorce, which would take place only in certain cases, regulated and determined by wise laws; these would be adultery, the malicious desertion of one of the conjoints, imperiling one's life by either poison or some other evil abuse, infamy incurred for some shameful deed, well-proven incompatibility of temperaments and characters, and still other cases left to the discretion of the laws. When the law pronounces divorce, the spouses liberated from their bonds will be free to contract happier marriages. This course conforms to natural law. In effect, is not the indissolubility of marriage repulsive to justice? Is it fair to irrevocably dispose of the liberty and happiness of inexperienced people in whom reason is not fully developed, without consulting them, except in form only? One knows that these cases are not rare among the rich and the powerful. Is it fair to attach death to the living, to leave a good, sensible, and virtuous wife united to a libertine, madman, monster? Is it fair that a reasonable and peaceful man, a friend of order and virtue, be condemned to pass his life with a shrewish, irascible, dissipated, and often debauched woman, whereas if he should seek separation, he will be deprived of the pleasures and of the consolation of sharing his existence? Among spouses, the one who first violates his faithfulness, does he not break the contract and disengage his other oaths? With what insensitive laws can one thus oppose us? Ah! that these inhumane laws should ever be prescribed for the earth which outrage nature, revolt good sense, and render unhappy the man that they should protect! . . .

How many scandals, injustices, troubles, and divisions in families are born of the fatal breakup of couples! How many crimes, outrages, and mistakes of every sort has the indissolubility of marriage brought into the world! How many scaffolds has she adorned! How many pyres has she inflamed! families covered in infamy, unfortunate victims perished in rage and despair! Can one relate without trembling that in the single year of 1769 the high court of the Parlement of Paris judged twenty-nine cases involving crimes of poison and murder between husbands and wives? . . .

All these reasons acquire new force if one takes population into account. Is it not evident that the indissolubility of marriage does much harm, that without it marriages would be more frequent and fruitful; that in weighing [marriages] down with impediments one deprives [the population] of a great number of persons? This assertion is demonstrated by the quantity of marriages and the numerous populations among peoples where divorce is established. Consider what takes place among the Protestants in Geneva, Switzerland, Holland, and in several German cantons, and see how much, in regard to the number of inhabitants, their population is superior to ours, how many marriages there are more frequent and happy than ours, how morals [are] purer, and the status of women elevated higher.

How can one tell us that the spirit of Christianity is opposed to a form of divorce wisely regulated by the law? It was permitted and practiced among Christians up to the ninth century; and without the ambition of Pope Leo VI, eager to attract to the faith every form of power, it would still be permitted among us. The Polish have retained the usage, even though Rome deprived them of communion, indisputable proof that divorce in certain cases has never been opposed to the true spirit of religion, which has in view the happiness and health of man. . . .

We demand to know how after these passages [previously cited], after these respected authorities, the so-called infallible Roman Church has been able to condemn priests to an absurd celibacy, contrary to nature, to the views of its author, and become the source of egoism, bad morals, scandals, and the majority of ecclesiastical disorders. O You! Immortal representatives of the French Nation, unite to avenge nature and her rights, annul the matrimonial despotism, a hundred times crueler than others. Render to society and to themselves these unhappy spouses who exist only to resent their fate and detest the barbarous laws which smother them. Spare the mistakes of these unfortunates in whom the excess of their misfortune can only lead to despair. Ah! if you could witness the lamentable scenes, secret horrors, unjust and barbarous treatments which reveal to your eyes the night shadows; if you could see all the acts of tyranny exercised on these unhappy spouses, occasioned by the antipathy of character, malice, dissipation, and debauchery, a profound indignation would seize your hearts and you would press for the abolition of a law which fills society with crime and misfortunes. So many victims, who up to the present have found only a feeble softening of their troubles by a separation which has been accorded them by civil justice and who are fallen from one misfortune to another, finding themselves isolated and who can approach someone who could bring them happiness only by dishonest bonds. Return them to good morals by according divorce; they join their benediction to those of all people you should make happy.

61. Decree Regulating Divorce
(SEPTEMBER 20, 1792)

Persuaded by arguments about the benefits of divorce to individuals and to the population as a whole (see previous selection), the Assembly finally legalized divorce in September 1792. This law, ahead of its time, endured until 1816. Following the Restoration, divorce would remain illegal in France until 1884.

The National Assembly, considering the importance of enabling Frenchmen to enjoy the privilege of divorce, a consequence of individual liberty which would be doomed by indissoluble engagements; considering that already a number of married couples have not waited, in order to enjoy the advantages of the constitutional provision according to which marriage is only a civil contract, until the law had regulated the manner and consequences of divorce, decrees as follows:

Grounds for Divorce

1. Marriage may be dissolved by divorce.
2. Divorce shall take place by mutual consent of husband and wife.
3. One of the parties may have divorce pronounced on the mere allegation of incompatibility of disposition or character.
4. Each of the parties likewise may have divorce pronounced on certain determined grounds, to wit: first, the insanity, madness, or violence of one of the parties; second, the sentence of one of them to corporal or ignominious punishments; third, crimes, cruelty, or serious injuries on the part of one against the other; fourth, notoriously dissolute morals; fifth, the desertion of the wife by the husband or of the husband by the wife for at least two years; sixth, the absence of one of them, without news, for at least five years; seventh, emigration, in the cases anticipated by law, particularly by the decree of April 8, 1792.
5. Married people now separated by a judgment executed, or in the last resort, shall have mutual right to have divorce pronounced.
6. All requests and suits for separation not granted are dismissed and abolished; each of the parties shall pay his (or her) expenses. Judgments of separation not executed, or impugned by appeal or through cassation, remain

Source: John Hall Stewart, ed., *A Documentary Survey of the French Revolution* (New York: Macmillan, 1951), pp. 333–334. Reprinted by permission.

as void, reserving to parties the right to have recourse to means of divorce according to the terms of the present law.

7. Henceforth, no separation may be pronounced; married parties may be disunited only by divorce.

Divorce Procedures: Divorce by Mutual Consent

1. The husband and wife who conjointly request divorce shall be required to convoke an assembly of at least six of the nearest relatives, or friends in default of relatives; three of the relatives or friends shall be chosen by the husband, the other three by the wife.

2. The assembly shall be convoked on an appointed day and at the place agreed upon with the relatives or friends; there shall be at least one month's interval between the day of the convocation and that of the assembly. A clerk shall serve the instrument of convocation upon the relatives or friends who are summoned.

3. If, on the day of convocation, one or more of the relatives or friends who are summoned cannot attend the assembly, the married parties shall have them replaced by other relatives or friends. . . .

62. Lebrun, "Republican Ode to the French People on the Supreme Being" (OCTOBER–NOVEMBER 1793)

The deist belief in a Supreme Being predates the Revolution, having been popular among many Enlightenment philosophes. Although some conceived of the deity as a great watchmaker who set the universe in motion and left it to run according to natural law, and others applied a more emotional language, most agreed that the Supreme Being was a more impersonal figure than the Christian god. During the Revolution, the cult of the Supreme Being reached its height in 1793–1794; it was, in part, a response to the popular movement of de-Christianization. Lebrun and others, most notably Robespierre, worked to associate the Supreme Being with republican ceremonies and principles. The cult died out shortly after Thermidor.

Source: P.-D.-E. Lebrun, *Ode républicaine au peuple français, sur l'Être Suprême* (Paris, n.d.). Translated by Laura Mason.

The French commemorated their Revolution in plays, speeches, and festivals, as well as in articles of daily life. Here the execution of Louis XVI is immortalized on a plate. *(Photo Bulloz)*

The most just indignation and most saintly love of the fatherland inspire this ode on the existence and necessity of a Supreme Being. The author composed the ode six months ago, at the most dangerous time; but even danger inspires genius. "At that time," Robespierre said with as much energy as truth in one of his best reports, "hooligans had usurped the political calling. One feared to propose a just idea. They had forbidden patriotism to use good sense. There was a time when it was forbidden to oppose the ruin of the fatherland, under threat of being considered a bad citizen. Liberty was, for them, free criminality, revolution was a trade, the people an instrument, the fatherland prey. . . . Did any legislator ever consider nationalizing atheism? The more that a man is endowed with sensitivity and genius, the more he cares for ideas that exalt his being and elevate his heart. But those who betrayed the fatherland wanted to *nationalize atheism.*... Who would believe in this excessive shamelessness! We heard a citizen denounced for having dared speak the name of providence; we heard of another charged with having written against atheism, as if they wanted to compensate for indulging tyranny by declaring war on the Divinity.... Admirable policy of Monsieur Pitt, who has his emissaries insult God so that he may then avenge him with bayonets.... Conspirators plan to exaggerate and corrupt everything. They flatter the people in order to oppress them.... It seems that they only relegated reason to the temples in order to banish it from the Republic."

In truth, what could be a more absurd and more impractical idea than that of a Republic of twenty-five million atheists! An idea which, if it could be realized, would make us the myth and the horror of all peoples.

To flatter the sovereign is to betray the fatherland.
If I had only dared, when the scepter armed tyranny,
To frighten kings with a republican verse,
If only the invincible genius of liberty
Had always known how to ignite my heart and my voice:
    If only, in spite of the Bastille and its threatening towers,
I, proclaiming this proud and saintly liberty,
Had dared then to pursue with my cruel rhymes
The usurping insect called *majesty:*
    If only, to advance freedom's conquest,
Into the tyrant's breast I had plunged the blade;
If only the civic palm leaf, in encircling my head,
Had dedicated it to glory and perhaps to death:
    French people, whose slow languors I awakened,
Sovereign, too long dethroned by kings,
No, you will not fear my vigorous tone;
You will lend an ear to he who crowned you.
    You reign! You are capable of all: fear this extraordinary power.
Above all, fear flatterers; they become drunk on pride:
They were the downfall of kings; they will be the downfall of you yourselves;
They are the ones who, beneath the throne, prepared the shroud.
    Truth; that is my beloved offering.
Far from you, for evermore, the base incense of courts.
To flatter the sovereign, is to betray the fatherland,
Public happiness poisons courts.
    People! without wisdom, blind power
Will, to their downfall, soon lead their steps.
Truth inspires me. O earth, be silent.
Woe to the fool who does not listen!

Particle of a moment, fleeting dust,
Man born for death, speak! Did you make the heavens?
Did you tell the sea: crash upon your shores?
Did you tell the sun: move and shine before my eyes?

[handwritten: philosophical]

It was a God who said so! This God of thought
Has no need of altars, priests, or incense.
But what proud and thoughtless ingratitude
Would dare deprive him of your grateful voices?

But, against the Eternal One, a mere worm conspires!
And, creeping in a corner of this vast universe,
Man would chase God from the bosom of his empire!
He would call wisdom a perverse delusion!

The impious vainly testify to nothingness or to the absence
Of a God that remorse reveals to infamy:
And I, I dare attest to the invisible presence
Of a God who showed his goodness to the universe.
These stars that you see, this orb on which you breathe,   *[handwritten: what he saw]*
Your days, your liberty, are the work of his hands.
From the heights of the heavens, he holds the reins of empires;
And watches with love over human frailty.

Flee Superstition! you thunderous brute;
Your foolish minister pledged you his fury.
He who makes the skies speak, always lies to the earth;
And the earth praised deception and error.

What! Europe on its knees quaked beneath the Crown!
And the pious fear of credulous mortals,
Pays the greedy luxury of a Roman Pontiff,
Who aspires to the shameful honor of enriching his altars!

Treacherous and sacred tyrant, proud of a tripart idol,
You who sold the too-long outraged heavens,
Wretched imposter, come down from the Capitol!
The priest has disappeared; the Eternal One is avenged.   *[handwritten: civil constitution of the clergy]*

Ah! independent Being, sole and fecund cause,
Not this tripart god enclosed by a jealous sky.
Father of nature, he animates the world.
We breathe in him, as he breathes in us.

No! God does not exist unless in our souls;
His immortal voice is there contained.
He lives in hearts; there, with burning strokes   *[handwritten: Enlightenment]*
He himself engraved our duties and their laws.

His religion is virtue; justice his image.
Mortal hypocrites too long distorted it.
Ah! that hearts give him homage,
Does it matter with what name this God is adored?

It is before heaven, before the being of beings,
That your legislators dethroned kings.
You yourself, O nation! free at last of your priests,
Wanted a present God to sanctify your rights.
　For this great creator who nourishes you, who loves you,
Never reserve criminal forgetfulness.
To rule over kings, serve this supreme king well;
Fall with the universe at the feet of the Eternal.
　Beyond the sun, beyond space,
There is nothing that he does not see; nothing that he does not embrace.
He alone among all is the principle and end;
And creation breathes in his breast.
　Could I be unhappy? I owe him my birth.
All is goodness, without doubt, in whom all is power.
　This God, so different from the God we composed,
Never sent black demons against armed men.
He never voiced his vengeance in thunder.
He never said to the skies, you shall instruct the earth.
But to conscience, he dictated its voice;
But within the heart of man, he engraved his laws;
But he made timid innocence blush;
But he made guilty license pale;
But in the place of hell, he created remorse,
And did not perpetuate suffering and death.

63. Benoît Monestier, "Decree Concerning Fanatical Priests or Troublemakers, and the Celebration of the Decades" (1794)

In October 1793 the government forbade public celebrations of Christianity, even as embodied in the Constitutional Church, thus launching a program of de-Christianization. In a deliberate effort to erase all traces of the Christian and royalist past, the radical Republic of Virtue was inaugurated to inspire patriotism as the sole basis for a new world order. Notre Dame was renamed the Temple of Reason, and a new calendar, organized around the ten-day week with terms from the natural world signifying the names of days and months, was propagated. The following decree is an example of the prohibitive legislation of de-Christian-

---

Source: Benoît Monestier, Représentant du Peuple dans les Départements de Lot, Garonne, et Landes, "Arrête Relatif aux Prêtes fanatiques ou perturbateurs, et à la célébration des Décades" (Agen, 1794). In the Bibliothèque nationale. Translated by Tracey Rizzo.

ization. Reactions were swift and virulent, especially in the south, as religious expression became tantamount to counter-revolution.

The representative of the people reports that the tranquillity of several communes has occasionally been disturbed by fanatical former priests and troublemakers, and that [tranquillity] is still subject to their disruptions;

Considering that the people prefer the most harmonious peace to trouble, and the unique cult of truth and reason to lies and superstition; whereas these men want to lead them into the dependence of error and to upset them out of the exclusive sentiment of domination or self-interest;

Considering that it is necessary, finally, to redeem the people from all the outrages committed up until now to the destiny and dignity for which nature and their author have made them; that consequently it is necessary to render their enemies powerless to harm them, and to treat them like renegade citizens who resist society and the law;

Decrees the following:

1. From the date of the publication of the present decree, all former priests or other ecclesiastics and ministers of any cult [who] incite citizens to fanaticism, whether in public or private, by remarks or actions or any other means; trouble or expose public or private tranquillity to disruptions; distract the people from the cult of reason and the celebration of the decades will be put under arrest and even brought before the tribunal according to the gravity of the cases of which they find themselves accused.

2. The district administrations are authorized and constrained to require all those whose presence might be dangerous in the communes to relocate to the department's major town to live there under the municipality's private surveillance. In the case of a refusal to obey, they will be transferred to the police; only public functionaries are excepted . . . unless they are fanatics or troublemakers.

3. For the execution of the preceding article, district administrations will, if they do not have knowledge of former priests or ministers who are in said circumstances, gather information of their whereabouts from constituted authorities charged with the application of revolutionary measures, or from popular societies, and from every good citizen.

4. The present decree hereby reiterates the celebration of the decades, and the decree of the people's representatives to public functionaries and the popular societies, dated 27 Pluviôse. It recommended that they deliver impassioned speeches to the people of love for country, the cult of reason, and the events which illustrate the Revolution's success. Unless [there is] a legitimate absence or other obstacle, those who fail to attend and to celebrate the former day of Sunday, because of their laziness or any other exterior condition will be

excluded from popular societies; what is more, if their example becomes dangerous, they will be deprived on that day of their bread ration which they have earned by their idleness.

5. All public information and instruction are expressly prohibited to former priests and other ministers of any cult whatsoever, under penalty of being considered suspects.

6. The present decree will be sent by rural routes to the directories of the departments of Lot, Garonne, and Landes, to be printed and then sent to the district administrations, and by these to the municipalities and popular societies; and finally to be read, publicized, and posted everywhere there is need.

Published at Agen, 25 Germinal, Year II of the one and indivisible Republic.

64. Maximilien Robespierre, "Report on the Principles of Political Morality" (FEBRUARY 5, 1794)

The revolutionary government had been confronting crises almost since the installation of the National Convention and, by the winter of 1793–1794, Robespierre stood accused of aspiring to dictatorship. He responded to both phenomena by giving a speech in which he sought to lift the Revolution above the confusion of circumstance and found its course on certain fundamental principles. Above all, he argues here, the republic must be founded on virtue, which, he idealistically believed, was a quality that naturally inhered in "the people." The historian R. R. Palmer has called this the most important of Robespierre's speeches, for it defines the purpose of the Terror and the kind of republic that the Committee of Public Safety was trying to create.

Citizens, representatives of the people.

A short time ago, we explained our principles of foreign policy: today, we will expand on the principles behind our domestic policy.

Having long moved forward aimlessly and as if propelled by opposing forces, the representatives of the French people finally show character and government. A sudden change in the nation's fortunes announced the regeneration of the national representation to Europe. But, until the very moment at which I speak, it must be admitted that, under such tumultuous circum-

Source: Maximilien Robespierre, *Textes choisies*, vol. 3 (Novembre 1793–Juillet 1794). Introduction and notes by Jean Poperen (Paris: Éditions sociales, 1973–1974), pp. 110–131. Translated by Laura Mason.

stances, we have more often been guided by the love of good and the sense of the fatherland's needs than by an exact theory and precise rules of conduct which we have not even had the leisure to sketch.

It is time to firmly trace the goal of the Revolution, and the time in which we mean to achieve it; it is time to take account of ourselves, of the obstacles that keep us from our goal, and of the means we must adopt to attain it. . . .

Toward what goal do we move? The peaceful enjoyment of liberty and equality; the reign of that eternal justice wherein laws are engraved not in marble or stone, but in the hearts of men, even in that of the slave who forgets them and the tyrant who denies them. . . .

In a word, we want to carry out nature's wishes, realize humanity's destiny, keep the promises of philosophy, absolve providence from the long reign of crime and tyranny. Let France, once illustrious among enslaved countries, eclipse the glory of all free peoples who ever existed, become the model of nations, the dread of oppressors, the consolation of the oppressed, the ornament of the universe and, in sealing our achievement with our blood, we may at least see the star of universal happiness shine. . . . That is our ambition, that is our goal.

What kind of government can realize these marvels? Only government that is democratic or republican: words that are synonymous. . . .

Democracy is a state in which the sovereign people, guided by the laws they have made, do all that they can do themselves, and all that they cannot do themselves through their delegates.

Therefore, you must seek the rules of your political conduct in the principles of democratic government. . . .

But what is the fundamental principle of democratic or popular government; in other words, the essential force that sustains and impels it? Virtue; I speak of the public virtue that accomplished so many marvels in Greece and Rome, and which should produce still more astounding ones in republican France; of that virtue which is nothing other than love of the fatherland and its laws.

But because the essence of the Republic or of democracy is equality, it follows that love of the fatherland necessarily embraces love of equality. . . .

Since the soul of the Republic is virtue and equality, and your goal is to establish and consolidate the Republic, it follows that the first rule of your political conduct should be to direct all your actions toward maintaining equality and improving virtue; because the legislator's principal care must be to fortify the principle of government. Thus, you should adopt all that tends to stir love of the fatherland, refine morals, elevate spirits, direct the passions of the human heart toward the public interest. You should reject or repress all that tends to focus attention on the abjection of personal interests, the awakening of the taste for little things and contempt for the great. In the system of the French Revolution, all that is immoral is impolitic, all that corrupts is counter-revolutionary. Weakness, vice, prejudice are the way of royalism. Perhaps too often led by the weight of our old habits, as well as by the imperceptible inclination of human weakness toward false ideas and base sentiments, we must defend ourselves less against excesses of energy than against excesses of weakness. Perhaps the greatest pitfall we have to avoid is not the zealotry of fervor but rather the lethargy of goodness, and the fear of our own courage. Thus, raise the sacred, motivating force of government again and again rather than letting it fall. I need not say that I do not want to justify excesses here. The most sacred principles are abused; it is up to the wisdom of government to consult circumstances, seize the moment, decide upon the means; because preparing great things properly is a fundamental part of accomplishing them, just as wisdom is itself a part of virtue. . . .

We may consider republican virtue in regard to the people and in regard to the government: it is necessary in one and the other. When government is deprived of it, the people's virtue remains a resource; but when the people itself is corrupted, liberty is already lost.

Happily, virtue comes naturally to the people, in spite of aristocratic prejudice. A nation is truly corrupt when, after having slowly lost its character and its liberty, it passes from democracy to aristocracy or monarchy; then the body politic dies by decaying. . . .

But when the people, by prodigious efforts of courage and reason, break the chains of despotism and transform them into trophies of liberty; when, by the force of moral temperament, the people abandon the arms of death to recapture all the vigor of youth; when, both sensitive and proud, bold and meek, they cannot be stopped by impregnable ramparts, nor by tyrants' innumerable battalions armed against them, battalions that they will themselves halt before the image of the law; if the people do not leap quickly to the pinnacle of their destiny, it can only be the fault of those who govern them.

It could even be said that, in a sense, the people do not need great virtue to love justice and equality; they need only love themselves.

But the magistrate must sacrifice his interest to the people's interest, and the pride of power to equality. The law must speak with authority, especially to those who are its mouthpieces. Government must weigh upon itself to keep all parts in harmony with the law. If a representative body exists, a primary authority constituted by the people, it is responsible for watching over and ceaselessly curbing all public functionaries. But who will curb that authority, if not its own virtue? The more this source of public order is elevated, the purer it must be; the representative body must thus begin by subjecting all the private passions it contains to the general passion of public good. Happy are the representatives when their glory and even their interest ties them as closely as does their duty to the cause of liberty!

Let us draw a great truth from all of this: that the character of popular government is to have confidence in the people, and to be strict with itself. . . .

If the motivating force of popular government in peacetime is virtue, the motivating force of popular government in revolution is both virtue and terror: virtue, without which terror is disastrous; terror, without which virtue is powerless. Terror is nothing other than prompt, stern, inflexible justice; terror thus issues from virtue; it is less a particular maxim than a consequence of the general principle of democracy applied to the most pressing needs of the fatherland.

Terror is said to be the motivating force of despotic government. Does your government resemble a despotic government? Yes, like the sword shining in the hands of liberty's hero resembles the sword with which tyranny's minions arm themselves. The despot who governs his dazed subjects with terror is right, as a despot; subdue the enemies of liberty with terror and you will be right, as the founders of the Republic. Revolutionary government is the despotism of liberty over tyranny. Does strength exist only to protect crime? and not to strike down the proud heads for which wrath is destined?

Nature imposes the law of self-preservation on every physical and moral being; crime murders innocence in order to reign, and innocence struggles with all its energy in the hands of crime. . . .

It is noteworthy that the fate of men who seek only public good is to become the victims of those who seek only for themselves, and there are two reasons for this: first, because schemers attack with the vices of the Old Regime; second, because patriots only defend themselves with the virtues of the new.

Such a domestic situation should seem worthy of all your attention, particularly when you consider that you must simultaneously fight the tyrants of Europe, maintain 1,200,000 men under arms, and that the government must continually repair, with energy and vigilance, the innumerable ills that our enemies prepared for us over the course of five years.

What is the remedy for all these ills? We know of none other than enhancing virtue, this general motivating force of the Republic.

Democracy perishes through two kinds of excess: the aristocracy of those who govern, or the people's contempt for authorities that they themselves established, contempt which results in each clique, each individual drawing public power to himself and leading the people, by chaotic excesses, to ruin or to the rule of a single person. . . .

But let us put our minds at rest; this is the sanctuary of truth; here reside the Republic's founders, the avengers of humanity, and the destroyers of tyrants.

Here, one need only point out an abuse to destroy it. We need only appeal to the virtue and glory of the National Convention in the name of the fatherland to guard against selfishness and the weakness of individuals.

We mean to excite a solemn discussion of all sources of the Convention's uneasiness and all that can influence the Revolution's progress; we beseech the Convention to prohibit any particular and hidden interest from usurping the ascendancy here of the general will of the assembly and the indestructible power of reason.

Today, we limit ourselves to moving that you consecrate, with your formal approval, the moral and political truths on which your domestic administration and the stability of the Republic should be founded, just as you have already consecrated the principles of your foreign policy: in that way, you will rally all good citizens, you will eradicate conspirators' hopes; you will insure your progress and outwit the schemes and lies of kings; you will do honor to your cause and your character in the eyes of all people.

Give the French people this new proof of your zeal to protect patriotism, of your inflexible justice against the guilty, and of your devotion to the people's cause. Order that the principles of political morals that we have just elaborated be proclaimed in your name, within the Republic and beyond its borders.

65. L.-A.-L. Saint-Just, "Report in the Name of the Committees of Public Safety and General Security Concerning Prisoners, Presented to the National Convention on 8 Ventôse Year II" (FEBRUARY 26, 1794)

Louis-Antoine-Léon de Saint-Just was known among revolutionaries for his oratorical skill and fervent commitment to revolutionary principle. When he was elected to the Convention in 1793, Saint-Just was its youngest member; he was elected to the Committee of Public Safety the following spring. In this speech, Saint-Just proclaims the government's commitment to redistributing wealth by promising to confiscate and share out the property of the republic's enemies. While Saint-Just himself was quite likely committed to what several of his colleagues on the Committee of Public Safety saw as an extremely radical measure, others treated this as a means to win over followers of Hébert.

You decreed, on the fourth of this month, that your combined committees of Public Safety and General Security would make a report to you on imprisonment, on the most immediate means to recognize and free oppressed innocence and patriotism and to punish the guilty.

I do not want to treat this question before you as if I were prosecutor or defender, or as if you were judges; because the imprisonments are rooted not in judicial relations but in the security of the people and the government. I do not want to speak of the storms of a revolution as if of a rhetorician's argu-

Source: Saint-Just, *Oeuvres complètes,* ed. Michèle Duval (Paris: Éditions Gérard Lebovici, 1984), pp. 698–707. Translated by Laura Mason.

ment; you are not judges, and you are not to decide according to civil interests but according to the security of the people, which is placed above us.

Nevertheless, justice is necessary; but justice that results from public rather than particular interests.

Therefore, you have less to decide what matters to this or that individual than to decide what matters to the Republic; less to cede to private opinions than to make universal notions triumph.

Imprisonment encompasses several political issues: the constitution and solidity of the sovereign; republican morals, virtues, and vices; the happiness or unhappiness of future generations; the economy, because of your notions of wealth and property; principles that lay forgotten until today, underrated reconciliations without which our Republic would be only a dream, destroyed upon awaking. Imprisonment encompasses the progress of reason and justice. Review the periods that brought it about: we have passed from contempt of the rebel minority to defiance, from defiance to the setting of examples, from the setting of examples to terror.

Imprisonment involves the defeat or triumph of our enemies. I do not know how to express my thought by halves; I am without leniency for my country's enemies, I know only justice. . . .

The foreigner has only one means to defeat us: by distorting and corrupting us, because a Republic can only be based on nature and its morals. It was Philip who shook Athens; it is the foreigner who wants to reestablish the throne, who responds to our soaring words with terrible crimes that remain with us.

When a Republic that neighbors a tyranny is troubled, it must have powerful laws; it need not care for the partisans of its enemies, nor even for the indifferent.

It is the foreigner who unofficially defends the criminals.

The natural agents of this perversity are men who make common cause with the Republic's enemies in their pursuit of vengeance and personal interest.

You wanted a Republic, but if you do not also want the means to constitute one, it will bury the people beneath its ruins. A Republic is constituted by the total destruction of all opponents. There are complaints about revolutionary measures! But we are moderates in comparison with other governments.

In 1788, Louis XVI sacrificed eight thousand people of all ages and both sexes in Paris, in the rue Mêlée and on the pont Neuf. The court revived the scenes at the Champ-de-Mars; it had hangings in the prisons; the drowned fished from the Seine were its victims; there were four hundred thousand prisoners; fifteen hundred smugglers a year were hanged; three thousand men were broken; there were more prisoners in Paris then than there are today. In times of famine, troops marched against the people. Travel across Europe: there are four million prisoners in Europe whose cries you do not hear, while your parricidal moderation allows the enemies of your government to triumph. Fools that we are, we take metaphysical luxury in showing off our principles while kings, a thousand times more cruel, sleep upon their crimes.

Citizens, how have you deluded yourselves into believing that you are inhuman? Your revolutionary tribunal made three hundred wretches perish in the past year: did not the Spanish Inquisition do more than that? And for what cause, good God! Have the tribunals of England not killed anyone this year? And what of Bender, who had Belgian babies roasted! No one speaks to you of the dungeons of Germany, where the people are buried! Does anyone counsel clemency to the kings of Europe? No, do not let yourselves weaken. . . .

To see the indulgence of some, one would think them the proprietors of our destiny and the pontiffs of liberty. Our history, since last May, is exemplary of the terrible extremities to which indulgence leads. Dumouriez had, at that time, overturned our conquests; patriots had been stabbed in Frankfurt; Custine had handed over Mayence, the Palatinate, and then the Rhine; Calvados was on fire; the Vendée was finally triumphant; . . . the whole world betrayed you, and it seemed that governing the state and commanding troops meant nothing more than handing them over and picking up the pieces. . . .

The Constitution rallied the sovereign. You mastered fortune and victory and you finally turned the same vigor against the enemies of liberty that they had turned on you; because while they counseled scrupulousness to you in defending the fatherland, Précy, Charette, and all other conspirators destroyed those who did not share their opinions and refused to rally to them; those who try to irritate us do nothing and propose nothing to irritate our enemies; to listen to them, one would think that Europe is peaceful and had not raised arms against you; to listen to them, one would think that the frontiers are as peaceful as our public squares.

Citizens, they want to bind and exhaust us to make our defeat easier. Seeing the smugness with which they keep you in the oppressor's thrall, it is tempting to believe that we are easily oppressed.

Such is the activity of the new factions: they are discreet because there is a tribunal which delivers death quickly; but they lay siege to all principles and sap the political body. For a long time we were attacked with living strength; now they want to undermine us with wasting diseases; because the Republic seems to have degenerated from the rigor that the execution of Brissot and his accomplices brought: then you were victorious everywhere; then the price of goods fell and money recovered some value.

The blossoming of revolutionary government, which created the dictatorship of justice, has wasted; one would think that the hearts of the guilty and those of fearful judges quietly agreed to freeze justice and escape it.

One would think that each person, frightened by his conscience and by the inflexibility of the laws, said to himself: "We are not virtuous enough to be so terrible; philosopher-legislators, take pity on my weakness; I do not dare say to you: I am depraved; I prefer to say: you are cruel!"

We will not achieve stability with such maxims. I told you that the system of the Republic is tied to the destruction of aristocracy. . . .

A few more strokes of genius are necessary to save us.

Is it out of care for their tyrants' pleasures, then, that the people spill their blood at the frontiers, and that families mourn their children? You recognize the principle that he alone has rights in our fatherland who helped to free it. Eliminate the poverty that dishonors a free state; the property of patriots is sacred but the goods of conspirators are there for the wretched. The wretched are the powerful of the earth; they have the right to speak as masters to the governments who neglect them. These principles are subversive of corrupt governments; they will destroy yours if you allow it to be corrupted; therefore, slay injustice and crime if you do not want it to slay you. . . .

I dare say that the Republic would soon flourish if the people and its representatives had the greatest influence, and if the sovereignty of the people were purged of the aristocrats and accountants who want to usurp it to win immunity. As William said, "Is there any hope of justice when wrongdoers have the power to condemn their judges?" Let no ill be pardoned or go unpunished by the government; justice is more formidable against the Republic's enemies than is terror alone. Let not the traitors who escaped terror and who speak, escape justice, which weighs their crimes in her hand! Justice condemns the people's enemies and the partisans of tyranny who are among us to eternal slavery. Terror allows them to hope for the end; because, as you have seen, all storms end. Justice condemns bureaucrats to integrity; justice makes the people happy and consolidates the new order of things. Terror is a double-edged sword, which some have used to avenge the people and others have used to serve tyranny; terror filled the prisons but the guilty went unpunished; terror passed like a storm. Do not expect to achieve lasting rigor in the public character except through the force of institutions; a terrible calm always follows our tempests, and we are always more lenient after terror than we were before.

The authors of this depravity are the Indulgents, who do not bother to demand accounts of anyone, because they fear that the same will be demanded of them; so, because of a tacit agreement among vices, the fatherland finds itself sacrificed to the interest of each rather than seeing all private interests sacrificed to the fatherland. . . .

How long will we be the dupes of our domestic enemies, of misplaced leniency, of foreign enemies whose projects we favor through our weakness? Spare the aristocracy, and you bring about fifty years of trouble. Dare! This word sums up the entire policy of our Revolution.

The foreigner wants to rule over us through discord: extinguish it by imprisoning our enemies and their partisans. Return war for war! Our enemies cannot long resist; they will make war against us to destroy one another. Pitt wants to destroy the house of Austria; Austria, Prussia; and everyone wants to destroy Spain; this is the horrible and false alliance that wants to destroy the Republics of Europe.

For your part, destroy the rebel faction; celebrate liberty; avenge the patriotic victims of intrigue; make good sense and modesty the order of the day; do not suffer there to be a single unfortunate or poor person in the state; only at this price will you make a Revolution and a true Republic. Oh! Who knows better than you the unhappiness of the good and the happiness of the evil?

Your committees present you with the following decree:

Article 1: The Committee of General Security is invested with the power to free detained patriots. Every person demanding liberty will give an account of his conduct since May 1, 1789.

Article 2: The property of patriots is inviolable and sacred. The goods of persons recognized as enemies of the Revolution will be sequestered for the Republic's profit; these persons will be detained until the declaration of peace and then banished in perpetuity.

CHAPTER 11

THE THERMIDORAN REACTION

66. J.-L. Tallien on the Terror (AUGUST 28, 1794)

Jean-Lambert Tallien was a representative on mission during the Terror. Recalled to Paris because of corruption and unable to redeem himself politically with Robespierre, Tallien became one of the architects of 9 Thermidor and an unabashed reactionary thereafter. The following speech had a precise political intent—it was associated with another deputy's motion to denounce several members of the Committees of Public Safety and General Security—but Tallien makes a broader argument as well. He suggests that the Terror should not be treated as a simple succession of events or as the outcome of critical legislation, but as a specific way of exercising power. Note the associations he draws between Terror and Old Regime.

The organization of your committees has been completed. The government is functioning once more; all parts of the public administration, supervised in a more active way, will finally set sail to the ship of state which has so long been tossed about by factions.

But we must not, we cannot hide the fact that Robespierre's shadow still hangs over the Republic; minds so long divided, so violently troubled by the infernal genius of this tyrant of opinion, this declared enemy of his country's liberty, are not yet reconciled as all good citizens wish them to be. A few disagreements over the adoption of a few measures, over the practical application

Source: Gazette Nationale, ou Le Moniteur universel, August 30, 1794. Translated by Laura Mason.

of a few principles, allowed our common enemies a moment of hope. Therefore, we must now explain ourselves frankly; here in the arena where the liberticidal projects of Capet and Robespierre were uncovered and punished, we must foil the projects of aristocratic malevolence as well; with a loyal exposition of our sentiments, we must prove to France and all of Europe that we are worthy of representing twenty-five million men and insuring their happiness after having established and consolidated public liberty. . . .

The only government capable of completing and guaranteeing the Revolution is one which knows how to make the Revolution loved, and how to instill fear in those who betray it. To make most people love a Revolution which is their own work, one need only refrain from corrupting it, from changing its fundamental principles, from thwarting its objective.

There are two means by which a government may make itself feared: it may limit itself to keeping watch over improper *actions*, threatening and punishing them with appropriate penalties; or it may threaten *individuals*, threaten them always and for everything, threaten them with the most cruel punishments imaginable. These two methods have different effects: the former raises the possibility of fear, the latter produces unceasing torment; the former is a promise of terror which follows upon crime, the latter is terror itself which settles over the soul despite a feeling of innocence; the former is a reasonable fear of laws, the latter an unreasoning fear of individuals.

The characteristics of terror are worth considering; terror is a perpetual and generalized trembling, an external trembling that affects the deepest fibers of the being, degrading man and making him like a beast; it is the weakening of all physical abilities, the disturbance of all moral faculties, the upheaval of all ideas, the inversion of all affection; [terror] strips [the spirit] of all the sweetness of hope and the resources of despair. An extreme emotion, terror can be neither anything more nor anything less. Fear of laws can, on the contrary, be augmented according to need.

Which of these two fears can best support, complete, guarantee the Revolution? That is the question I will consider.

Let us begin with terror; judge it by its means, its effects: a government can only inspire terror by threatening capital punishment, by threatening it endlessly, and by threatening everyone with it. . . .

To make everyone fearful, it is necessary not only to propose a torment for every action, a threat for every word, a suspicion for every silence, but as well to set a trap for each step, to place a spy in each house, a traitor in each family, murderers in the court. In a word, it is necessary to know how to torture all citizens by tormenting a few, how to take the lives of the latter in such a way as to shorten those of the former: this is the art of spreading terror; is this the art of a steady, free, humane government, or is it one of tyranny?

But I hear the question: Cannot the system of terror be deployed against *suspect groups* without touching others? I ask in turn how anyone can be secure where there is not justice for all, where deeds are judged by who commits

"The Mirror of the Past to Protect the Future": A reactionary's graphic attack on the horrors of the Terror. *(Musée Carnavalet/Photo Bulloz)*

them and persons are not judged by their actions; as for the rest, I add that terror must be everywhere or it is nowhere.

The Convention must not suffer the Republic to remain any longer divided between two classes: those who create fear and those who fear, those who persecute and those who are persecuted. Couthon and Robespierre can no longer prohibit the defense of the principles of equality and justice. I am asked once more, is it possible to instill terror in the hearts of evil-doers without disturbing the good citizens of no matter what class? Again, I say no; because if the government of terror pursues a few citizens for their presumed intentions, it will frighten all citizens; and if it limits itself to supervising deeds and their punishment, it does not inspire terror but that other kind of fear of which I spoke earlier, the healthy fear of punishments that follow crime. Therefore, one may truly say that the system of terror presupposes that those charged with spreading it will exercise arbitrary power. . . .

The system of terror presupposes two excesses which are always new and always increasing: one did nothing by striking off twenty heads yesterday unless one strikes off thirty today, and sixty tomorrow; and, no matter how rapid the progression, it will never outpace the progression of the resentments kindled daily.

Moreover, the more hateful one makes life, the more hateful must one make death so that it will be feared. At first, the idea of hemlock is enough to frighten the imagination; then, to strike the imagination the idea of death must be joined with that of bloodshed; next, the victim must be surrounded by other victims, who are made to fall one after the other; then their numbers must be extended, and a man must witness the deaths of fifty others before he is himself put to death; then vary the victims with cruel artfulness, putting to death a virtuous artisan with someone who sucked the blood of the people, a good man with the greatest wretch, finally extend the refinement to killing the father after his son, the husband after his wife, the brother after his sister. . . .

The system of terror presupposes power that is as concentrated as possible, as unitary as possible, and which tends necessarily to monarchy. Unity of action or will can exist in a council or a committee when it is concerned with a regular and suitable administration whose activity is guided by law or by reason; but in a bureau of terror, where there are no fixed rules, where each may accuse the other of doing or wanting to do too much or too little, unity can only emerge from the blind subjection of all to a single person, whose will takes the place of law: but that unity of action is especially necessary to villains, speeding their movements, facilitating their undertakings, hiding their projects, preserving them against their enemies, against justice; just as all enslaved peoples have a king, all thieves have a leader.

Once more, what kind of system presupposes or entails this kind of political organization and these means of leading men? What other system than tyranny, and what system other than tyranny has an interest in terror? Legitimate authority, which has the consent of the majority, needs only that consent to triumph, to avert particular opposition. Terror is only useful to a minority which wants to oppress the majority; it does not matter whether such tyranny is exercised by a king, [or] a triumvirate . . . ; it is tyranny in all of its foulness, and the fatherland calls the knife of Brutus or the sword of Virginius . . . down upon those who exercise it. And the security of French liberty should be placed under a shelter such as this! What! The Revolution can only be completed by Counter-Revolution! The triumph of the Republic can only be achieved by obliterating every trace of the Republic! The sovereignty of the people can only be guaranteed by taking sovereignty from them! [. . . I]f this is how republics are founded, the infamous Nero deserved another fate.

And if it were possible to imagine a tyranny that was only temporary, a dictatorship which necessarily restored sovereignty after having guaranteed political liberty by means of terror, what reasonable mind would want it? There are two reasons to reject this: in the first place, the power of tyranny and terror, as violent as it is, is nonetheless too fragile to serve as a guarantee; in the second place, once tyranny was in a position to restore liberty to the nation, the nation might be in no state to receive it. . . .

[T]he bureau of terror . . . renders the people incapable of receiving liberty and enjoying its benefits. Terror, by repressing the mind, saps it of energy; by revealing danger in everything, it predisposes the mind always to see danger in something; by making existence uncertain, it makes the mind insensitive to liberty and ready to trade servitude against death. When terror is disseminated in the name of liberty, it does worse than create indifference to liberty, it makes it hated; and it makes this hatred not only an incurable, but a hereditary ill which fathers, in the name of prudence, cowardice, and servitude, transmit to their children. Terror, when it becomes a habitual state of mind, focuses man on himself and on the meanest part of himself, which is to say on his physical existence; it breaks all ties, destroys all affection; it destroys fraternity, sociability, morality; it reduces the spirit to pure egoism. . . .

[T]his system [of terror] was Robespierre's system; he was the one who put it into practice with the help of a few subordinates, some of whom perished with him and others of whom were buried beneath public contempt. The Convention was a victim of it, never an accomplice. The nation and Europe have charged Robespierre with crimes that were the result of this system, seeing that they now give Robespierre's name to this infernal system. Public and private resentments were satisfied by the punishment of this monster and his accomplices.

Certainly, the Convention will not lend an ear to orators who dare to suggest that it take responsibility for some of Robespierre's crimes by calling itself his successor; that it call down upon itself some of the hostility it should not share with the wretch it punished; that it provoke a reaction for which there has been neither object nor pretext since the execution of the guilty; only those who shared in tyranny can still counsel resort to it; only those who require justice dread outraged justice; only those who have plunged themselves into the mire want to drag the Convention through it.

I come now to the kind of fear that must be employed to complete and consolidate the Revolution: it is the fear of laws for actions against the law.

1. Fear of laws can be heightened by creating a police force to supervise their observance.

2. This fear can be directed toward the interests of the Revolution, by making specific laws in its favor; therefore a revolutionary government can and must exist; but rather than being arbitrary, this government should, in a word, complement the essential order of political society; it should be a stern institution and yet one sufficiently just to lay the groundwork of a free constitution.

It is presumptuous to distinguish two kinds of liberty at the podium of the Convention; there is only one justice, citizens; that which does not recognize men but which weighs deeds; that kind of justice alone sits in judgment, all else murders. . . .

67. P. Gaveaux and J.-M. Souriguières, "The Alarm of the People" (JANUARY 1795)

"The Alarm of the People," first performed in January 1795, was quickly adopted by young men who called themselves "gilded youth." Arguing that the Convention was not acting quickly enough to dismantle the policies of the Terror, the "gilded youth" took it upon themselves to "purge" cafés and theaters of radical republican symbols and personnel; in other words, they often overturned busts of Marat, tore down café signs, and publicly humiliated Jacobin actors while singing "The Alarm of the People." The song went on to experience brief popularity as the tune of all French men and women who were opposed to the Terror, but it was later labeled counter-revolutionary and outlawed by the government.

French people, people of brothers,
Can you see without a shudder of horror,
Crime unfurling its banners
Of carnage and Terror?
You suffer that an abominable horde,
Of assassins and brigands,
Soils with its ferocious breath,
The lands of the living!

What! this cannibalistic horde,
Vomited up from the depths of hell,
Preaches murder and carnage!
It is covered with your blood!
Before your eyes, before those of the fatherland,
It murders children,
And contemplates a slaughter
Of your dignified legislators.

What is this barbaric languor?
Make haste sovereign people,
To return to the monsters of Tenairon
All these drinkers of human blood.
War against all emissaries of crime!
Hound them unto death;
Share the horror that impels me,
They will not escape us.

Ah! they will perish, these malefactors,
And these raging murderers,
Who carry in the depths of their souls,
Crime and the love of tyrants!
Plaintive shades of innocence,
Soothe yourselves in your tombs,
The belated day of vengeance
Will at last blanche your executioner.

See already how they tremble;
They don't dare flee the scoundrels!
The traces of blood that they vomit
Will soon slow their steps.
Yes; we swear upon your tomb,
By our unhappy land,
To do nothing other than massacre
These horrible cannibals.

Representatives of a just people,
O you humane legislators,
Whose august countenances
Make our vile assassins tremble,
Follow the path of your glory,
Your names, beloved by humanity,
Fly to the temple of remembrance,
In the bosom of immortality.

68. The Prairial Uprising (MAY 20–23, 1795)

As bread prices rose and supplies shrank during the spring of 1795, many work-ing women and men recalled that essentials had been available under the con-trolled economy of 1793–1794. Therefore, it is hardly surprising that during the last two popular insurrections of the Revolution—those of Germinal and Prai-rial—many of the insurgents called for "bread and the constitution of 1793." During both insurrections, women played a key role (as they always did when subsistence was at issue) and crowds invaded the Convention in an effort to elicit favorable legislation like that which they had won in September 1793. They had limited success during the Germinal insurrection, and the Prairial events were followed by a harsh repression that reached into the heavily working-class neigh-borhoods of the faubourg Antoine. About seventeen hundred militants were dis-armed and twelve hundred imprisoned. The defeat of the Prairial insurgents marked the end of the sans-culottes movement.

National Convention, Session of 1 Prairial

Vicious rumors, seditious words, brazen complaints, and horrible threats punctuated the night of 30 Germinal; only groups were visible, almost all composed of women who promised an uprising for the following day. They said loudly that it was necessary to attack the National Convention; that the Convention had allowed people to die of hunger for far too long; that it only had Robespierre and his accomplices executed so it could take over the gov-ernment, tyrannize the people, and subject them to famine by raising the prices of essentials and protecting the merchants who feed on the sweat of the poor. A pamphlet was circulated containing plans for the uprising, the means to be used, and the demands that ought to be made. People announced that women would be placed in the lead, because they were certain that the Con-vention would not dare open fire on them; they added that once the women had prepared the way, men would come to help them. This plan was entirely successful.

Today, there was a call to arms and the alarm was sounded in the faubourgs Antoine and Marcel at five in the morning; the crowd gathered. The Committee of General Security, informed of this movement, sounded the recall for soldiers at about eight o'clock; it was almost noon before the forces were gathered. At eleven o'clock, the Convention opened the session that we are about to describe. . . .

Source: Gazette Nationale, ou Le Moniteur universel, May 23, 1795. Translated by Laura Mason.

ISABEAU: Citizens, you are aware of the rebellion that is being organized; the Committee of General Security has commissioned me to inform you of the plan of insurrection that is being circulated widely in this city. [He reads.]

Insurrection of the People, to Obtain Bread and Recover Their Rights

The people, considering that the government has inhumanely allowed them to die of hunger; that the government's repeated promises are misleading and false;

Considering that each citizen is reduced to envying the unhappy fate of those whom famine sends daily to their graves;

Considering that the people will fail themselves and future generations if they do not hasten to guarantee their subsistence and recover their rights;

Considering that the government is illegitimate, unjust, and tyrannical when it arbitrarily arrests those who have the courage and the virtue to lay claim to bread and common rights, transferring them from dungeon to dungeon, from town to town, and massacring them in the prisons;

Considering that an illegitimate and tyrannical government only founds its criminal hopes and strength on the weakness, ignorance, and misery of the people;

Considering that such a terrible government can only last as long as we have the weakness to fear and obey it; . . .

Considering that the republicans in the departments and in the army are watching Paris, which is responsible to them for any delay;

Considering that insurrection is *the most sacred of rights, the most essential of duties*, a need of the first order for all people and for each oppressed part of the people;

Considering that it belongs to that portion of the people closest to the oppressors to recall them to their duties, because the people's position allows them to know the source of ills:

The people decree the following:

Article 1: Today, without further delay, the citizens and citizenesses of Paris come en masse to the Convention to demand of them:

1. Bread;
2. The abolition of revolutionary government, which each faction abuses in turn to ruin, starve, and subjugate the people;
3. To demand that the National Convention immediately proclaim and establish the democratic constitution of 1793;
4. The dismissal of the current government, its immediate replacement by other members of the National Convention, and the arrest of each member of the current committees of government as guilty of crimes against the nation and tyranny against the people;

5. The immediate release of citizens detained for having demanded bread and having freely expressed their opinions;

6. The convocation of primary assemblies for next 25 Prairial, to renew all authorities, who must behave and act constitutionally until that period;

7. The convocation of a national, legislative assembly to replace the Convention next 25 Messidor. . . .

Note: Undoubtedly, the government will try to inhibit the effect of the above-mentioned measures; but it will not be able to do so. It will not in any way succeed in undermining the people's indignation and its own just punishment; at the same time, the government will open the storehouses that it has kept closed and which it reserves for its own infamous projects.

(*Loud applause sounds in several parts of the galleries. The assembly maintains the deepest silence.*) . . .

Clauzel bares his chest to the citizens in the galleries and shouts: "Those who replace us by marching over our corpses will not work with any greater zeal for the good of the people. Citizens, think hard: the leaders of the movement will be punished, and the sun will not set on their trespasses." (*More applause*) . . .

BOURDON (of the Oise): Today is a repetition of 12 Germinal; today we find ourselves in the same circumstances as we did then. On 12 Germinal, we were on the eve of peace with the king of Prussia. Today, we are on the eve of having peace with most of the allied powers. That is what they want to prevent. They use every means to disgust all their agents, who make up Paris, and to persuade them that we are close to a general upheaval. They want us to tear ourselves apart once more to prolong our ills. (*Applause*)

I can see nothing in all of this but the fury of royalists, the fury of unsworn priests who will not breathe easily unless they do so over the corpses of republicans and the ruins of the fatherland. (*Applause*)

They ask for the constitution of 1793; we want it as well; but it must be made to work, we must be able to put it into action: organic laws are being considered at this very moment and they will soon be completed.

People, I beg you, in the name of the liberty that you conquered, do not dishonor the glory of so much work. Do not make five years of privation and sacrifice useless! After having done so much for liberty, can you refuse to put up with a few difficult moments on its behalf? Just a few days more, and your suffering will end. (*Applause*) . . .

ANDRÉ DUMONT: This disturbance has long been in preparation; the public papers provoke revolt. Opinion is manipulated in every way; above all, the class of workers is led astray; they are led to believe that you wait for them to come demand a king so that you can proclaim one immediately. . . .

Issue a call to all good citizens of Paris, do not allow the preaching of pillage and murder, as is done every day. I ask that as soon as the committees give you a proclamation, it be circulated as widely as possible and soon you will see the crowds designate you as their leaders. Punish Raffet's assassins, punish all those who have watered the soil with blood and tears; let the rich aid the poor, let the poor defend the rich, and union will reign among you. (*Applause*)

... I ask that a proclamation be drafted to enlighten the citizens. ...
The National Convention decrees:

Article I: The Commune of Paris is responsible to the entire Republic for any attack against the national representation.

[Article] II: All citizens, individually and collectively, must go immediately to the headquarters of their section with arms in hand, to receive the National Convention's orders from their commanders.

[Article] III: Those who have not gone to their respective sections within an hour of the publication of this decree will be held particularly responsible for events. ...

[Article] V: The leaders of the crowds are outlawed; good citizens are charged with arresting them and, in case of resistance, chasing them down.

[Article] VI: The first twenty people marching at the head of a crowd will be considered its leaders.

[Article] VII: The National Convention declares that it will not inhibit the rights of citizens to present petitions, as long as such petitions are presented in the number and manner prescribed by the law. ...

This proposal is put to a voice vote and adopted.
(*The women who are in the galleries laugh ironically.*)

National Convention, Session of 4 Prairial

Last night, as the assassin of the people's representative, Ferraud, was being led to his death, a mob of furies appeared and carried him away from beneath the scaffold; immediately, the cry *To arms!* was heard in several quarters. During the night, the government gathered and organized troops. Since four o'clock in the morning, the troops have been advancing silently and without drums; they have surrounded the faubourg Antoine; the rest of the city is calm.

At ten o'clock, the assembly resumed its session.

LAPORTE, in the name of the Committee of Public Safety: The audacity of the factionals is so great, and they have revealed their evil plots with such wickedness, that any sign of weakness on your part would be a crime.

Your committees have charged me to propose the following decree:

"The National Convention, in light of the report of the combined committees of Public Safety, General Security, and the Military, considering that the factionals of the faubourg Antoine did, on the first and second days of this month, march under arms against the National Convention and aim their cannons at its meeting hall, with the intent of extracting decrees from the representatives of twenty-five million Frenchmen; decrees which should not under any circumstances be produced by constraint but should always be the product of the free will of the majority;

"Considering that the factionals threatened once more to raise before France the spectacle of a small portion of the people seeking to impose law on the majority of the nation; that they have insulted the national majesty in the person of its representatives; that they threatened to cover France once more in the funereal crepe that the revolution of 9 Thermidor ought to have torn away forever; that their liberticidal projects are clearly to tear France from the happy epoch when it may finally enjoy a free and democratic constitution, consolidated by peace treaties already concluded and those about to be accomplished, to carry out instead the dissolution of the social body by perpetual anarchy in order to feed once more on blood and pillage, and to give advantages to the enemies of the French name that they would not dare dream of achieving with an army's strength;

"Considering that . . . it is of great import to restore authority to the law; dignity to the national majesty; security and peace to all good citizens; and liberty and respect to the representatives of a great people, without which they may not accomplish their duties, decrees the following:

Article I: The inhabitants of the faubourg Antoine will be summoned, in the name of the law, to deliver immediately the assassins of the representative Ferraud into the hands of justice, and especially to hand over those who shielded him from the execution of the judgment passed against him.

[Article] II: They are similarly summoned to hand over the cannons of the three sections that compose the faubourg to the general commander.

[Article] III: If these summons are refused by the faubourg Antoine, it is to be considered to be in a state of rebellion.

"Consequently, Paris sections are ordered to march under generals' orders to forcefully subdue the rebels; henceforth, all distribution of essentials in the three sections in revolt will cease.". . .

(This project is enthusiastically applauded and unanimously adopted, to the cries of "Long live the Republic! Long live the Convention!") . . .

ANDRÉ DUMONT: I demand that all those who wore any unlawful sign of rallying be arrested immediately, handed over to the courts, and judged as counter-revolutionaries.

This proposal is adopted. . . .

Génissieux had the following decree pronounced:

"The National Convention, after having heard the report of its committees of Public Safety, General Security, and the Military, considering that amidst the troubles that shook Paris, the agitators dressed themselves in women's clothing, in hopes of acting with impunity; that moreover reckless women, incited by the enemies of liberty, abused respect for the weakness of their sex by running through the streets, gathering themselves together, lining up, and disordering all activities of police and military;

"Decrees that all women will retire to their respective domiciles until otherwise ordered; that, one hour after the posting of the present decree, those found in the streets, gathered together in groups of more than five persons will be dispersed by armed force and placed under arrest until public tranquillity is restored to Paris."

The present decree will be printed and posted immediately.

69. Louis XVIII, "Declaration of Verona" (June 24, 1795)

The Comte de Provence, brother of Louis XVI, assumed the title Louis XVIII on June 8, 1795, following the death of the son of Marie Antoinette and Louis XVI. The Comte de Provence had emigrated from France on June 20, 1791, the same day that the king's flight was aborted at Varennes. Once abroad, he quickly moved to the center of the émigré royalist reaction, where his intransigent neo-absolutism, exemplified below, alienated him from constitutional monarchists and helped to stifle royalist attempts at Restoration. Restoration would come only in 1814 when, having defeated Napoleon, the allied powers of Europe returned the Bourbons to the throne of France.

Louis, By the Grace of God, King of France and Navarre

To All Our Subjects, greeting.

In depriving you of a king, whose whole reign was passed in captivity but even whose infancy afforded sufficient grounds for believing that he would

Source: The Annual Register, or a View of the History, Politics, and Literature for the Year 1795 (London: T. Burton, 1800), pp. 254–262.

prove a worthy successor to the best of kings, the impenetrable decrees of Providence, at the same time that they have transmitted his crown to us, have imposed on us the necessity of tearing it from the hands of revolt, and the duty of saving the country, reduced by a disastrous revolution to the brink of ruin.

. . . Our love for you is the only sentiment by which we are moved; our heart delightfully obeys the dictates of clemency; and since it has pleased Heaven to reserve us, like Henry the Great, to reestablish in our empire the reign of order and laws, like him we will execute this divine task, with the assistance of our faithful subjects, by uniting kindness with justice.

Your minds have, by dreadful experience, been sufficiently informed of the extent and origin of our misfortunes. Impious and factious men, after having seduced you with lying declamations and deceitful promises, hurried you into irreligion and revolt. Since that time a torrent of calamities has rushed in upon you from every side. You proved faithless to the God of your forefathers; and that God, justly offended, has made you feel the weight of his anger; you rebelled against the authority which he had established, and a sanguinary despotism, and an anarchy no less fatal have alternately continued to harass you with incessant rage.

. . . You have changed sanguinary despots whom you abhorred for hypocritical despots whom you despise. They conceal their weakness beneath an appearance of mildness, but they are motivated by the same ambition which influenced the conduct of their predecessors. The reign of terror has suspended its ravages, but they have been replaced by the disorders of anarchy. Less blood is shed in France, but greater misery prevails. In short, your slavery only changed its form, and your disasters have been aggravated. You have lent a favorable ear to the calumnious reports that have been propagated against that ancient race which, during a long period, reigned as much in your hearts as over France. . . .

To that ancient and wise constitution, whose fall has proved your ruin, we wish to restore all its purity which time has corrupted; all its vigor which time has impaired: but it has fortunately deprived us of the ability to change it; it is your happiness and our glory: it is the wish of all true Frenchmen; and the knowledge we have acquired in the school of misfortune, all tend to confirm in our mind the necessity of restoring it entire. . . .

The nobility, who have only left their country the better to defend it; who have only drawn their swords in the firm persuasion that they were fighting for France, and not against it; who offer you assistance even when duty compels them to fight you; who oppose to the attacks of calumny their firmness in adversity, intrepidity in battle, humanity in the moment of victory, and their invincible attachment to the principles of honor—those nobles, against whom every effort is made to excite your hatred, will not forget that they are destined to enlighten, to assist, to support the people. . . .

We are called hither by our rights and we know how to defend them. We may there be able to promote the happiness of France, and that motive gives us courage to proceed. If we shall be reduced to the necessity of conquering our country, confiding in the justice of our cause, and in the zeal of true Frenchmen, we will advance to the conquest with indefatigable perseverance and with undaunted courage; we will advance to the conquest, should it be necessary, through the cohorts of rebels, and the knives of assassins. The God of St. Louis, that God whom we call to witness the purity of our intentions, will be our guide and support.

But no—we shall not be reduced to the necessity of using arms against deluded subjects. No: to themselves alone, to their regret, to their love, shall we be indebted for the reestablishment of our throne; and the mercy of heaven, moved by their tears, will make religion once more flourish in the empire of the most Christian Kings.

This pleasing hope revives our heart. Misfortune has removed the veil which was placed before your eyes; the harsh lessons of experience have taught you to regret the advantages you have lost. Already do the sentiments of religion, which show themselves with éclat in all the provinces of the kingdom, present to our sight the image of the glorious ages of the Church! Already does the impulse of your hearts, which brings you back to your king, declare that you feel the want of being governed by a father.

Delivered in the month of June, in the Year of Grace, 1795, and the first of our reign.

70. Nicolas Toussaint le Moyne des Essarts

Des Essarts (see document 7) had participated actively in the Revolution until the fall of the monarchy. He only resumed public life after the fall of Robespierre. Continuing to publish court cases, he turned away from the dramas of private life to the trials of the famous and infamous. These polemical prefaces to his new enterprises are typical of the vehement anti-Jacobin rhetoric of the post-Thermidoran period. Of special interest here is his view of the historian's responsibility to posterity.

Source: Nicolas Toussaint le Moyne des Essarts, "Introduction" to *Procès fameux jugés depuis la Révolution* (Paris, 1796), and "Introduction" to *La vie et les crimes de Robespierre et de ses principaux complices, avec le détail des circonstances qui ont accompagné leur supplice* (Paris, 1797). Translated by Tracey Rizzo.

A. "Introduction," *Famous Trials Judged Since the Revolution* (1796)

Oh, my country! What crimes have been committed in your bosom! Oh, Liberty, the most precious of gifts which man takes from nature, how the heinous deeds of anarchy are permitted in your name!

Will posterity believe that the French have let an innumerable multitude of prisons cover their soil, after having toppled the Bastille? Will it learn, without shuddering, that the cruelty of our ancient criminal laws were replaced, for twenty months, by all the most ferocious [elements] of tyranny, and that our public places were drowned in the blood of the best citizens? Finally, will it recall, without horror, all the outrages committed by cannibals during the too-long reign of anarchy?

Sensible souls will not peruse these annals of crime without being torn with grief; but nature and humanity command [us] to engrave the memory of all these crimes in history, in order to spare future generations their return.

If the condemnation of an innocent has always been regarded as a public calamity, in what abyss of misery, oh, my country, have monsters plunged you to satisfy their furor and ambition!

Liberty of the press, imprescriptible right of man, it is under your auspices that I will write this terrible history!

Finally the odious phantom of anarchy has fallen, losing the prestige which enveloped it in the people's eyes. Its long calamities have taught the people to recognize its enemies. It senses the need to love the truth. I will have the courage to tell it to them and to expose in their hideous deformity those who, after having so cruelly deceived, ended their days by expiating their crimes on the scaffold.

Powerful [are] these terrifying examples that I will show the people, inspiring in them the love of virtue, and persuading scoundrels that rarely do they escape the punishment they deserve!

B. "Introduction," *The Life and Crimes of Robespierre and His Principal Accomplices* (1797)

I will trace the history of the most hypocritical, cowardly, and ferocious of monsters who has appeared on the world's scene for the misfortune of humanity.

Can posterity believe that for eighteen months France groaned under the iron rod of the vilest scoundrel, under Robespierre's abominable tyranny?

However, we can say with a painful sentiment that what appears improbable to our nephews became for us a terrifying truth. Frenchmen! Men of all nations! Have the courage to read this distressing history. Put these terrible lessons of crime in the hands of your children so that they will inspire the horror of anarchy in remotest posterity. While sketching this tableau, the pen fell from my hands twenty times, and I would never have had the courage to finish this work if the idea of being useful to humanity had not sustained me. But, I said to myself, Robespierre dealt the most terrible blows to public morale and to all social institutions; for future generations to avoid the return of the calamities which we witnessed or suffered, it is important to engrave in bronze the history of the tyranny of this impudent tyrant of the French. It is this which determined me to undertake this work.

En me violant trois fois ils m'ont causé la mort !!!

CONSTITUTION DE L'AN III.

PART

FOUR

Directory and Consulate
1795–1803

*L*ong neglected by historians, the Directory seemed the poor relation of the Revolution to those who were attracted by the drama of its early years or eager to move on to the exploits of Napoleon Bonaparte during the Consulate and the Empire. The situation has begun to change, however, as a growing number of scholars turn their attention to the workings of Directorial politics, culture, and society. The picture that is emerging is one of a period rich in complexity and paradox. For, after six years of revolution, the republic was finally endowed with a working constitution which established a separation of powers, promised rule of law, and guaranteed regular elections; but the same legislators and Directors who praised the constitution as the foundation of order and legitimacy violated it repeatedly. After years of bitter and violent opposition, public officials and private citizens alike were creating new arenas of consensus and new ways to understand politics; but old hostilities, tensions, and suspicions persisted, fragmenting the political community and creating a political seesaw that sent the nation careening between left and right. In the end, the Directory would succeed in institutionalizing and preserving many of the Revolution's innovations even as it laid the foundation for subversion of the republic from within.

The New Government

The Directory came into being because the deputies of the Thermidoran Convention refused to revive the constitution of 1793, which had been suspended only

"Having Violated Me Three Times, They Have Killed Me" A cartoonist condemns the government's practice of annulling the results of legal elections. *(Musée Carnavalet/ Photo Bulloz)*

weeks after its adoption. Instead, they drafted France's third constitution in less than five years. The constitution of 1795 was distinct from its predecessors in several ways. Most noteworthy were its restrictions on suffrage, for the new constitution abandoned the universal male suffrage promised in 1793 and created a two-tiered electoral system that would serve as a bulwark against popular government. Accordingly, qualified voters—men who paid direct taxes or who had served in the army—only chose electors, while the electors—a far more elite group of men who paid taxes equal to 150–200 days of labor—actually chose the nation's political representatives. The constitution also restructured government. For the first time, France had a two-chambered legislature, divided between the lower Council of Five Hundred and the upper Council of Ancients. Executive power was exercised by a five-man Directory whose members were chosen by the Council of Five Hundred.

The new Directors, in sharp contrast to the great figures who had led the National Assembly and the National Convention, tended to be men of limited political vision with mediocre careers. Their shifting political sympathies reflected the tumultuous course of revolutionary politics. So, for example, La Réveillière-Lépeaux's ambitions were unknown upon his election because he had been expelled from the Convention as a Girondin in 1793 and only recently reintegrated; Carnot, who had been a loyal Jacobin during the Terror, was in flight from his political past and so moving quickly to the right. Those who were most cynical about the Directory considered Paul Barras its exemplary figure: a venal ex-noble, he placed his own interests above those of the republic and would prove to have few scruples about constitutionality. The other two Directors, Reubell and Letourneur, were noteworthy principally as the allies of, respectively, Barras and Carnot.

The Directors may have been mediocre and selfish politicians, but it is undeniable that they, in company with the deputies of both councils, faced an enormous political task: the economy was in shambles, the nation still at war, and the population fragmented by bitter political divisions. The government rebuilt the economy slowly and steadily. In part, it benefited from favorable conditions as harvests improved after 1795. But concerted action reinforced nature's favors: the Directory abolished the grossly inflated assignat early in 1796 and restored metal currency in 1797; it rationalized tax collection; it wrote off more than half of the public debt. In short, it stabilized the economy. We must not forget, however, that the general picture of a more stable economy was offset by appalling extremes of wealth and poverty: ex-nobles and government contractors displayed their riches at formal dinners and elegant balls while the poor continued to commit suicide at unusually high rates, even in the relatively prosperous years of 1797 and 1798, and to experience infant mortality that was probably well over the national average of 23.3 percent.

Militarily and diplomatically, the nation was experiencing great successes. French armies had taken the offensive in the winter of 1794–1795, and when Prussia signed the Peace of Basel in April, it became the first European power to recognize republican France as an equal. This did not, however, put an end to the military ambitions of a nation that had embarked on a strictly defensive war a mere three years earlier. French armies moved south and east in Europe, creating "sister republics," which they propped up militarily, and pillaging occupied territories of wealth and artistic treasures. It was during the years after 1795 that the army became truly professionalized: soldiers increasingly lost contact with civil society, while their commanders—able to finance themselves by conquest—became impatient with domestic supervision.

While the Directory could claim economic and military successes, the threat of the political seesaw proved its most difficult challenge. By 1795 the French citizenry had fractured into a dizzying array of opinions that traced the whole spectrum of political thought. What might seem like abstract political labels to us—Girondin, Jacobin, royalist, Orléanist—were acutely real to the men and women of the Directory, as much because of the past violence they recalled as because of the futures to which each aspired.

The first tip of the political seesaw came from the left, in the person of a radical journalist who called himself Gracchus Babeuf. Babeuf was part of a loose coalition of former Jacobins and Montagnards who met together to discuss politics and encourage the working people of Paris to revive a more radical republic. Babeuf himself hoped to restore the controlled economy of 1793 and eventually to create an agrarian community of goods. When the Director Carnot received a denunciation in the spring of 1796 that Babeuf and others (who came to be known as the "Equals") were planning to overthrow the government, he acted quickly. The Paris police arrested the "Equals," while authorities throughout France used news of the reputed conspiracy as occasion to arrest and question local radicals who had reemerged during the political thaw following the Vendémiaire insurrection. The denouement took the form of a lengthy show trial, through which the Directors hoped to make clear their commitment to the rule of law and their ability to deal firmly with any excesses of the left.

Meanwhile, royalism, a persistent feature of the political landscape since 1789, continued to threaten as well. Republican armies had effectively repressed rebellion in the west but royalist sympathies persisted there and in the south, offering fertile ground to propagandists who hoped to bring down the republic by constitutional means. In Paris the Clichy Club brought together royalists in the capital, who paired electoral aspirations with secret alliances with émigrés and British agents. In the end, royalist propagandizing throughout the nation was reinforced by the profoundly conservative tendencies of the electors, and the elections of the year V became a humiliating defeat for the republicans. Low voter turnout suggested political apathy but, worse still, the candidates returned suggested outright hostility: 228 of the 234 deputies elected had no political experience whatsoever; 182 were avowed royalists.

Rather than accept a constitutionally legal restoration, three of the Directors—Barras, Reubell, and La Réveillière—set out to tip the seesaw. On the night of September 3–4 (17–18 Fructidor Year V), they ordered troops to surround the legislature and arrest the other two Directors and fifty-three deputies. Barras and his allies completed the Fructidor coup by annulling election results and initiating a political and cultural purge. The police closed down right-wing newspapers, and the courts had prominent royalists executed or deported, while government officials reinvigorated republican rhetoric and tried to renew de-Christianization. The remaining Directors argued that they had saved the republic—a refrain that was becoming all too familiar to French citizens—but they had done so by breaching the constitution and relying on the force of the army yet again.

Seeking a Center

The paradox and enduring strength of the Directory is that the political seesawing and military alliances that would ultimately bring down the republic coexisted with purposeful projects—by public officials and private citizens alike—to create a viable political arena capable of producing legitimate consensus, and a postrevolutionary, republican culture. These projects would constitute the Directory's legacy to the nineteenth century.

Royalist efforts to create a constitutional opposition had been squashed by the Fructidor coup, but their defeat did not bring an end to what may have been nascent efforts to create political parties. Now, however, these efforts were concentrated on the left. With the installation of the more vigorously republican second Directory, Jacobins reemerged to involve themselves in political life. Gathering in small constitutional clubs across the country, neo-Jacobins celebrated political equality and a greater measure of economic fairness. Although there was little contact between individual clubs, which served primarily as political refuges from local conservatism, a handful of neo-Jacobin newspapers provided national links, sharing news, aspirations for a more democratic republic, and strategies for working within the existing system. Before the elections of 1798, the neo-Jacobins went further still, energetically organizing voters and electors alike, perhaps laying the foundation for what might, under other circumstances, have led to the development of a multiparty system.

While an important but relatively small fraction of the population involved itself in the reform of formal political practices, a great many people participated in the ongoing search for compromise between church and republic. Many officials continued to regard Catholicism with skepticism and even suspicion, and the government gave expression to these attitudes with a 1795 law that prohibited public religious displays—such as processions or the wearing of clerical vestments—and with the deportation, after Fructidor, of eighteen hundred priests who had refused to swear loyalty to the constitution. Certainly, Catholic hostility against the republic had persisted, especially in those parts of France that had been counter-revolutionary, but, at the same time, other parts of the country were witnessing efforts to reconcile Catholic practice with republican loyalty and to create a postrevolutionary church. Worshippers married traditional means of protest with revolutionary ideologies of liberty and popular sovereignty to demand the right to practice their religion freely and openly. And the synergy between republicanism and Catholicism moved in both directions, for as worshippers broadened republican rhetoric to defend religious practices, they also created new practices and empowered new groups, especially women, in ways that would shape nineteenth-century French Catholicism.

Perhaps the best known of Directorial efforts to reconstruct and renew were in the cultural arena, although here too the results were mixed. The Thermidoran Convention and the Directory echoed the aspirations of earlier legislators when they passed decrees that emphasized the need for free, nonclerical primary education. In practice, however, they fell far short of the aspiration: without adequate commitment of money, teacher training, or school buildings, basic literacy remained a privilege rather than a right.

Meanwhile, France witnessed a flourishing of creativity at the opposite end of the spectrum of intellectual activity. Philosophically, the Directory is best known for the prominence of the Ideologues. Meeting privately in salons and cafés, and delivering lectures at the recently organized École Normale, they built on traditions within Enlightenment philosophy: they celebrated inductive reasoning and argued that all thought, even morality, can be traced to its origins in sensory experience. Many men of science during this period shared the Ideologues' utilitarian emphases and their respect for prerevolutionary innovation. The work of these men had practical applications that were of great import to the broader population: they standardized French weights and measures by creating a metric system, made innovations in chemistry that were to have important applications in the creation of firearms, and developed improved surgical techniques, better midwifery, and the smallpox vaccine.

Less utilitarian culture also flourished. While some critics argued that literature and theater ought to improve citizens by calming their passions and offering them models of moral behavior, others believed that providing an escape from politics would be enough, and they fled to aimless jokes or romantic and pastoral images. Painting showed greater continuity with the preceding ten years and Jacques-Louis David—whose subjects stretched from the classical "Oath of the Horatii" through the death of Marat and on to Napoleon's coronation—played a profoundly important role as painter and teacher throughout the period. Fashion, on the other hand, reflected the new visibility of wealth as surely as the liberty caps and long pants of 1793 had reflected the importance of the sansculottes. Working people continued to dress as they had throughout the Revolution, but the well-to-do took up wigs, elaborate hats, and cravats, and very delicate, almost transparent gowns that were stylized evocations of classical Greek tunics.

The End of the Republic

The electoral efforts of the neo-Jacobins in 1798 were moderately successful, and they gained seats in a number of departments, although once again few voters turned out and once again they favored men with limited political experience. More problematic still, the Directory once again took issue with the election results, which, they believed, had now inclined too far to the left: the government annulled elections in almost half of France's ninety-eight departments and put its own candidates in place. But the Jacobins recovered somewhat in the elections of the following year, and in the summer of 1799, the legislature turned on the Directors, purging three of them and creating harsh laws against counter-revolutionaries and their relatives, which revived fears of a return to the Terror.

By the late summer of 1799, hopes for stability were vanishing quickly. Several men within the government—among them the abbé Sieyès, who had penned *What Is the Third Estate?* in 1789—surveyed the political seesawing, the breaches of the constitution, and the renewal of war that were shaking the nation and began to conspire to establish a stronger, more authoritarian government. Casting about for a figurehead, Sieyès and his allies fixed upon Napoleon Bonaparte, the enormously popular general who returned to France from Egypt in October. Thus, in early November 1799 (18–19 Brumaire) the conspirators persuaded the Council of Five Hundred to meet in a special session in the town of Saint-Cloud, outside of Paris. Once there, they commanded troops to purge hostile deputies and left the remaining few to abolish the legislature and create a three-man executive, composed of Sieyès, Napoleon Bonaparte, and the former Director, Roger Ducos. Although Sieyès had engineered the Brumaire coup with the intention of making himself head of the government, he soon found himself outmaneuvered by the shrewd and popular Bonaparte. By the time the constitution was drawn up, Napoleon had negotiated the powerful position of First Consul for himself, while Sieyès was left with the meaningless position of president of the Senate.

Napoleon Bonaparte is probably one of the most famous figures of French history, and even to contemporaries, he seemed to embody the promise of a revolution that claimed to value talent over birth. Born to an impoverished noble family in Corsica, Napoleon received a military education as a youth and joined the French army before the Revolution. Although the Old Regime army provided few opportunities for advancement to a soldier without wealth or patrons, the armies of the Revolution sped the talented young man along: with the officers' corps decimated by emigration and the pressing needs of the war, Napoleon was made captain by 1793. His career stalled briefly during the Thermidoran reaction until he was given command of the Army of Italy. There he began to build his reputation as a brilliant and successful general, his popularity becoming so great that not even his abandonment of thousands of French troops in Egypt in 1799 could dull his aura.

Napoleon and his supporters claimed that the coup of Brumaire allowed them to preserve the accomplishments of the Revolution, but this was only half true, for even as Napoleon oversaw the consolidation of revolutionary administration and bureaucracy, he initiated the abolition of free press and free elections, two of the most fundamental of the Revolution's accomplishments. What is closer to the truth is that Napoleon and his allies (and, it must be admitted, many of France's citizens) were most interested in domestic order and national glory. Napoleon had already brought glory with the successes of the Army of Italy, and he continued to do so. Thanks to his spectacular victory at Marengo, the French were able to sign the Peace of Lunéville in 1801, which granted French dominance in northern Italy and on the left bank of the Rhine, and fortified Napoleon's strength at home.

Within France, the First Consul developed national administration and attended to revolutionary legacies. As the nineteenth-century historian Alexis de Tocqueville pointed out, Napoleon completed a process of centralization that had been initiated by the kings of France in the seventeenth century, creating a system of prefects who supervised local government and were answerable only to the Minister of the Interior. Like the Directors before him, and the kings before them, Napoleon appointed ministers and bureaucrats to improve assessments and collection of taxes. And he closed the religious rift that had divided the nation since 1791 by signing a Concordat with the Pope. Under the terms of this agreement, the church had to accept the permanent loss of its lands and the legal presence of other faiths in France, but it regained a singularly important place in the nation's public life.

One of the most lasting achievements of this period was the drafting of the Civil Code, which continues to shape French law today. As with so much else, the Code simultaneously institutionalized and corrupted revolutionary principles. Prior to the Revolution, law in France had been a patchwork of royal edicts, local traditions, and personal and group privileges. In sweeping away this welter of regulations, the revolutionaries hoped to ratify the principle of equality before the law and to impose a single, uniform code on the entire nation. Undeniably, the Civil Code accomplished the latter. However, on such crucial matters as divorce and inheritance, its authors reined in revolutionary aspirations by creating more conservative provisions than had been envisioned in 1793 or 1795. And although the authors of the Code paid lip service to the notion of equality, they drafted laws which replaced the castelike hierarchies of the Old Regime with hierarchies of wealth and gender, privileging wealthy employers over tenant farmers and workers, and burdening married women with nearly insurmountable legal and economic disabilities.

While Napoleon accomplished a great deal in France and Europe during his tenure as First Consul, he met with far less success in the Caribbean. By 1800, Toussaint l'Ouverture ruled all of French Saint Domingue, and by 1801 he had conquered the Spanish half of the island. Rather than accepting this revolution, Napoleon sought to turn the clock back by reinstating plantation and slave systems. French troops defeated Toussaint fairly quickly—holding him imprisoned in France until his death in 1803—but they were unable to defeat the people of Saint Domingue. When news arrived that the Consulate had already restored slavery and the slave trade in Guadeloupe, the blacks rose again. The French, finding their troops decimated by war and tropical fevers, retreated and abandoned the island in 1803, leaving Toussaint's former second-in-command, J. J. Dessalines, to found the state of Haiti.

Napoleon could afford to ignore his defeat in the Caribbean in light of his successes at home. Having achieved victory in Europe and mollified or forcibly silenced his opponents in France, he organized a plebiscite in 1804 that asked the population to approve the de facto abolition of the republic. And by a majority so overwhelming as to deny plausibility (3,572,329 votes in favor; 2,569 against) the citizens of France did just that, accepting Napoleon as Emperor and postponing the hard work of creating and preserving a republic for almost a half century.

CHAPTER 12

ORCHESTRATING POLITICS FROM ABOVE

71. Declaration of the Rights and Duties of Citizens
(AUGUST 22, 1795)

The government had been operating without a constitution since suspending that of 1793. Although the members of the Thermidoran Convention initially proposed to revise and restore the existing constitution, they abandoned the project after the Prairial insurrection and drafted the constitution of the year III, which would remain in place for the duration of the Revolution. Besides once again restricting suffrage, the new constitution no longer guaranteed the rights to free expression or assembly, not to mention insurrection; it also dropped the right to education and the guarantee of public relief. Most significantly, in contradistinction to previous declarations of rights, this declaration defined the general will as the simple will of the majority.

Declaration of the Rights and Duties of Citizens

The French People proclaim in the presence of the Supreme Being the following declaration of the rights of man and citizen:

Source: Frank Maloy Anderson, ed., *The Constitution and Other Select Documents Illustrative of the History of France, 1789–1907* (New York: Russell and Russell, 1908; reprinted 1967), pp. 212–214.

Conservative

Rights

added

1. The rights of man in society are liberty, equality, security, and property.
2. Liberty consists in the power to do that which does not injure the rights of others.
3. Equality consists in this, that the law is the same for all, whether it protects or punishes.
4. Security results from the cooperation of all in order to assure the rights of each.
5. Property is the right to enjoy and to dispose of one's goods, income, and the fruits of one's labor and industry.
6. The law is the general will expressed by the majority of citizens or their representatives.
7. That which is not forbidden by the law cannot be prevented. No one can be constrained to do that which it does not ordain.
8. No one can be summoned into court, accused, arrested, or detained except in the cases determined by the law and according to the forms which it has prescribed.
9. Those who incite, promote, sign, execute, or cause to be executed arbitrary acts are guilty and ought to be punished.
10. Every severity which may not be necessary to secure the person of a prisoner ought to be severely repressed by the law.
11. No one can be tried until he has been heard or legally summoned.
12. The law ought to decree only such penalties as are strictly necessary and proportionate to the offense.
13. All punishment which increases the penalty fixed by the law is a crime.
14. No law, either civil or criminal, can have retroactive effect.
15. Every man can contract his time and his services, but he cannot sell himself nor be sold; his person is not an alienable property.
16. Every tax is established for the public utility; it ought to be apportioned among those liable for taxes, according to their means.
17. Sovereignty resides essentially in the totality of citizens.
18. No individual or assembly or part of the citizens can assume the sovereignty.
19. No one can without legal delegation exercise any authority or fill any public function.
20. Each citizen has a legal right to participate directly or indirectly in the formation of the law and in the selection of the representatives of the people and of the public functionaries.
21. Public offices cannot become the property of those who hold them.

This member of the Court of Cassation is dressed, like other men of government and administration, in newly designed robes. *(From* Costumes des Représentants du Peuple, *by Labrousse. By permission of the Houghton Library, Harvard University)*

22. The social guarantee cannot exist if the division of powers is not established, if their limits are not fixed, and if the responsibility of the public functionaries is not assured.

Duties

1. The declaration of rights contains the obligations of the legislators; the maintenance of society requires that those who compose it should both know and fulfill their duties.

2. All the duties of man and citizen spring from these two principles graven by nature in every heart: Not to do to others that which you would not that they should do to you. Do continually for others the good that you would wish to receive from them. *[handwritten: attributing to nature]*

3. The obligations of each person to society consist in defending it, serving it, living in submission to the laws, and respecting those who are the agents of them.

4. No one is a good citizen unless he is a good son, good father, good brother, good friend, good husband. *[handwritten: gender roles + hierarchy]*

5. No one is a virtuous man unless he is unreservedly and religiously an observer of the laws.

6. The one who violates the law openly declares himself in a state of war with society.

7. The one who, without transgressing the laws, eludes them by stratagem or ingenuity wounds the interests of all; he makes himself unworthy of their good will and their esteem.

8. It is upon the maintenance of property that the cultivation of the land, all the productions, all means of labor, and the whole social order rest.

9. Every citizen owes his services to the fatherland and to the maintenance of liberty, equality, and property whenever the law summons him to defend them.

72. Law Against Provocation to Dissolution of Government (APRIL 1796)

The Directory had only been in place six months when it passed the following law. In the wake of two dangerous royalist offensives, at Quiberon and during the Vendémiaire insurrection, the new government had begun to tolerate the

Source: Moniteur universel, April 15, 1796. Translated by Tracey Rizzo.

resurgence of radical press and clubs as a bulwark against monarchism. During the winter of 1796, however, Gracchus Babeuf's *The People's Tribune* and the newly established Pantheon Club began to promote increasingly democratic and Jacobin reforms. As their idealization of Robespierre as a defender of the poor and their efforts to reinvigorate sans-culottism spread in Paris and several provincial towns, the Directory began to fear for its reputation as the guarantor of order. Hence, the following decree, which strikes at political left and right alike.

Council of Five Hundred, Continuation of the Meeting of 26 Germinal (April 14, 1796)

A secretary reads a message from the Directory:

"Citizen legislators,

We have already brought to your attention the necessity of passing a law against the malevolents who violate or elude the dispositions of the constitutional act, who provoke scorn for and the dissolution of authority, [who seek] the reestablishment of royalty or the return of the infamous and anarchical constitution of 1793; it is important, citizen legislators, that you pronounce on this matter. You do not have even a moment to lose, if you want to prevent the seditious from leading good citizens astray. Numerous mobs are formed every day; the perfidious orators who maintain them augment audacity and overtly provoke the massacre and destruction of the legislative corps and the government.

We do not have sufficient means to repress these offenses, which intensify the fears of good citizens. The constituted authorities can only arrest the leaders and bring them before a judge; but the judge, in the absence of penal laws, is then forced to release them.

We require a law, citizen legislators, that pronounces the punishment due to he who would provoke and mislead the crowds by his discourse; it is necessary that the law promise to inflict this on those who, joining the crowd, do not withdraw after the first command of the authorities or of the armed force sent by them.

Made aware of this state of things, the Directory must act responsibly. It thus urgently reminds you of the demand it already submitted to you on this matter, and invites you to take it in the most serious and prompt consideration.

Signed, President Letourneur, and Secretary General Lagarde (of the Executive Directory)"

SAVARY: I believe it is important to propose a law against crowds and against those who want to overthrow the government. I will cite a fact that will doubtless provoke you to take into serious consideration the message which was just read: I have breathed the free air of the camps, I know the soldiers and the spirit which animates them, they are republicans, I do not fear that they want to topple liberty; but I should tell you that the malevolents do everything to mislead them, and to make them partake of the spirit of rebellion that torments them; they will not succeed, but it is necessary to reprimand their audacity. I demand that a commission be named, and that it make its report on this message tomorrow.

TALOT: We have the project of bringing the quarter-general of the Chouans to Paris, and nothing has been neglected to call in the troops in this abominable plot; but those who want to lead the soldiers away from liberty do not know them well.

Decorated with laurels and wounds, and faithful to their victory, they have ever fought for the republic, they will be victors, as during Vendémiaire; but in order to buttress their valor the Legislative Corps and the Directory must bring down the royalists and the anarchists.

The enemies of the Republic redouble their efforts just when a campaign is about to begin, or when you are about to propose a financial plan to save the Republic. People, these are the perfidious journalists, these are the agitators who seek to deceive you. We toil for you, we need your confidence, rally to your representatives. I support Savary's proposal.

LECOINTE: Five years of experience have taught us to recognize the symptoms of popular agitation fomented by the royalists. These symptoms have reappeared in the last eight days; danger is less potent when it is known, but it is less a question of speaking up than of acting.

Pass severe laws against those who excite the reestablishment of royalty or the Constitution of 1793.

All public enemies appear to diverge in their opinions; but they tend to the same goal, to overturn the Republic and its constitution. Therefore, pass laws against criminal provocation, against written provocation, against verbal provocation. You have been prevented by orators' phrases from striking the evil at the root, from wresting the sword from the hand of perfidious journalists who . . .

PHILIPPE DELVILLE: Order! I demand the podium to recall the speaker to order.

LECOINTE: I have spoken all my thoughts; future events will prove perhaps only too well that I was right.

I demand the formation of a commission right away that will report to you tomorrow.

This proposal was adopted. . . .

Meeting of 27 Germinal

Treilhard proposed, and the Council adopted, a resolution which called for the death penalty against instigators of royalty or the reestablishment of the Constitution of 1793, and the dissolution of the Legislative Corps or the Directory.

73. Council of Five Hundred Decrees the Closure of All Political Clubs (JULY 24–25, 1797)

The following is an excerpt from a long and contentious debate that revolves around the right of a free citizenry to assemble. Recovering from Babeuf's Conspiracy of the Equals, which had ended in Babeuf's execution that spring, the government sought to exert greater control over the increasingly restive populace. This included suspending the police legion, which was perceived to be Babouviste, arresting hundreds of subscribers to Babeuf's newspaper, and using the army to put down a Jacobin rising at Grenelle. These repressive measures culminated in the closure of political clubs. At the level of the symbolic, the closure of the clubs foreshadows the Revolution's end, since the clubs had always played a major role in every phase of the Revolution.

THE PRESIDENT: Today's agenda calls for the discussion of societies occupied with political questions. The podium is turned over to the secretary for an address.

SECRETARY DUPLANTIER: This is an address from the central administration of Allier, which has forwarded to the council documents transmitted to it by the municipal administration of Mont-Luçon and which prove that a correspondence exists between the constitutional circle in Paris and that established in Mont-Luçon.

"This meeting," say the administrators, "is the only one to be found in this department, thanks to the vigilance of the constituted authorities. However, it presides over a secret fermentation; above all, we fear the revival of the popular societies of 1793. Our efforts to suppress them will be useless if the Legislative Corps does not promptly come to our aid."

PASTORET: Political associations, these tools of destruction, are not worth protecting. Agitation and change are the essence of these numerous meetings. Moreover, how many times have they disturbed order, prepared and organized revolts? Where was May 31 concocted, for example? Who provided the impetus for that atrocious day? Are not their objectives hatred, vengeance,

Source: Journal des débats et lois du Corps législatif (Paris, 1797), pp. 55–59, 93–95. Translated by Tracey Rizzo.

and the ambitions of the leaders of these infamous societies? On 9 Thermidor, didn't this same society dare to struggle against the return of justice and humanity, and in favor of crime?

After 9 Thermidor, the restriction of popular societies was one of the surest means to return to public order. Thus were closed the bronze doors of this anarchic temple, which had been for three years the capital of all factions. This decision was followed by the dissolution of all political assemblies. Was there any other way to elevate the constitutional edifice without reducing their power? Usurpers of the tribunal, they denounced to the people's fury members of the senate who repelled their ambitious anarchy. Usurpers of the censure, they degraded those whose probity frightened their audacity.

Many passions are weak when they are solitary; united they ferment and are fortified. Facility of calumny, restless need for turbulence, hatred of established government, hypocritical and harassing fanaticism, favored idleness, organized defiance, the perfection of the art of denunciation—that is the history of popular societies. Everything was criminal there, except crime itself.

These were their leaders who established this aristocratic demagoguery, unrivaled in the annals of the world.

Here, Robespierre had the genius and Couthon the virtue. Here one insulted Montesquieu and demanded the honors of the Pantheon for Marat. Here finally, by means of a clever contrivance and after a long reign of impiety, they wanted to accord to the eternal one a certificate of existence, and to the soul a diploma of immortality.

Unanimous opinion, strongly expressed in the constitutional act, is opposed to the revival of popular societies.

[The following day . . .]

PASTORET: After an in-depth analysis of the articles of the constitution concerning political associations, I conclude that where the constitution has recognized these sorts of associations, it has taken and used the most severe precautions against them in order to remove all influence. . . .

But it is said that the abuses I complain of are also linked to the liberty of the press, and yet I defend it. . . . The liberty of the press is for the advantage of all, while the liberty of the clubs is the privilege of a few. The former is in essence a representative of the government as it establishes a correspondence of views and opinions between the member and his constituents; the latter is the opposite because it tends to the usurpation of delegated powers. . . .

JEAN DEBRY: I do not deny the ills which it is just to impute to the popular societies, but I think it is poor reasoning to speak always of the wrongs they have done without ever mentioning the services they have rendered to liberty.

It is not less unjust to attribute to the orators and friends of the peaceful clubs the intention to favor anarchy. If this logic were admitted, we would also be accusing of royalism those who proscribed it, since we can prove that we owe the Republic to the patriotic energy of the diehard Jacobins. But reason speaks another language, and never does it draw conclusions from the particular to the general. . . .

Good governments do not fear the shedding of light, and it is in the peaceful meetings that the rays of light shine with the greatest consistency. Only tyrants fear the vigilant eye of the people. Cromwell prohibited every meeting of more than four persons.

[The following day . . .]

SIMEON (makes a motion): The clubs are not necessary to liberty. If you tolerate them, who guarantees that along with those who appear devoted to the Republic others will not be elevated who defend the anarchic regime of 1793 or the royal constitution of 1791? I fear the weakness of administrations. By what sign do they recognize which clubs are contrary to public order? . . .

The greater the liberty of the press, the less it is necessary to tolerate that of particular associations. . . . I propose to provisionally suspend all popular societies.

The Council, after having declared urgency, passed the following resolution:

Article I. Every particular society occupied with political questions is provisionally closed.

Article II. The individuals who meet in such societies will be brought before the tribunal of the correctional police to be punished for the crime of unlawful assembly.

Article III. Proprietors or principal tenants of locations where these societies assemble will be condemned by the same tribunal to a fine of one thousand francs and to three months' imprisonment.

Article IV: The present resolution will be printed and carried to the Council of Ancients by a state messenger.

74. Proclamation of the Directory to the French People (SEPTEMBER 14, 1797)

Convinced that plots, both royalist and Jacobin, were being hatched against the government, the reigning triumvirate in the Directory launched a military-backed coup d'état on September 4, 1797 (18 Fructidor). In its wake, two Directors were deported to Guiana, along with fifty-three deputies. Moreover, forty-nine departmental elections were nullified, forty-two newspapers were banned, and thirty-

Source: Moniteur universel, September 14, 1797. Translated by Tracey Rizzo.

two journalists were arrested. Provincial administrations were also purged. Here the newly formed Directory justifies its actions and urges patriotic citizens to respect the arts and adhere to familial values.

Citizens,

The French people have above all entrusted its Constitution to the fidelity of the Legislative Corps and the executive power.

The integrity of this trust has been threatened by a royalist plot, organized for a long time, fabricated with skill, pursued with dedication. The Executive Directory discovered the conspiracy; the guilty have been seized: on this matter, the Legislative Corps has taken measures which the circumstances command.

No blood has been spilled; wisdom has guided force; valor and discipline have regulated the mission. National justice has been consecrated to the tranquillity of the people. It was evident to everyone that [we] did not want to displace anything, but to return it to its place.

The Legislative Corps, the Executive Directory have fulfilled their duty.

But the French people have also entrusted its fundamental charge to the fidelity of administrators and judges, to the enlightened vigilance of fathers of the family, to wives and mothers, to the virtuous affection of young citizens, and finally to the courage which distinguishes all the French.

Administrators, judges, fathers, wives, mothers, young citizens, Frenchmen of any age and profession, have you fulfilled your oaths? Have you guarded the deposit that has been entrusted to you?

Frenchmen, open your eyes; it is time to acknowledge the snares in which the king's friends and the enemies of France want to entrap you.

To return you to the yoke you have broken, to lead you there by yourselves, in a manner, they have introduced into all the magistracies corrupt men, as clever as they are perverse, cunning at turning the power they have received for defending and strengthening the people's liberty against it.

They have dishonest judges in your tribunals [who] abuse the independence that the Constitution has given them, and [who] use their rights only to absolve or protect the country's enemies.

Above all they have omitted nothing to return France to monarchical principles, and despotic institutions, holidays, morals, and practices. They know well that man is a creature of habit and that in changing habits one changes man himself.

Without a doubt monarchical principles suit exactly the objective of the conspirators; it was important to them to fit the mass of the nation into a royal mold, but the indignant nation repelled them far from her. The Republic has triumphed and republican principles should manifest and consolidate this triumph; this should be signaled as the fruit of victory.

The republican spirit, republican morale and institutions, republican practices should prevail today: but to embrace them it is necessary to know them better, and to begin by forming the truest ideas of them.

The republican spirit gathers together all interests in the sacred foyer of public interest, composed of all that is just, fair, good, and amiable among men.

Among a people animated by this divine spirit, justice presides over social relations; none seeks to wound the interests of another; the equality of citizens inspires them to mutual aid. If contestation is born, the right to judge is never a lucrative practice which inspires the desire to self-perpetuate; republican justice is the sister of peace.

The sweetest and purest sentiments of nature, the respect for advanced age, the conjugal union, paternal tenderness and filial piety [are] honored in public [and] reign in the bosom of families, and forge all the blood ties of fraternal lineages, love, and happiness.

In homage to the public, the arts bring the treasure of their enjoyments and the pomp of their masterpieces. Eloquence, poetry, and music come together to excite love for country, and to exalt courage in all hearts. Valor and genius are liberty's children; the paintbrush, the chisel, and noble architecture elevate monuments to it. The stage echoes the oracles of morality, the sacred maxims of philosophy, the grand examples of virtue.

The fine arts triumph above all during the national holidays, popular and fraternal solemnities, and august and touching gatherings where a single sentiment unites and imposes silence on an immense people: imposing ceremonies, which would never take place in the palaces of kings and which are an object of horror for the proponents of despotism, but which have an invincible charm for republicans.

In a Republic, writers and men of letters are honored by liberty, profess its maxims, oppose instruction and Enlightenment to error, fanaticism, and lies, lend the support of their talents to the reign of law, [and] to its force the supplement of their genius. They search for the true principles of morals and liberty; it inspires them, propagates them. They teach citizens to love each other more, and to better love the country.

It is here where public instruction should flourish: this invigorating source flows like pure milk throughout all parts of society; all parents are urged to send their children there to drink and to be nourished. Individual instruction is always accorded there with public instruction; the one prepares for and leads to the other. The one and the other are surveyed by the magistrates; and these magistrates in their turn are also the teachers of the people, either by the public readings of government acts, or by their efforts to spread enlightenment, or their zeal to instigate the celebration of republican games and national holidays, above all by the living example of their conduct and their morals.

Finally it is here that reigns the most powerful resort, and the greatest motive for laudable actions and courageous traits, this holy emulation which engages citizens to vie with one another for individual virtue and public utility. The universal right to the best state jobs is the first clause of the pact of equality; no distinction of birth or privilege: merit alone is honored, an imperious motive to elevate men to form great thoughts and undertake great deeds.

People of France, here is what you should be! You would already be this if you had imbibed the spirit of your constitutional act, if you had not listened to those who have defamed the republican spirit in order to reestablish the yoke of priests and kings.

Ah! Cease to believe them. Hasten to quit the path they have traced for you, and which can only lead you to shame and ruin. You should be the model and arbiter for all peoples; they want, on the contrary, to cover you in opprobrium. See how they have deceived you! See for yourselves if the Republic is the reign of terrorism. The Republic has triumphed and yet the blood of traitors has been spared. No, it is not blood which holds republics together. It is necessary to shed blood for an autocratic despotism, but only laws are necessary to build a republic.

The Constitution should be the rule of your morals and your life's compass. Therefore, make your children learn it and recite and practice the declaration of rights and duties yourself: eagerly relearn republican practices which well distinguish you among peoples, and render you forever the example among free nations.

Abjure servile abuses; honor your calendar, a division of time so clear, so convenient, and which, by an admirable trait of republican destinies, reminds you that the year begins anew the day the Republic was born.

For your days of rest unceasingly prefer those indicated by law; these days recall you home, not only for sweet repose, a consequence of and compensation for your work, but also for innocent pleasures, family reunions, the reading of the laws, holidays, and games.

Commercial meetings, fairs, and markets should hereafter be in accord with the republican era. All civic affairs should be regulated only by civil laws. Any usurpation of the domain of the law should cease in the Republic.

Wear the badge of citizen with legitimate pride: this fine title has sacred rights: under despotism, our fathers long desired it; they regretted and deplored the fact that they were not citizens. This name should be dear to you; never give it away, if this is out of scorn. Your speech, finally free, should never be soiled by feudal dispositions, or by shameful distinctions which formerly vilified you, the most modest of which should still wound you as it recalls slavery.

Hereafter the national spirit is formed among you and is raised to the level of your sublime destiny. Be the first free people, and let the distinction "French citizen" be the finest of your titles.

Let taste and propriety preside over your clothing; admirable simplicity should never be banished, let youth avoid ostentation and affectation; [youth] does not need to renounce rallying signs [in favor of] the revolting costumes of the armed enemy; let gentle and modest beauty, adorned with decency, prefer for its ornaments those which have been woven by French hands.

Defend yourself against intemperance, because it is the vice of slaves; frugality is one of the virtues which distinguishes a free people.

Be humane and compassionate; humanity breathes easy among free people, [but is] trod underfoot by despots; the altar of mercy is in the heart of the free man.

Remember the principles that your immortal Montesquieu assigned to the three governments: he gave to despotism the basis for terror; honor is the phantom which kings pursue; but virtue is the basis, the essence, of republics.

People of France! see by this word that which the Constitution, your government, your country demands of you today; do not say to others or to yourself that you are not republican, because virtue is the basis of republics; do not calumniate yourself, and suppress calumny. French people! Be virtuous, love your Constitution, your government, your country, and you will be a republican and nothing will outshine your glory and happiness.

You should be attached to your government, as the two supreme powers, instituted by you, are now attached to one another.

Be awestruck by this grand example.

The royalist conspirators had disunited these two powers; and in breaking this bond, this key to the vault of the social edifice, they were nearly able to dissolve the Republic. Thanks to your destiny, the conspirators are no more, neither in the Directory, nor in the two Councils. The Councils and the Directory finally march onward together, and the Republic is saved!

Long live the Republic!

DISSENTERS AND OPPONENTS

commoner

75. Gracchus Babeuf, *The Plebeians' Manifesto*
(NOVEMBER 30, 1795)

Gracchus Babeuf involved himself in the Revolution from its outset, becoming a self-appointed champion of peasants and urban working people. By the time that he published *The Plebeians' Manifesto*, Babeuf had begun to marry his attacks on the Directory's political and economic arrangements to an increasingly pointed critique of private property. He published this treatise in his newspaper, *The People's Tribune*, which had a subscription of about two thousand people and was quite probably still more widely read. Babeuf was arrested the following year and charged with conspiring against the government; he was executed in 1797.

. . . It is time to speak of democracy; to explain what we mean by it, and what we want it to bring us; finally, to make a plan with everyone to establish and maintain it.

advocating for another constitution

Those who think that I act only to replace one constitution with another are mistaken. We have much greater need of institutions than of constitutions. The constitution of '93 only merited the praise of all good people because it made way for institutions. If that constitution had been unable to achieve that goal, I would have ceased to admire it. Any constitution that allows inhumane

Source: Pages choisies de Babeuf, collected and annotated by Maurice Dommanget (Paris: Armand Colin, 1935), pp. 250–262. Translated by Laura Mason.

and abusive institutions to persist, no longer excites my enthusiasm; any man called upon to revive his peers who only drags himself through the tired routines of old legislation that was given to the happy and unhappy alike by barbarians, will not be a legislator in my eyes; he will not win my respect.

First, let us work to found good institutions, plebeian institutions, and we will always be sure that a good constitution will follow.

Plebeian institutions must insure general happiness, equal affluence for all associates.

Let us recall a few of the fundamental principles developed in our last issue, in the article "Concerning the War of Rich and Poor." Repetitions of this sort do not tire as many as they interest.

We determined that *perfect equality* is a primitive right; that the social contract, far from undermining this natural right, should guarantee each individual that it will never be violated; that, consequently, there should never be institutions which favor inequality and greed, which allow the necessities of some to be diminished to increase the superfluous wealth of others. That, nevertheless, the reverse took place; ridiculous conventions were introduced into society which protected inequality and permitted the spoliation of the greater number by the few; there were eras when the final results of such murderous social rules were that the totality of everyone's wealth came to be grasped by the hands of a few; peace, which is natural when all are happy, inevitably became troubled; the masses, no longer able to exist, finding nothing within reach, meeting only pitiless hearts among the caste that monopolized everything, these outcomes caused the era of the great revolutions, established those memorable periods foretold in the book of Time and Destiny, when a general upheaval in the system of property becomes necessary, when the revolt of the poor against the rich becomes so necessary that nothing can stop it.

We demonstrated that we had reached this point by '89, and that is why the Revolution broke out then. We demonstrated that, since '89 and especially since '94 and '95, the accumulation of calamities and public oppression has made the majestic tumult of the people against its spoliators and oppressors evermore urgent. . . .

True equality is not a dream. The great tribune, Lycurgus, happily undertook the practical test of it. It is well-known how he came to institute this admirable system, in which the advantages and disadvantages of society were shared equally, in which abundance was the permanent share of all, in which none could acquire superfluous wealth.

All well-meaning moralists acknowledged this great principle, and sought to sanction it. Those who expressed it most clearly were, in my opinion, the most estimable men and the most distinguished tribunes. The Jew, Jesus Christ, earned the title but poorly for having expressed the idea too obscurely in a maxim: "Love your brother as you would love yourself," he said. The implication is there but the saying does not express clearly enough that the most important law of all is that no man may legitimately claim that any of his peers ought to be less fortunate than he.

N°. 39.

Le
Tribun du Peuple,

OU

LE DEFENSEUR

DES

DROITS DE L'HOMME.

Par GRACCHUS BABEUF.

Le but de la société est le bonheur commun.
Droits de l'Homme, (de 93) art. Ier.

Tableau critique et analytique des actes du Gouvernement,
et Observations sur la marche de la révolution, depuis
le 13 Vendémiaire.
Effets de la journée de Vendémiaire sur l'esprit public.
Estimation de l'énergie populaire actuelle. Vérité triste
et épouvantable : La liberté, par l'astuce horrible du
Patriciat, a pour ennemis les patriciens, et le gouvernement, et la majorité du Peuple. — Il n'est qu'une
seule ressource pour la sauver; c'est de lui reconquérir
cette majorité du Peuple. Moyens.
But de la narration historique, offerte par le Tribun,
des actes des Trois Pouvoirs, résolutif approbatif et
exécutif, depuis le 13 Vendémiaire : il est démontré
par là que le Peuple ne peut attendre son bien, ni des
institutions, ni des hommes publics qui existent.
Assignation du rang que doit occuper le 13 Vendémiaire
dans les époques révolutionnaires. Ce que ce jour devoit
être et ce qu'il fut. Réflexions et observations atten-
Tome II.   M

Title page for Gracchus Babeuf's newspaper, *The People's Tribune*. Note the epigraph: "The goal of society is the happiness of all." *(Le Tribun du Peuple, no. 39. Reprinted by Éditions d'Histoire Sociale [Paris, 1966]).*

Jean-Jacques expressed this very principle best when he wrote, "In a perfect society, each must have enough, and no one may have too much." This short passage is, in my opinion, the essence of the social contract. The author expressed it as clearly as he could at that time, and these few words suffice for those who know how to listen.

. . . The time has come for the thronging, abused people to express its will in a greater, more solemn, and more general way than ever before so that not only the signs and symbols, but the reality of poverty itself will be eliminated. For the people to proclaim its Manifesto. For them to define democracy as it should be, in accordance with flawless principles, and they want it. For them to prove that democracy is an obligation to be fulfilled, by those who have too much, those who lack, and those who do not have enough! and that all deficits in the wealth of the latter exist only because others have stolen from them. Stolen legitimately, if you like; in other words, stolen with the help of the laws of bandits who, under the last regimes as under the most ancient, authorized every theft; with the help of laws like those that exist at this very moment; with the help of laws that force me to live by stripping my household of furniture each day and carrying it to the homes of the thieves the laws protect, down to the very last rag off my back! Let the people announce that they mean to have restitution for all this theft, for these shameful confiscations of the poor by the rich. . . .

We will explain clearly what we mean by *general happiness, the purpose of society.*

We will show that man's destiny should not deteriorate when he leaves the natural state for society. . . .

We will prove that everything an individual monopolizes beyond his needs is theft from society. . . .

We will prove that *heredity within families* is no less an abomination; that it cuts off all members of the association, transforming each household into a tiny republic that can only conspire against the great and sanction inequality.

We will prove that whatever a member of the social body lacks to meet his daily needs of any sort is the consequence of the spoliation of his natural, individual property by the monopolizers of common goods.

That, by the same reasoning, whatever a member of the social body possesses above his daily needs of any sort is the result of theft from his associates which necessarily deprives a greater or lesser number of their portion of common goods. . . .

That superiority of talent and labor is only a dream and specious illusion that has always wrongfully served conspirators' plots against equality.

That the different values and merits attached to the products of men's labor is only based on the opinions of a few who knew how to make themselves heard.

That it is certainly wrong for such opinion to place a value twenty times greater on a watchmaker's day than on the day of the man who sows.

That, nevertheless, this false estimation helped the watchmaker earn enough to acquire the patrimony of the men of the plough who were, consequently, expropriated.

That all proletarians did not become so except through the same combination of proportional relationships, which were founded on the different values placed on things by the authority of opinion alone.

That it is an absurd and unjust claim that earnings should be greater for those whose tasks require more intelligence, diligence, and concentration than those who listen only to their stomachs.

That there is no justification for earning more than what meets one's needs.

That the value of intelligence is only a matter of opinion, and that it is perhaps worth considering whether natural and physical strength do not also have the same value.

That it is intellectuals who have placed such a high price on the ideas from their brains and that if the strong regulated matters, they would undoubtedly value arms as highly as the head and would compensate fatigue of the whole body as generously as that of the thinking part alone.

That without this proposed equalization, the most intelligent and most industrious are given license to monopolize, entitling them to fleece the less intelligent and the less industrious with impunity.

That this is how the equilibrium of affluence is destroyed, overturned in society because nothing is more easily proved than our great maxim: *that some acquire too much only through others not having enough.*

That all of our civil institutions, our reciprocal transactions are nothing but acts of perpetual theft authorized by absurd and barbarous laws, in the shadows of which we busy ourselves with stealing from one another.

That our society of thieves brings about, as a consequence of its heinous, primordial agreements, all species of vice, crime, and unhappiness against which good men join together to fight in vain; that these men will never triumph because they do not attack the evil at its root but only apply palliatives drawn from the reservoir of false ideas concerning our innate depravity.

That the preceding makes clear that all possessions of those who have more than their individual share of society's goods are the results of theft and usurpation.

That, consequently, it is just to take such possessions back from them. . . .

That the products of ingenuity and genius also become the property of all, the property of the entire association from the very moment that inventors and workers bring them to light; because they are only compensation for previous inventions of genius and ingenuity that these new inventors and workers profited from in social life, and which helped them in their discoveries.

That because acquired knowledge is the property of all, it must therefore be shared equally among all. . . .

That education is monstrous when it is unequal, when it is the exclusive patrimony of a part of the association; because, in the hands of that part, education becomes a heap of instruments, a supply of weapons of all kinds with which they combat the others, who are unarmed, and so easily succeed in repressing them, fooling them, robbing them, enslaving them with the most shameful chains.

That no truth is more important than the one we have already cited and which a philosophe proclaimed in these terms: "Talk as much as you like about the best form of government, you will not accomplish anything until you destroy the seeds of greed and ambition." [Diderot]

That social institutions must therefore strive to take the hope from each individual of ever becoming richer, more powerful, or more distinguished for his abilities than his equals.

That, to be still more precise, it is necessary to succeed in *binding up fate*; in making each associate independent of all chance and circumstance, happy or unhappy; *in guaranteeing sufficiency, and only sufficiency to each person and his descendants, no matter how numerous*; in closing off all possible means for anyone to gain more than his individual share of the products of nature and of work.

That the only way to accomplish this is to establish *communal administration*; to suppress private property; to join each man to the talent or industry with which he is familiar; to require him to place the raw products of his labor in a common storehouse; and to establish a simple distributive administration, an administration of subsistence which, by registering all individuals and all things, will divide the latter with the most scrupulous equality and have them delivered to the homes of each citizen. . . .

People! arise to hope, do not any longer remain numb and plunged in despair. . . .

76. Marc-Antoine Jullien, *Some Advice to the Cisalpine Patriots* (1797?)

Discredited after 9 Thermidor, Jacobins began to revive and reorganize themselves under the Directory. Celebrating the democratic and egalitarian ideals of the year II, they nonetheless accepted the constitution of the year III, which they simultaneously hoped to defend from antidemocratic forces and reform through proper legislative channels. This pamphlet, ostensibly addressed to the republicans of Italy, describes the program by which French Jacobins hoped to organize themselves into a reformist political party.

Publisher's Forward

Some Advice to the Cisalpine Patriots, which we publish today, is composed of fragments that were initially intended to serve as part of a more extended

Source: [Marc-Antoine Jullien], *Quelques conseils aux patriotes cisalpins* (n.p., n.d.). National Archives, F7 3054. Translated by Laura Mason.

work, so the reader should not be surprised by the want of order and connections among the ideas. But, however incomplete this composition, if it offers nothing new, we thought it best not to postpone publicizing it because at least it brings together many of the lessons that seven years of experience have made familiar to the French and which now interest the patriots of all countries.

1. Henceforth, Italy's destiny resides in the cisalpine legislative corps.

2. Once she has proclaimed her complete independence and organized a great republic, one and indivisible, Italy may in her turn exercise great influence on the world's destiny.

3. The new legislators should have recourse to the lessons of experience and the history of the French Revolution, to protect themselves against deviations that could compromise liberty.

4. First faults are irreparable; it is necessary to make a plan, formulate it carefully, amplify it, and so guide all developments by the gradual steps through which they must pass to be successfully executed. . . .

7. All thoughtless or false steps by republicans are that many victories for royalists.

8. In revolutions, prudence supplements strength.

9. Tyrants and their henchmen have machiavellism and intrigue on their side, corruption, calumny, and the art of dividing to conquer; republicans must oppose unity and prudence against tyrants.

10. If republicans are not united, they will be weak and will perish.

11. If republicans are not prudent, they will be like a naked, unarmed man who stands before an enemy armed with a dagger and clothed in armor.

12. Patriotism and enlightenment are almost always in the minority in large assemblies.

13. Unity and prudence can insure the minority's ascendancy over the majority.

14. There must be a secret, directing committee. The different members of the two councils should often meet together privately, to study and know one another, to prevent unjust suspicion and unfounded mistrust, in short to organize themselves, find common motivation, and base all their actions on uniform and unvarying principles.

15. If deputies were isolated, they would have no power, would do no good; they could even do much harm through thoughtless, haphazard, or inopportune motions.

16. Isolated proposals, raised one after another without rhyme or reason, do not bring about a union of men who want the good of the fatherland, but

rather a group of associated measures adapted to current circumstances and in exact proportion to public opinion.

17. Legislators must never forget Solon's words: "I did not," he said, "give Athenians the best possible laws, but those that they could best use."

18. A legislative corps has tactics just as an army does.

19. Patriotic deputies should only assemble in small groups . . . in one another's homes, at dinners, at receptions, without appearing to form private clubs or committees . . . because such things should exist without seeming to.

20. One must never give any hint of coalition, even coalition for good, for fear of giving rise to factions, which are the scourge of a state.

21. Once factions have arisen, they are not long in corrupting and destroying a revolution's principles. Public spirit is extinguished; the good and the bad are mingled, or thrown indiscriminately into the most oppositional parties. Regulation no longer exists, public opinion goes astray, the national conscience degenerates, the only choice remaining to citizens is between one crime and another.

If, on the contrary, the question of the general good is clearly and simply posed, if truth is not obscured nor virtue slandered, if all those who should assist in directing government activity could know and understand one another, if they could inspire that reciprocal trust which arises from the intimate relations of private life and from the clear language of private explanations shorn of the often confusing verbiage of the political tribune: then, all the good will be on one side, all evil on another. The rights and interests of the people would no longer be ignored, they would no longer be abandoned to the passions and caprices of corrupt men; intrigue and slander would no longer reign by sowing discord. *Misunderstandings cause the crime and unhappiness of the world.*

22. Republicans, especially in a state newly organized as a republic, must carefully avoid the appearance of being a party. *The nation, the people*: they must ceaselessly identify themselves with the mass of citizens, always attach themselves loyally to the constitution and the republic, and use only these arms to fight their enemies.

23. Even those who might secretly intend to modify or change the constitution, must not support it any less until peaceful and legal means to correct it become available. . . .

35. It is necessary to consult together so that a patriot never makes a thoughtless or harmful motion.

36. One must be careful when choosing influential personalities and distributing roles. Something that is good in itself can appear bad or may not have the desired effect coming from the mouth of a particular speaker. Sacrifice yourselves so that success is never in doubt.

A member has a good idea; but if it concerns a branch of administration with which he is not familiar—the military or finance, for example—he should have it presented by a colleague who has the reputation of being well-versed in that area, and who can encourage a favorable reception of the proposal.

Is it necessary to attack some abuse or a powerful person? Choose a man who will not appear to plead either the cause of his own interest or that of personal hatred.

37. There are decisions that must be made immediately; there are questions that must be adjourned: it is agreed in advance, the means and actors are prepared. Sometimes a false attack is called for, the better to mislead and confuse those who watch us. Those are the ruses of the art and the secrets of tactics.

38. Those who share the same opinion never place themselves in the same part of the hall, to avoid the appearance of being a faction. But, once divided, they gain greater influence over the assembly in general because they have a certain number of partisans on all sides, who often carry their neighbors. Signals are agreed upon for important occasions; they are given in turn, according to the more or less visible place that each happens to have in the hall, to the most enlightened patriots who, with the single action of sitting or standing, decide the important questions for their colleagues who do not have enough insight to resist shrewd speakers but who, through purity of intent, always side with the republican minority. This minority, I repeat, will only become a majority through the prudence of the men who lead it and the close unity of those who constitute it. . . .

41. In keeping with the principle that one does not want to seem to be in opposition, you must never start out by repealing all existing laws; rather appoint different committees to examine them and propose renewing or modifying them, in order to have stable and uniform legislation.

42. Always keep an eye on the directory and its ministers, but do not engage in unsuitable argument with them. Always show a desire for concord and a willingness to work to maintain it. Strictly prohibit all insulting personalities; do not attack a man without positive actions and proof, then be inflexible and strike concerted blows that will have sure results. When a denunciation is based on evidence, you have on your side the truth, justice, and opinion that rule the world.

43. Never take a step without having tried the ground and without a clear idea of your course; never backtrack.

44. It is necessary to restrain the prerogative of the executive power, which always tends to encroach upon legislative power. Fulfill this responsibility with strict laws, communications, frequent requests for accounts, but without affectation and without ever giving the impression that the two powers are rivals and enemies. . . .

48. It is necessary to make the laws popular, adapted to locales and to the people's spirit, in favor of the poor, farmers, laborers, defenders of the

fatherland; but never make a direct attack on the interests of the rich and large landholders.

49. *One of the secrets of the art of governing is to know how to use even what is harmful.* Direct huge fortunes, which exist, to the benefit of agriculture, commerce, industry, artistry, those establishments suited to developing national activity. You will have more success consolidating the republic by this means than by watering the seeds of internal discord, by irritating and alienating a whole class of citizens with systematic persecution and proscription.

50. Carefully oversee national finances, the apportionment and use of taxes; lighten their burden on the poor. Avoid revolting disproportion when appointing functionaries; put a brake on the rapid accumulation of fortunes; eliminate begging. Make yourselves examples of austere integrity, and fear enriching yourselves: the people always model themselves on those who govern. Woe to you if you neglect to practice the virtues that you should inspire in others! . . .

60. If you infuse your souls with the counsel I have offered you, which is the result of careful thought and experience, if you make it the foundation of your conduct, you will triumph. . . .

77. Old Enemies

By the beginning of 1796, France had a new government and a new constitution. New institutions could not, however, obliterate memories of the violence of terror, civil war, and reaction that had touched the lives of so many citizens since 1792. The two accounts that follow reflect the persistence of tensions in different parts of the country. Chouans were peasants in western France who had organized themselves into guerrilla bands to resist the revolutionary state's efforts to levy troops in 1793–1794; these men and women hoped to restore the Old Regime. Although the Chouans were defeated in 1795, hostility persisted; the movement would reemerge in 1799. Meanwhile, the citizens of Lyons bitterly recalled their experience of the Terror. Having rebelled against local Jacobins and the National Convention in 1793, the Lyonnais were besieged by national troops for almost two months. When the city was defeated, the Committee of Public Safety demanded that it be destroyed; although the orders were not completely effected, many parts of the city were ruined and its citizens subjected to an extremely violent repression.

A. A Chouan in Caen (September 4, 1797)

18 Fructidor, Year V of the Republic

To General Dumeny

Citizen General,

The law has charged you with the surveillance of amnestied Chouans: a man named Gueret, one of their dignitaries, the enormity of whose crimes forced him and his family to take refuge in Caen, has come to live close to our home in the Union section. His terrible hatred of republicans, whom he prides himself on having murdered, is the same as ever; it is likely that he has judged me worthy of being one of his victims.

Yesterday, about 3 o'clock in the afternoon, having opened my door and left my house with my nephew to attend to business, this amnestied Chouan—who was imprisoned a while ago for having disturbed the peace at the Comédie—walked about ten steps behind me and appeared to be very animated; his mother and sister followed him; he took the street of the old church of St. Nicholas; crossing this street, I saw him backtracking with his mother and sister, mumbling the curses "monster" and "criminal." I could not believe that he had given me right of way. Nonetheless, he gratified me. A moment later, he left his mother and sister, who kept telling him to keep quiet. He ran to his house, changed clothes and, not thinking himself sufficiently armed with a thick club, he returned to the attack with his hand in one of his pockets, telling me he had a gun. I waited peacefully until, at the cries of Gueret's mother, a citizen stopped him and prevented him from executing his criminal project. Gueret thought up his project eight days ago in a letter, without place or date, that his brother gave to citizeness Le Mercier: this letter . . . was seized by the citizen Mercier, who had the weakness to burn it when his wife begged him to, but this citizen did not fail to reveal the horrors that it enclosed: two of his servants certify that it existed, and Le Mercier certifies that its contents described me as a criminal, a monster who should have been reduced to ashes long ago.

Citizen General, I ask you for justice against this draft-dodging Chouan, who was amnestied more than a year ago. The law requires him to live in his home in Vire, the scene of his crimes, and he is in Caen. The law forbids him to carry arms, and he is armed day and night.

If there were question of portraying his crimes, which his relative Allais has revealed publicly, you would tremble with horror. The least of them are having murdered both parish priests of Gouvay, and having the watch of one of them sold to Marie, watchmaker in Caen, although the mother Gueret still wears the steel watch chain; having forced women to hold plates beneath their

Source: National Archives, F7 7237. Translated by Laura Mason.

husbands whose throats he slit, to catch the blood, etc. etc. That is a part of the *amusements* attributed to him in front of twenty people, which he did not dare disavow.

Citizen General, protect peaceful citizens whose only crime is that of being unshakable friends of the government; do not allow attacks against their persons; that is one of the finest prerogatives of your duties and your patriotism.

Signed, Hardy.

B. A Jacobin in Lyons (March 11, 1797)

21 Ventôse, Year V

Central Bureau of Police for the Canton of Lyons

To the Citizen Minister of the General Police of the Republic

Citizen Minister,

Our canton recently came quite close to being raked over by one of those horrible attacks that only factionalism can produce and which makes clear the degree of prejudice, blindness, and fury it has reached. On 15 Ventôse, the citizen Julien, chief warrant officer in the army of the Rhine and Moselle, who was passing through our city on his way to Saint-Esprit, took a walk along the quai St. Clair at about 4 o'clock at night; he had a mustache and a circular haircut; but he was in regulation uniform with the proper braided hat; and everyone knows that a mustache is common in the army, and that a short, circular haircut is the simplest and easiest kind, especially for a soldier. Under other circumstances, those parts of the officer's uniform would not have attracted any attention; but the disturbances associated with everything put him in the position of being noticed and considered a Jacobin, a judge of the revolutionary tribunals, and of being associated with the actor Dorfeuille, who is famous in this commune for the violence he exercised at the time of the Terror. This chief warrant officer, in spite of his uniform and hat which visibly attested to his status and rank, was immediately greeted with howls, a huge crowd came running, and there was question of doing no less than throwing him into the Rhône. Happily, he was not far from city hall and an officer accompanying him urged him to go there before the excitement and commotion, which precedes these sorts of attacks, could reach the point of madness that completes them. If we can congratulate ourselves on the outcome of this scene, there is much to bemoan in the predispositions that gave rise to it; they are the fruit of the fury with which some devote themselves to sustaining and renewing hatred with posters and theatrical productions. There is no end to

---

Source: National Archives, F7 7237. Translated by Laura Mason.

the public reminders of the anarchists' terrible acts, as if they still reigned or were about to return; no one ever speaks of the enormous distance or, better yet, of the fundamental opposition that exists between the current government and the revolutionary government that it succeeded in eliminating; all disturbances, all plots, all assaults are blamed on the anarchists, even those that directly and intentionally have anarchists as their victims; the result is that people see Jacobins everywhere at the smallest provocation, they see them even in defenders of the fatherland and in the best citizens. This conduct and the silence that has been maintained regarding the most recent royalist conspiracy makes quite clear that there is remarkable bad faith here and a desire to envelop the current government in the same hatred that is turned against the anarchists. We will not take these thoughts any further, but they will always guide our surveillance and make it deadly for all factions.

Greetings and fraternity,

M. Blanc

78. Anonymous, "On the True Cause of the Revolution" (1797)

Thermidor marked the beginning of popular chaos and counter-revolutionary activism in the south of France that would persist until Napoleon's administrators reimposed order in the early nineteenth century. In many towns and villages, embittered royalists waged a violent campaign of "White Terror" against former Jacobins, whom they harassed, robbed, and assassinated, perpetuating the revolutionary cycle of bloodshed and revenge for years to come. Simultaneously, this part of the country witnessed the return of many refractory priests who joined with and encouraged local villagers' continuing opposition to the Civil Constitution of the Clergy. Much of this activity was initiated under the blind eye of the conservative Thermidoran Convention and First Directory, but the Second Directory would find it enormously difficult to organize the force necessary to reimpose order. The following pamphlet, written in 1797, contains a catalogue of some of the counter-revolutionary grievances that lay behind the ongoing violence and disorder.

A discourse presenting a sketch of the calamities which have plagued France for eight years, and which war perpetuates, in the form of a prayer to God so

Source: "De la véritable cause de la Révolution." Par un citoyen d'un Département du Midi soumis aux Lois, mais attaché à la Religion de ses pères et ami de la vérité (1797). In the Bibliothèque de la ville de Toulouse. Translated by Tracey Rizzo.

that he will relent, have pity on this unfortunate Empire, finally bring peace to it, and bless the French people to choose good deputies in the next elections.

By a citizen from the department of the Midi, humble before the law, but attached to the religion of his fathers and a friend of truth.

Oh, God, infinitely patient because you are eternal! but who sometimes suddenly manifests your justice for the instruction and the conversion of the impious and the wicked. The multiplied crimes and conspicuous irreligion displayed by the French nation for several years have attracted the scourge of your just indignation; you have not spared it calamities and you have spread a spirit of vertigo and madness among this impious and sacrilegious people. . . .

By the arrogance and injustice of its proceedings, the first legislature excited the indignation of neighboring peoples, forcing them to form coalitions and take up arms to halt the progress of the French epidemic which began to engulf them. Yes, astonishing event! The allied powers have often been forced to cede terrain to the French armies, which, like torrents, have burst forth with an unrivaled rapidity and fury which nothing is able to resist; these armies have also had the fate of torrents which are dispersed and disappear. What sad laurels won by these armies! Alas! They have been covered and buried under a heap of cypress. Instead victory chants, moans, wails, and cries of despair have been heard from the orient to the occident, from the north to the south. Aggrieved fathers and mothers vainly demand from the Republic those to whom they gave birth, [those who would] support them in their advanced age; wives uselessly reclaim their husbands, children their fathers. They are no more. . . .

But, Lord! in the midst of the blows which you are forced to deal a rebellious people, have you forgotten that you are still its father? . . . Because we have not obeyed your commandments we have been delivered to pillage, to death, and have become a laughing stock and the object of every nation's scorn. . . .

Then you permitted, good God, the toppling of the throne and the abolition of the monarchy! Then you permitted philosophers to seize the reins of government and elevate themselves to the legislature. . . . Today these haughty men have resolved to substitute a constitution of their fashion for the ancient constitution of the monarchy, maintained for fourteen centuries. . . . Never has an assembly of men more resembled the famous architects of the Tower of Babel, or of confusion. . . .

Good God! Is this then the fruit of this sweet and amiable liberty with which our philosophes love to delude us in their fatuous proclamations? Do they not know that liberty can belong only to the well-born man, and that the wicked and the corrupt are necessarily slaves? What fruits of death has this tree so vaunting of liberty produced? Does it not suffice to be rich, upright, or virtuous to become suspect, to be delivered to the dagger, or to the hatchet's sharp edge? . . .

For several years the French people, naturally lively, careless, and curious, developed a puerile curiosity for all the fables and rhapsodies that it pleased the philosopher-jugglers to yield up to them. . . .

Therefore, o my God! to attempt to make [them] return from this sort of drunkenness and bestiality, you deemed it necessary to bring down your hand on them. By a terrible but lovable severity you have made them feel the weight of your just indignation, from the king who wielded the scepter to the last of his subjects; from the one who lived in palaces and donned crimson to the one who slept on straw, covered with vulgar clothes and rags. . . .

But because these superb and blind wits have blushed of you, o my God! and of your Son [who was] humiliated until his death on the cross, they have insulted your wisdom and scorned the excess of your love for man. For your part, you have been shamed by this species of degraded being, fallen from his primitive reason, more ingrate than the beast who recognizes his master and bites the hand that feeds and cares for him. You are sorry to have placed on earth a creature who dishonors his creator by so strangely abusing his reason, an unnatural creature, ingrate and insolent toward his benefactor, and who has no other desire than to satisfy his sensual and gross appetites just like a beast. . . .

You began by striking the French nobility. Suddenly it became like a drunkard who staggers at each step; he vacillates, he errs on the right and left; he does not know where to place his foot, he can hardly support himself and is incapable of any sane judgment or any determination. The same [goes for] the majority of nobles, vacillating, in a stupor and delirious, uncertain as to which part they should take, divided among themselves, able only to search for asylum in foreign lands. . . . Thus you wanted to punish the bad examples and the scandals that a great number of nobles gave to the Nation. This nobility, degenerated from its ancestors, had almost no religion or morals; they debased themselves and were rendered contemptible.

You have not spared the ministers consecrated to your cult. You had reproached them in general for a scandalous luxury and an abusive use of their riches. . . .

You then abandoned the French Nation to the Empire of the demon. The Prince of darkness and confusion reigned sovereign over a people blinded by its passions and the long-felt desire to withdraw from your domination. . . .

Then to make the first revolution, the Demon conjured a man without morals or principles whom he animated with his genius and endowed with that sort of eloquence which seduces and misleads the people. . . . Similar to the Pharaoh's magicians, his prestige mystified the blind and ignorant multitude, and led them to execute his projects. The besieged clergy and nobility nearly fell both at once before his blows.

The success of this first revolution demanded that he persuade the people that paper is worth gold. The diabolical orator goes further: he persuades them that paper is worth more than gold. At that moment gold and specie disappeared; under the name of "assignats," paper tissues of different colors and values steal into every corner of the Empire and replace them. . . .

Little satisfied with the deluge of evils with which he inundated France, the demon spills anew still more horrible calamities over her. Knowing the feebleness of the human heart, he knows that all men are dominated by interest and vanity. . . . By exaggerating the abuses of the old administration, financial disorders, the tyranny of the ministers and the powerful courtiers, the despotism of the *lettres de cachet*,* religious intolerance, and the obstacles erected by the government to freedom of the press, it was easy to render the king, his ministers, and their circle odious. With the vague and insignificant word "aristocracy," applied to nobles, clergy, and the rich, [the demon] makes them the target of insults and the fury of the populace and rabble. By calling white "black," lies "truth," and "patriotism" the hatred of the country, authority and laws, he makes [them] honor as patriots and regard as good citizens all bandits, scoundrels, and cutthroats whom he lets out of the prisons. He lets them loose on republican soil and makes them carry flame and iron, terror and death in bouts of frenetic liberty. This troop of cannibals, in its blind fury, butchers without distinction of age, sex, status, rank, or fortune. It pillages, burns, tears apart the heart of the country, retraces the horrors of civil war in the middle of peace, and places terrible dearth in the heart of abundance. . . .

Nothing is spared: the loveliest monuments, masterpieces of art, edifices, statues, and paintings are broken and reduced to cinders. Temples [are] profaned and despoiled with horrible testimonies, blasphemies, and execrable imprecations. The pontiff, the priest, the levite, the virgin devoted to the lord, the religious man, and the honest and virtuous wife, [all] cruelly insulted, beaten, incarcerated, and butchered in cold blood. . . .

Then holy days were transformed into a day of mourning, and the solemnity of Sunday was converted into a day of shame and persecution for all Christians. . . .

Good God, you permitted orders to close your churches, and to end the celebration of holy days or Sundays. In their place, the Devil ordered the celebration of the decades. His project was to uproot all that it pleases modern philosophy to call prejudice and religious fanaticism, only to substitute for them the oblivion of all principles, libertinism, and a desolate atheism. . . . All free citizens were forced to dress their tables before their houses and to make public feasts in honor of the goddess "Equality." . . .

Divine Peace, let your voice, banished from France, hurl barbarous discord forever into the infernal abyss. Plunge the spirit of faction, sedition, persecution, ambition, blind and insatiable cupidity [into that abyss]! Make the White Terror disappear! Let the Furies henceforth search in vain to quench their thirst in streams of human blood! O beloved peace, make your charitable olive branch blossom, and pour all your blessings on the French land!

These are the wishes that I long ago made for my country: may they be granted! You who read the depths of my heart, you see, O my God, that they are sincere; that I desire only the well-being of my fellow citizens, and that I demand of you only peace, forgetfulness and pardon for the past, the reunion

---

Lettres de cachet were, under the Old Regime, orders issued directly by the king. Such orders were overwhelmingly for exile or imprisonment for an indeterminate period of time.

of spirits and hearts, the reestablishment of order and just government! The form of this government matters little, as long as it is equitable, clear, a friend of peace, protector of innocence, conservator of property, and favorable to religion and morals.

Oh, Heaven! Deign to grant these wishes of a simple citizen humble before the law and whom you know to be attached to the religion of his fathers and a friend of truth.

79. Public Opinion in Paris (1796–1799)

After the defeat of the Prairial insurrection, Parisian sans-culottes and other working people retreated from politics. The following snapshots of the popular mood under the Directory are taken from reports by police spies whose job it was to wander the city daily, reading newspapers, surveying the markets, and listening in on the conversations of passers-by to determine, and report on, the contours of "public opinion."

Report of Police Agent 4 for December 13, 1796

In the evening, I wandered through the rue Mouffetard which cuts across the faubourg Marcel. The greatest peacefulness reigned there; I noticed that there were not many people in the cabarets. Only one cabaret, at the corner of rue Neuve Étienne and rue des Fossés Victor was full of people who were singing. That is normal.

I went in there and stayed for a half hour. I saw workers of all sorts there, but most were workers from the ports. They spoke very little of current affairs, saying only, "It doesn't matter what kind of government there is as long as we can eat and work," and they finished by saying, "We helped to put those fuckers in place who don't give a shit about us now," and they all went back to singing.

Report of the Central Bureau of Police for October 30, 1797

Mood of the Public

If one judges patriotism by the hatred felt for the Republic's enemies, external as well as internal, then it is possible to say that patriotism has recently made

Sources: Report of December 13, 1796, from National Archives, F7 3688/11; Reports of October 30, 1797, and February 19, 1798, from Alphonse Aulard, *Paris pendant la réaction thermidorienne et sous le Directoire*, vol. 4 (Paris: Librairie Léopold Cerf, 1900); Report of November 14, 1798, from National Archives, F7 3688/15; Report of October 20, 1799, from National Archives, F7 3688/20. Translated by Laura Mason.

great strides. People want an attack on England, they want the British government, pushed back to its last entrenchments, to be punished for the Machiavellianism with which it found the means to rend the heart of our fatherland. Patriots condemn the British government for the Vendée; royalists for Quiberon. People want Hanover taken from the list of British possessions; they want the Saint James cabinet to restore all conquests and pay the costs of the war or to be annihilated; they want the Directory to push our allies to arm as many ships as possible and to encourage the merchants of the ports to devote themselves energetically to this by leaving them all that they capture. . . . The continuing discussions over [the peace] treaty are peaceful and free of partisan spirit; it is even clear that the patriots object to several dispositions out of concern for the government; some fear that the cession of Istria and Dalmatia will offend our Ottoman allies; others fear the consequences for the cisalpine republic of being next to the Austrian house in Italy. In a word, it seems that no one has any intention of opposing his opinions against the government.

Report of the Central Bureau of Police for February 19, 1798

If peaceful emotions, and the absence of the passions, hatreds, and personalities of parties work to the benefit of public opinion, there can be no doubt of the happy progress they have made; better still, one can well say that this is one of those moments when the Revolution's progress has a decisive character. The government's influence is palpable; people recognize the already certain activity of the administration while citizens of every class of society profit, in ever greater numbers and with a perfect knowledge of the source, from the benefits of the constitution of the year III. Such, in essence, are the opinions that have been expressed recently in public places; busier than ever, they are more peaceful than ever. Royalism vainly affects foolish hopes: the public order that it hoped to ruin seems beyond its reach. Restricted to shadowy meetings, or faithful to gathering places to which they give a bad reputation, royalists sigh with regrets and impotent hopes. The ever-growing union of patriotism is the source of their despair. Such is the political appearance of this commune today and it is in the midst of such attitudes, so favorable to public prosperity, that the ideas are formed and ripened which will make the next elections new mortar for the constitution of the year III.

Report of Police Agent 1 for November 14, 1798

I was in the rue Charenton in that cabaret where a lot of people go. A small grocer tends that cabaret . . . ; there were a lot of people, especially workers who drank and sang a few patriotic songs; but they didn't say anything against anyone; I think this place attracts so many more drunks than anywhere else because wine only costs six sols a pint, which attracts all the people who will go anywhere they can find a better deal of a single sol.

As I was leaving this place, at about 8 o'clock, I heard a lot of noise outside. It was because of the director, Barras, who was passing in a lighted carriage. He was returning from his country estate, Gros Bois. As he was passing, I heard a group of men and women who were standing by say, "Look at that thief there. He would happily drive over us with his carriage that sprawls across the ground; he comes on foot into the faubourg when he needs us. The thieves, they have their goods and we're left with the troubles. . . ."

Report of Police Agent 13 for October 20, 1799

I went to the faubourg Antoine quite early and I stayed there for most of the morning. [The workers from the manufactories] were all in the cabarets of the rue de Lappe and the rue de la Roquette. I went into several of these cabarets. I saw the workers all seated at tables.

Drink and sing. It looked to me as if that was their principal occupation. They said, "We are celebrating our armies' victories and the arrival of our father, our savior Bonaparte. . . . We don't have work; okay, then, we'll march together under the command of our good father Bonaparte. We are sure to return bringing peace with us. Then, we'll no longer lack work and republican France will become the warehouse of commerce and the meeting-point of all nations."

chapter 14

CULTURAL LIFE

80. The Revival of Religious Practice

Although the law of February 21, 1795, permitted freedom of conscience, it placed firm restrictions on religious expression: priests could not wear their liturgical clothes outdoors and open-air processions and public displays of banners and crosses were prohibited. At the same time, much of the citizenry was committed to recovering religious buildings and reviving ceremony. Here, as with subsistence crises, women were leading figures. Many revolutionary officials, as well as subsequent historians, have tended to see this religious revival as necessarily opposed to the Revolution but that was not always the case; in many instances, local parishioners believed that their efforts to renew religious practice merely fulfilled the revolutionary guarantee of freedom of conscience.

A. Letter from Commune of Loudun (Vienne) Concerning Refractory Priests (FEBRUARY 23, 1797)

We cannot hide from you the ills that refractory priests are committing here: since the department freed them, they incite the people to fanaticism more than ever. They provoke the people to regard the Republic and those who love it with horror. They urge them to choose, in the next elections, royalist administrators, electors, and deputies capable of overturning the Republic and reestablishing the throne.

Source: National Archives, F7 7237. Translated by Laura Mason.

The people are naturally good in this part of the country, but the priests make them fundamentally bad with their fanatical talk. If you do not take action promptly to restrain those monsters, we are not afraid to tell you that we are on the eve of open counter-revolution or civil war. A certain Maurice was chosen among them to call himself a papal envoy; he wears a three-tier cross, he goes into the countryside to baptize, marry, preach, and pardon all those he indoctrinates who once swore love and fidelity to the Republic, and hatred of royalty. You may judge the possible consequences of all this for yourselves.

B. Letter from the Commissioner in Krignac (Morbihan) Concerning Local Religious Practices (FEBRUARY 27, 1797)

Citizen,

Certain of the duties of a sincere republican who is attached to the constitution of the year III and stationed to assist the government, which is itself charged with solidifying the Republic and making it dear to all Frenchmen; certain, I say, that such a man must devote himself entirely to the public good, I am committed to having full knowledge of the attitudes and character of the inhabitants of this canton; and I believe that I have already noted in my reports that it would be easy to loosen their ties to all factions opposed to the Republic, but with the condition that I believe they will never abandon these factions entirely; they want the ministers of their cult left free; they assert that the two who live in their part of the country do not in any way incite them against the government but rather ceaselessly advise them to obey the laws of the Republic.

I have investigated these priests as fully as possible; the evidence is that they conduct themselves as peaceful men who want to be protected and supervised by the authorities.

The Directory's last message concerning priests alarmed many people, who fear that the Legislative Corps will proscribe all priests indiscriminately because of the oath that was abolished by our constitution. I wanted to reassure the people and encourage them to persuade their ministers that indiscriminate proscriptions will never take place; that henceforth the law holds only the individual accountable. My conduct won me an interview with them, they admitted their uneasiness to me, I let them know of the Minister of Police's letter of 22 Fructidor, which forbids disturbing, for oaths or statements, priests who are peaceful and who encourage the people to obey the laws; that the government, having reason to complain of the conduct of some among them, will always know how to distinguish between the innocent and the guilty; that the Legislative Corps, religiously observant of the constitution, will only pass laws based on principles of equity and justice. I told them that the influence they have over the masses is well known and that they would always be judged according to the peacefulness of the commune in which they live, unless it was very clear that the cause of trouble had come from elsewhere. They assured me that they did not fear their public conduct being known. And privately, they even wished that the constituted authorities were present when they speak to the people; they do not fear laws that punish men who have been proven guilty because they want those who desecrate the laws to be punished, but that they also feared that they would be surprised with a law of general proscription.

I thought it useful to share the knowledge furnished me by these remarks.

In the parts of the country where the priests are well behaved, and where the people seem as attached to their religious institutions as they are to life itself, the priests must be given great security:

1. Because they communicate easily with the people, informing them of laws that instruct them on their rights and duties, and without regular gatherings, the people live in an isolation that would soon cast them into pitiable ignorance.

2. Because, enjoying all the freedoms of worship, the citizens will no longer welcome enemies of the republican government, and the laws will be received and executed with respect everywhere.

C. Letter from the Commissioner in Maguy (Calvados)
Concerning Religious Processions (JULY 11, 1797)

Citizen,

Fanatics and bandits are stronger than the law: the trees of liberty topple in this canton and are replaced with anticivic crowns, symbol of the worship of a couple of old saints of the town and the work of the apostolic mob.

On 21 Messidor, warned that two hundred men or women had gathered in the commune of St. Vigor to make a pilgrimage to a saint that used to make miracles, I asked the commandant of the armed forces of the canton of Bayeux to join his troops with ours to disperse a crowd that should have proceeded to the commune of Sommervien. . . . The commandant who was, unfortunately, absent did not receive my letter in time to gather sufficient force, he said, to disperse a bunch of crazies whipped up by a crowd of backward priests who were going to clear the way for every crime. Only fifteen men from the standing armed forces were sent to meet the gathering; but either spite was involved or the men were badly directed because they did not arrive until the moment when commander Lefèvre, who had taken the right road, advanced alone and forced the crowd to disperse with threats or prayers. I do not know exactly what he did: he alone succeeded in making them hide their trinkets, crosses, and banners and pass through Bayeux in an orderly fashion. It was a nice piece of work for a commander to put two hundred pilgrims in marching order and to have protected the law and public interest without a shot being fired. Everyone applauded his tactics and his learned maneuver. The passage through Bayeux took place, as I told you, in a very orderly way, and the general, relying on the word of a female general of the opposing party, wished them good night at about 7:30 and gave me an exact account of his progress with the art of conciliation. I said to him, "But citizen, the assembly reformed upon leaving the city, why did you not take action to disperse it? The bells sounded, the banners were unfurled, a cross. . . was raised, an Our Mother of Deliverance, in plate and decorated with the jewels of all the local fanatics, majestically reappeared on a cart, and the cortege entered its town in a procession accompanied by the sound of the bells of the church of St. Loup." He replied that he did not know that. I believe, citizen commissioner, that worship should be respected for two reasons; the first, because it does not produce conspirators; the second, because it does not disturb morals or integrity, but the law of 7 Vendémiaire which wisely foresaw everything, requires that worship be kept indoors. . . .

81. Anonymous, "Bloody Combat Between Sunday and Décadi"

This anonymous pamphlet leaves few clues as to its origin. The perspectives of the two interlocutors suggest that its author was prorevolutionary. While Sunday evinces a clichéd Catholic reactionary position, Décadi (the tenth day of the ten-day week) is more subtle. The disagreement is nominally over the revolutionary calendar, adopted by the Convention on October 5, 1793, and abolished January 1, 1806.

SUNDAY (to himself): To the devil with this meeting! I will again find myself nose to nose with this great lout Décadi; when, then, will my friends deliver me? . . . God bless you, citizen.

DÉCADI: Honored, M. Sunday. For a holy day you seem quite sad.

SUNDAY: That may be . . . why do you meddle?

DÉCADI: Hey, M. Sunday, do not forget your profession so soon. I do not tell you to be Christian; only be devout and do not quit your benign tone; it has always served you so well!

Source: Anonymous, "Combat sanglant entre le Dimanche et le Décadi." Translated by Tracey Rizzo.

SUNDAY: You are a fool, my friend, a philosophe, a scamp, an atheist ... enough. I was created to reign over the impious, to crush them from head to toe, and perhaps to make you understand misery one day. (To himself): How content I would be if I saw this wretch burn!

DÉCADI: Oh, such a blow ... there's priestly charity for you. ... You attack me ... if I don't fear to offend your humility. ...

SUNDAY: I do not speak to the enemies of God.

DÉCADI: One moment! Are you afraid of being eaten?

SUNDAY: Eaten! Eaten! Curses! ... By our holy father the Pope, Décadi will not eat Sunday; I swear it on my Lord. Your kingdom is neither of this world nor the other, my dear friend; you must yield to me the place you have usurped from me.

DÉCADI: Show your authority, Lord's day, and I will abandon to you on the field all of my pretensions.

SUNDAY, presenting a ream of paper: The profane Décadi, son of Baal, is ordered to evacuate the land of true believers in twenty-four hours ... and if you make the appearance of resisting, I hope to call all the Saints of my calendar to march against you and eat all of yours. ...

DÉCADI: Oh, how I love the saints! How I want to see them honored, served, imitated with more zeal than one displays in your temples! You have one, thank God, for every day of the year. But the greatest, without contradiction, are those for whom the boutiques are closed in the cities, as in a day of insurrection, and where one leaves the land fallow to run to the cabaret.

Agree nevertheless that one could say of the manner in which one honors the patrons of your sublime Gregorian calendar: they have all been drinking bouts.

SUNDAY: I deny all your conclusions because they are based on facts. ... Come, come, my dear Décadi, one cannot reverse the work of sixteen centuries in a moment. ...

DÉCADI: ... I will repeat it to you often: do not rely upon your sixteen centuries of existence; they are a great reason for terminating that which has endured too long; I will often deny to you that your calendar is easier to calculate; and ...

SUNDAY: Come, then ... he dreams ... the good citizen with your calendar and your calculations in tenths. Good women no longer know anything of the moon, and the devout souls no longer know what day to go to confession, nor when to be disciplined. ... Respond to my people, and let your Euler and your Lagrange calculate as much as you want, they will not prove that a calendar is simpler when it is less amusing.

DÉCADI: I agree with you, M. Sunday, that there is nothing comparable to the month of January, a sonorous and very intelligible word, which incontestably signifies two-faced Janus, representing the year which ends and begins. The month the ancients consecrated to Aphrodite, to this Venus, to this principle which rejuvenates nature is the palpable emblem of our month of April: "Vendredi" [Friday] and "Mercredi" [Wednesday] still recall the idea of Venus and Mercury, so much has fable always imitated history.

Why, then, o great Lord's day, have your calendar and your saints not yet traversed the globe, if they are so powerful? Why have they scorned the Indians, the Chinese, the Persians, the Egyptians, the Mohammedans? Why does Europe alone, subject to Christianity, blindly obey the sublime institutions of your thaumaturges? Finally, why do you cry so forcefully against the heathens, when this calendar which is so dear to you, is that of the very profane Greece, which you and your priests have mutilated, but whose months, days, holidays even recall the ancient cult of nature still?

SUNDAY: Good lord! Friend, you are funny with your "why"s. . . . Why sing to me with your Greek priests and my pagan names? Have not theology and Catholic religion been parodied by all these tellers of tales and mythology?

Finally, if I have not yet conquered the world, it is the fault of your villainous reason, obstinate as a devil, and stubborn as a mule. This is why nations reject the folly of the cross, and the number of the elect is so small. . . . But the gates of Hell will not prevail over the Church though it is chased from three quarters of Europe, reviled in the other quarter, and is quite unknown in the rest of the world. Novelty can well please the human species, but it cherishes, caresses its old errors.

DÉCADI: Tell me, between us, how have you arranged yourself with Rome? I see you in a difficulty: many men claim that in wanting to appear as citizens, you become schismatic and damned; others think that for the health of your soul you should be royalist and aristocratic. I will be discreet, come then, frankly, are you?

SUNDAY: I am . . . I am M. Sunday.

DÉCADI: That is well said . . . but still . . . what is a Sunday? Must I help you? Come, avow your debt. You are passably aristocratic.

SUNDAY: Aristocrat!

DÉCADI: Hey! Yes. Why dissimulate? Your saints, your books, your legends, your evangelists, don't they preach the most perfect and monotonous obedience? Are not kings sacred, deriving everything from God and their swords?

Has not faith, this brilliant flame, blinded you to the point of making you believe the most subtle sleights of hand? Is it not agreed that the first act of a Christian is to renounce his reason, and to have none other than that of his priest? . . .

SUNDAY: Devil! what you just said was villainous, though there may be a grain of truth. It was at that time, by God, the sweet days of my glory. . . . But, come on, I am reasonable, and I want to be Citizen Sunday, but above all Sunday. . . .

My God is the God of Abraham, Isaac, and Jacob.

DÉCADI: Mine is the God of the universe, and I offer as incense to the Supreme Being his own work.

SUNDAY: I am supported by miracles so illuminating that they have converted thousands of wretches, all the rabble of Rome, above all women and children.

DÉCADI: You have lost a little of the secret of miracles; mine are eternal, and I present those of nature and of the seasons.

SUNDAY: I have lost, you say, the secret of miracles? Come, come, they are not so difficult to do, and if I just wish hard enough, I have more than half done it.

DÉCADI: Oh! for the rarity of the act, demonstrate to me then half a miracle; who knows, this might begin my conversion!

SUNDAY: I consent to it, but only on the condition that you will not call me an aristocrat.

DÉCADI: Let it be, and even in advance I assure you that I take you for a very good man. But do tell?

SUNDAY: Listen, the day that Madame Elizabeth [the Queen's sister] conserved in her features all the pride of innocence and all the vigor of a chaste and robust temperament . . . the day that her virginal blood . . .

DÉCADI: Virginal! Ha, ha. I have heard it told of certain accidents . . . of a certain general . . .

SUNDAY: To the devil with interruption! By God, M. Décadi, read your catechism and you will see if similar trifle is made for touching [on the topic of] virginity.

DÉCADI: Pardon me, but I read so little of the catechism. . . . But continue . . .

SUNDAY: Well, at the moment where her virtuous "head" was struck . . . I was perfumed by the scent of rose, and I believed I sensed the soul of a celestial being who ascended earth.

DÉCADI: Sensed a soul! Good heavens! It is miraculous. You have a fine nose, M. Sunday . . . and yet this soul was not the color of rose then . . .

SUNDAY: Alas, no! and to tell you the final word, I turned; from there I saw a woman who had a bouquet at her bosom. . . . But you see that if I had not turned, I would have had a miracle, and I was in the right to say: Miracle! Miracle! I sensed a soul the color of rose.

DÉCADI: It is, good lord, quite a shame that this woman did not also turn at the same time as you; then you would not have seen her bosom, nor her bouquet of roses, but you would have seen your miracle.

SUNDAY: Agree then, after all this, that you cannot resist me. You should perceive that the first rose I saw this year, recalled to me the memory of Madame Elizabeth. . . .

DÉCADI: So it goes, my good M. Sunday! Sit down and take a deep breath. . . . There, thank God, a pretty enough series of absurdities.

SUNDAY: Let us finish. Just as well that I will gain nothing from you. I have listened too much to your profane banter; I see well that you are a hardened atheist, an unbeliever, a heretic, a philosophe.

DÉCADI: Ah, M. Sunday, you become ecclesiastic, but at least order your insults, and by God conclude before we part: you want to be M. Sunday, and let the poor Décadi exist?

SUNDAY: No.

DÉCADI: Then you want me to be abolished?

SUNDAY: Yes.

DÉCADI: I testify to you that I am not exclusive and that I consent to exist with you.

SUNDAY: I do not want to share. Farewell, may the devil take you. It is time for mass and I am to sing it.

DÉCADI: May the good lord accompany you. Since you still have no organ, if you want, I offer to whistle it.

82. Magazine of the Muses (1797)

Under the Directory, many men and women of letters turned their attention to idealized notions of Old Regime literary culture. Believing that the marriage of politics and culture that characterized the first half of the Revolution had undermined French taste and gaiety, many editors and writers determined to make aesthetics and wit the sole criteria by which literary production would be judged. The outcome of such decisions was, of course, that only the creative productions of the educated and the cultivated would be considered truly worthy of attention. The *Magazine of the Muses*, which published poetry, songs, and short prose pieces, was one of the leading exemplars of this movement.

Foreword

We have occupied ourselves with carefully collecting scattered blossoms from the great field of literature, in order to bring them together in a flowerbed whose choice, variety, and freshness may perhaps attract the friends of sweet and peaceful enjoyments.

Each month, we will publish a small volume of *light literary productions* from the different genres. We will not allow our choices to be affected by prejudices based on the personalities and opinions of the authors; on the contrary, we will try to mingle spirits that were once divided into helpful reconciliations, and *we will allow nothing that may flatter or exasperate party hatreds.*

It is in so offering pleasant distractions to persons who are tired of their activities or of their leisure that we hope to contribute to the project of restoring our fellow citizens to their natural tastes and gaiety.

Many men and women of letters have already hastened to open their notebooks to us. We invite them all to contribute to the activities of an enterprise which, by creating a repository for their frivolous writings and permitting them to arrange and preserve them in libraries, has earned the right to a favorable welcome.

Competition from other collections of the same genre, but created with a less far-ranging vision, will undoubtedly produce that noble emulation which always benefits the glory of letters and the pleasures of the public.

Source: Journal des muses, no. 1 (1797). Translated by Laura Mason.

"The Marvelous and the Incredible": the men and women of Directorial high society. *(Musée Carnavalet/Photo Bulloz)*

Response to the Verse on Fickleness

  Made to be loved tenderly,
why praise inconstant love,
And of the pleasures of change,
Why embellish the image?
Anacreon, laughing always,
treated love as a jest;
Like him, to be fickle,
One must at least be his age.
  It is true that pleasure,
like time itself, has wings;
Those who claim to hold it
Open themselves to cruel pains.
Do you want to feel its return?
Pleasure is the child of love,
and Happiness that of constancy.

            Fanni Beauharnais

83. The Philosophical, Literary, and Political Decade (1796)

La décade philosophique, politique, et littéraire was published between 1794 and 1807, but it exerted its greatest cultural influence during the Directorial period. Most of the editors were Ideologues, philosophers who believed that the acquisition of knowledge, the formation of ideas, and even the development of moral judgments were linked to the experience of the senses. Politically, the editors were moderately republican, and socially they were conservative: they accepted the constitution of the year III and were critical of excessive wealth and luxury, but they believed that social hierarchy was natural. In regard to literature and the arts generally, the editors—like those of the *Magazine of the Muses*—hoped to revive traditional aesthetic judgments and improve French culture.

Boniface Veridick to Polyscope, Concerning His Project for a Theater for the People

Hey! For once, my dear Polyscope, I do not share your opinion. I do not deny that you have given a wealth of good advice in the *Philosophical Decade*;

Source: La décade philosophique, politique, et littéraire, no. 70, March 30, 1796. Translated by Laura Mason.

you have satirized several absurdities that dishonor the human race, and offered excellent thoughts on the beaux arts; but I do not approve of your *theater for the people.*

In the name of the fatherland, cultivate the earth, perfect the useful arts, behave yourselves, and go rarely, very rarely, to the theater. You said it well, the education found there is not worth the time lost and, for myself, I think that since the Revolution the taste for the theater has very much spread among all classes of people. Our loges and the seats on the floor are now filled only with shopgirls, laundresses, cutlers, or market porters who go to waste time and, occasionally, to show off their wares. . . .

You say, my dear Polyscope, that there are not enough schools to educate our children; that even more schools are needed for the *big children*, whose means or circumstances prevented them from learning the principles of morality and politics. Let us separate the issues, be precise in our thinking. There are, without a doubt, many very ignorant people; there are many neglected educations; three quarters of the inhabitants of our so-called ordered society know neither how to read nor write; I agree; but what sort of instruction do they need? It seems to me that first they need instruction that will make them more skillful in their profession, whatever it may be; the more they produce, the better the products will be, and the better off they and their families are, the more the fatherland will be enriched by their work. And where will they learn that? They are consistent and hardworking at home, not in the theater. Next, they must know how to write and count to keep their little affairs in order and, if need be, know how to write a letter or make out a bill. Certainly, the theater will not teach them those things.

You think that they will, at least, acquire the principles of morality and politics. But, setting aside the *phrase* and considering the *idea*, what kind of conduct is most common among men? The art of behaving properly under the ordinary circumstances of life; I say "ordinary" because life is made up of ordinary circumstances: for, do not be displeased with this, it is still in his home, in the bosom of his family, in the company of his father, his brothers, his wife, his children, his friends that one learns to know and love his duties. O my friends! Virtue is in the household; prefer homely life above everything else. What do you do elsewhere? Dissipate yourself, spend money, catch diseases, store up bad moods; and all the while, talent gets rusty, money leaves, the baby cries in its cradle, and the mother is burdened with hardship and worry. Find your pleasures near these interesting beings; they will teach you true morality and their caresses will be the source of your happiness.

Where will our citizens learn politics, you add? But what political talent does ninety-nine one-hundredths of the nation need? To know how to make a good choice of electors once a year: ha! let them choose the men around them who have good sense, integrity, and are friends of republican government, I do not ask any more of them; that is all the political talent that the fatherland needs; and they will certainly learn more in this regard in a small group of respectable men than in a theater.

And, you say to me, what of shaping those upon whom such choices should fall; do you not think the theater useful for shaping good administrators, honest judges, enlightened legislators? Perhaps, but in a very attenuated and indirect way. Reading carefully, thinking often, and working steadily will teach them far more; and I doubt that there are many among those who are currently distinguished for their work in a public post who owe their abilities to regular attendance at the theater, not even those you imagine.

What, then, are theaters good for? For disseminating good taste in the arts and in literature, and for improving manners. We should sustain the theater, as we do sculptors and painters, to embellish our country and the imaginations of our inhabitants. We should encourage the one and the other to give us objects worthy of the majesty of a great people, and able to make the people love their laws and their fatherland; and on this point, my dear Polyscope, we are in complete agreement; with the caveat that our government never be director of the troupe; no national theaters, no *theaters for the people*.

Those circuses, those popular spectacles were fine among the ancients, where a class of unemployed citizens—especially in the cities—disdained the useful arts and, when they were not under arms, knew of nothing other than conspiring in the public squares, eating wheat distributed for free from conquered provinces, and parading their idleness through festivals given by magistrates eager to win their favor. These people were the true nobles; they were, in truth, real rogues at times, but they were noble; and the slaves, the laboring class of the society, formed the Third Estate. Things should be entirely different among us: forget the desire and hope of making our fellow citizens Greeks or Romans. We can be much better than that. Modern mores, our more northerly position, the greatness of our estates, their almost equal degree of civilization and the nature of relations between them, the invention of paper and printing, the progress of the sciences, navigation, commerce, and the post, all impose upon us the law of refusing to servilely copy the ancients, of being ourselves, of attaining the only degree of perfection and happiness for which we are suited.

Here is something close to how I imagine such a state of perfection and happiness in a great modern state, like France, for example.

First, I want it to have domestic peace, I want a shared confidence, a general good will to unite all its citizens; I want a stable government to guarantee its independence abroad and security at home. I want agriculture and all forms of industry to have the most illustrious activity; the seaports to be filled with ships, canals and rivers covered with boats, the markets clean and well provisioned, providing a vision of abundance. I want each laborer in the countryside, each artisan of the towns to have, if not his own property, at least the possibility of procuring one for his old age, if only a small life annuity. I want each household to have proper utensils that are well cared for, clothes of solid fabric, and white linen, everywhere giving the appearance not of opulence but of ease; I want everyone to know how to read and to have at least a few volumes in his cupboard, to enlighten him on the processes of the arts and crafts, and a few newspapers, so that he will not be a stranger to the interests of his fatherland. I want public establishments, distinguished by their utility, to inspire those who come to observe them not with the sadness produced by the appearance of suffering humanity but with the contentment offered by the spectacle of humanity relieved. In a word, I want there not to be a single idler in this great republic, whose unproductive existence is a burden for society, nor a single wretch who can complain of not being able to earn an easy living with work and good conduct, and lead a life that the English would call "comfortable.". . .

CHAPTER
15

NAPOLEON CLOSES
THE REVOLUTION

84. Napoleon Bonaparte, "Proclamation to the French Nation" (NOVEMBER 10, 1799)

The widespread popularity enjoyed by Bonaparte since his military successes in Italy (1795–1796) won him immunity to criticism of the recent Egyptian debacle. Returning to Paris from Egypt a hero in the fall of 1799, he was Sieyès's obvious choice for a military member of the triumvirate that would overthrow the Directory. The coup d'état of 18 Brumaire has been thought by many to signal the end of the Revolution. Yet here Napoleon attempts to portray himself as a devotee of the Revolution who means to wrest liberty from the grip of a corrupt government.

On my return to Paris I found all authority in chaos and agreement only on the one truth that the constitution was half destroyed and incapable of preserving liberty.

Men of every party came to me, confided their plans, disclosed their secrets, and asked for my support: I refused to be a man of party.

The Council of Ancients called upon me, and I responded to its appeal. A plan for general reform has been drawn up by men upon whom the nation is

Source: John Eldred Howard, ed. and trans., *Letters and Documents of Napoleon*, vol. I (London: Cresset Press, 1961), pp. 313–314.

Napoleon Bonaparte as emperor. *(The Granger Collection, New York)*

accustomed to look as the defenders of liberty, equality, and property. That plan needed calm examination, free from all fear and partisan influence. Therefore, the Council of Ancients resolved to transfer the legislative body to Saint-Cloud and charged me to deploy the force necessary to ensure its independence. I believed it my duty to my fellow citizens, to the soldiers laying down their lives in our armies, to the national glory gained at the price of their blood to accept this command.

The Councils reassembled at Saint-Cloud. The troops of the Republic guaranteed their security from without. But assassins created terror within. Several deputies of the Council of Five Hundred, bearing daggers and firearms, uttered threats of death all around them. Discussion of the plans was halted, the majority became disorganized, the most intrepid orators hesitated, and the hopelessness of any wise proposal was evident.

I carried my indignation and sorrow to the Council of Ancients. I urged it to ensure the execution of its liberal designs. I recalled to it the ills of the nation which had led it to conceive them. The Council joined with me in renewed assurance of its steadfast resolve.

I then appeared before the Council of Five Hundred, alone, unarmed, bareheaded, just as the Ancients had received and applauded me. I came to recall the majority to its purpose and assure it of its power.

The daggers which threatened the deputies were immediately raised against their liberator: a score of assassins threw themselves upon me, seeking my breast. The grenadiers of the legislative guard, whom I had left at the door of the chamber, ran up, came between us, and bore me out. One of the grenadiers had his coat pierced by a dagger.

At that moment cries of "outlaw" were heard against the defender of the law, the savage cry of the assassins against the force destined to crush them. They pressed round the president, threatening, arms in their hands, ordering him to declare my outlawry. Told of this, I ordered him to be saved from their fury and six grenadiers rescued him. Immediately afterwards the legislative guard entered at the charge and cleared the chamber.

Intimidated, the seditious dispersed and disappeared. The majority, safe from their threats, returned freely and peacefully to the chamber, heard the proposals made to them for the public good, debated and prepared the salutary resolution which must become the new, provisional law of the Republic.

Frenchmen, you will no doubt recognize in my conduct the zeal of a soldier of liberty and of a devoted citizen of the Republic. Liberal, beneficent, and traditional ideas have returned to their rightful place through the dispersal of the odious and despicable factions which sought to overawe the Councils.

85. The Imperial Religious Settlement

Religious conflict had plagued revolutionaries since the promulgation of the Civil Constitution of the Clergy in 1791. In 1800, hoping to end rebellion in western France and win over the peasantry, most of whom remained loyal to the church, Napoleon initiated secret negotiations with the Papacy. In the resulting Concordat (signed in July 1801), Napoleon recognized Catholicism as the religion of the majority of the French and allowed bishops to appoint lower clergy. In return, the Pope agreed to recognize purchases of former church lands as irrevocable. Because many ex-revolutionaries remained opposed to conciliation

Source: E. A. Arnold, ed. and trans., *A Documentary Survey of Napoleonic France* (Lanham, Md.: University Press of America, 1993), pp. 114–120. © University Press of America. Reprinted by permission.

with the church, Napoleon delayed announcing the Concordat until Easter Sunday of 1802, and even then (as the second selection makes clear) he suggested that it was the Pope who had finally sought compromise.

A. Concordat with the Papacy (July 1801)

The First Consul of the French Republic and His Holiness the sovereign Pontiff, Pius VII, have named as their respective plenipotentiaries. . . .

Who, after the exchange of their full respective powers and credentials, have settled on the following convention:

The Government of the French Republic acknowledges that the Catholic, Apostolic, and Roman religion is the religion of the great majority of French citizens.

His Holiness equally recognizes that this same religion has derived from and at this moment expects the greatest good and the greatest fame from the establishment of the Catholic worship in France, and from the personal profession of it made by the Consuls of the Republic.

Consequently, after this mutual recognition, as much for the benefit of religion as for the maintenance of internal tranquillity, they have agreed to what follows:

1. The Catholic, Apostolic, and Roman religion will be freely practiced in France: Its worship will be public and in conformity with police regulations that the Government will judge necessary for public tranquillity.

2. The Holy See, in concert with the [French] Government, will make a new division of French dioceses.

3. His Holiness will declare to the titular French bishops that, with firm confidence, he expects of them, for the benefit of peace and tranquillity, all manner of sacrifices, even that of their Sees.

   After this exhortation, if they should refuse this sacrifice commanded for the good of the Church (nonetheless, a refusal is not anticipated by His Holiness), he will provide government of the bishops of the new division by new titularies in the following manner:

4. The First Consul of the Republic will name, in the three months which will follow the publication of the Bull of His Holness, the archbishoprics of the new division. His Holiness will confer canonic institution, following the established forms regarding France before the change of Government [i.e., before the Revolution].

5. Nominations to bishoprics which will be vacant in the future will equally be made by the First Consul, and canonic institution will be granted by the Holy See in conformity with the previous article.

6. Before assuming their functions, the bishops will swear directly, at the hands of the First Consul, the oath of loyalty which was in use before the change in Government, expressed in the following terms:

   "I swear and promise before God, on the Holy Gospel, to observe obedience and loyalty to the Government established by the constitution of the French Republic. I also promise to have no correspondence, nor to assist by counsel, nor to support any league, either inside or outside, which is against public tranquillity, and if, in my diocese or elsewhere, I learn that anything prejudicial to the State is being plotted, I will make it known to the Government."

7. Ecclesiastics of the second rank will swear the same oath at the hands of the civil authorities designated by the Government.

8. The following form of prayer will be recited at the end of divine service in all Catholic Churches in France: "*Domine, salvam fac Republiam; Domine, salvos fac consules.*"

9. Bishops will make new divisions of parishes in their dioceses, which will only have effect after the Government's approval.

10. The bishops will nominate the priests. Their choice may only include those men approved by the Government.

11. The bishops may have a chapter in their cathedrals, and a seminary for their diocese, without the Government being obliged to endow it.

12. All metropolitan, cathedral, parochial, and nonalienated Churches necessary for worship will be placed at the disposal of the bishops.

13. His Holiness, for the good of peace and the happy reestablishment of the Catholic religion, declares that neither he nor his successors will in any way disturb the purchasers of alienated ecclesiastical property and that, as a consequence, the ownership of this same property, the rights and revenues attached to them, will remain untransferable in their hands or those of their assigns.

14. The Government will guarantee an appropriate salary to bishops and priests whose dioceses and parishes are included in the new division.

15. The Government will likewise take measures so that French Catholics may, if they wish, act in favor of Church foundations.

16. His Holiness recognizes in the First Consul of the French Republic the same rights enjoyed by the previous government [i.e., the pre-1789 monarchy].

17. It is agreed by the contracting parties that, in case one of the successors of the present First Consul will not be Catholic, the rights and prerogatives in the previous article, and the nomination of French bishops will be, in regard to him, regulated by a new convention.

Ratification will be exchanged at Paris within the space of forty days.

Done at Paris, July 15, 1801.

B. Napoleon's Proclamation to the French on the Religious Settlement (APRIL 1802)

Frenchmen:

From the bosom of a revolution inspired by love of the fatherland suddenly exploded in your midst religious dissensions, which became the plague of your families, the nourishment of factions, and the hope of your enemies.

An insane policy tried to stifle them under the debris of altars, under the very ruins of religion. At its voice, pious solemnities ceased where citizens were called by the sweet name of brothers, and all were recognized as equal under the hand of God who created them. The dying, alone with this grief, no longer heard this consoling voice which calls Christians to a better life, and even God seemed exiled from nature.

But the public conscience, the sentiment of the independence of opinion, rose up and soon, distracted by external enemies, their explosion brought devastation into our departments; Frenchmen forgot that they were French and became the instruments of foreign hate.

On the other hand, passions were unchained, morals were without support, woes were without hope in the future, all were united to bring confusion into society.

To stop this confusion, it was necessary to set religion on its base again and to take only measures accepted by religion itself.

It was the sovereign Pontiff whom the example of centuries and reason directed to appeal to bring together opinions and reconcile hearts.

The head of the Church pondered in his wisdom and in the interest of the Church the proposition that the interest of the State had dictated.

His voice was heard by the pastors; what he approved, the Government agreed to, and the Legislators passed a law of the Republic. Thus vanished all the elements of confusion; thus faded all qualms which could alarm consciences, and all obstacles that malevolence could oppose to the return of internal peace.

Ministers of a religion of peace, may the most profound forgetfulness cover your dissensions, your woes, and your faults, may this religion that unites you, attach you by the same ties, by indissoluble ties, to the interest of your fatherland.

Exert for it all the force and ascendancy of spirit that your ministry gives you; that your lessons and examples may form in young citizens the love of our institutions, respect for and attachment to the tutelary authorities which have been created to protect them; may they learn from you that the God of peace is also the God of armies, and that He fights alongside those who defend the independence and liberty of France.

Citizens who profess Protestant religions, the law equally extends to you its care. Let this moral, common to all Christians, this moral so holy, so pure, so fraternal, unite them all in the same affection for all the members of its great family.

Never let doctrinal struggles alter the sentiments that religion inspires and commands.

Frenchmen, let us all be united for the happiness of the fatherland and humanity; let this religion, which civilized Europe, still be the bond which brings humanity together, and let the virtue it demands always be associated with the light that illuminates us.

86. The French Civil Code (1803–1804)

Even before the Revolution, French kings and their subjects had considered replacing the approximately four hundred law codes effective in France with a single, unified system of law. This project was finally realized under the Empire. The Civil Code was drafted by a legislative committee; although Napoleon only attended about half of the sessions, his influence was decisive in several matters. In particular, the Civil Code is noteworthy for its provisions favoring the division of estates among heirs (rather than restoring the traditional practice of primogeniture), the subordination of wives to the authority of husbands, and its ratification of the Revolution's guarantee of equality before the law.

Preliminary Title: Of the Publication, Effect, and Application of the Laws in General

1. The laws are executory throughout the whole French territory, by virtue of the promulgation thereof made by the First Consul.

They shall be executed in every part of the Republic, from the moment at which their promulgation can have been known.

The promulgation made by the First Consul shall be taken to be known in the department which shall be the seat of government, one day after the promulgation; and in each of the other departments, after the expiration of the same interval augmented by one day for every ten myriameters (about twenty ancient leagues) between the town in which the promulgation shall have been made, and the chief place of each department.

2. The law ordains for the future only; it has no retrospective operation.

Source: E. A. Arnold, ed. and trans., *A Documentary Survey of Napoleonic France* (Lanham, Md.: University Press of America, 1993), pp. 151–164. © University Press of America. Reprinted by permission.

3. The laws of police and public security bind all the inhabitants of the territory. Immovable property, although in the possession of foreigners, is governed by the French law. The laws relating to the condition and privileges of persons govern Frenchmen, although residing in a foreign country. . . .

6. Private agreements must not contravene the laws which concern public order and good morals.

Book I: Of Persons

Title I: Of the Enjoyment and Privation of Civil Rights

7. The exercise of civil rights is independent of the quality of citizen, which is only acquired and preserved conformably to the constitutional law.

8. Every Frenchman shall enjoy civil rights.

Chapter VI: Of the Respective Rights and Duties of Married Persons

212. Married persons owe to each other fidelity, succor, assistance.

213. The husband owes protection to his wife, the wife obedience to her husband.

214. The wife is obliged to live with her husband, and to follow him to every place where he may judge it convenient to reside: the husband is obliged to receive her, and to furnish her with every necessity for the wants of life, according to his means and station.

215. The wife cannot plead in her own name, without the authority of her husband, even though she should be a public trader, or noncommunicant, or separate in property.

216. The authority of the husband is not necessary when the wife is prosecuted in a criminal manner, or relating to police.

217. A wife, although noncommunicant or separate in property, cannot give, pledge, or acquire by free or chargeable title, without the concurrence of her husband in the act, or his consent in writing.

218. If the husband refuses to authorize his wife to plead in her own name, the judge may give her authority.

219. If the husband refuses to authorize his wife to pass an act, the wife may cause her husband to be cited directly before the court of the first instance, of the circle of their common domicil[e], which may give or refuse its authority, after the husband shall have been heard, or duly summoned before the chamber of council.

220. The wife, if she is a public trader, may, without the authority of her husband, bind herself for that which concerns her trade; and in the said case she binds also her husband, if there be a community between them.

   She is not reputed a public trader if she merely retails goods in her husband's trade, but only when she carries on a separate business.

221. When the husband is subjected to a condemnation, carrying with it an afflictive or infamous punishment, although it may have been pronounced merely for contumacy, the wife, though of age, cannot, during the continuance of such punishment, plead in her own name or contract, until after authority given by the judge, who may in such case give his authority without hearing or summoning the husband.

222. If the husband is interdicted or absent, the judge, on cognizance of the cause, may authorize . . . [the] wife either to plead in her own name or to contract.

223. Every general authority, though stipulated by the contract of marriage, is invalid, except as respects the administration of the property of the wife.

224. If the husband is a minor, the authority of the judge is necessary for his wife, either to appear in court, or to contract.

225. A nullity, founded on defect of authority, can be opposed by the wife, by the husband, or by their heirs.

226. The wife may make a will without the authority of her husband.

Title VI: Of Divorce

Section II: Of the Provisional Measures to Which the Petition for Cause Determinate May Give Rise

267. The provisional management of the children shall rest with the husband, petitioner, or defendant, in the suit for divorce, unless it be otherwise ordered for the greater advantage of the children, on petition of either the mother, or the family, or the government commissioner.

268. The wife, petitioner or defendant in divorce, shall be at liberty to quit the residence of her husband during the prosecution, and demand an alimentary pension proportioned to the means of the husband. The court shall point out the house in which the wife shall be bound to reside, and shall fix, if there be ground, the alimentary provision which the husband shall be obliged to pay her.

269. The wife shall be bound to prove her residence in the house appointed. As often as she shall be thereto required; in default of such proof, the husband may refuse the alimentary pension and if the wife is the petitioner for divorce, may cause her to be declared incapable of continuing her prosecution.

270. The wife having community of goods, plaintiff or defendant in divorce, shall be at liberty, in every stage of the cause, commencing with the date of the order mentioned in article 238, to require, for the preservation of her rights, that seals should be affixed to the movable goods in community. These seals shall not be taken off until an inventory and appraisal is made, and on the undertaking of the husband to produce the article contained in the inventory, or to answer for their value, as their legal keeper.

271. Every obligation contracted by the husband at the expense of the community, every alienation made by him of immovable property dependent upon it, subsequent to the date of the order mentioned in article 238, shall be declared void, if proof be given, moreover, that it has been made or contracted in fraud of the rights of the wife.

Section III: Of Exceptions of Law Against the Suit of Divorce for Cause Determinate

272. The suit for divorce shall be extinguished by the reconciliation of the parties, whether occurring subsequently to the facts which might have authorized such suit, or subsequently to the petition for divorce.

273. In either case the petitioner shall be declared incapable of pursuing the action; a new one may, nevertheless, be instituted for cause accruing subsequently to the reconciliation, and the ancient causes may then be employed in support of such new petition.

297. In case of divorce by mutual consent, neither of the parties shall be allowed to contract a new marriage until the expiration of three years from the pronunciation of the divorce.

298. In case of divorce admitted by law for cause of adultery, the guilty party shall never be permitted to marry with his accomplice. The wife adulteress shall be condemned in the same judgment; and, on the request of the public minister, to confinement in a house of correction, for a determined period, which shall not be less than three months nor exceed two years.

299. For whatever cause a divorce shall take place, except in the case of mutual consent, the married party against whom the divorce shall have been established shall lose all the advantage conferred by the other party, whether by their contract or marriage, or since the marriage contracted.

300. The married party who shall have obtained the divorce shall preserve the advantages conferred by the other spouse, although they may have made stipulations and such reciprocity has not taken place.

301. If the married parties shall have conferred no advantage, or of those stipulated do not appear deficient to secure the subsistence of the married party who has obtained the divorce, the court may award to such party, from the

property of the other, an alimentary pension, which shall not exceed the third part of the revenues of such order. This pension shall be revocable in a case where it shall cease to be necessary.

302. The children shall be entrusted to the married party who has obtained the divorce, unless the court, on petition of the family, or by the commissioner of government, gives order, for the greater benefit of the children, that all or some of them shall be committed to the care either of the other married party, or of a third person.

303. Whoever may be the person to whom the children shall be committed, their father and mother shall preserve respectively the right to watch over the maintenance and education of their children, and shall be bound to contribute thereto in proportion to their means.

304. The dissolution of a marriage by divorce admitted by law shall not deprive children, the fruit of such marriage, of any of the benefits secured to them by the laws, or by the matrimonial covenants of their father and mother; but there shall be no admission of claims by the children except in the same manner and in the same circumstances in which they would have been admitted if the divorce had not taken place.

305. In the case of divorce by mutual consent, a property in half the possessions of each of the two married parties shall be acquired in full right, from the day of their first declaration, by the children born of their marriage: the father and mother shall nevertheless retain the enjoyment of such moiety until their children's majority, on condition of providing for their nourishment, maintenance, and education, in a manner suitable to their fortune and condition; the whole without prejudice to the other advantages which may have been secured to the said children by the matrimonial covenants of their father and mother.

Title IX: Of Paternal Power

375. A father who shall have cause of grievous dissatisfaction at the conduct of a child, shall have the following means of correction.

376. If the child has not commenced his sixteenth year, the father may cause him to be confined for a period which shall not exceed one month; and to this effect the president of the court of the circle shall be bound, on his petition, to deliver an order of arrest.

377. From the age of sixteen years commenced to the majority or emancipation, the father is only empowered to require the confinement of his child during six months at the most; he shall apply to the president of the aforesaid court, who, after having conferred thereon with the commissioner of government, shall deliver an order of arrest or refuse the same, and may in the first case abridge the time of confinement required by the father.

378. There shall not be in either case, any writing or judicial formality, except the order itself for arrest, in which the reasons thereof shall not be set forth.

The father shall only be required to subscribe an undertaking to defray all expenses and to supply suitable support.

379. The father is always at liberty to abridge the duration of the confinement by him ordered or required. If the child after his liberation fall into new irregularities, his confinement may be ordered anew, according to the manner prescribed in the preceding articles.

380. If the father be remarried, he shall be bound to conform to article 377, in order to procure the confinement of his child by the first bed, though under the age of sixteen years.

381. The mother surviving and not married again is not empowered to cause the confinement of a child, except with the concurrence of the two nearest paternal relations, and by means of requisition, conformably to article 377.

382. When the child shall possess personal property, or when he shall exercise an office, his confinement shall not take place, even under the age of sixteen years, except by way of requisition in the form prescribed by article 377.

The child confined may address a memorial to the commissioner of government in the court of appeal. This commissioner shall cause the child to render a detail in the court of first instance, and shall make his report to the president of the court of appeal, who, after having given intimation thereof to the father, and after having collected the proofs, may revoke or modify the order delivered by the president of the court of the first instance.

383. Articles 376, 377, 378, and 379 shall be common to fathers and mothers of natural children, legally recognized.

384. The father during marriage, and, after the dissolution of marriage, the father or mother surviving, shall have the enjoyment of the property of their children, until the full age of eighteen years, or until emancipation, which may take place before the age of eighteen years.

385. The conditions of such enjoyment shall be, first, those by which usufructuaries are bound; second, nourishment, maintenance, and education of children, according to their fortune; third, the payment of arrears or interest on capital; fourth, funeral expenses, and those of the last sickness.

386. This enjoyment shall not take place for the benefit of a father or mother against whom a divorce shall have been pronounced; and it shall cease with regard to the mother in the case of a second marriage.

387. It shall not extend to property which children may have acquired by separate labor and industry, nor to such as shall be given or bequeathed to them under the express condition that their father and mother shall not enjoy it.

Book III: Modes of Acquiring Property

Title I: Of Successions

818. The husband may, without the concurrence of his wife, claim a distribution of objects movable or immovable fallen to her and which come into community; with respect to objects which do not come into community, the husband cannot claim the distribution thereof without the concurrence of his wife; he can only demand a provisional distribution in case he has a right to the enjoyment of her property.

The co-heirs of the wife cannot claim final distribution without suing the husband and his wife.

Title II: Donations and Wills

905. A married woman cannot make donation during life without the assistance or the special consent of her husband, or without being thereto authorized by the law, conformably to what is prescribed by articles 217 and 219, under the title "Of Marriage."

She shall not need either the consent of her husband, or the authorization of the law, in order to dispose by will.

Chapter IV: Of Donations During Life

Section I: Of the Form of Donations During Life

934. A married woman shall not be allowed to accept a donation without the consent of her husband, or, in case of her husband's refusal, without the authorization of the law, conformably to what is prescribed by articles 217 and 219, under the title "Of Marriage."

1094. The husband shall be allowed, either by marriage contract, or during the marriage, in the case where he shall have neither children nor descendants, to dispose in favor of his wife, absolutely, of every thing which he might dispose of in favor of a stranger, and in addition of the usufruct of the entirety of the portion of which the law prohibits the disposition to the prejudice of heirs.

And in the case where the husband donor shall leave children or descendants, he may give to his wife either a fourth absolutely, and another fourth in usufruct, or the moiety of his property in usufruct only.

Section II: Of the Administration of the Community, and of the Effect of the Acts of Either of the Married Parties Relating to the Conjugal Union

1421. The husband alone administers the property of the community. He may sell it, alienate and pledge it without the concurrence of his wife.

1424. Fines incurred by the husband for a crime not importing civil death, may be sued for out of the property of the community, saving the compensation due to the wife; such as are incurred by the wife cannot be put in execution except out of her bare property in her personal goods, so long as the community continues.

1427. The wife cannot bind herself nor engage the property of the community, even to free her husband from prison, or for the establishment of their children in case of her husband's absence, until she shall have been thereto authorized by the law.

1428. The husband has the management of all the personal property of the wife.

He may prosecute alone all possessory actions and those relating to movables, which belong to his wife.

He cannot alienate the personal immovables of his wife without her consent.

He is responsible for all waste in the personal goods of his wife, occasioned by the neglect of conservatory acts.

Section VI: Of the Renunciation of Community and of Its Effects

1492. The wife who renounces forfeits every description of claim upon the goods of the community, and even upon the movables which have become part thereof in her right. She retains only linen and clothes for her own use. . . .

Section V: Of the Power Granted to the Wife of Resuming Her Contribution Free and Unencumbered

1530. The article importing that the parties marry without community does not confer upon the wife a right to administer her property, nor to enjoy the fruits thereof; such fruits are deemed to have been given to the husband to sustain the expenses of marriage.

Section II: Of the Rights of the Husband over the Property in Dowry, and of the Inalienable Nature of the Funds of the Dower

1549. The husband alone has the management of the property in dowry, during the marriage.

He has alone the right to use the debtors and detainers thereof, to enjoy the fruits and interest thereof, and to receive reimbursements of capital.

Nevertheless it may be agreed, by the marriage contract, that the wife shall receive annually, on her single acquaintance, a part of her revenues for her maintenance and personal wants.

87. Napoleon's Policies Toward Saint Domingue

Violent civil and foreign war had plagued Saint Domingue for nearly ten years by the time Napoleon came to power; agricultural productivity in France's once wealthiest colony had come to a standstill. As in France, so also in her colonies, Napoleon intended to restore order. Although he reassured Saint Dominguans that their freedom would not be threatened, he launched an expeditionary force in 1802 and had Toussaint L'Ouverture arrested. Once his ultimate goal—the reestablishment of slavery—became known, intense fighting broke out, and Napoleon's forces were repelled. Unsuccessful in Saint Domingue, Napoleon did restore slavery in France's other colonies. This policy was consistent with other decrees that reversed many of the civil and political liberties gained during the Revolution.

A. Proclamation to the Citizens of Saint Domingue
     (DECEMBER 25, 1799)

Citizens, a Constitution which could not be maintained in the face of repeated violations has been replaced by a new pact designed to strengthen freedom.

Article 91 lays down that the French colonies will be governed by special laws.

This disposition derives from the nature of things and the differences of climate. The inhabitants of French colonies situated in America, Asia, and Africa cannot be ruled by the same laws. Distinctions of tradition, of custom, of interest, the diversity of soil, of culture, of production demand various modifications.

One of the first acts of the new legislature will be to prepare the laws destined to govern you. Far from these being a cause for alarm among you, you will recognize in them the wisdom and depth of view which inspires the legislators of France.

In announcing the new social pact to you, the Consuls of the Republic declare that the sacred principles of the liberty and equality of the black peoples will never undergo any threat or modification among you.

If there are any who maintain relations with the enemy powers, remember, brave blacks, that the French people alone recognize your freedom and the equality of your rights.

Bonaparte

Source: John Eldred Howard, ed. and trans., *Letters and Documents of Napoleon*, vol. I (London: Cresset Press, 1961), pp. 329, 506.

B. To Citizen Talleyrand, Minister of Foreign Affairs
(OCTOBER 30, 1801)

You will send a courier to Citizen Otto, Citizen Minister; you will tell him that he can inform the English cabinet confidentially, in exchange for the communication they have made to us of the dispatch of five ships to Jamaica, that six ships and four frigates of the Rochefort squadron . . . will leave for Saint Domingue during the last decade of Brumaire; the whole will carry about twenty thousand landing troops under the orders of General Leclerc. I wish the British Government to give orders at Jamaica that he is to be supplied with all the foodstuffs he may need, for it is to the interest of civilization to destroy the new Algiers that has been growing up in the middle of America.

Bonaparte

C. To Consul Cambacérès (APRIL 27, 1802)

Citizen-Consul, attached you will find notes that will serve to complete a sketch of a decree which will be converted into a senatus-consulte: (1) one for Île-de-France [Mauritius]; (2) one for Tobago, Martinique, and Sainte-Lucie; (3) one for Guadeloupe; (4) one for Saint Domingue; finally a fifth for preventing the arrival of blacks on the continent of the Republic, and vigorously reinstating the rules which already exist.

I ask you to draft these five ordinances, and to confer with citizens Regnier, Dupuy, and Roederer so that these drafts will be finalized after tomorrow.

Warm regards, Bonaparte

First Enclosure

According to the report of the rules pertaining to blacks, the colonies should be divided into two types: those where the laws on black emancipation have been publicized and more or less perfectly executed, and those where the old order is conserved. I propose rule number one for the first, and number two for the second.

Number One

The consuls of the Republic and the informed council of State decree:

Article One: According to the reports made to the captain-general of the colony of _____ by those individuals who will commit to this result, a

Source: Correspondance de Napoléon I, publiée par ordre de l'Empereur Napoléon III. 7 vols (Paris: Henri Plon and J. Dumaine, 1861), pp. 444–447. Translated by Tracey Rizzo.

list will be composed comprising first the names of black people who enjoyed freedom before 26 Pluviôse, Year II, and second, the names of blacks who have united to defend the territory of the Republic from its enemies, or who, in any other matter, have served the State.

Article Two: All the individuals named on this list will be declared free.

Article Three: Those among them who do not own property, and who have no trade or skill which can assure their subsistence, will be subjected to the regulations of the police who will assign them to property owners who will support them in agricultural work, determine their pay, and who will stipulate above all arrangements for preventing vagabondage and insubordination.

Article Four: Insubordinates and outspoken vagabonds will be, in cases determined by the regulations, struck from the list and deprived of the advantages which result from it. One can substitute for this arrangement deportation to colonies where the emancipation laws have not been enacted.

Article Five: All blacks not included on the aforementioned list in article one will be subjected to the laws which in 1789 comprised the Black Code in the colonies.

Article Six: It will be permitted to import blacks in the colony of _____ in accordance with the laws and regulations of the trade which were in place in 1789. The minister of the marine is charged with the execution of the present order.

Number Two

The consuls of the Republic and the informed council of State decree:

Article One: The laws and regulations to which the blacks were subjected in 1789 continue to be in effect in the colony of _____.

Article Two: It will be permitted to import blacks in conformity with the laws and regulations formerly established on this matter. The minister of the marine is charged with the execution of the present order.

Second Enclosure

The consuls of the Republic and the informed council of State decree:

Article One: Blacks on the islands of Martinique, Sainte-Lucie, Tobago, and Île-de-France will continue to live under the regime in place in 1789.

Article Two: Laws which have been rendered by different legislative bodies, under various constitutions, are declared null and inapplicable to the aforementioned colonies.

Article Three: The slave trade and all the laws pertaining to the trade existing in 1789 will be vigorously reenforced until the French government is able to confer with the English government and with other governments for a common accord to suppress the slave trade.

Article Four: All laws contrary to the present senatus-consulte, rendered by previous constitutions, are declared null as irreconcilable with article 91 of the Constitution.

Third Enclosure

The consuls of the Republic and the informed council of State decree:

Article One: All blacks issuing from the trade who arrive in the colonies of Martinique and Saint Domingue will be treated as they would in other European colonies, and in the same manner as they would have been in 1789 in these same colonies.

Article Two: All blacks who defended our colonies against the enemies of the Republic, and who have rendered service to the State are definitively considered free. For this purpose, the government will take measures convenient to distinguishing those who are worthy of liberty.

Article Three: All the regulations of the government discussed in council of State will have the force of law for five years.

Suggestions for Further Reading

General Histories

Doyle, William. *Oxford History of the French Revolution*. Oxford & New York: Oxford University Press, 1989.

Lefebvre, Georges. *The French Revolution*, trans. Elizabeth Moss Evanson. New York: Columbia University Press, 1962–1964.

Popkin, Jeremy D. *A Short History of the French Revolution*. Upper Saddle River, N.J.: Prentice-Hall, 1995.

Sutherland, Donald. *France 1789–1815: Revolution and Counter-Revolution*. Oxford & New York: Oxford University Press, 1985.

Origins of the Revolution

Baker, Keith M. *Inventing the French Revolution*. Cambridge & New York: Cambridge University Press, 1990.

Chartier, Roger. *The Cultural Origins of the French Revolution*, trans. Lydia G. Cochrane. Durham, N.C. & London: Duke University Press, 1991.

Doyle, William. *Origins of the French Revolution*. Oxford & New York: Oxford University Press, 1980; 1988.

Jones, Peter. *Reform & Revolution in France: The Politics of Transition, 1774–1791*. Cambridge & New York: Cambridge University Press, 1994.

Lefebvre, Georges. *The Coming of the French Revolution*, trans. R. R. Palmer. Princeton, N.J.: Princeton University Press, 1947.

Sewell, William. *A Rhetoric of Bourgeois Revolution: The Abbé Sieyès and What Is the Third Estate?*. Durham, N.C. & London: Duke University Press, 1994.

Legislative Politics

Hampson, Norman. *Danton*. New York: Holmes & Meier, 1978.

Hardman, John. *Louis XVI*. New Haven, Conn.: Yale University Press, 1993.

Jordan, David P. *The King's Trial: The French Revolution vs. Louis XVI*. Berkeley & Los Angeles: University of California Press, 1979.

———. *The Revolutionary Career of Maximilien Robespierre*. Chicago: University of Chicago Press, 1989.

Palmer, R. R. *Twelve Who Ruled: The Year of the Terror in the French Revolution*. Princeton, N.J.: Princeton University Press, 1989.

Tackett, Timothy. *Becoming a Revolutionary: The Deputies of the French National Assembly and the Emergence of a Revolutionary Culture*. Princeton, N.J.: Princeton University Press, 1996.

Walzer, Michael, ed. *Regicide and Revolution: Speeches at the Trial of Louis XVI*. New York: Columbia University Press, 1992.

Rural Life and the Destruction of Feudalism

Jones, Peter. *The Peasantry in the French Revolution*. New York & Cambridge: Cambridge University Press, 1988.

Lefebvre, Georges. *The Great Fear of 1789: Rural Panic in Revolutionary France*, trans. Joan White. Princeton, N.J.: Princeton University Press, 1973.

Markoff, John. *The Abolition of Feudalism: Peasants, Lords, and Legislators in the French Revolution*. University Park, Pa.: Pennsylvania State University Press, 1996.

Ramsay, Clay. *The Ideology of the Great Fear: The Soissonnais in 1789*. Baltimore: Johns Hopkins University Press, 1992.

Religion

Desan, Suzanne. *Reclaiming the Sacred: Lay Religion and Popular Politics in Revolutionary France*. Ithaca, N.Y.: Cornell University Press, 1990.

McManners, John. *The French Revolution and the Church*. New York: Harper & Row, 1970.

Tackett, Timothy. *Religion, Revolution, and Regional Culture in Eighteenth-Century France: The Ecclesiastical Oath of 1791*. Princeton, N.J.: Princeton University Press, 1986.

Van Kley, Dale. *The Religious Origins of the French Revolution: From Calvin to the Civil Constitution, 1560–1791*. New Haven, Conn.: Yale University Press, 1996.

Women and Gender

Godineau, Dominique. *The Women of Paris and Their French Revolution*, trans. Katherine Streip. Berkeley & Los Angeles: University of California Press, 1998.

Hufton, Olwen. *Women and the Limits of Citizenship in the French Revolution*. Toronto & Buffalo: University of Toronto Press, 1992.

Hunt, Lynn. *The Family Romance of the French Revolution*. Berkeley & Los Angeles: University of California Press, 1992.

Landes, Joan. *Women and the Public Sphere in the Age of the French Revolution*. Ithaca, N.Y.: Cornell University Press, 1988.

Levy, Darlene, and Harriet Applewhite, eds. *Women in Revolutionary Paris, 1789–1795: Selected Documents*. Urbana: University of Illinois Press, 1979.

Melzer, Sara, and Leslie Rabine, eds. *Rebel Daughters: Women and the French Revolution*. New York & Oxford: Oxford University Press, 1992.

Sans-Culottes and Other Activists

Cobb, Richard. *The People's Armies*, trans. Marianne Elliott. New Haven, Conn.: Yale University Press, 1987.

———. *The Police and the People: French Popular Protest, 1789–1820*. Oxford & New York: Oxford University Press, 1970.

Kennedy, Michael. *The Jacobin Clubs in the French Revolution.* 2 vols. Princeton, N.J.: Princeton University Press, 1982; 1988.

Rudé, George. *The Crowd in the French Revolution.* Oxford & New York: Oxford University Press, 1972.

Soboul, Albert. *The Sans-Culottes: The Popular Movement and Revolutionary Government, 1793–1794,* trans. Remy Inglis Hall. Princeton, N.J.: Princeton University Press, 1980.

Revolution in the Provinces

Hanson, Paul. *Provincial Politics in the French Revolution: Caen and Limoges, 1789–1794.* Baton Rouge, La.: Louisiana State University Press, 1989.

Hunt, Lynn. *Revolution and Urban Politics in Provincial France: Troyes and Reims, 1786–1790.* Stanford, Calif.: Stanford University Press, 1978.

Margadant, Ted. *Urban Rivalries in the French Revolution.* Princeton, N.J.: Princeton University Press, 1992.

Culture and Political Culture

Baker, Keith M., and Colin Lucas, eds. *The French Revolution and the Creation of Modern Political Culture,* vols. 1 and 2. Oxford & New York: Pergamon Press, 1987; 1989.

Darnton, Robert, and Daniel Roche, eds. *Revolution in Print: The Press in France.* Berkeley & Los Angeles: University of California Press, 1989.

Hunt, Lynn. *Politics, Culture, and Class in the French Revolution.* Berkeley & Los Angeles: University of California Press, 1984.

Kennedy, Emmett. *A Cultural History of the French Revolution.* New Haven, Conn.: Yale University Press, 1989.

Mason, Laura. *Singing the French Revolution: Popular Songs and Revolutionary Politics in Paris.* Ithaca, N.Y.: Cornell University Press, 1996.

Ozouf, Mona. *Festivals and the French Revolution,* trans. Alan Sheridan. Cambridge, Mass.: Harvard University Press, 1988.

Popkin, Jeremy D. *Revolutionary News: The Press in France, 1789–1799.* Durham, N.C. & London: Duke University Press, 1990.

The Revolution in the Caribbean

Fick, Carolyn E. *The Making of Haiti: The Saint Domingue Revolution from Below.* Knoxville: University of Tennessee Press, 1990.

Gaspar, David, and David P. Geggus, eds. *A Turbulent Time: The French Revolution and the Greater Caribbean.* Bloomington: Indiana University Press, 1997.

Geggus, David P. *Slavery, War, and Revolution: The British Occupation of Saint Domingue, 1793–1798.* Oxford & New York: Oxford University Press, 1982.

James, C.L.R. *The Black Jacobins: Toussaint L'Ouverture and the San Domingo Revolution.* London: Allison & Busby, 1980.

Langley, Lester D. *The Americas in the Age of Revolution, 1750–1850*. New Haven, Conn.: Yale University Press, 1996.

Counter-Revolution

Godechot, Jacques. *The Counter-Revolution: Doctrine and Action, 1789–1804*, trans. Salvator Attanasio. Princeton, N.J.: Princeton University Press, 1971.

Popkin, Jeremy D. *The Right-Wing Press in France, 1792–1800*. Chapel Hill: University of North Carolina Press, 1980.

Sutherland, Donald. *The Chouans: The Social Origins of Popular Counter-Revolution in Upper Brittany, 1770–1796*. Oxford & New York: Oxford University Press, 1982.

Tilly, Charles. *The Vendée*. Cambridge, Mass.: Harvard University Press, 1964.

The Army

Bertaud, Jean-Paul. *The Army of the French Revolution: From Citizen-Soldiers to Instrument of Power*, trans. R. R. Palmer. Princeton, N.J.: Princeton University Press, 1988.

Forrest, Alan. *Conscripts and Deserters: The Army and French Society During the Revolution and Empire*. Oxford & New York: Oxford University Press, 1989.

———. *The Soldiers of the French Revolution*. Durham, N.C. & London: Duke University Press, 1990.

Lynn, John. *The Bayonets of the Republic: Motivation and Tactics in the Army of Revolutionary France, 1791–94*. Urbana: University of Illinois Press, 1984.

The Thermidoran Reaction and the Directory

Gendron, François. *The Gilded Youth of Thermidor*, trans. James Cookson. Montreal: McGill-Queen's University Press, 1993.

Lucas, Colin, and Gwynne Lewis, eds. *Beyond the Terror: Essays in French Regional and Social History, 1794–1815*. Cambridge & New York: Cambridge University Press, 1983.

Lyons, Martyn. *France Under the Directory*. Cambridge & New York: Cambridge University Press, 1975.

Rose, R. B. *Gracchus Babeuf*. Stanford, Calif.: Stanford University Press, 1978.

Woloch, Isser. *Jacobin Legacy: The Democratic Movement Under the Directory*. Princeton, N.J.: Princeton University Press, 1970.

Napoleon: Consulate and Empire

Arnold, E. A., ed. *A Documentary Survey of Napoleonic France*. Lanham, Md.: University Press of America, 1993.

Bergeron, Louis. *France Under Napoleon*, trans. R. R. Palmer. Princeton, N.J.: Princeton University Press, 1981.

Ellis, Geoffrey. *Napoleon*. London & New York: Longman, 1997.

Lefebvre, Georges. *Napoleon*, trans. J. E. Anderson and Henry F. Stockhold. New York: Columbia University Press, 1969.

Lyons, Martyn. *Napoleon Bonaparte and the Legacy of the French Revolution*. New York: St. Martin's Press, 1994.

Walter, Jakob. *The Diary of a Napoleonic Foot Soldier*, ed. Marc Raeff. New York: Penguin Books, 1993.

Long-Term Impact of the Revolution

Fraisse, Geneviève. *Reason's Muse: Sexual Difference and the Birth of Democracy*, trans. Jane Marie Todd. Chicago & London: University of Chicago Press, 1994.

Ragan, Bryant T., Jr., and Elizabeth A. Williams, eds. *Re-Creating Authority in Revolutionary France*. New Brunswick, N.J.: Rutgers University Press, 1992.

Scott, Joan Wallach. *Only Paradoxes to Offer: French Feminists and the Rights of Man*. Cambridge, Mass.: Harvard University Press, 1996.

Tocqueville, Alexis de. *The Old Regime & the French Revolution*, trans. Stuart Gilbert. Garden City, N.Y.: Doubleday Books, 1955.

Woloch, Isser. *The New Regime: Transformations of the French Civic Order, 1789–1820s*. New York: W.W. Norton, 1994.

Assessing and Commemorating the Revolution

Burke, Edmund. *Reflections on the Revolution in France*. Oxford & London: Oxford University Press, 1993.

Furet, François. *Interpreting the French Revolution*, trans. Elborg Forster. Cambridge & New York: Cambridge University Press, 1981.

Hobsbawm, Eric. *Echoes of the Marseillaise: Two Centuries Look Back on the French Revolution*. New Brunswick, N.J.: Rutgers University Press, 1990.

Kaplan, Steven. *Farewell Revolution, 1789/1989*. Ithaca, N.Y.: Cornell University Press, 1995.